The People of God's Presence

An Introduction to Ecclesiology

TERRY L. CROSS

Baker Academic
a division of Baker Publishing Group
Grand Rapids, Michigan

Published by Baker Academic
a division of Baker Publishing Group
PO Box 6287, Grand Rapids, MI 49516-6287
www.bakeracademic.com

Printed in the United States of America

Library of Congress Cataloging-in-Publication Data
Names: Cross, Terry L., author.
Title: The people of God's presence : an introduction to ecclesiology / Terry L. Cross.
Description: Grand Rapids : Baker Academic, a division of Baker Publishing Group, 2019. |
    Includes bibliographical references and index.
Identifiers: LCCN 2019002830 | ISBN 9781540960573 (pbk.)
Subjects: LCSH: Church.
Classification: LCC BV600.3 .C76 2019 | DDC 262—dc23
LC record available at https://lccn.loc.gov/2019002830

ISBN 978-1-5409-6220-1 (casebound)

In keeping with biblical principles of creation stewardship, Baker Publishing Group advocates the responsible use of our natural resources. As a member of the Green Press Initiative, our company uses recycled paper when possible. The text paper of this book is composed in part of post-consumer waste.

19   20   21   22   23   24   25   7   6   5   4   3   2   1

To the memory of my grandparents,
who taught me to love God's presence and God's people

Rev. Arthur L. Cross (1895–1984)
Essie Thomas Cross (1892–1976)
John H. Stockwell (1876–1943)
Cora Parks Stockwell (1884–1971)

Contents

Preface

This work offers a doctrine of the church for Christians in the twenty-first century. The precise theological location of this ecclesiology will be explained throughout this book and its companion volume, *Serving the People of God's Presence*. However, in terms of type or genre, this work is one of constructive theology—like building a house with rooms that are fitting to both one's environment and personal taste. Nonetheless, the theological foundation will be built on Scripture and in particular on the revelation of God in human flesh, Jesus Christ. The style of the house and the features will be informed by those thinkers within the movement of Christianity who have gone before us and blazed a trail of ideas in relation to their times. Constructing a theological house is a rather apt metaphor for the task of this work, but writing a constructive theology of the church that others will read is quite daunting. It is like inviting strangers into one's mental construction to render judgment on the dimensions of each room, the placement of doors and windows, and the adequacy of the decor.

A number of years ago, David Ford expressed rather precisely the sentiment with which I wrote this book: "It is riskier to come up with a constructive position, an attempt to design a habitable contemporary dwelling. At every step in the process one is aware of the immense power of the demolition experts with flourishing businesses, of the overcautious insurance and lending companies, of those who protest at one's building going anywhere near their own . . . , and those who seem quite content that no actual dwellings be built at all if they cannot meet their own impossibly ideal specifications."[1] Such second-guessing

---

1. David F. Ford, *Self and Salvation: Being Transformed*, Cambridge Studies in Christian Doctrine 1, ed. Colin Gunton and Daniel W. Hardy (Cambridge: Cambridge University Press, 1999), 6.

is an important part of the writing process to be sure, but too much focus on how others will perceive one's theological house can halt construction.

So why am I daring to construct a house that details my understanding of the church? Why not just critique other houses—something with which I am vastly more comfortable? As will be shared in the introduction, I believe that radical shifts are required of the Christian church in this century, the most fundamental of which is a theological renewal of understanding the nature and mission of the church.

Therefore, the reader should understand that my writing is in the form of a proposal, not a set-in-stone system that is always "right." Even in my most stringent writing I recognize that I could be wrong—that I may need the engagement of others to help flesh out the reality of the community of faith for our times. Nevertheless, the church seems to be in such a condition today (especially in Western societies) that changing the drapery over the windows is not going to help. What I am proposing is really nothing less than building a new theological house from the foundation up, not rearranging furniture or dressing up our already existing houses with laser light shows and condensed fog to create a sense of mystery that we think will appeal to people.

Perhaps it is important at this point that I share some aspects of my church background so that the reader may better understand some influences for the concepts in this book. My own approach to the doctrine of the church arises from three major arenas: my pastoral experience with three different local churches; my theological and biblical study; and my early years of being shaped by Christians in a small, rural church in Michigan. Trained in systematic theology, I engaged in almost twelve years of pastoral ministry during different segments of my career. Raised as a Pentecostal, I have served classical Pentecostal churches as well as an independent charismatic church. I have been connected with the Church of God (Cleveland, TN) all my life and am currently an ordained bishop in that denomination. However, I have also worked across denominational lines in the ecumenical movement, representing the Society for Pentecostal Studies at the Faith and Order Commission of the National Council of Churches of Christ in the USA for nine years. I am well aware that the proposal in this book will not fit many communions of the Christian faith, but I believe that parts of the proposal may provide a beneficial dialogue partner for them.

My training at Lee College (TN) introduced me to hermeneutical and language skills to begin a lifetime of Scripture study.[2] My training at Ash-

---

2. Professor Donald N. Bowdle (religion and history) provided ample and appropriate models for biblical and theological studies that remain with me to this day. Professor French Arrington

land Theological Seminary (OH) taught me how to do ministry in a church setting—in particular, how to lead body ministry (that is, ministry that arises from and through the body of Christ). Much of what I offer here as a proposal for the church would never have come to mind without the humble, steadfast example of these Anabaptist brothers and sisters in Christ.[3] Added to this approach to ministry was the commitment of the Reformed churches to the work of the church as a witness of Christ's reconciliation and desire for justice in the world. Their reliance on and respect for Scripture expanded my grasp of what was important from a theological point of view. During my PhD studies at Princeton Theological Seminary, the nature and mission of the church came more clearly into view.[4]

Yet it was only as I engaged in the day-to-day task of pastoral work that I began to ask questions of my theological training and of Scripture. From among the conflicting duties demanding my time, how was I supposed to choose which to perform first—if at all? Why did the work of ministry seem to fall entirely on me, the pastor? Should the people of God also be involved in doing the work of ministry? How might that come about? I began to engage in a desperate search to determine what God intended the church to be and do. That search, begun in the throes of pastoral work in the 1990s, has continued over the years as I have shifted from pastoring to teaching theology at Lee University to future pastors, teachers, missionaries, and ministers of God's work.

What I have discovered from looking into the Scriptures and engaging various theological works on the church has grounded my suspicion that we need a re-formation of the church. It has become the basis for this work.

A word of thanks is due to many people who have contributed to this book, sometimes without knowing they were doing so. President Paul Conn and the board of directors at Lee University gave me a sabbatical to help complete the work presented here. This was the incentive and time I needed as an academic

---

(New Testament and Greek) taught me three years of New Testament Greek that provided the basis not only for the next forty years of reading the New Testament but also for reading the Greek fathers. Their commitment to training future leaders in the church provided the foundation for my own career at Lee University today.

3. In particular, the lifelong friendship and mentoring example of Professor Jerry R. Flora remains paramount among the influences on my theological and spiritual formation.

4. My indebtedness to several professors at Princeton Theological Seminary will be evident throughout this book, especially my reliance on ideas from Daniel Migliore, along with Diogenes Allen, David Willis, Karlfried Froehlich, Ed Dowey, and Mark K. Taylor. More recently, work and interaction with Darrell Guder on a translation team for Karl Barth's three-volume *Gespräche* (*Barth in Conversation*) from German to English has profited me immensely in understanding the mission and evangelism of the church.

administrator to engage in research, reflection, and writing. I am most appreciative of their continued support. Colleagues and students in the School of Religion have sparked numerous rewrites of my ideas, always making them better conceived along the way. Various secretaries have worked on parts of this manuscript in its primitive stages. Thanks are due to them for assisting me in getting this manuscript in shape—even though it has changed immensely since I began it in 1992. Dori Salvador from the church in Connecticut and Dana Crutchfield, my executive secretary for seventeen years at Lee University, have both assisted me immensely in this work. Student workers and teaching assistants have also contributed to the process of putting thoughts onto the page. Many aspects of this work have been improved by their input. Also, the editors and staff at Baker Academic have been exceptional to work with, especially Dave Nelson, who has been supportive and enthusiastic about this project from the beginning, and project editor Jennifer Hale, whose stellar attention to detail has made this text a much easier document to read.

My family has offered support for my writing in so many ways that my thanks for their time and love seem especially vacuous here. Without their love and encouragement, this effort would still be a collection of notes instead of the work it is today. To my wife, Linda, to my daughter, Tara, and to my son-in-law, Kevin, I offer sincere thanks. To my grandson, Luke, is owed a great debt for joyous relief from the weariness of writing, reminding me that play is a vital part of life too.

Finally, I dedicate this book to my grandparents, who provided me the greatest example of love for the people of God in our little country church in North Woodville, Michigan. They loved and served the people of God throughout their long lives, teaching me by their example to do the same.

Abbreviations

General

¶	paragraph	n.d.	no date
§	section	no.	number
alt.	altered	NS	New Series
ca.	*circa*, around	NT	New Testament
cf.	*confer*, compare	orig.	original
chap(s).	chapter(s)	OT	Old Testament
col.	column	pl.	plural
dist.	distinction	ques.	question
ed(s).	editor(s), edited by, edition	report.	reprinted
e.g.	*exempli gratia*, for example	rev.	revised
esp.	especially	sg.	singular
ET	English translation	s.v.	*sub verbo*, under the word
et al.	*et alii*, and others	trans.	translation, translator, translated by
etc.	*et cetera*, and so forth		
i.e.	*id est*, that is	vol(s).	volume(s)
lib.	book	v(v).	verse(s)
LXX	Septuagint		

Bible Versions

CEB	Common English Bible	NEB	New English Bible
CEV	Contemporary English Version	NIV	New International Version
ESV	English Standard Version	NKJV	New King James Version
HCSB	Holman Christian Standard Bible	NRSV	New Revised Standard Version
KJV	King James Version	Phillips	*The New Testament in Modern English*, J. B. Phillips
NASB	New American Standard Bible	RSV	Revised Standard Version
NCV	New Century Version		

Old Testament

Gen.	Genesis	Eccles.	Ecclesiastes
Exod.	Exodus	Song	Song of Songs
Lev.	Leviticus	Isa.	Isaiah
Num.	Numbers	Jer.	Jeremiah
Deut.	Deuteronomy	Lam.	Lamentations
Josh.	Joshua	Ezek.	Ezekiel
Judg.	Judges	Dan.	Daniel
Ruth	Ruth	Hosea	Hosea
1 Sam.	1 Samuel	Joel	Joel
2 Sam.	2 Samuel	Amos	Amos
1 Kings	1 Kings	Obad.	Obadiah
2 Kings	2 Kings	Jon.	Jonah
1 Chron.	1 Chronicles	Mic.	Micah
2 Chron.	2 Chronicles	Nah.	Nahum
Ezra	Ezra	Hab.	Habakkuk
Neh.	Nehemiah	Zeph.	Zephaniah
Esther	Esther	Hag.	Haggai
Job	Job	Zech.	Zechariah
Ps(s).	Psalm(s)	Mal.	Malachi
Prov.	Proverbs		

New Testament

Matt.	Matthew	1 Tim.	1 Timothy
Mark	Mark	2 Tim.	2 Timothy
Luke	Luke	Titus	Titus
John	John	Philem.	Philemon
Acts	Acts	Heb.	Hebrews
Rom.	Romans	James	James
1 Cor.	1 Corinthians	1 Pet.	1 Peter
2 Cor.	2 Corinthians	2 Pet.	2 Peter
Gal.	Galatians	1 John	1 John
Eph.	Ephesians	2 John	2 John
Phil.	Philippians	3 John	3 John
Col.	Colossians	Jude	Jude
1 Thess.	1 Thessalonians	Rev.	Revelation
2 Thess.	2 Thessalonians		

Bibliographic Sources

BDAG   Bauer, W., W. F. Arndt, and F. W. Gingrich, editors and translators. *A Greek-English Lexicon of the New Testament and Other Early Christian Literature.* Chicago: University of Chicago Press, 1957.

BDB *The New Brown-Driver-Briggs-Gesenius Hebrew and English Lexicon.* Edited by Francis Brown, S. R. Driver, and Charles A. Briggs. Translated by Edward Robinson. Lafayette, IN: Associated Publishers and Authors, 1978.

CD Barth, Karl. *Church Dogmatics.* Edited by T. F. Torrance and G. W. Bromiley. Translated by G. W. Bromiley et al. 13 vols. Edinburgh: T&T Clark, 1936–.

Inst. Calvin, John. *Institutes of the Christian Religion.* Edited by John T. McNeill. Translated by Ford Lewis Battles. 2 vols. Library of Christian Classics 20–21. Philadelphia: Westminster, 1975.

KD Barth, Karl. *Die kirchliche Dogmatik.* 13 vols. Munich: Kaiser, 1932; Zurich: Evangelischer Verlag, 1938–.

OS Calvin, John. *Joannis Calvini Opera selecta.* Edited by Peter Barth, Wilhelm Niesel, and Dora Scheuner. 5 vols. Munich: Kaiser, 1926–52.

Sermons Wesley, John. *Sermons.* Edited by Albert C. Outler. 4 vols. Bicentennial Edition of the Works of John Wesley 1–4. Nashville: Abingdon, 1984–87. Repr. Grand Rapids: Baker Books, 2002.

TDNT *Theological Dictionary of the New Testament.* Edited by G. Kittel and G. Friedrich. Translated and edited by G. W. Bromiley. 10 vols. Grand Rapids: Eerdmans, 1974–2006.

TDOT *Theological Dictionary of the Old Testament.* Edited by G. J. Botterweck, H. Ringgren, and J.-J. Fabry. Translated by J. T. Willis, G. W. Bromiley, D. E. Green, and D. W. Stott. 15 vols. Grand Rapids: Eerdmans, 1974–2006.

TWOT *Theological Wordbook of the Old Testament.* Edited by R. Laird Harris, Gleason L. Archer Jr., and Bruce K. Waltke. 2 vols. Chicago: Moody, 1980.

WA Weimarer Ausgabe. *D. Martin Luthers Werke: Kritische Gesammtausgabe.* Weimar: Hermann Böhlau & successors, 1883–2009.

Introduction

A Re-formation of the Church?

It was shocking to hear Josh McDowell say this in 1998, but I knew it was true: "If the church does not change its method and keep in touch with the times, in five years we could be *irrelevant* to an entire generation of young people."[1] After almost twenty years of massive cultural shifts in North America, as well as the enormous increase of social media during this time, it seems likely that this timetable of the church's relevancy should move from five *years* to five *days*! Not only is the church's appeal to youth at stake, but also its relevancy to our entire society. In light of such rapid and far-reaching shifts, what is the church to do? At the very least, it seems that a new re-formation[2] is in order—one that reshapes our understanding of the nature and mission of the church today. Change of some sort seems necessary, but what should that look like?

Perhaps a first step is an attitude adjustment—one that engagement with young adults over the past twenty years has helped to fine-tune in me. An essential aspect of needed change is for the church to become more authentic.[3] Many people today are cynical of churches. While for some people a

1. My paraphrase of his statement made at a conference at Lee University, Cleveland, TN, in January 1998.

2. The word "re-formation" used throughout this work points to a renewal of the structural framework of the church. It attempts a wordplay on the Protestant Reformation that began such reform of the church but in many ways became stalled. Therefore, ecclesiology awaits a renewal in the way the church is set up, based on a theological and biblical foundation.

3. Surveys of young people since 2007 tend to underscore this specific perception—the church is "hypocritical." Research done by the Barna Group notes that 66% of millennials

1

relationship with God or some type of general spirituality is perceived as beneficial, for others a connection with the Christian church is seen as unnecessary or even harmful to one's well-being. Unfortunately, on a number of occasions the church has earned its reputation for harming instead of healing. A stance of genuineness seems vital to begin any internal reform in the church so that it operates with integrity both within and without its doors. Yet beyond adjusting our willingness as the church to examine ourselves and begin seeing ourselves as others see us, there remains an even more important task of assessing ourselves from God's perspective. Such a self-assessment requires a theological review of who the church was meant to be and how the church was meant to operate in the world. Re-formation of the church must begin with penetrating theological introspection before it proposes any practical solutions. Therefore, our proposal coincides well with the saying that Karl Barth made famous: *ecclesia semper reformanda est* (The church must always be reforming).[4]

The church has often had an ambiguous and sometimes difficult relationship with the world in which it operates. At times we became so like the world that we lost our prophetic stance; at other times we spoke so harshly to people that we lost our loving posture. While the message of the good

---

(born between 1984 and 1998) make this claim about churchgoers ("What Millennials Want When They Visit Church," March 4, 2015, https://www.barna.com/research/what-millennials -want-when-they-visit-church/). This is also supported by information from Pew Research Center, "America's Changing Religious Landscape," May 12, 2015, http://www.pewforum .org/2015/05/12/americas-changing-religious-landscape/. In 2016, Pew Research conducted a new survey related to the Religious Landscape survey, attempting to discover more detail for why people are nonaffiliated ("nones"). About 78% of the nones were raised in a religious household but left their faith behind, no longer identifying with a religious group. By allowing for extended answers instead of preset answers to questions, Pew learned that about 49% of the nones were disenchanted with faith and no longer believed. About 20% of the nones disliked organized religion. See Michael Lipka, "Why America's 'Nones' Left Religion Behind," August 24, 2016, http://www.pewresearch.org/fact-tank/2016/08/24/why -americas-nones-left-religion-behind/. Finally, research from the Barna Group also focuses on the question of church in relation to the newer youth group "Gen Z" (born between 1999 and 2015). A study from 2016 of the thirteen- to eighteen-year-olds in this segment revealed some important data. For non-Christians, the second most common (23%) barrier to faith was the perception of Christians as hypocrites. The most common barrier was the problem of evil (29%). Most respondents who said, "Church is not important," felt that "church is not relevant to me personally" (64%) or "I find God elsewhere" (61%). For the latter information, see "Gen-Z: Your Questions Answered," February 6, 2018, https://www.barna.com /research/gen-z-questions-answered/.

4. For a thorough recent history of this Latin phrase, see Theodor Mahlmann: "'Ecclesia semper reformanda': Eine historische Aufarbeitung; Neue Bearbeitung," in *Hermeneutica sacra: Studien zur Auslegung der Heiligen Schrift im 16. und 17. Jahrhundert*, ed. Torbjörn Johansson, Robert Kolb, and Johann Anselm Steiger (Berlin: de Gruyter, 2010), 381–442.

news of Jesus Christ need not change, the method by which it is disseminated *must* change if it is to remain relevant to the people among whom the church lives. That has been an "old saw" for many years, but there is still some truth to it. However, what I am proposing in this book goes beyond that old remedy of keeping the message and tweaking the method of delivery. What I propose has to do with transformation of our understanding of the church itself—not just its methods or programs—as well as a transformation of our communal lives together. Such transformation requires a major *theological* overhaul of the doctrine of the church as well as a major *existential* overhaul of our expectations of the life of the Spirit together as the people of God. In other words, before we fiddle with our methods, we must return to a theological task that searches out the basis of the church's being and doing. It is my belief that by turning to such a theological inquiry about the church, we will also turn to a renewal of our own commitment to life together in the presence of God.

Consequently, this book arises out of a desire to contribute to a theological discussion about the direction of the church in the twenty-first century. Other voices have already provided some impetus for this discussion since the last quarter of the previous century, yet a great deal of change has occurred in culture and the way we "do" church since then.[5] In the past twenty years, we have witnessed new forms of doing church—the "emergent" church as well as the "emerging" church.[6] We have seen a rise in the theological and practical discussion of churches viewing their own mission as an extension of the mission of God (*missio Dei*).[7] In the United States, however, we have also seen a rather drastic drop in church attendance and a strong trend toward spirituality but not the institutional church (i.e., the "nones," as they are called in Pew's survey, who are not affiliated with institutional religion).[8] People in Western societies, especially in the United States, seem to continue moving toward being spiritual but not religious.

5. Consider Howard A. Snyder, *The Problems of Wineskins: Church Structure in a Technological Age* (Downers Grove, IL: InterVarsity, 1975); also Greg Ogden, *The New Reformation: Returning the Ministry to the People of God* (Grand Rapids: Zondervan, 1990).

6. See E. Gibbs and R. Bolger, *Emerging Churches: Creating Christian Community in Postmodern Cultures* (Grand Rapids: Baker Academic, 2005); also Tony Jones, *The New Christians: Dispatches from the Emergent Frontier* (San Francisco: Jossey-Bass, 2008).

7. See, e.g., Darrell L. Guder, ed., *Missional Church: A Vision for the Sending of the Church in North America* (Grand Rapids: Eerdmans, 1998).

8. Pew Research Center, "America's Changing Religious Landscape," May 12, 2015. Accessed from www.pewresearch.org. Weekly church attendance dropped by 3.7% in just seven years (from 2007–14), according to this survey. Also, the category of "nones" rose dramatically to 19% in the same period of time. About one out of five adults in the United States do not affiliate with institutional religion or church.

So what is the church to do? Are we to stick our heads in the sand, ignoring what is happening in the culture around us? Do we batten down the hatches and attempt to make sink-proof churches? Some have suggested that a new approach to Christianity is needed.[9] Others have a refrain that runs something like the following proposals: *If only the church would become less judgmental and more tolerant, then people would return to it. If only the church would be more open to other religions and less focused on Jesus Christ as the way, then society would appreciate the church's role in helping people in the world. If only the church would shed its view of salvation as procured by a violent "bloody sacrifice" through Christ's death in appeasement of the wrath of God the Father and would take up a view of atonement that is peaceable, then the world would be less violent. If only the church would jettison its rhetoric about lifestyles and welcome all styles of living, then we could truly be an inclusive home for lost souls.* These proposals are not crafted from my imagination but have arisen recently.[10] As if to put an exclamation point on his article, the author of these challenges and proposals has offered a prophetic warning: "It is this kind of church that will emerge and thrive. The others will die a slow and agonizing painful death."[11] While I disagree with this assessment and some of the proposals he offers, I do recognize the pressure that the church faces to become something that fits the needs of more people today. But is this the answer—changing our theological bases along with our methods so that people like us more? Is the church supposed to adjust its purpose and function for the sake of wider appeal?

We certainly need to reform more than just the methods and programs we utilize while we *do* church; we need to reassess the very *theological* foundation on which those methods stand. We need to grasp a deeper biblical and theological understanding of the nature of the church—who we *are* as the church—in order to engage the world with God's mission. Therefore, in this book I offer the following two lenses to examine the current state of the church and to provide a proposal for each:

9. Sources as diverse as John Shelby Spong's *Why Christianity Must Change or Die: A Bishop Speaks to Believers in Exile* (San Francisco: HarperCollins, 1998) and Michael L. Brown's *Revolution in the Church: Challenging the Religious System with a Call for Radical Change* (Grand Rapids: Chosen, 2002) provide differing criteria for their goal of making the church relevant or effective in this century.

10. See Steve McSwain, "Why Christianity Is Dying While Spirituality Is Thriving," *Huffington Post*, Dec. 10, 2012, http://www.huffingtonpost.com/steve-mcswain/christianity-is-dying-spirituality-is-thriving_b_1950804.html. All of these suggestions above stem from this article. McSwain thinks that new churches—like the emerging church movement—hold the best hope for the "nones," those who want spirituality without religion.

11. McSwain, "Why Christianity Is Dying."

1. a reassessment of a theology of the church with regard to the *nature* of the church;
2. a reconsideration of the tasks and worship of the church with regard to its *mission*.[12]

On the one hand, I have no illusions about the apparent impracticality of my overall proposal. On the other hand, I also have no illusions about the result awaiting us if we do not attempt to bring theological and practical change to the church with something like what is proposed here. The church needs a re-formation of ecclesiology today as surely as it needed a re-formation of soteriology five hundred years ago.

From Individual Believers to a Believers' Church?

The basic ecclesial model upon which our discussion in this book stands is located within the larger framework of what is called the believers' church. Founded after the Protestant Reformation by groups of Anabaptists who felt that the main (or so-called magisterial) Reformers did not renew the structure of the church far enough, the believers' church stressed the need for its members to be *believers*—regenerated persons in Christ—who have followed Christ in baptism.[13] The immediate difficulty with this model for building a doctrine of the Christian *community* is that it leans so heavily toward *individual* decision for Christ that the church becomes more of an afterthought to which individual Christians are somehow tied. Given the rampant individualism of modern Western society and the clear communalism of the people of faith in the Scriptures, this becomes a major concern for building a healthy, more biblically attuned model for the church. Therefore, readers will see that there are features of the believers' church model that need to be tweaked and perhaps even overcome before we can imitate some of the corporate aspects of the church in the New Testament. However, as I will propose, we cannot escape the fact that salvation is *individual*, not corporate.

12. In a companion volume entitled *Serving the People of God's Presence: A Theology of Ministry* (Grand Rapids: Baker Academic, forthcoming), I sketch out in more detail the practical ramifications of the theology presented in this book.

13. Some sources refer to this as the free-church model in order to contrast it with the state-church model, in which being baptized as infants within a certain geographical region "made" one a Christian. While this last description is an oversimplification, I engage it further in *Serving the People of God's Presence*. For more information on the believers' church model, see Franklin H. Littell, "The Concept of the Believers' Church," in *The Concept of the Believers' Church: Addresses from the 1968 Louisville Conference*, ed. James Leo Garrett Jr. (Scottdale, PA: Herald Press, 1969), 15–32.

Given this proposition, then, how can we develop an ecclesiology that is not fraught with individualism?[14]

I deny any automatic conclusion that such a focus on *individual* decision in salvation requires an *individualistic* ecclesiology. Indeed, the theological features of this book were developed in order to craft an ecclesiology where the church

1. is based on each member/participant of a local church being a Christian who has been directly encountered and birthed anew by the Spirit of God and has chosen to respond to this grace given them by being baptized in water (often called believers' baptism);

2. is constituted by the Spirit drawing and binding together the people of God into a newly empowered community (the body of Christ) to fulfill the mission of God in the world; and

3. is crafted both individually and *especially* communally by the Spirit into the shape and image of Christ (attaining to the full stature of Christ, as Paul says in Eph. 4:13, 15).

It is such growing "up into him . . . , which is the head" (KJV) of the church that is the continual process toward the goal not just of individuals but also of the entire community (Eph. 4:15). When *all of us* in the local congregation "continually reflect the glory of the Lord with an unveiled face,"[15] we begin to demonstrate the reality of God's being and nature in the finite world of our human existence (2 Cor. 3:18). When *all of us* in the congregation "are constantly being transformed into the image of the Lord from one stage of glory to another," we begin to witness to the unbelieving world with the presence and power of the God who has encountered us through our collective lives and loving relationships. The metamorphosis (μεταμορφούμεθα | *metamorphoumetha*) required for humans in a congregation to reflect accurately and appropriately their Lord's glory can be accomplished only by that Lord, who is the Spirit. Living and dwelling in the presence of God's glory transforms

---

14. This is also the challenge for developing an evangelical ecclesiology. Stanley Grenz suggests that the focus on personal experience in the new birth influenced this individualistic flavor among evangelicals to the extent that it created a "benign neglect of the church, if not a certain anti-church bias." See Grenz, *Renewing the Center: Evangelical Theology in a Post-Theological Era* (Grand Rapids: Baker Books, 2000), 291.

15. The Greek used in this sentence makes it clear that it is the *group together* that is the subject: "*We all* with *a single unveiled face* reflect the glory of the Lord." The word "face" is in the singular, describing how we all together (plural) are to reflect (or contemplate) God's glory. The Greek reads, ἡμεῖς δὲ πάντες ἀνακεκαλυμμένῳ προσώπῳ τὴν δόξαν κυρίου κατοπτριζόμενοι. When this passage is used in the next few sentences, it is my translation of 2 Cor. 3:18 from the Greek.

us into the people of God—a people who grow up together to look like their God in terms of nature and action. Hence, the Christian community is not a voluntary association, which individual believers may choose to join or not. It is a gathering of those called out by the Spirit into fellowship, discipleship, and comradeship in the body of Christ in order to reflect God's nature and to fulfill God's mission on earth.

A Pneumatic Ecclesiology

The dimension whereby I propose to overcome some of the challenges to a believers' church model, or evangelical ecclesiology, is what I call a *pneumatic* approach to the church. While this will be developed more fully throughout the pages of this book, the essential idea highlights the role of the Spirit in creating believers who are new creatures in Christ; in grafting us into the body of Christ, his church; in shaping this new community into the likeness of Christ; and in constituting this new community with such love, unity, and power that the *missio Dei* (mission of God) is being fulfilled in this world by its actions. The reason this is *pneumatic* is because it relies heavily on the Spirit's work in individuals and in the community; it is the Spirit of God who creates both Christians *and* Christian communities. It is the Spirit of God who brings into our finite, sinful world a direct encounter with God's presence and power so that the new community formed by God's hand continues the ministry of Christ here and now. To say that this ecclesiology is pneumatic is *not* to imply that the church is merely an invisible fellowship. Just as encounters with the Spirit happen within our human bodies in time and space so that we are being transformed in our earthly, historical existence day by day (2 Cor. 4:7), so too the Spirit's operation in knitting together human lives into the body of Christ occurs within visible communities in human history.[16]

Hopefully, my proposal will provide some new insight to help resolve some of the difficulties for a believers' church model, while at the same time offering more than just a believers' church ecclesiology. Moreover, it will be evident that

16. To make the church entirely into an invisible communion of believers is to offer an ecclesial form of docetism, in which the true essence of the church lies in its invisible, spiritual nature. The trappings of human institutions or structure or order are something less than or other than the true body of Christ. Swiss theologian Emil Brunner comes very close to this idea, emphasizing the spiritual, invisible nature of the true church as a fellowship of brothers and sisters in Christ. See Emil Brunner, *Das Mißverständnis der Kirche* (Stuttgart: Evangelisches Verlagswerk, 1951), 12, where the church is identified as a "community of Christ," or a "pure fellowship of persons," not an "institution, a Something [*ein Etwas*]." While I think Brunner offers a powerful concept regarding the spiritual dimension of the church's existence, I also believe he is mistaken since the church in his mind seems to hover over the reality of existence in time and space without any concrete order for its existence.

Pentecostal concepts flood my proposal, yet this project is designed to be more than a Pentecostal ecclesiology. It is my conviction that the situation of the church today is so dire that a new way of conceiving the local body of Christ in theological and practical dimensions is necessary for the future well-being of the gospel of Christ in the Western world (and perhaps even more broadly than that). For any relevant and effective church bearing the name "Christian" in the twenty-first century, at least some of the features proposed here will need to be incorporated. Essentially, I propose the following major points:

1. *If the church is the people of God, then <u>we should reflect the nature of the God we serve</u> in all aspects of our lives.* From our understanding of God should come our understanding of the church; insight from trinitarian relations should offer some insight into and paradigms for human relations within the body of Christ. It only makes sense that the people of God should reflect the character of their God. But *how* can God's people act and think like God? This discussion is engaged in chapters 1–2 of this book.

2. *If the people of God are to reflect God's nature, then <u>we must be transformed</u> by the presence and power of God.* The presence of God is the necessary requisite for accomplishing God's will as a community of believers. As I will show, the Spirit of God brings God's presence to believers both in their individual lives and in their corporate life. Along with this presence comes a power to accomplish what God calls us to do. This material is explained further in chapter 3 of this book.

3. *If the people of God are to do the work of God, then they <u>must be gathered for worship</u> to glorify God and <u>be trained to reach out</u> to others in the body of Christ and the world.* As we, the people of God, dwell together in God's presence, we align our hearts with God's heart, which shapes us with proper motivation for loving others. We practice this love first in the community of fellow believers, and then we move out together to witness and serve the people of the world. We proclaim and hear proclaimed the Word of God, and through the Spirit's help, we share this Word with others. This is the focus of chapters 4–6.

4. *If the people of God are to be equipped to do the work of ministry, then they must be <u>led by servants</u> who reflect Jesus's own reversal of worldly power and tend the flock of God entrusted to their care with love and respect, thereby opening space for God's presence and power both within and without the congregation.* Church leaders are given by Christ to local congregations and the church as a whole for the purpose

of equipping disciples to serve. The entire body of Christ is meant to be ministers—servants of their Lord and of people. The leaders are not meant to perform all the work to be done but to train disciples of Christ to live and work in the world by the power of the Spirit. Successful business models of leadership and secular CEOs may provide some insight into managing people, but they cannot be the basis for leadership training in the church. It is this material that the book *Serving the People of God's Presence* develops, along with a proposal for restructuring the church based on the pneumatic empowerment of the Spirit.

God's Presence and Power

A further word needs to be said about the title of the book: *The People of God's Presence*. While there are other important New Testament images of the church that carry significant messages about our nature—*who* the church is to be—I have chosen the phrase "people of God" as a primary image since it is one that readily brings continuity to both the old and new covenants, speaking directly to a major point of this book.[17] God desired to have a people with whom he could share fellowship and face-to-face communication; as we will see, this intent was delayed in the old covenant (Exod. 19–24) but revisited in the new covenant, where it was fulfilled in Christ (1 Pet. 2:9–10). Due to the Spirit's mediatorial role between the risen Christ and believers today, we no longer need any human go-between office since that has been filled by our high priest, Jesus Christ. It is the Spirit who is the bridge between heaven and earth, between the spiritual realm and the terrestrial realm. When he ascended to heaven, Christ sent the promised Counselor, the Holy Spirit, to reside with us and in us, being called alongside us to help (John 14–16).

Here two key concepts come into play: the presence and power of God. From how I read the New Testament *and* how I have experienced the risen Lord in my life and the life of the church, the *presence of God* is necessary for us to experience transformation (being "born again" by the Spirit; John 3), to understand who Christ is and what he has taught (being led by the Spirit, who "will guide" us "into all truth"; John 16:13; Rom. 8:14, 16), and to follow the guidance of the Scripture as genuine children of God—true disciples of

---

17. An older but definitive study of the various images for church used in the New Testament remains Paul S. Minear's *Images of the Church in the New Testament*, New Testament Library, ed. C. Clifton Black, John T. Carroll, and Beverly Roberts Gaventa (Louisville: Westminster John Knox, 2004; orig. ed., 1960). Minear's chapter on "minor images" of the church is especially intriguing. I have also benefited from Everett Ferguson's discussion of this topic: *The Church of Christ: A Biblical Ecclesiology for Today* (Grand Rapids: Eerdmans, 1996), esp. 73–91 on the people of God.

Jesus Christ (being adopted into the family of God by the Spirit and crying, "Abba, Father," as did Jesus himself; Rom. 8:14–15). In what may be the most magisterial study of Paul and the Spirit in recent times, New Testament scholar Gordon Fee has concluded that when Paul uses the motif of "presence" in his writings, it is essentially synonymous with the Spirit of God. He states that central to Paul's theology of the Spirit is the idea

> that the Spirit is the fulfillment of the promises found in Jeremiah and Ezekiel: that God himself would breathe on us and we would live; that he would write his law in our hearts; and especially that he would give his Spirit "unto us," so that we are indwelt by him. What is crucial for Paul is that we are thus indwelt by the eternal God. The gathered church and the individual believer are the new locus of God's own presence with his people; and the Spirit is the way God is now present.[18]

Fee notes that the Spirit is God—a person, a presence, and a power. While I have no conscious memory of how I arrived at understanding the important role that "presence" and "power" play in this book, I believe it was somewhat influenced by Fee's depiction of Paul's ideas.

My proposal will attempt to demonstrate the necessity of God's *direct presence* for individual believers and for the gathering of believers locally in a community of faith. Just as Moses understood the disaster awaiting the people of Israel if God's presence would not go with them, we, too, grasp the significance of God being with us: "If your Presence does not go with us, do not send us up from here. How will anyone know that you are pleased with me and with your people unless you go with us? What else will distinguish me and your people from all the other people on the face of the earth?" (Exod. 33:15–16). While it is true that God's presence is actually everywhere (Ps. 139), it is not this omnipresent reality of God's life that we are noting here with the word "presence." Instead, it is more akin to the glory of God filling the temple of Solomon so that the priests could not minister in the temple (1 Kings 8:11).[19] It is the presence of God indwelling believers individually *and* corporately that distinguishes us from all other peoples on the earth.

18. Gordon D. Fee, *God's Empowering Presence: The Holy Spirit in the Letters of Paul* (Peabody, MA: Hendrickson, 1994), 6–7. I call this work magisterial for three reasons: (1) its scope—the entire corpus of Paul's Letters in search of how the Spirit is understood in them; (2) its length—915 pages of intense, non-repetitive study; and (3) its evidence marshaled to substantiate its thesis—an overwhelming argument sustained throughout the text, bringing a powerful conclusion to the unity on this theme of God's presence in Paul's writings.

19. The layout of these Scriptures follows what Fee has written in *God's Empowering Presence*, 7–9.

We belong to God because we have been encountered by God's presence and have responded positively to his gracious overtures. If the church is to remain relevant and a vital part of the life of any society, it must stop searching for programs that appeal to those who either are or are not attending church and instead start engaging in a search for the presence of God in their lives within the corporate life of the local body of Christ.[20]

This brings us to the word "power" itself. Fee's use of the word "empowering" to describe God's presence is quite ingenious, since it seems to characterize Paul's own understanding of the Spirit's power in our lives. As Fee summarizes Paul's thoughts on power, he states, "We are not left on our own as far as our relationship with God is concerned; neither are we left on our own to 'slug it out in the trenches,' as it were, with regard to the Christian life. Life in the present is empowered by the God who dwells among us and in us."[21] These words reflect Paul's own optimism about life in the Spirit, both individually and corporately. Humans who are believers in Jesus Christ have been indwelt with God's presence through the work of the Spirit and should find that they have the power to live the life of a disciple of Christ, assisted in this endeavor by the family of God in the community of faith. This is the power necessary to transform us from self-centered sinners to other-centered givers. However, just as we humans cannot live the Christian life without the Spirit's presence and power, so too the church cannot reflect the nature of God without the Spirit's presence and power.

One recurring issue that I have experienced in ministry is the challenge of leadership. In many cases, the way we have structured congregations affects the way we experience the church. Here I am referring not to styles of *governance* (such as episcopal, congregational, or presbyterian) but to the structure of leadership in the overall internal operations of a local church gathering. Rather than ignore the issue of leadership in this book on ecclesiology, I have set aside an entire companion volume (*Serving the People of God's Presence*) to deal with it in the context of power. In the companion volume,

20. As an example of one group that is definitely not heeding the revamping of church through programs, bells, or whistles, see Jonathan Aigner's blog *Ponder Anew* (also located at patheos.com). Speaking to the church today, he states, "In modeling worship after commercial entertainment, you've compromised your identity, and we're still not coming back. And even if we did, would there be any church left? Would there be anything beyond the frills, the lights, the performance, the affected vocals? Would we still see a cross? Would we still find our place among the saints who have come before? Would we find reminders of our life-long need of grace?" "Dear Church: An Open Letter from One of Those Millennials You Can't Figure Out," May 13, 2015, http://www.patheos.com/blogs/ponderanew/2015/05/13/dear-church-an-open-letter-from-one-of-those-millennials-you-cant-figure-out/.

21. Fee, *God's Empowering Presence*, 8.

I ask questions about theory and praxis in relation to leadership as well as questions about the New Testament and church leadership. Yet perhaps the most important thing in this companion volume will be a call for a different approach to understanding "power" and "authority" among God's people. As Daniel Migliore has noted with regard to issues of power, "To be moved by the Spirit of resurrection and new life is to undergo a *metanoia*, a conversion, a complete turnaround in one's understanding of power and in one's exercise of power. Nothing in one's daily life and practice is left undisturbed."[22] It is that "conversion" and how it can be implemented in the church that I consider in *Serving the People of God's Presence*.

Therefore, I will propose some radical changes in the way we consider leaders (clergy) and even in the way we consider followers (laity).[23] One thing is clear to me: the way we have done things in the structuring of the church frequently has led to power struggles in local congregations and to some of God's people being seriously harmed. While these things may never be completely overcome in this life, shouldn't the church work toward imitating the Lord so that such a worldly view of "power" could be diminished and the true, authentic understanding of power as servanthood be realized?

The result of this *theological and practical* reorientation of the church could be no less impactful than the Reformation of the 1500s on the doctrines of salvation and justification. It is time for the church to be reformed, because if it is not, it may find itself preaching to a disinterested, deafened world.

Sitting On Our Past?

Several times during seminary training in Ohio, I was asked to fill in for a pastor about thirty miles away. The pastor was a fellow seminarian. This particular church refused to get a permanent pastor, so they would come down to the seminary and pluck one of us for a plush job for the two or three years we were there. While I was never chosen for the more permanent

22. Daniel L. Migliore, *The Power of God and the gods of Power* (Louisville: Westminster John Knox, 2008), 56.

23. My choice of the biblical image "people of God" for the primary image to describe the church in this book is due in part to a desire to rethink the concept of λαός | *laos* (Greek for "people") for today's church, especially over against the troublesome divide of God's people into "clergy" and "laity." As we shall see, even the English word "clergy" derives from the Greek word κλῆρος | *klēros*, which refers to "a lot, a portion, a possession, or something assigned," as in 1 Pet. 5:3. The people of God are the *klēroi*, the flock allotted to the care of shepherds. So the people (the *laos*) of God are also the "clergy" (*klēroi*) in the more biblical sense of that term. See Everett Ferguson, *The Church of Christ*, 75. These concepts are clarified and supported further in *Serving the People of God's Presence*.

assignment, I was asked several times to fill in while my friend was away or on vacation.

The church was one of a kind. It had eight members—the same eight members for dozens of years. They met every Sunday morning to perform their liturgy precisely as they had for decades. (It was made clear to me that changing or adding one syllable would place my honorarium at risk!) Each member filed in on Sunday until all eight found their pew spots in this 125-year-old building. The architecture and grounds were exquisite. The place, however, was lifeless. All of the members were over seventy years old, and it was clear that newcomers were not welcomed. Once, it had been the largest church in the town; now it was the smallest. It lived off the past—quite literally. In its heyday, an endowment fund was established; by the time I preached there, it had accumulated almost three million dollars! And eight people sat on it every Sunday, keeping up the appearance of a church. There was no evangelism, no outreach, no benevolence for the poor in town, no hands outstretched to the community. Only eight souls were keeping the status quo. I wondered, Could the church as a whole—*the* body of Christ—become like this church?

It is my belief that a renewed theological dialogue is needed to ensure that such an outcome does not happen to the church. Not until our *theology of the church* begins to affect the *life of the church* will we engage the world around us in a manner that is both relevant and effective. This book heads toward that goal of engaging a theological conversation, especially by providing theological and practical proposals for a renewed doctrine of the church.

This book begins by examining the traditional model of the church as the mediator of God's presence and moves forward to lay a theological foundation for the church as the people of God's direct presence and power. *Serving the People of God's Presence* continues in this direction by asking how the church could be structured and led as a people of God's presence and power. It is my hope that the radical nature of the overall proposal will generate discussion among God's people so that we can be light and salt to a world that desperately needs the message of Christ—the good news.

The Church as *the* Means of Connecting with God?

Direct Encounters with God and Secondary Mediation in the Church

Encounters between God and Humans: Direct or Indirect?

The people of God have experienced the presence of the risen Christ *directly* through the presence of the Holy Spirit and the instrumentality of the Word of God; they have been (and are being) transformed by this encounter. Moreover, the people of God continue to experience the presence of God *directly* through the presence of the Spirit and within the gathering of God's people for worship, instruction, ministry, and sending. Overall, this is the proposal of this book. The initial encounters with God's Spirit in order to bring about salvation may come all at once or over many years through many means. Within such experiences, as God uses various means to connect with a human, the Spirit makes *direct* connection with the unbeliever's spirit and therefore reveals the truth of the gospel in Jesus Christ. While God may have used a person sharing their experience with God, a worship service in a local church, a sunset over the Rocky Mountains, the preaching of the Scriptures on the radio, "a flute concerto, the blossoming shrub, or a dead dog"[1] to initiate

---

1. *CD* I/1:55 (2nd ed.). Here we find Barth stressing the sovereignty of God to speak to humans outside of the Word of God as proclaimed by the church; he suggests that we would do well to listen if it really is God. Yet we cannot build our theology based on these experiences. In the context of arguing for the proclamation of the Word of God, then, Barth raises several

these encounters with us, these were *secondary means* to the *primary or direct* encounter with God. By using the words "primary" and "secondary," I do not mean to denigrate the latter, since both are ways in which God operates in our midst. However, what I am suggesting is that within such indirect, secondary means, God confronts us in a direct, primal encounter of an "I" and a "Thou." The Holy Spirit connects with our spirits *directly*. Jürgen Moltmann offers a clear description of what he calls experiences of the Holy Spirit: "We are saying that these experiences [of the Spirit] are of unfathomable depth, because in them God himself is present in us [*weil in ihnen Gott selbst in uns anwesend ist*], so that in the immanence of our hearts we discover a transcendent depth."[2] This heads toward what I mean by experiencing the direct presence of God. While it is true that God accommodates to us by stooping to our level with signs and symbols to mediate his presence to us, it is also true that we may experience God directly even within that mediation. Thus, while utilizing indirect means of physical, tangible signs, God still encounters us directly through his Spirit. The difficulty with this proposal is that many understandings of the church have focused on the church itself as *the only* means of connecting with God; the church somehow becomes the *primary* way by which humans can connect with God and God with them. I find this conclusion to be problematic.

It seems true to say that physical signs (media) may indeed participate in some way with the thing they are signifying, thereby *opening up space for God to enter and truly encounter us*. However, if the focus of our attention is on the sign and not on the presence of God within, behind, or beyond the symbol, then we have somehow missed the occasion for God's presence to confront us *directly*. To be sure, missing the direct presence of God by focusing on the secondary means may not have been the intent of the authors we will survey in this chapter, but it certainly is the result of their ecclesiological proposals. The origin and continuance of the Christian life are not found in the secondary accoutrements of the church's rituals or activities; the origin and continuance of the Christian life are found in a direct encounter of the Spirit of God with a human being, such that a transformation occurs—a passing from death to life, created anew in Christ Jesus by the power of the Spirit. "The experience of the Spirit makes Christ—the risen Christ—

---

quotes from the Gallic Confession (1559) that deal with the need for pastors to instruct the faithful in the gospel of Christ.

2. Jürgen Moltmann, *The Spirit of Life: A Universal Affirmation*, trans. Margaret Kohl (Minneapolis: Fortress, 1992), 155. The original German work is *Der Geist des Lebens: Eine ganzheitliche Pneumatologie*, Werke 7 (Gütersloh: Gütersloher Verlagshaus, 2016; orig. ed., 1991), 169.

present, and with him makes the eschatological future present too."[3] It is my contention that this initial, salvific encounter with God—rebirth or regeneration, if you will—is the basis for calling ourselves Christians and the foundation for being engrafted into the body of Christ. "In the moment of 'rebirth,' eternity touches time."[4] Without such an experience in God, we are left circulating around things that look and sound churchy, but without a truly life-changing movement from death to life. Only the Spirit of God can birth us a second time and engraft us into the body of Christ (John 3:3–8). *To become a Christian* can take a moment when the presence of Christ encounters us and we respond positively to God's gracious Spirit; *to become Christlike*, however, takes a lifetime of continual divine encounters and a life-response of obedience within the context of a community of believers where we learn together how to spend our lives for God and others, where we share life together while following Christ, and where we continue to experience together the empowering presence of the Spirit leading us away from our self-centeredness and into a life that is other-centered, just like the Triune God. To accomplish this *becoming*, we need the body of Christ—the church.

So then, is the church only good for making us better followers of Christ? It is certainly more than that. Through the secondary mediation of signs and symbols, I contend that God's Spirit may encounter us directly. These are instruments through which God himself[5] has chosen to meet with us. This encounter does not, however, make the instruments themselves holy—just useful. The church, then, has a role to play in spreading the gospel of Christ so that people who are encountered by the Spirit may be able to discern who this One is who confronted them.

As already noted, this proposal for a direct encounter with God does not mean there is no indirect or mediated avenue through which God engages humankind. God continues to speak and encounter us through these secondary means, but at the same time believers have something more. God has also given us his own Spirit—the same Spirit who raised Christ from the dead and now works with power in us to raise us from the death of sin to the life of God (Rom. 8:9–11). The Spirit of God lives within us, assuring us that we

---

3. Moltmann, *Spirit of Life*, 147.

4. Moltmann, *Spirit of Life*, 147.

5. Throughout the book, I vary the reflexive pronoun for God from "Godself" to "himself." The former term is a recent neologism meant to overcome the difficulty in English of not having a genderless reflexive pronoun to refer to God. I acknowledge that God is neither male nor female but is above these designations, because God is Spirit. Whenever possible, I have used "Godself." But in those instances where the use of "Godself" leads to awkward syntax and cadence, I use "himself" as the reflexive pronoun for God.

belong to Christ (8:9). Therefore, those who are led by this indwelling Spirit of God are truly God's children (8:14). The Spirit within us does not bring fear, but instead the certainty of our adoption into God's family, whereby we cry "Abba, Father," as did Jesus (8:15). This same indwelling Spirit "testifies with our spirit that we are God's children" (8:16). Finally, the indwelling Spirit also "intercedes for us through wordless groans" (8:26b). Through the power of the *indwelling Spirit of God*, then, believers have the direct, immediate presence of the living God in Jesus Christ, assuring them of their salvation and adoption into God's family as well as attesting to the Spirit's own presence within them by praying through them with groans from their inner beings. We have the privilege of experiencing God face-to-face in this new covenant—and not solely through mediation; such encounters continue throughout the Christian life because the Spirit lives within us, leading, guiding, and assuring us of God's very presence. This is what it means to live *in Christ* and have Christ live *in us*. I can think of no clearer biblical expression than this to describe the *direct encounter* with God.

Two Challenges to a Direct Encounter with God

In speaking of a *direct encounter* with God, I face two major challenges. First, there seem to be only *indirect encounters* with God, since the infinite God uses (or must use) media in order to connect with finite humans. At best, then, humans have an encounter with God that is not really with God but with the media used by God.[6] This becomes problematic because humans seem to have an interpretive network centered in our brains and coordinated by means of our social network to give meaning to these media and to any experience we might have of them. Therefore, the thorny issue of subjectivism raises its head: how can we know that our interpretation of the God whom we experienced is genuine or merely a warped interpretation of the medium through which God has chosen to operate? How can we even say we have experienced a *direct* encounter with God when such an experience would undoubtedly be impossible in this life (rendering us dead; to use a biblical concept: "No one may see [God] and live!" Exod. 33:20)? Yet if we only have *indirect* encounters with God, how can we know that what we experienced was truly God and not some undigested piece of cheese (to quote Ebenezer Scrooge upon seeing one of the spirits that visited him on Christmas Eve)?

The second challenge to a direct encounter relates to the instrumentality itself, especially in terms of the way the Christian church has tended to view

---

6. A thorough examination of what I mean by "direct encounter with God" will be offered in chap. 3.

itself as a mediator of God's presence to humans. When the church sets itself up as *the* medium through which God connects to humans in this world, the danger of making the instrument itself into something sacred becomes apparent. When the church is seen as *the* mediator of God's presence, then humans tend to look for God *in the church*—that is, in the medium—rather than *within the instrument*. I have no desire to nullify the church's important role in assisting people in coming to salvation—preaching the gospel, spreading the good news everywhere, engaging in love of neighbor, publishing the text of the Bible, and so forth. Without these things, an encounter with the living Christ might be strangely unrecognizable. However, by using these media in the community of believers, the Spirit is able to encounter humans *directly* by bringing to their hearts the certitude that what they have heard in a sermon, testimony, or Scripture itself is truly the God who loves them and wants to deliver them. Such truth does not make the medium into something sacred, however, or even sacramental. It merely points beyond itself to the presence of God *within* the medium. This is what creates a *direct awareness* or *perception* of God in people, thereby forging a *direct encounter* that opens the possibility for transformation of life. Thus, I am not denying that God uses media, but I refuse to allow these media to take the place of the Holy Spirit, who directly encounters our whole beings.

While this entire book works toward sharpening our thesis and dealing with challenges to it, the remainder of this chapter will focus on the role of the church as a mediator between God and humans (the second challenge). After dealing with the nature of God and God's people in chapter 2, I turn in chapter 3 to explicate direct experiences further and respond to the question of whether there can be only indirect encounters with God (the first challenge). By engaging these challenges to the thesis, I will also be laying out a doctrine of the church along the way.

Is the Church a Mediator between God and Humans?

"The one Christ is the mediator and the way of salvation: he is present to us in his body which is the Church."[7] It has been a long-held tradition in Christianity to view the church as the mediating presence of Christ to the world. The invisible, risen Christ is made visible through the physical reality of the church. "The one mediator, Christ, established and ever sustains here on earth his holy Church . . . as a visible organization through which he communicates

7. *Catechism of the Catholic Church* (New York: Doubleday, 1995), 244, ¶846.

truth and grace to all men."[8] According to this tradition, if humans desire to connect with God or if God wants to speak to humans, it will always be done *through* the church, which is itself a means of distributing grace.

This view was succinctly described by Cyprian, bishop of Carthage (ca. 200–258 CE). He suggested that apart from the church, there is no salvation, because "those who do not have the church as Mother cannot have God as Father."[9] For him, the church is our mother, because we are born to eternal life through her ministry. The church is not Christ, but rather his body—his representation on earth. Through the church, then, "faith comes from God's grace."[10] The souls of humans are saved by entrance into this institution.[11]

A variation of this institutional view—although still a model of mediation—emphasizes the sacramental nature of the church itself. Jesus Christ himself ministers through the liturgy, sacraments, and the rites of the church.[12] The church, then, is the mediator of God's presence to the world as a means of grace. The Second Vatican Council taught, "The Church is in Christ like a sacrament or as a sign and instrument [*veluti sacramentum seu signum et instrumentum*] both of a very closely knit union with God and of the unity of the whole human race."[13] Later in the same document, Vatican II

---

8. *Lumen gentium* 1.8 (*Dogmatic Constitution on the Church*, Nov. 21, 1964), in *Vatican Council II: The Conciliar and Post Conciliar Documents*, ed. Austin Flannery, trans. Colman O'Neill (Collegeville, MN: Liturgical Press, 1980), 357; hereafter cited as *Vatican Council II* (Flannery). Also see Heinrich Denzinger, *Lumen gentium*, in *Enchiridion symbolorum definitionum et declarationum de rebus fidei et morum / Compendium of Creeds, Definitions, and Declarations on Matters of Faith and Morals*, ed. Peter Hünermann, Robert Fastiggi, and Anne Englund Nash, 43rd ed. (San Francisco: Ignatius, 2012), 866, §4118; hereafter cited as *Lumen gentium*, in Denzinger, *Enchiridion*. This is a bilingual edition of the approved Latin and English translations for the major documents of the Catholic Church.

9. Cyprian, *De catholicae ecclesiae unitate* 6, in *S. Thasci Caecili Cypriani: Opera Omnia*, Corpus Scriptorum Ecclesiasticorum Latinorum, vol. 3, part 1, ed. Guilelmus Hartel (Vindobonae: Apud C. Geroldi Filium Bibliopolam Academiae, 1867), 214, lines 23–24. The Latin for this translation reads, "*Habere non potest Deum patrem qui ecclesiam non habet matrem.*" See also Paul Tillich, *A History of Christian Thought: From Its Judaic and Hellenistic Origins to Existentialism*, ed. Carl E. Braaten (New York: Simon & Schuster, 1968), 100.

10. Hans Küng, *The Church* (Garden City, NY: Doubleday, 1976), 57.

11. Avery Cardinal Dulles describes this model of the church as "institutional." See Dulles, *Models of the Church*, expanded ed. (New York: Doubleday, 1987), 41–42.

12. *Sacrosanctum Concilium* 1.7 (*The Constitution on the Sacred Liturgy*, Dec. 4, 1963), trans. Joseph Rodgers, Clifford Howell, and Austin Flannery, in *Vatican Council II* (Flannery), 4–5. Vatican II states that Christ is "always present in his Church, especially in her [the Church's] liturgical celebrations" (4). The liturgy is even called the "exercise of the priestly office of Jesus Christ" (5). Also, *Sacrosanctum Concilium*, in Denzinger, *Enchiridion*, 849, §4007.

13. *Lumen gentium* 1.1, in Denzinger, *Enchiridion*, 860, §4101; also cf. *Vatican Council II* (Flannery), 350. See also Robert W. Jenson, "The Church and the Sacraments," in *The Cambridge Companion to Christian Doctrine*, ed. Colin E. Gunton (Cambridge: Cambridge University Press, 1997), 207. Jenson translates this phrase as follows: "a sacrament, as it were," or "a sort

says that Christ sent the Spirit to the disciples, and through the Spirit, he "has established his Body which is the Church as the universal sacrament of salvation."[14] Henri de Lubac, a twentieth-century Catholic theologian, had held the same view fifteen years prior: "If Christ is the sacrament of God, the Church is for us the sacrament of Christ; she represents him in the full and ancient meaning of the term, she really makes him present."[15] It is clear that both Vatican II and Henri de Lubac saw the church as a mediator of Christ or even as a sacramental means of grace. Many others in the twentieth century took this view. Perhaps the most influential theologian of this ilk has been the Austrian Catholic Karl Rahner, who viewed the church as a "primal sacrament."[16] Christ is the "primordial sacrament," because he is precisely "what is signified (God in God's self-communication to human beings)."[17] What is the church, then, in terms of a sacrament? Rahner explains: "God is so present in the church that the church can be called a sacrament of God's self-communication; or to distinguish it from the seven sacraments, we can say that the church is the most important, the primal sacrament."[18] To paraphrase Rahner's interpretation, "As Christ was the sacrament of the Father, so the Church was the sacrament of Christ himself."[19] Christ is a sacrament of God because he represents God's love and grace to humanity. Christ, in his visible flesh, reveals this love. "Only in exteriorizing itself does grace achieve the highest intensity of its realization."[20] Christ contains the grace he represents in exterior and visible form. In this way, the church is a sacrament, a sign of God's grace in Christ. It, too, contains the grace it represents, although as Rahner concedes, not in exactly the same way that Christ does.

---

of sacrament." He also suggests that this sacramental view of the church has become central to Catholic ecclesiology and even ecumenical ecclesiology.

14. *Lumen gentium* 7.48, in Denzinger, *Enchiridion*, 900, §4168; also, *Vatican II Council* (Flannery), 407. The Latin phrase of interest is *"per eum Corpus suum quod est Ecclesia ut universale salutis sacramentum constituit."*

15. Henri de Lubac, *Catholicism: Christ and the Common Destiny of Man*, trans. Lancelot C. Sheppard and Sr. Elizabeth Englund (San Francisco: Ignatius, 1988; orig. French ed., 1947), 76. Cf. also Dulles, *Models of the Church*, 63.

16. Karl Rahner, "The Church: Basis of Pastoral Action," in *Karl Rahner: Theologian of the Graced Search for Meaning*, ed. Geffrey B. Kelly, The Making of Modern Theology: Nineteenth- and Twentieth-Century Texts, ed. John W. de Gruchy (Minneapolis: Fortress, 1992), 265. This reading comes from Rahner's 1964 text, *Theology of Pastoral Action*.

17. Rahner, "The Church," 265.

18. Rahner, "The Church," 265.

19. See Richard Lennan, *The Ecclesiology of Karl Rahner* (Oxford: Clarendon, 1997), 24. Rahner broadens the concept of sacrament to mean a deep symbol of a thing signified. There is reality in the symbol itself, and therefore Christ can be seen as the symbol of the Father. Now, however, Christ's presence is symbolized (or sacramentalized) in the church.

20. Dulles, *Models of the Church*, 67.

One upshot of these sacramental views is that since the cross-resurrection event, God does not deal *directly* with people, but only *indirectly* through the institutional, visible church. Obviously, this is primarily a position of Roman Catholicism, but not exclusively so. The Protestant Reformation did not dramatically alter this view. For all of his talk of the priesthood of individual believers and of focus on the human self before God, Luther never really solidified a place for a re-formation of the doctrine of the church. While he viewed the church as a *Gemeinde*—a community of believers with little need for outward forms to give it identity—he neither developed this fully nor established it in Wittenberg or anywhere else in Germany.[21]

Luther did, however, provide a brief description of what a group of earnest Christians who gather together might look like. *Ecclesiola*, or "little church," was Luther's way of expressing this smaller covenantal community. Hilbert argues that Luther held this *ecclesiola* to be a realistic option yet did not put it into an embodied reality.[22] In the twentieth century, several theologians, such as Emil Brunner and Dietrich Bonhoeffer, emphasized the church as community, attempting to place more emphasis on the *invisible* union of the body of Christ. Brunner even "rejected all law, sacrament, and priestly office as incompatible with the true being of the Church."[23] In Lutheran ecclesiology today, there seems to exist a tension between the church as a ritualistic institution and as a "brotherhood." The fact that Luther suggested the priesthood of all believers but never fleshed out its practical implications in the real, concrete ecclesial life of churches in Germany feeds this tension, though it is interesting to note in this regard that George H. Williams has described the believers' church as having "some of the characteristics of an *ecclesiola in ecclesia*."[24]

Due to the ramifications of the doctrine of justification by faith alone, not only did the change of soteriology open the door to an emphasis on individual

21. Martin Luther, *Liturgy and Hymns*, ed. Ulrich S. Leupold, in *Luther's Works*, ed. Helmut T. Lehman et al. (Philadelphia: Fortress, 1965), 53:53–55.

22. Although it is almost one hundred years old, the definitive work on this subject is that of Gerhard Hilbert, *Ecclesiola in Ecclesia: Luthers Anschauungen von Volkskirche und Freiwilligkeitskirche in ihrer Bedeutung für die Gegenwart* (Leipzig: A. Deichert, 1920), see esp. 1–3. See also Howard A. Snyder, *Signs of the Spirit: How God Reshapes the Church* (Eugene, OR: Wipf & Stock, 1997), 37; and J. S. Whale, *The Protestant Tradition: An Essay in Interpretation* (Cambridge: Cambridge University Press, 1955), 163.

23. Dulles, *Models of the Church*, 48. Also see Emil Brunner, *Das Mißverständnis der Kirche* (Stuttgart: Evangelisches Verlagswerk, 1951); ET, Brunner, *The Misunderstanding of the Church*, trans. Harold Knight (Philadelphia: Westminster, 1953).

24. See Williams, "A People in Community: Historical Background," in *The Concept of a Believers' Church: Addresses from the 1968 Louisville Conference*, ed. James Leo Garrett Jr. (Scottdale, PA: Herald Press, 1969), 100.

belief, but it also lessened the role the church played in one's salvation. Radical Reformers (Anabaptists, Mennonites, Brethren, and the like) transformed their understanding of the church and its structure completely. Indeed, emphasis was placed on an individual's ability to interpret Scripture for oneself and to pray *directly* to God without the necessity of "Mother Church."[25] The resulting ecclesiology is frequently referred to as "free church" or even "low church." As George Williams suggests, these Radicals felt that the doctrines of justification, original sin, and predestination that spawned the Protestant Reformation seemed "to undercut the significance of their personal religious experience and their continuous exercise of those personal and corporate disciplines by which they strove to imitate in their midst what they construed from the New Testament texts to have been the life of the original apostolic community."[26] This became the basis of their ecclesiological endeavors.

In contrast to the muted ecclesiology of Luther and the radical ecclesiology of the Anabaptists, John Calvin provided a very high view of the church. Echoing the sentiment of Cyprian, Calvin says that the church is our mother.[27] As John Hesselink appropriately comments, "Here Calvin sounds more like a Roman Catholic than a Protestant!"[28] When Jesus ministers today, Calvin argues, it is through the human institution of the church. God did not usher in an age of the Spirit whereby we are "allowed to enjoy an immediate and so-called spiritual relation with God."[29] The fanatics and ecstatics of all ages have presumed this spiritual and direct connection with God, but Calvin argues that God does not work this way. God chooses to use humans as instruments to deliver his Word.[30] If God chose to take the form of human flesh and not reveal himself directly, then it is logical to conclude that God would operate analogously by using earthly vessels to communicate a heavenly gospel. Wilhelm Niesel summarizes Calvin's thought in this regard: "No pure reality of the Spirit has been promised us apart from the work of the Incarnate Son of God nor in independence of the message, which, obediently to His command, His witnesses spread abroad, or apart from the earthly sacraments which He

---

25. George H. Williams, *The Radical Reformation* (Philadelphia: Westminster, 1967), xxv. Other Reformers held similar views with regard to the individual's ability to interpret Scripture, but these had varying arbiters added as a type of "safety net" to deal with those who were handling Scripture too strangely.

26. Williams, *The Radical Reformation*, xxv.

27. *Inst.* 4.1.4 (1016).

28. John I. Hesselink, *Calvin's First Catechism: A Commentary* (Louisville: Westminster John Knox, 1997), 155.

29. Wilhelm Niesel, *The Theology of Calvin*, trans. Harold Knight (Grand Rapids: Baker, 1980), 184.

30. *Inst.* 4.1.5 (1016–18).

has instituted."[31] In other words, God only communicates to us through the mediation of the church—more specifically, through the Word and sacraments. To make this even clearer, Calvin sees the church as a mother who births and nurtures us until we die. "Furthermore, away from her bosom one cannot hope for any forgiveness of sins or any salvation."[32] And this pronouncement caused J. S. Whale to call Calvin the "Cyprian of the Reformation era."[33]

Fanatics who have overstepped their bounds have no use for the church, Calvin thinks. They focus on experience, private reading, and inner meditation.[34] But God has condescended to human need; instead of terrifying us with his thunderous presence, he speaks to us through the mouths of human servants. The church becomes the "mirror" of God's presence, an indirect reflection. Again, Niesel describes Calvin's thought succinctly: "The church is the sphere of the self-revelation of God and of the encounter between Christ and ourselves."[35] Thus, there is no direct experience of Christ by believers; only through the church can we encounter Christ. Only where the Word of God is preached and heard and the sacraments administered rightly does a church exist.[36]

Is the Church Our Mother?

Henri de Lubac rightly noted that the notion of the church as "our mother" is held by Protestants "even after their secession."[37] In terms of the doctrine

---

31. Niesel, *Theology of Calvin*, 184.
32. *Inst.* 4.1.4 (1016).
33. Whale, *The Protestant Tradition*, 161.
34. *Inst.* 4.1.5 (1018).
35. Niesel, *Theology of Calvin*, 185.
36. *Inst.* 4.1.9 (1023).
37. Henri de Lubac, *The Motherhood of the Church*, trans. Sergia Englund (San Francisco: Ignatius, 1982), 75. This quote begins the chapter titled "The Motherhood of the Entire Church" and is followed by a chapter on "The Fatherhood of the Clergy," in which de Lubac extends the metaphor of family to the clergy being the "father," who (in this case) represent God as Father to the people. Elsewhere, de Lubac makes the dimension of the motherhood of the church even clearer:

> The Church is a community, but in order to be that community she is first a hierarchy. The Church we call our Mother is not some ideal and unreal Church but this hierarchical Church herself; not the Church as we might dream her but the Church as she exists in fact, here and now. Thus the obedience which we pledge her in the persons of those who rule her cannot be anything else but a filial obedience. She has not brought us to birth only so as to abandon us and let us take our chance on our own; rather she guards us and keeps us together in a maternal heart. (Henri de Lubac, "Ecclesia Mater," in *The Splendor of the Church*, trans. Michael Mason [San Francisco: Ignatius, 2006; orig. ed., 1956], 264–65)

of the church since the Protestant Reformation, Christian thinkers have apparently fallen into two camps: (1) those who view the church as a mediator of God's presence as well as the "mother" (instrument) of our salvation, and (2) those who view the church as people who *directly* experience God's presence with or without churchly or even sacramental mediation.[38]

This second view is the presupposition on which the proposal of this book rests. In other words, I am proposing a believers' church model in which the church consists of those people who have been regenerated by God's Spirit and adopted into God's family by the same Spirit. While the kingdom of God may appear as a mixture of tares and wheat, the body of Christ has no such mixture. However, this view holds some difficulties. Are we saying that everyone who is a part of *our* local church is "saved" or "regenerated," and therefore those who are part of other churches where mixture is allowed (even expected) are not regenerated? This could be the implication and probably has been the way the believers' church has sensed its distinctiveness in the past. However, this need not be the implication or explication. Of course, there will be people who are not really disciples of Christ but have come to be part of a local church—even a believers' church—for whatever reasons. My intent is not to emphasize that type of person but rather to suggest (along with Friedrich Schleiermacher!) that regeneration is a prerequisite for being a true part of the body of Christ.[39] Here *regeneration* is my term for transformation of a human being who is encountered by the Spirit of God directly, being confronted by the truth of Jesus Christ in the Spirit's *re*-presentation of Christ to him/her, and who thereby believes on the Lord Jesus Christ for salvation, producing a new birth of resurrection life into that human's existence here and now as wrought by the Spirit. Is the church our mother? In terms of nurturing and nourishing our growth in the Christian life, yes; in terms of birthing us into God's kingdom, no. The "mothering"

38. While this may be a broad-stroke depiction of Protestant ecclesiology since the 1500s, it depicts the various views within the movement well enough.

39. Friedrich D. E. Schleiermacher, *Christian Faith: A New Translation and Critical Edition*, ed. Catherine L. Kelsey and Terrence N. Tice, trans. Terrence N. Tice, Catherine L. Kelsey, and Edwina Lawler (Louisville: Westminster John Knox, 2016), 2:761, § 115. Schleiermacher states, "The Christian church is formed by the joining together of individual regenerate persons to affect one another and to cooperate, both in an orderly fashion." To be "regenerate" for Schleiermacher is to partake "of the Holy Spirit, so that there is no vital community with Christ without an indwelling of the Holy Spirit, and vice versa." Schleiermacher, *Christian Faith*, 2:813, §124. Also, cf. §125, in Schleiermacher, *Christian Faith*, 2:818. Perhaps the Moravian influence in Schleiermacher's youth continued with him on this point. I am grateful to Gregor Etzelmüller for pointing out this passage in Schleiermacher when I offered a lecture at Heidelberg University in April 2008.

described in this second aspect is the work of the Holy Spirit, who brings about the new birth (John 3).

How does this relate to our proposal for ecclesiology? Most believers' church ecclesiologies have been crafted—if crafted at all—from the Radical Reformers (chiefly Anabaptists) through very different cultural and historical lenses.[40] Numerous evangelical churches in North America today come from this church movement, emphasizing regeneration followed by believer's baptism (credobaptism). However, the challenge for these churches has been to develop a believers' church ecclesiology that does not wallow in individualism, on the one hand, or puff up into a holier-than-thou triumphalism, on the other. Our proposal submits that not only is such an ecclesiology possible, but it also is essential for overcoming the negative image that the church currently possesses in increasingly post-Christian societies.

The Church—a Voluntary Society of Individual Christians?

In order to tease out the direction our proposal heads, it will be helpful to interact with a theologian who has ties to the evangelical movement yet may not consider himself entirely at home within segments of it. Miroslav Volf has engaged aspects of ecclesiology with a proposal that provides fitting insight for and appropriate contrast to our own proposal here. Volf attempts to craft what he calls a "nonindividualistic Protestant ecclesiology."[41]

Miroslav Volf's Nonhierarchical Ecclesiology

Having presented and analyzed the doctrine of the Trinity from the perspectives of Joseph Cardinal Ratzinger (later, Pope Benedict XVI) and John Zizioulas (Orthodox Metropolitan Bishop of Pergamum) in relation to their doctrines of the church, Miroslav Volf presents his own proposal in contrast to them. His goal is to "develop a nonhierarchical but truly communal ecclesiology based on a nonhierarchical doctrine of the Trinity."[42] His proposal points in the direction of providing the free-church tradition an ecclesiology that does not result in individualism.

40. For a history of the movement, see Donald F. Durnbaugh, *The Believers' Church: The History and Character of Radical Protestantism* (Scottdale, PA: Herald Press, 1985; orig. ed., 1968).

41. Miroslav Volf, *After Our Likeness: The Church as the Image of the Trinity*, Sacra Doctrina: Christian Theology for a Postmodern Age, gen. ed. Alan G. Padgett (Grand Rapids: Eerdmans, 1998), 191.

42. Volf, *After Our Likeness*, 4.

Without detailing the layers of excellent insight that Volf offers, I will summarize and interact with his proposal as it seems germane to my own. Volf views the inner life of the Trinity as a model for building an ecclesiology. While he does not believe we can exactly mimic the life of God here and now, he does believe the Trinity points us toward something of the future eschatological life here and now in the community of faith. He analyzes faith and its connection to salvation by using the early English separatist (Baptist) John Smyth. Volf portrays Smyth as the classic believers' church theologian because he points to individuals experiencing regeneration by the Spirit and then being drawn into voluntary societies called churches. Coming about as a "direct influence" on the individual,[43] salvation occurs for Smyth "between individual souls and God."[44] Volf disparages this approach: "If salvation takes place between the lonely soul and its God, as John Smyth maintains, then it is individualistic."[45] Within such a framework, the church comes about through the voluntary choice of people of faith to join together. As Smyth labels it, a person is "churching himself."[46] The question then becomes one of how the church is used in such an encounter of salvation: Is there any purpose for its existence or any instrumentality in salvation at all?

By way of contrast, Ratzinger suggests that the faith of a person never arises from one's own person but is a gift of God *from the church*. Hence, the church "appears as a mother giving birth to sons and daughters who live with her and through her."[47] Faith is given not taken; humans are passive receivers of the grace handed to them by the collective church.[48] In this way, faith is "co-faith."[49] The individual seems lost in this array of the "whole Christ" (*totus Christus*).

Volf's own approach to faith and the mediation of the church remains rather nuanced. He uses Matthew 18:20 as his guiding principle for ecclesiality: "For where two or three gather in my name, there am I with them." His first comment on this suggests the direction he will head: "According to this text, Christ's presence is promised not to the believing individual directly, but rather to the entire congregation, and only through the latter to the individual. This is why no one can come to faith alone and no one can live in

---

43. Volf, *After Our Likeness*, 161.
44. Volf, *After Our Likeness*, 162.
45. Volf, *After Our Likeness*, 172.
46. Volf, *After Our Likeness*, 175.
47. Volf, *After Our Likeness*, 162.
48. Volf, *After Our Likeness*, 44, 64.
49. Volf, *After Our Likeness*, 33, 35, 37. In this context, the passive mode of reception is clearly underscored through infant baptism.

The Presence of Christ in Matthew 18:20

I am unsure that the context of Matthew 18:20 is about *believing* faith. It seems rather to concern the restoration of someone who has fallen out of fellowship with God and others because of sin. The presence of Christ is there with the disciplining church (even the two or three representatives who have attempted to restore the individual) to underscore the authority with which the entire process is handled. Hence, in the context of this Matthean passage, I agree with the latter half of Volf's statement ("no one can live in faith alone") but not entirely with the former statement ("no one can come to faith alone"). As I suggest below, coming to faith demands more nuance than is offered here.[a]

I have often heard this verse from Jesus repeated at worship gatherings: "For where two or three gather in my name, there am I with them" (Matt. 18:20). It is often used to communicate the idea that whenever we gather in Jesus's name, he has promised to be with us. While I believe the concept itself is true, this verse is not the one to prooftext that idea. Within the context of 18:15–20, Jesus describes a brother or sister who sins and the process that should be followed to deal with that (first, privately, one-on-one; then take two others with you; then take it to the church, the *ekklēsia*). Verse 18 then underscores the authority that the gathered church has to deal with such issues of discipline: "Whatever you bind on earth will be bound in heaven, and whatever you loose on earth will be loosed in heaven" (18:18). Verse 19 continues with the foundation for the gathering's

faith alone."[50] Volf then continues to describe the church as a daughter (*filia*) of faith and then also the mother (*mater*) of faith.[51] For Volf, faith provided to individuals must be ecclesially mediated. "The faith with which I believe is shaped by the ecclesially mediated forms in which it is expressed; there is no pure, ecclesially unmediated faith consisting of pure feeling."[52] Therefore, from the church we receive the *content of faith*, and through the church we learn how to live out that faith. Yet in the same paragraph, Volf maintains that a person's own faith-as-trust (*fiducia*), which brings one to entrust one's life to God, is something only the Spirit—not the church—can give. If the church were to do so, then it would "participate actively in God's salvific activity," which is what Volf understands to be happening with the Catholic Church,

50. Volf, *After Our Likeness*, 162.
51. Volf, *After Our Likeness*, 162.
52. Volf, *After Our Likeness*, 163.

authority for such discipline: "If two of you on earth agree about anything they ask for, it will be done for them by my Father in heaven." The agreement here is commonly understood to be concerning items requested in prayer, but the context has been set by verse 16 (a matter is established in the mouth of two or three witnesses). Now if two or three bring a request to God related to the matter of discipline (binding and loosing), then the Father will do it.

Finally comes 18:20: "For where two or three gather in my name, there am I with them." It is true that Jesus has promised to be "with us" to the end of the ages, even if any believer is alone! He will never leave or forsake us (28:20). Through the power of his Spirit, his presence abides with us both as individuals and in corporate meetings. We do not need to take 18:20 out of context in order to achieve an understanding of God meeting us in our gatherings. What Jesus is addressing in 18:20 is the authoritative right for congregations to deal with believers who sin, as if he himself were there dealing with them—and he is there when two or three gather to provide testimony to the entire church. The church, then, has the authority to disown them as believers—treating them just like the unbeliever (or worse, a pagan or tax collector).

a. See also M. Eugene Boring, *Matthew*, New Interpreter's Bible, ed. Leander E. Keck et al. (Nashville: Abingdon, 1994), 8:379: "With a pair of solemn *amen* sayings the Matthean Jesus assures the church of the divine ratification of its decisions."

especially as reflected in Vatican II's document *Lumen gentium*.[53] Christ must be the *only subject* in the salvific activity, Volf affirms. In this position, or even alongside it, the church can never take Christ's place.

Within this overall approach and critique, Volf strongly suggests that the *totus Christus* of Ratzinger (and others) must be replaced with the more Protestant *solus Christus*: "Precisely in order to preserve the principle *solus Christus*, 'the loneliness of the believing "yes" to God,' a 'yes' that must be pronounced by the self and nobody else, is soteriologically indispensable."[54] Then Volf concludes with this rather astounding statement: "The exclusivity of divine salvific activity requires direct personal acceptance of saving grace by human beings."[55] I use the word "astounding" because it seems that Volf

53. Volf, *After Our Likeness*, 163–64.
54. Volf, *After Our Likeness*, 164.
55. Volf, *After Our Likeness*, 164.

has been arguing against direct experience of God all along, except now, when he comes to the problem of the church somehow joining in the salvific activity, he wants to resort quickly to the direct and personal experience of believers in accepting the grace that saves them through Christ.[56]

However, Volf continues to clarify his point with even greater nuance. No one receives *fiducia from* the church, and the church is not (therefore) another "secondary subject of salvific activity" alongside God.[57] Yet humans receive *fiducia through* the church "because the church is a communion of persons rather than a subject."[58] Volf's main difficulty with Ratzinger's idea of "co-faith" and redemption is that the church becomes the "whole Christ" (*totus Christus*) and as such can be confused with God as some type of co-redeemer of humans. Volf urges that there is no priestly office that hands out *fiducia* or salvation; this must be the work of God in individuals. On the other hand, he asserts that "the word of God that creates faith always comes to individuals through the multidimensional confession of faith of *others*."[59] Precisely what does this mean? How do I come to faith *through* the confession of faith of others? Perhaps he means nothing more than the fact that my hearing the Word creates faith in me, as Romans 10:17 says, and that preaching is a confession of faith of others about and in Jesus Christ. Volf concludes with some words based on Eberhard Jüngel: "Understood in this way, the mother church does *not* stand *over against* individual Christians; rather, Christians *are* the mother church; the mother church is the communion of brothers and sisters that has always existed vis-à-vis the individual Christian. The universal priesthood of believers implies the 'universal motherhood of believers.'"[60] What is the difference here between "Christians *are* the mother church" and "the mother church does *not* stand *over against* individual Christians"? Does Volf mean that the church as mother is *the individual Christian gathered in community*? Further, in what way does the universal priesthood of all believers *imply* the universal motherhood of the church? To call this communion of brothers and sisters the "mother church" seems to redefine the meaning of motherhood—and perhaps even church. The image of motherhood remains a tainted one for the church since it automatically implies birthing rather than simply nurturing or nourishing.

---

56. His footnote 32 infers another point we shall engage: "This is not to deny that every experience of God is mediated. There is no immediate directness; one's own socially mediated self-experience flows into every experience of God" (Volf, *After Our Likeness*, 164n32). It is precisely this claim that I wish to challenge in this book, especially as it relates to ecclesiology.

57. Volf, *After Our Likeness*, 166.

58. Volf, *After Our Likeness*, 166.

59. Volf, *After Our Likeness*, 166 (his emphasis).

60. Volf, *After Our Likeness*, 166 (his emphasis).

And here is the crux of the matter. What is the role of the church in the way a person comes to faith in Jesus Christ? What I find lacking in Volf's proposal is severalfold: (1) the appreciation for the individual decision about Jesus Christ seems ambiguous at best in Volf's account; (2) the concept of "mother" for the church continues to lead people into an understanding of the church as an acting subject of salvation alongside Christ, regardless of how many qualifications Volf attempts to provide; (3) the "confession of faith of *others*" remains sketchy and unclear in its portrayal; and (4) the role of the Spirit in mediating salvation to individuals who are confronted by God's presence seems inchoate, and therefore dimensions of the Spirit's role in establishing the church are also lacking.[61]

While there is more that we will engage throughout this book with Volf's fecund proposal, enough has been said so far to give an introductory glance at the potential problem facing proposals that deal with the traditional mediatorial role of the church within the context of a free-church or believers' church tradition.[62] Allow me to sketch my own approach as to how one comes to faith and the role of the church in that process; such a sketch will provide a sense of where we are going in future chapters, a broad map of the forest that may provide a glimpse of the journey ahead through the trees.

To say the church is our mother and to state there is no salvation outside of the church is to lessen the role of the Holy Spirit in the operation of salvation. To say the church functions now as the chief mediator of God's grace in the world is to denigrate the role of God the Father to draw people to Christ and of the Holy Spirit to woo and convince people of their sin in relation to Christ. Since much of this segment of our ecclesial discussion revolves around aspects of soteriology, I shall clarify my own approach to salvation and then speak to how that relates to the church.

Christians are those who have been confronted by the person of the risen Christ as *re*-presented to them by the Holy Spirit; they have responded positively to this confrontation by saying yes to Christ. Such an ability to respond requires both faith and the will of a human being. It is my contention that salvation is *individual* yet not individualistic. God's presence confronts

---

61. This last point is clarified by Volf later in the chapter, but its absence here is rather glaring. See Volf, *After Our Likeness*, 176: "It is *the Spirit* who constitutes the church. *People*, however, must accept the gifts of God in faith . . . ; *they* must come together, and *they* must remain together" (his emphasis).

62. For all my criticism of Volf's proposal thus far, his overall conclusion to use the life of the Trinity as paradigmatic for a nonhierarchical, nonindividualistic ecclesiology for free-church traditions is precisely the direction toward which I am heading. Indeed, the reason I am heading that way at all is due to Volf's powerful critique of Ratzinger and Zizioulas, as well as his own potent proposal for the free church, which has engaged my own ecclesial thoughts.

individuals with the gospel. Whether God uses physical or human instruments to reach out to individuals is not the point here, even though it does seem quite usual for God to use such "secondary" means in order to reach humans at their level. What is crucial here is that in every encounter with God's presence in the Spirit by whatever means used to initiate that encounter, it is God himself who confronts us directly. Volf and others seem wrapped up in *socially mediated* ways that humans interpret all of life, including this divine-human encounter. They assert that there can be no immediate experiences of God since this is impossible for human beings. We are always interpreting objects we perceive through our own interpretive lenses. "There is no immediate directness; one's own socially mediated self-experience flows into every experience of God."[63] The difficulty with this statement is that it is a concession to human limitations not a profession of divine ability to overcome that limitation within the encounter. God's presence in the power of the Spirit brings the impossible to pass; that is precisely what it means to be a Christian who has experienced here and now the exuberant and surging new life of the age to come.[64]

Why should we deem it impossible for God to overcome our limitation and confront us directly? To be sure, there is much, even in this encounter, that can and will come to us through social mediation. There is the interpretation of Scripture, the understanding of what a community is to be, the perceiving of who this God is who confronts us, and the grasping of ideals of moral values. Yet we are not talking here about a *human* initiative or *human* endeavor; rather, we are talking about a *divine* initiative and a *human* response. It seems to me that the incarnation of the Son of God quashes any notion of limitation in God's effort to meet us directly.[65]

Christians are also those who are regenerated by the Holy Spirit and "inserted" or "engrafted" into Christ (*insitio in Christum*), having been joined in a holy and mystical union with Christ (*unio cum Christo*).[66] It is this regenera-

---

63. Volf, *After Our Likeness*, 164n32.

64. Jürgen Moltmann aptly describes this divine-human encounter: "The heart expands. The goals of hope in our own lives, and what we ourselves expect of life, fuse with God's promises for a new creation of all things. This gives our own finite and limited life an infinite meaning." See Moltmann, *Spirit of Life: A Universal Affirmation*, trans. Margaret Kohl (Minneapolis: Fortress, 1992), 155; cf. Moltmann, *Der Geist des Lebens*, 169.

65. To be sure, the incarnation was an event in which God was with us "incognito," but for those with faith it was God present in their midst, overcoming the vast chasm that humans cannot bridge.

66. I have learned much from John Calvin on this concept, but also from the Reformed dogmaticians who followed him. See *Inst.*, esp. 3.1–3. Also see Dennis E. Tamburello, *Union with Christ: John Calvin and the Mysticism of St. Bernard*, Columbia Series in Reformed Theology, ed. Shirley Guthrie et al. (Louisville: Westminster John Knox, 1994), esp. 90–92.

tion and insertion into Christ that forms the basis on which one is engrafted into the body of Christ. Through the power of the Spirit, "Christ is internal to Christians as persons without suspending their status as selves."[67] We have been baptized by (or "in") one Spirit so as to form one body; we have been "given the one Spirit to drink" (1 Cor. 12:13). Believers experience a conversion, therefore, from their old direction away from God to a new direction that lives within the life of Christ itself and within the body of Christ as well. It is Christ in us and we in Christ that forms a mutuality of relationship, establishing a Christian's essence and directing our existence. As Volf says, "To experience faith means to become ecclesial beings."[68] How else could we be the people *of* God?

The nature of this regenerative encounter is personal with God. In some manner that is quite indescribable, God stoops to our form and accommodates himself to our ways so that God might be revealed to us in Jesus Christ. Yet this accommodation does not make God's presence *indirect* or *mediated*; God comes to us *directly* with his presence. This revelation of Christ is brought to us by the Holy Spirit, whose task as the "Go-Between-God" is to bridge the gap between the Infinite and finite.[69] The Spirit *re*-presents Christ to us as found in the Gospels, giving us a leap over the historical Grand Canyon that separates our century from his. Christ stands before us as the One who was crucified, buried, and raised again *for our sakes*. This portrayal by the Spirit in connection with the Word of God propels us toward making a decision for or against this Christ. The faith that arises in us who believe is not our own concoction but a gift from God. God initiates the movement toward humans and graciously provides us with the faith that we need to respond positively to God's call on our lives. There is no earning of our salvation here. However, *in response to that calling and gracious overture*, humans freely and of their own accord may choose to believe and accept Christ or not. It is not the church that gives a person faith to believe in such situations; it is not the church as a sacrament or means of grace that confronts the person. It is the living Lord of all creation, the Triune God, who initiates the encounter and

---

Tamburello notes that terms like *insero* or *insitio* (referring to engrafting) and *communio* or *societas* (referring to fellowship) are used in that order of frequency to refer to this insertion of believers into Christ. Moreover, words like *participes* and *unio* speak to the direct relationships between Christ and his people. For the discussion from later Reformed theologians, see Heinrich Heppe, *Reformed Dogmatics Set Out and Illustrated from the Sources*, ed. Ernst Bizer, trans. G. T. Thomson (Grand Rapids: Baker, 1978), 511.

67. Volf, *After Our Likeness*, 188.

68. Volf, *After Our Likeness*, 174.

69. This phrase comes from John V. Taylor, *The Go-Between-God: The Holy Spirit and Christian Mission*, 2nd ed. (London: SCM, 2004; orig. ed., 1972).

presents Christ directly to a person, cutting through the socially mediated modes of interpretation for the event and displaying the true nature of God to this person in a manner we may, in biblical terms, call "face-to-face."

It is the Spirit of God who brings God's presence to us in a way that is direct and unmediated. It is the Spirit of God who "implants" persons into Jesus Christ, instantaneously regenerating them and illuminating their minds to assent to the truth they have heard.[70] Further, it is the Spirit who changes persons, "bending their wills"[71] toward him, "changing them and inflaming them to love him."[72] The result is conversion where the will operates with spontaneity toward favorably choosing God.

Yet simultaneously as persons are converted and regenerated, they are engrafted into the body of Christ. How is this different from some "need for association" by individual believing Christians?[73] It is the Spirit who inserts us into Christ *and* into his body. Christians, then, have a "twofold communion"—one with God and one with other Christians.[74] It is the Lord of the church who adds to the church daily those who are being saved (Acts 2:46–47), but as Miroslav Volf reminds us, the human willingness to *come together* with others and *remain together* is a human response to God's grace given to us in the church.[75]

There is one additional aspect of the church's instrumentality in salvation that needs to be addressed here. Paul describes this aspect in the Epistle to the Romans:

> For it is with your heart that you believe and are justified, and it is with your mouth that you profess your faith and are saved. . . . How, then, can they call on the one they have not believed in? And how can they believe in the one of whom they have not heard? And how can they hear without someone preaching to them? And how can anyone preach unless they are sent? As it is written: "How beautiful are the feet of those who bring good news!" . . . Consequently, faith comes from hearing the message, and the message is heard through the word about Christ. (Rom. 10:10, 14–15, 17)

How can people believe in the one of whom they have not heard? Without the preaching of the message about Christ, how can anyone believe?

---

70. Heppe, *Reformed Dogmatics*, 518. These words and ideas come from Amandus Polanus (1624).

71. Heppe, *Reformed Dogmatics*, 521. This phrase is from Bartholomaeus Keckermann Dantiscanus (1611).

72. Heppe, *Reformed Dogmatics*, 512. These words are from Johannes Henricus Heideggerus (1700).

73. Volf, *After Our Likeness*, 177.

74. Volf, *After Our Likeness*, 177.

75. Volf, *After Our Likeness*, 176–77.

What appears to be in front of us here is the important role the community of faith must play in passing along the message about Christ. Without such organized sharing of the good news, how can people come to believe in Christ, since faith arises from hearing the Word? In context, the point Paul is making relates to the parts of the paragraph that I have skipped over in the above quotation from Romans 10. Paul argues that the Israelites have heard the good news, but not every one of them accepted it (10:16). "But I ask: Did they not hear? Of course they did" (10:18a). So the direct application of this pericope seems to be the agency of sharing God's news to Israel— something that Israel had already heard from the company of preachers who had gone throughout the earth. Is such a specific reference meant also to be understood as preaching the Word about Christ? Perhaps. In this respect, it is true that the church is responsible for some aspect of the *content* of the message that God uses to encounter people, but only as the church faithfully exegetes, expounds, and proclaims the written Word of God.[76] To speak of the church as mediating all of the content of faith is to misplace its role and perhaps misunderstand the role of the Word and Spirit in the experience of faith when God encounters humans. Volf contends that "even my most personal faith" is "ecclesially mediated" *and* that it is "only through life in the congregation in whose confession I participate that I discover the meaning of the confession of faith."[77] Leaving the entirety of the experience with God to the role of the church dismisses the role of the Spirit in teaching and leading individuals to Christ. While I may have learned *about* Jesus Christ from Sunday school lessons that my parents forced me to attend as a child or from movies like *The Passion of the Christ*, I may have learned them incorrectly, or the exposure may have warped my understanding of them. When I am confronted by the Spirit concerning Jesus Christ, those lessons and images may or may not help me to assess the idea about God and Christ (in other words, I may or may not more quickly grasp what the Spirit is trying to tell me), but the Spirit's encounter with me is not empty of content itself. To say that the content must come solely from the church's witness of preaching presumes that God himself need not engage a person face-to-face. If I say that the Word is the sole efficient cause of salvation, I miss the causative power of the Spirit.

76. Volf seems to overstate this point: "Hence, even my most personal faith can only be that which is ecclesially mediated. . . . It is from the church that one receives the content of faith, and it is in the church that one learns how faith is to be understood and lived. . . . The faith with which I believe is shaped by the ecclesially mediated forms in which it is expressed; there is no pure, ecclesially unmediated faith consisting of pure feeling." Volf, *After Our Likeness*, 163.

77. Volf, *After Our Likeness*, 163.

Is the content of any encounter between God and humans only cognitive information that is able to be "socialized" in ecclesial settings? Is it not feasible that an encounter with the living God is one in which more than cognitive dimensions of the human being are engaged? To be sure, there is content in this event, but I submit that content is much more of a *personal* nature, of God's own being encountering us face-to-face, than it is a list of propositions to be inculcated. When we are encountered directly by the living God, we come to know this God personally in ways that may not fit all our categories of epistemology yet provide real and genuine knowledge nonetheless. The person of God (in the Spirit) connects immediately with the innermost core of my person, thereby creating an intimacy of "joy unspeakable and full of glory" (1 Pet. 1:8 KJV). However, *after* this encounter is the time for the church to expand and elucidate the meaning of that encounter. The local community of believers works together to assist one another by listening to the narratives about encounters with God from fellow believers and to help the community grasp together the best ways to place such encounters and narratives within their own life stories.[78] To be sure, the church may be used by God *before* such an encounter in terms of preaching, teaching, worship, acts of benevolence, or even the translation and publication of the Scriptures. I am not downplaying these instrumental aspects of the church's calling and ministry. However, the point is that these cannot be primary in terms of salvation—only God, not the church, can be the *subject* of the encounter. The church is *used by God* to accomplish the goal for which God established it. Thus, the church becomes a *secondary* contributor in the encounter of salvation and subsequent spiritual growth. Whenever it supplants the place of God, the church becomes an idol, and experiences within it become stale and sterile. Only the living Christ can bring abundant life to humans.

Is an understanding of the "language of faith" or of the church's grasp of the content of the gospel prerequisite to experiencing an encounter with God? I should think not. Some of our "socially mediated" understandings of the Christian God may have been *mis*understandings. However, I do understand the rather chicken-and-egg nature of ecclesial socialization that Volf explains: in some sense, one must be ecclesially socialized in order to understand the language of faith and thereby experience God with some content that is not sheer emptiness but portrayed to people by the community itself. Still, there remains the question as to the nature of this "language of faith" that is necessary before one encounters the living God, as opposed to after

---

78. In chap. 3, "The Encounter between God and Humans," we shall return to this discussion concerning a direct encounter in order to clarify the terms.

this encounter. It is my contention that when God's presence encounters us directly, we experience God's person and nature, which is full of "content" of some sort, although such content may not be easily described in language that explains what this means cognitively.[79]

Therefore, throughout this book the idea of God's *direct* presence will be repeated as an essential aspect of God's life among his people. Volf is helpful in providing the setting for such a discussion, even if I disagree with the specific aspect of the role of the church itself in the encounter with God. Perhaps his most riveting discussion concentrates on the use of the doctrine of the Trinity as a potential paradigm for human relationships in the church. As he notes, the idea that there can be correspondence between the Trinity and the life of the church "has remained largely alien to the Free Church tradition."[80] With this book, it is my hope to mitigate this "alien" aspect. How can humans take on the correspondence of God's inner-trinitarian relations as a model for their own life together? To this end, Volf provides a succinct and yet profound thesis: "The correspondence between the trinitarian and ecclesial relationships is not simply formal. Rather, it is 'ontological' because it is soteriologically grounded."[81] In other words, if the basis of our being the church is the regenerative encounter of the Spirit and the engrafting insertion by the Spirit into the body of Christ, then what the Trinity is doing in its own personal relationships can realistically become a pattern for our lives (within certain limits, to be sure, since we are not God and cannot fully understand the inner life of God). It is the Spirit of God who brings God's presence to us and dwells as God's Shekinah within us (both individually *and* corporately). Therefore, the communal and relational Triune God can be the basis for our interpersonal relationships with believers in the church, because the nature of God is increasingly present in our own lives as we submit to the Spirit's work in us, making us more like Christ. The entire point of my proposal in this regard is that the Spirit is the centerpiece for encountering us, indwelling us, and engrafting us into Christ and into his body.[82]

79. Whatever else was happening on the day of Pentecost in Acts 2, I think the Spirit's presence on them and in them was explosive of their usual cognitive communication and overflowed into languages they did not learn. Yet within these languages, there was content (they heard them praising God in their own tongue). Moreover, it seems that the disciples' experience of Pentecost transformed their understanding of God and the mission to which God was calling them.

80. Volf, *After Our Likeness*, 196. He also notes that the free-church tradition has left largely unexplored the element of "human will in belonging to a concrete church." Volf, *After Our Likeness*, 177.

81. Volf, *After Our Likeness*, 195.

82. In a recent book, Daniel Castelo has argued against my description of the use of the life of the Trinity or even the doctrine of the Trinity as an integrating principle for theology. For

A Working Definition of the Church

So where does the church fit in all of this discussion? Indeed, why do we need the church if we can go directly to God? In the model proposed in this book, the church cannot be viewed as the sole mediator between God and humans or even as their spiritual mother. However, if that mediatorial role is no longer primary or prominent, then why do we need the church?

At this point, some need for definition of the nature and mission of the church becomes necessary. In general terms, the church is an assembly of those called out (ἐκκλήσια | *ekklēsia*) by the Spirit to engage in fellowship with the Triune God as God's own people, to share with and care for others who have also experienced this direct connection with God, and to preach the good news of reconciliation to those who have not experienced it. The church is a fellowship in the Spirit of those who have experienced God's immediate presence and thus sense that a new age has dawned in human history. Therefore, the church is the people of God's immediate presence, the people who live in fellowship with the Trinity and each other, and who live in the eschatological mystery between this age and the age to come. This community of love gathers together regularly in rich fellowship to worship God; likewise, it reaches out to others in evangelism and service to extend the ministry of Christ's presence to the world today through the power of the Spirit. Such a community of love will reflect the true image of God on this earth.

Toward an Ecclesiology of Experiencing God's Presence

Isn't all this talk of "presence" and "Spirit" and "experience" simply not germane to the subject at hand—namely, an ecclesiology that presses the body of Christ toward relevance in this century? I recognize that discussion about spiritual encounters and experiences can be downright uncomfortable for many (perhaps most) Western Christians. Something like this discomfort

---

him, the triune life "cannot be reduced to a theological *concept*" because a life cannot be "put to use as a rubric." See Daniel Castelo, *Pentecostalism as a Christian Mystical Tradition* (Grand Rapids: Eerdmans, 2017), 27, esp. n. 67. My proposal had been that the Trinity could assist Pentecostals in forming an integrating principle for their own approach to systematic theology. While I understand the critique that Castelo has made against my proposal, in some ways I think he missed my point—or I hadn't clearly relayed it. I was not proposing that a life (the triune life, in fact) be "used" as a thing, even a *conceptual* thing; rather, I was proposing that the nature of the God we confess, we study, and with fear and trembling we attempt to describe according to the revelation given us is such that *the triune life of God* confronts us as a life that can transform us in the encounter. If God as this Subject has condescended to our level to allow Godself to become (in his grace) an object of our reflection, then why can't the nature of this God serve as a paradigm for theological consideration?

may have hampered a bestselling book titled *Experiencing God*, written by Henry Blackaby and Claude King.[83] While phrases like "experience" and "love relationship" and "God is speaking" pepper the book, there is also a clear message that despite these experiential tones, the reality of experiencing God comes only through *indirect* means.[84] In a book titled *Experiencing God*, why is there no discussion of *direct* experiences with God?

In our project, we are proposing that God's Spirit connects with humans *directly* and that every believer experiences this transforming power, making each a child of God and therefore a member of the family of God. The New Testament is full of such references to direct religious experience. Why do we awkwardly ignore them and focus on mediation or some alternative to experiencing God instead?

However, at this point I must underscore what I am *not* proposing. I do not believe that all people must experience God the same way; indeed, God encounters us all in very different manners according to the needs of our lives at any given moment as well as the context of our life stories. The all-wise God knows precisely how to confront us at any given time. My point is that in whatever manner this encounter takes shape, there must be such an experience in the lives of those who call themselves believers. The encounter may be so minimally invasive that I do not fully realize what is happening to me; it also could be so maximally confrontational that I am knocked to the ground like Paul.

In the context of discussing regeneration, Jürgen Moltmann provides a foundation for the boldness with which we need to talk about experiences in God:

> It would be presumptuous to describe the ways in which people experience the rebirth to life. They are as multifarious and protean as human life itself. Nor can we make particular inward experiences a yardstick for regeneration, as a way of testing the state of faith of other people. Yet theology must not be prevented from describing the experiences of the Spirit out of fear of singular experiences and pietistic introspection. In the New Testament, at least, believers and apostles talk extensively about their experiences.[85]

83. Henry Blackaby and Claude King, *Experiencing God: How to Love the Full Adventure of Knowing and Doing the Will of God* (Nashville: Broadman & Holman, 1994).

84. For example, the fourth point of seven realities of experiencing God is this: "God speaks by the Holy Spirit through the Bible, prayer, circumstances, and the Church to reveal Himself, His purposes, and His ways." Blackaby and King, *Experiencing God*, 50. These are clearly indirect means by which we encounter God, but not one of them is direct. To be sure, these indirect mediations are proper and healthy ways to experience God through secondary means, but there is nothing here about direct encounters.

85. Jürgen Moltmann, *Spirit of Life*, 153; cf. Moltmann, *Der Geist des Lebens*, 167. The phrase translated "singular experiences" I might rather translate as "peculiar" or "curious"

Following a similar line of thought, New Testament scholar Luke Timothy Johnson has highlighted an analogous problem with the biblical disciplines in the last hundred years. He notes that the "history of religions school" and "historical criticism" were two prominent methods of New Testament study. Each bypasses the enormous amount of language and reference to religious experience in the New Testament. He argues that because of their philosophical predispositions, they ignored the Christian claims to experiencing the Divine. In order to compensate for a lack of "real evidence," Johnson suggests that the historical-critical method has viewed religious experience in the New Testament as too "overly subjective and elusive to serve the cause of historical reconstruction."[86] Yet the New Testament is filled with language of power, experience, and the Spirit. As Johnson states, "It is literally impossible to read the New Testament at any length without encountering claims that something is happening to these people, and it is happening *now*."[87]

In the New Testament church, there is an infusion of the Spirit into the lives of common folk; there is an "invasion" of God's presence that propels unlearned people into sharing their faith with others; there is the shaking of a place where the saints are praying; there is the presence of the Lord in their midst to heal people; there is *God* in direct encounter with human beings. This *is* the New Testament story. Therefore, why can it not be *our* story?[88] Are we to expect that the faith and experience of believers in the New Testament are to be so different from ours that such encounters never occur—at least, not without the aid of special rituals or symbols or "the church"? The very heart of the Christian faith seems to drive this point home: God encounters us wherever we are and enters our lives (if we are willing), offering

---

experiences in order to bring out the presumed nuance of Moltmann's point. The German reads: "*Aber die Theologie darf aus Angst vor eigentümlichen Erfahrungen und pietisticher Introspektion nicht auf die Beschreibung der Erfahrungen des Geistes verzichten.*" Admittedly, the difference is minimal; in the end it depends on whether or not Moltmann *meant* "singular" experiences or "curious" ones. The latter I took to refer to the Pentecostal/charismatic types of experiences, but perhaps he didn't mean this.

86. Luke Timothy Johnson, *Religious Experience in Earliest Christianity: A Missing Dimension in New Testament Studies* (Minneapolis: Fortress, 1998), 13.

87. Johnson, *Religious Experience in Earliest Christianity*, 5 (his emphasis).

88. James McClendon notes in his systematic theology that a *baptistic* form of interpretation of Scripture follows an approach to reading what happened in the Bible as something that can still happen today. He calls such an approach a "this-is-that" hermeneutic. I find this to be true of many free-church or believers' church adherents, as well as many evangelicals and Pentecostals that I know. It was an exceptional insight by McClendon. See James W. McClendon Jr., *Systematic Theology*, vol. 2, *Doctrine* (Nashville: Abingdon, 1994), 44–46. McClendon states, "There is a strong link between the plain sense of Scripture and the church's self-understanding as a continuation of the biblical story" (44).

us a transformation of thought and life so compelling that others notice the change in us.[89]

James Loder speaks of these encounters as "transforming moments" that produce "convictional experiences."[90] When the human spirit confronts issues it cannot resolve or faces absurd situations filled with tension, it attempts to construct a resolution. Loder describes this pattern in detail. However, he also adds a further dimension to transformation: the human ego. We cannot change our own ego, but the "logic of transformation" allows for the divine agency to alter our ego. Loder comments, "In this the Holy Spirit as *Spiritus Creator*, whose mission begins and ends in the inner life of God, transforms the human ego—and by implication, then, all human transformations which issue from the ego are themselves transformed."[91] This is clearly the type of religious experience that occurs in the narrative of the New Testament. It seems to be the expectation of the believers described in the New Testament narrative that transforming moments in the presence of the Holy Spirit are available to all who call on God's name in faith. This is the "normal" experience of believers.

Given this approach to the New Testament story, what kind of people ought we to be? We will continue our inquiry by examining the very nature of God, since it is my contention that the people of God should reflect the nature of this God who both made humans in his likeness at creation (Gen. 1:26) and now transforms them into his likeness through the new creation in Christ (Col. 3:10).

89. Gregory J. Polan has described the experiences recorded for us of God's presence among the Hebrews as reading something about God, yet they also may be considered "as an enticement for us to enter into the mystery of knowing God ourselves, not vicariously through another's written account but through our own entry into the realm of the sacred, wherever and however that may come about in our lives." See Gregory J. Polan, "Divine Presence: A Biblical Perspective," *Liturgical Ministry* 3 (Winter 1994): 13–21, here 14.

90. James E. Loder, *The Transforming Moment*, 2nd ed. (Colorado Springs: Helmers & Howard, 1989), 13.

91. Loder, *The Transforming Moment*, 4.

2

The Nature of God
and the People of God

Introduction

The foundation for the doctrine of the church relies almost entirely on the doctrine of God.[1] Why is this the case? It is because the person of God informs our conception of who the people *of God* should be. In an insightful essay, Daniel Migliore offers a bold thesis in this regard: "The primary mission of the church is to participate in the missionary activity of the triune God in the

---

1. Consider Miroslav Volf's statement that "the way one thinks about God will decisively shape not only ecclesiology, but the entirety of Christian thought." Volf, *After Our Likeness: The Church as the Image of the Trinity*, Sacra Doctrina: Christian Theology for a Postmodern Age, ed. Alan G. Padgett (Grand Rapids: Eerdmans, 1998), 193. Also, compare John Webster's statement: "A doctrine of the church is only as good as the doctrine of God which underlies it." Webster, "The Church and the Perfection of God," in *The Community of the Word: Toward an Evangelical Ecclesiology*, ed. Mark Husbands and Daniel J. Trier (Downers Grove, IL: InterVarsity, 2005), 78. Added to this is a similar comment by Amy Plantinga Pauw on the relation of theology proper to ecclesiology: "A defective doctrine of the church suggests a defective doctrine of God." Amy Plantinga Pauw, "Eccentric Ecclesiology," in *The Theological Anthropology of David Kelsey: Responses to Eccentric Existence*, ed. Gene Outka (Grand Rapids: Eerdmans, 2016), 99. Finally, consider Colin Gunton's thought that "the manifest inadequacy of the theology of the church derives from the fact that it has never seriously and consistently been rooted in a conception of the being of God as triune." Colin E. Gunton, "The Church on Earth: The Roots of Community," in *On Being the Church: Essays on the Christian Community*, ed. Colin E. Gunton and Daniel W. Hardy (Edinburgh: T&T Clark, 1990), 48.

world."[2] He describes the nature and mission of the church as being grounded in the nature and mission of God. To his thesis, which is primarily focused on mission, I would like to add a parallel thesis on the nature of the church, something perhaps already implicit in Migliore's original claim. Because God is triune, existing in a perfect society of perpetual unity and community, the nature of the church must have its basis in this God. Both the nature and mission of the church are grounded in the nature and mission of the Triune God.

However, I am not proposing that humans *are* God or even that they can fully become *like* God in this life. To be sure, the people of God are and remain human beings, albeit transformed by the power and presence of the Spirit. Therefore, it is essential to clarify the distinction between creature and Creator in order to grasp an understanding of both the doctrine of God and the doctrine of the human being. In the first sentence of this chapter, I said that the doctrine of the church "relies almost entirely" on the doctrine of God. The small part that fills this remaining gap, noted by the word "almost," is theological anthropology. Although understanding the God who encounters us with his presence is the basis for building most of the doctrine of the church, understanding who the *people* of God are as human beings in relationship is also essential. Hence, in this chapter we will consider first the nature of God and implications for the doctrine of the church; then we will examine what it means to be a human person called by the Spirit into community with other humans.

The Doctrine of the Church Relies on the Doctrine of the Triune God

Across the landscape of theology today, ecclesiologies dot the Protestant scene. Some follow patterns of their denominations' founders while others trace their doctrine of the church to interpretations of Scripture. For the most part, there is little integration between ecclesiology and the other doctrines in their theological scheme. The result is that the doctrine of the church remains

---

2. Daniel Migliore, "The Missionary God and the Missionary Church," *Princeton Seminary Bulletin*, NS, 19, no. 1 (1998): 14–25, here 17. While this is not a new idea with Migliore, he does develop it in a way that is unique in this article. It is also found in David J. Bosch, *Transforming Mission: Paradigm Shifts in Theology of Mission*, 20th anniv. ed. (Maryknoll, NY: Orbis, 2016), 400. Bosch states, "Mission is not primarily an activity of the church, but an attribute of God. God is a missionary God." Also, Jürgen Moltmann, *The Church in the Power of the Spirit: A Contribution to Messianic Ecclesiology*, trans. Margaret Kohl (Minneapolis: Fortress, 1993; orig. German ed., 1975), 64: "It is not the church that has a mission of salvation to fulfill to the world; it is the mission of the Son and the Spirit through the Father that includes the church, creating a church as it goes on its way."

unconsidered or becomes relegated to the realm of practitioners alone; even more commonly, it can be seen protruding out of their theological agenda like an extra appendage on an already complete body. It just does not seem to fit.

Since we are proposing that the people of God have directly experienced the God of the Scriptures and since it is clear from the Scriptures that such an experience with God begins to transform the person who is encountered by God, it is necessary to understand the nature of the God who confronts us directly and thereby begins to transform us into his likeness. Who God is should inform our understanding of what God's people should be (or become) like. The nature of God shapes the people of God, which in turn informs our doctrinal reflection on the people of God. Hence, the nature of God will clarify the nature of the church. In this way, the doctrine of the church relies on the doctrine of God.

While one could merely list the obvious attributes of God as seen through Scripture and conclude that the people of God should possess these qualities (such as love, holiness, mercy, et al.) to a lesser degree, this bypasses a more fundamental aspect of God's nature that is necessary to examine for the doctrine of the church. The God of the New Testament is fundamentally portrayed as triune.[3] It is this aspect of God's being that will inform all other aspects of our consideration of God and the people of God.

How does one describe the indescribable, ineffable God? In one sense, we cannot do so since God exists in a dimension far beyond ours. Yet in another sense we can describe God because of the revelation that has occurred in Jesus Christ and Scripture. In Jesus Christ lived the fullness of the Godhead in bodily form (Col. 2:9). Seeing Jesus allows us to say that we have seen the Father (John 14:9).

One clear message we have about God through Jesus is that Jesus does not live or work alone. "I tell you the truth," said Jesus, "the Son can do nothing by himself; he can do only what he sees his Father doing, because whatever the Father does the Son also does" (John 5:19). Indeed, Jesus cannot even do his ministry without the Spirit: "The Spirit of the Lord is on me, because he has anointed me to proclaim . . . freedom for the prisoners and recovery of sight for the blind, to set the oppressed free, to proclaim the year of the Lord's favor" (Luke 4:18–19). Thus, a fundamental message of the revelation of God found in Jesus Christ is that he (and therefore God) is not alone. God exists in community, we might say, not in some monistic simplicity but in the

---

3. While there may not be a fully developed trinitarian language or doctrine in the New Testament as there would be by the end of the fourth century, what comes through clearly enough is an inchoate trinitarianism.

variegated richness of trinitarian life, in which there is reciprocal relationality. A definitive characteristic of God, therefore, is that God dwells in perfect communion as Father, Son, and Spirit.

While the church has struggled and perhaps even stuttered with how to express this truth, it has maintained it as a faithful reading of Scripture and as a faithful reading of our experience with the Triune God. Probing too deeply into this mystery with the limited logic of our monochromatic capacity will cause us to miss the beauty of God's multifaceted technicolor dimensions. However, this essential truth becomes the foundation for all other truths of the faith: God exists in rich fellowship of Father, Son, and Spirit, with perfect communion and equality of essence within these distinctions. Therefore, we must say something about this God who is beyond us. God is one, yet God is three.

The British theologian Leonard Hodgson compares the complexity of human personhood with the immensely greater complexity of the Trinity. In some sense, a human reflects the Trinity by possessing the capacity for "thinking, feeling, and willing."[4] One difficulty in understanding humans is that we desire to see these varied and complex activities as part of a greater whole, the unified concept of a human person. In an analogous manner, Hodgson suggests that the divine life is constituted by unification of three aspects: Father, Son, and Spirit. Hodgson explains,

> It is the main thesis of these lectures that the act of faith required for acceptance of the doctrine of the Trinity is faith in this unification, faith that the Divine unity is a dynamic unity actively unifying in the one Divine life the lives of the three Divine persons. It is a mystery, but not an irrational mystery. It is a mystery, because on earth we have no experience of any unity which so perfectly unites so wide and rich a diversity of content: our experience does not go beyond the imperfect unification of activities in single personal selves and we by no means fully understand that. . . . Mysterious as the unity may be, it is the kind of unity postulated by our reason to account for the observed and recorded evidence. The essence of our faith is that there is in the Godhead the perfect instance of the kind of unity of which we have imperfect analogues on earth.[5]

Thus, the unity we see and experience in the Triune God is unlike any unity we have on earth. This is the God with whom we have to do—a being who is

4. Leonard Hodgson, *The Doctrine of the Trinity: Croall Lectures, 1942–1943* (London: Nisbet, 1943), 85.

5. Hodgson, *The Doctrine of the Trinity*, 95–96.

in some way one and yet three. As Clark Pinnock has said, "It is the essence of God's nature to be relational. This is primordial in God and defines who God is. God is triadic community, not a single, undifferentiated unity."[6]

The Relational Nature of the Triune God

What does all of this mean for our doctrinal construction to say that God is "social" or "communal"? There are obvious ramifications for this in almost every avenue of theology, but some of the clearest connections are related to the doctrine of the church. If the essential nature of God is communal, what does God expect of his people? If we directly experience a relational God, how does that shape our relations with others? Without tracing the history of the doctrine of the Trinity or its more recent developments in trinitarian theology,[7] let us consider more closely the nature of this triune, communal God.

The "Dance" of the Trinity

The Triune God is uniquely united. The early Greek theologians used the term *perichōrēsis* (περιχώρησις) to describe this union. Following passages in John (e.g., 17:21), they saw the three distinctions or persons as "mutually giving and receiving."[8] Jesus had described his relationship with the Father in these terms: "the Father is in me, and I am in the Father." There is a reciprocal interiority of this relationship between the divine persons. Utilized as a way to counteract the subordinationism of Arius (that Christ was inferior in essence to God the Father), the concept of *perichōrēsis* "expressed the idea that the three divine persons mutually inhere in one another, draw life from one another, are what they are by relation to one another. *Perichōrēsis* means being-in-one another, permeation without confusion."[9] Deriving from two

---

6. Clark Pinnock, *Flame of Love: A Theology of the Holy Spirit* (Downers Grove, IL: InterVarsity, 1996), 35.

7. For a thorough discussion of the doctrine's development in the early church, see R. P. C. Hanson, *The Search for the Christian Doctrine of God: The Arian Controversy, 318–381* (Edinburgh: T&T Clark, 1988). For clarification on the resurgence of trinitarian theology in recent decades, see Colin Gunton, *The Promise of Trinitarian Theology* (Edinburgh: T&T Clark, 1991); also Christoph Schwöbel, "Introduction: The Renaissance of Trinitarian Theology: Reasons, Problems and Tasks," in *Trinitarian Theology Today*, ed. Christoph Schwöbel (Edinburgh: T&T Clark, 1995), 1–30.

8. Miroslav Volf, *After Our Likeness*, 208.

9. Catherine Mowry LaCugna, *God for Us: The Trinity and Christian Life* (San Francisco: Harper & Row, 1991), 270–71.

Two Forms of *Perichōrēsis*

In the fourth century the concept of *perichōrēsis* | περιχώρησις arose from the debates over the essential nature of the Trinity, especially in relation to Christology. G. L. Prestige, a well-known writer on the patristic era of the church, has posited two forms of the use of *perichōrēsis*. The "weak" form, he suggests, was used in a manner similar to the *communicatio idiomatum*—that is, to denote the close relationship between the two natures of Christ (divine and human). The metaphoric usage of this term struck the image of the rotation or revolution of "two opposites" of the two sides of a coin. To achieve this "weak" form of relationality or *perichōrēsis*, there is a prior hypostatic union presupposed in the person of Christ.

The "strong" form is quite different. It suggests a real and "ontological interpenetration of two entities (not simply their close association and reciprocation) such that *it is itself* the process whereby a union exists, and not the result of a distinct and prior union."[a] Trevor Hart analyzes this: "As Prestige observes, in the Christological context, this concept led inevitably to the danger of monophysitism, but it provided trinitarian theology with an invaluable tool with which to secure the avoidance both of Sabellian modalism and tritheism, pointing to a genuine

Greek terms, *peri* and *chōreō*, this term has a root idea of movement (dance) around something or someone. The verb *chōreō* can also mean "to make room for another."[10] We can see the English word "choreography" deriving from the second Greek term. While *perichōrēsis* referred primarily to the inner-trinitarian relations, it also was expanded to suggest that divinity itself could be communicated: it could "move outside itself, even indwell that which

10. S.v. "*perichōreō* [περιχωρέω]" in Henry G. Liddell and Robert Scott, eds., *Greek-English Lexicon with a Revised Supplement*, 9th rev. ed., ed. Henry Stuart Jones and Roderick McKenzie (Oxford: Clarendon, 1996), 1394. This meaning of "making room for one another" will be important for development in later chapters. It was referenced by Molly Truman Marshall, *Joining the Dance: A Theology of the Spirit* (Valley Forge, PA: Judson, 2003), 17n30, from the 1980 edition of Liddell and Scott. Also s.v. "χωρέω," in *Bagster's Analytical Greek Lexicon* (London: Samuel Bagster & Sons, n.d.), 440, where it means "to make room for"; with the prefix *peri*, it can mean "to make room for (someone) around (someone/something)." Also, s.v. "περιχορεύω" and "περιχωρέω," in G. W. H. Lampe, ed., *A Patristic Greek Lexicon* (Oxford: Clarendon, 1961), 1077, where the former verb means "to dance around" or metaphorically can mean "to circle around," and the latter verb means generally "to encompass," or "alternate by revolution," or "to pass into reciprocally." These both give rise to the patristic use of the noun "περιχώρησις," which means "cyclical movement," "reciprocity," or "interpenetration." Lampe, *A Patristic Greek Lexicon*, 1077–78).

unity which yet presupposed an absolute hypostatic diversity."[b] Hart then assesses Karl Barth's approach as using the "weaker" side of *perichōrēsis* and thereby positing (as Jürgen Moltmann has earlier charged) a prior ontological oneness of the divine subject.

Using the stronger side, we could see mutual interpenetration of the persons as constituting the divine substance without any "God" of sorts lurking in the background. We are suggesting that the stronger sense of *perichōrēsis* is appropriate to the ontological relationality between the members of the Trinity, but the weaker sense of it illuminates the way we humans participate in the fellowship of the Triune God—namely, with an ontic and prior union of the divine Godhead staging the backdrop for our own participation with God.[c]

a. Trevor Hart, "Person and Prerogative in Perichoretic Perspective: The Triunity of God," in *Regarding Karl Barth: Toward a Reading of His Theology* (Downers Grove, IL: InterVarsity, 1999), 112–13.

b. Hart, "Person and Prerogative," 113.

c. See also G. L. Prestige, "*Perichoreo* and *perichoresis* in the Fathers," *Journal of Theological Studies* 29 (1928): 242. (This is the article referenced by Trevor Hart above.) In addition, one should refer to Prestige's magisterial work on God among the early church fathers, particularly his last chapter, which deals with *perichōrēsis*. See G. L. Prestige, *God in Patristic Thought*, 2nd ed. (London: SPCK, 1959).

is other and not be thereby diminished."[11] If the joyous dance of the life of God is merely self-contained—that is, unrelated to creation or to humans—then, as LaCugna intimates, the doctrine of the Trinity is defeated.[12] It spins around itself with no impact on our history or lives. The rich fellowship of the Trinity is more than a model for our own human lives; it is a real opportunity for finite humans to experience the transcendent God in ways that are almost palpable. Incorporating humans into the life of the Trinity is a real event in which our mundane lives are forever transformed and being transformed in the life of God, where there is joy in the presence of God forevermore and "eternal pleasures at [God's] right hand" (Ps. 16:11).

While it may be unusual to picture the life of the Triune God as one of dancing movement among Father, Son, and Spirit, it is a spatial metaphor that assists us greatly in picturing the Trinity from our finite perspective. Swiss

11. Molly Truman Marshall, "Participating in the Life of God: A Trinitarian Pneumatology," *Perspectives in Religious Studies* 30, no. 2 (Summer 2003): 139–50, here 146. Marshall notes that Athanasius was responsible for this "move."

12. LaCugna, *God for Us*, 198. Marshall cites LaCugna here in "Participating in the Life of God," 146.

theologian Hans Urs von Balthasar (1905–88) speaks of the inner-trinitarian life as one of "infinite circulation."[13] There is movement within the life of God. A contemporary German theologian, Jürgen Moltmann, has described *perichōrēsis* as an ancient concept that speaks to "community without uniformity, and personality without individualism."[14] The semantic background of *perichōrēsis* is a noun that refers to a "whirl or rotation," while the verb points to "going from one to another, walking around, . . . encircling, embracing, or enclosing."[15] So how does all of this help us better understand the Trinity—and the church?

Four Points on the God Who Makes Room for the Other

First, the Trinity lives in circulatory movement—but not some chaotic churning; instead, God's life in movement "makes room for the other."[16] We have seen how this phrase can depict both the life of the Trinity and our own human reflection of that life. In what way, then, does the Trinity make room for the other? Initially, the Father makes room for the other in the Triune Godhead by begetting the Son. This is not to be understood in some sequence of time, as if the Father was God first and the Son was God second. This begetting of the Son is brought about in eternity without any sequence of time to mark its occurrence. It is a mystery yet also a truth that is revealed in Scripture: the Son is the only begotten one of the Father. This is a form of making room for one who is exactly the same in substance (whatever that may mean) yet distinct in person (whatever that may mean). In other words, the Christian God is not a lonely *monad* who exists in solitariness as Father. The Christian God is One who is God in the mystery of three persons, whose functions and "faces" are differentiated so that there are neither three gods nor one undifferentiated god. In the richness of the triune life, the Father "makes room" for the Son with love and great joy. From the Father also proceeds the Holy Spirit through the

13. Hans Urs von Balthasar, *Explorations in Theology*, vol. 4, *Spirit and Institution*, trans. Edward T. Oakes (San Francisco: Ignatius, 1995; orig. German ed., 1974), 4:40.

14. Jürgen Moltmann, "Perichoresis: An Old Magic Word for a New Trinitarian Theology," in *Trinity, Community, and Power: Mapping Trajectories in Wesleyan Theology*, ed. M. Douglas Meeks (Nashville: Abingdon, 2000), 113; in this chapter, Moltmann goes on to support the "validity [of *perichōrēsis*] for envisioning a trinitarian understanding of God, the inhabitation of the Holy Spirit, the human community, and the community of culture and nature on earth within a 'sustainable society'" (113).

15. Moltmann, "Perichoresis," 113; Moltmann notes that Gregory of Nazianzus was the first to use the word in a theological sense, but John of Damascus used it for his Christology and doctrine of the Trinity. See also Nonna Verna Harrison, "Perichoresis in the Greek Fathers," *St. Vladimir's Theological Quarterly* 35, no. 1 (1991): 53–65.

16. As noted in n. 10 above, *perichōrein* | περιχώρειν can mean "to make room for [another]."

Son. Through the agency of the Son, the Father spirates or breathes out the Spirit, thereby making room for a third distinction. Here is the movement, the "infinite circulation" within the Triune God. The Son, moreover, makes room for the Father and the Spirit by willingly agreeing to the wish of the Father that the Son become flesh and to the prompting of the Spirit to continue living in obedience to that desire. Hence, the Son does only what he hears and sees the Father telling him to do (John 5:19). The Son makes room for the Father by obeying the Spirit. The Spirit urges the circulation to continue within the Godhead but also extends this loving relationality to the other—that is, to humans, who are made according to God's image and likeness but who are not themselves God. The Triune God reaches outward because the inner nature of love that shapes the character of this God is to make room for the other, first within the triune persons themselves but then by reaching out to those unlike themselves—namely, human creatures. It is this making-room-for-the-other that must become the very essence of the life of the church in the twenty-first century. The people of God make room for God, the ultimate form of the other, and are so transformed by God's presence that they are drawn into the life of the world in order to make room for the other. As Balthasar has suggested, a number of religions have this concept of making room for the Absolute, but

> what distinguishes Christianity is that the God for whom room is being made is himself already the God who makes room for: he is God the Father who makes room for the Son in God; he is God the Son who knows himself as the one made room for by the Father, and thus he hands over to the Father all the room in himself . . . ; and he is the Spirit who proves that this mutual making room for is the inner divinity of God. It is this process of handing over and making room for that is the highest capacity, the absolute power, but the power *of* self-surrendering love.[17]

A truly *Christian* church follows its Lord into the depths of loving self-surrender to God, which in turn propels it into the world to love and serve the neighbor. This divine characteristic of "making room for the other" becomes the essential feature of the people of God's presence and power.

Allow me to suggest, then, a further analogy to assist us here with the idea of movement in God. Imagine that we could take a picture of the Trinity. Were it even possible to do so, we would end up with a snapshot that captured only a blur of movement. In order to grasp something of the rich fellowship and reciprocal movement of the Triune God, we would require something more like a movie camera, with which we could begin to trace the constant Oneness

17. Balthasar, *Explorations in Theology*, 4:341 (his emphasis).

in Threeness and Threeness in Oneness, yet still this would not be adequate. The Triune God of Christians is not a static, motionless being but a dynamic being with such unity of will and energy of movement that "still shots" are impossible to capture the richness of the fellowship among Father, Son, and Spirit. In the trinitarian dance, there is no person stumbling over the toes of another (to stretch the analogy for a moment); no person not in agreement with the direction of the dance; no person with arms folded, unwilling to participate in the dance; and especially no person unwilling to invite humans into the joyous communion of the perichoretic dance.

As a second point regarding "making room for the other," the Triune God consists of three distinctions equal in essence but differentiated in function. As Gregory of Nyssa has said, the Father is not the Son, the Son is not the Father, and the Holy Spirit is neither Father nor Son.[18] It is clear from the narrative of Scripture that each person of the Godhead has distinctive tasks. Nevertheless it is also clear that the persons function in such unity that there is no rift in their nature—no tug in opposite directions.

Third, the fellowship between Father, Son, and Spirit is so rich that it naturally overflows. The fullness of the divine love is so great that it bursts outward to the creation of the world and the gracious redemption of human-kind.[19] Canadian theologian Clark Pinnock describes this overflow as the "ecstasy" of God, coming from the Greek word meaning "to stand outside of oneself."[20] He sees the Spirit as directing this abundant overflow outward from the inner-trinitarian fellowship to the creative acts of world-making and the redemptive acts of mission-seeking. God chooses to add members to the fellowship—inferior members, to be sure, but invited nonetheless! This ecstatic overflow of love issues from the inner trinitarian, perichoretic dance. "The church is a missionary community because God is a missionary God."[21] God's loving being is such that it naturally reaches out to the other—the estranged, the marginalized, the outcast. God's mission takes the shape and direction of God's love—namely, other-regarding love.

Finally, the other-centered nature of God's perichoretic life turns toward those who are unlike God. God makes room for the other when he creates

18. Gregory of Nyssa, *Against Eunomius* 2.2, in *Nicene and Post-Nicene Fathers of the Christian Church*, 2nd series, ed. Philip Schaff and Henry Wace (Grand Rapids: Eerdmans, 1979), 5:102.

19. Cornelius Plantinga Jr., *Engaging God's World: A Christian Vision of Faith, Learning, and Living* (Grand Rapids: Eerdmans, 2002), 22–23. Plantinga is especially gifted in describing the role of grace within the creation and the fact that God did not create out of loneliness or need but out of an overflow of the richness of his trinitarian fellowship.

20. Pinnock, *Flame of Love*, 38.

21. Migliore, "The Missionary God," 17.

the worlds. While creation may point toward its Creator, it is fundamental to the Judeo-Christian faith that the creation is not God.[22] Yet this making-room-for-the-other begins in the inner trinitarian life of God, where the richness of fellowship and singularity of purpose is not disturbed by the dimensions of differentiation of Father, Son, and Spirit. Hence, the Triune God makes room for the other with such richness of loving other-regard that it overflows toward creation, making room for the radically other. Further, God not only makes room for humans by creating them, but he also *invites them to the dance of trinitarian life by making them in the image of Godself.* Whatever else *imago Dei* (image of God) might mean, it must at least mean that God desired communion with a part of his creation.[23] According to Scripture, only the human being is called to such a privileged position. Due to sin, humans experience brokenness of that image, making the possibility for fellowship with God and each other severely strained. The new creation in Christ Jesus brings renewed life to believers as well as creates them anew in the image of their Creator (Col. 3:10). So now, the Spirit invites all to join the dance. Molly Marshall reminds us of the reciprocal nature of this event: "It is by the Spirit that we participate in the life of God and God participates in our life together."[24] In this way, the Spirit operates with a mission directed outward toward the created order. God is a "missionary God," searching the highways and byways to urge people to join God's party. With respect to this, Daniel Migliore comments, "The triune God who lives eternally in mutual self-giving love wills to include creatures in that community of love. The welcoming of the other that marks the life of the Trinity in all eternity is extended outward to us. Through the divine missions of Word and Spirit, God welcomes creatures to share the triune life of love and community."[25]

With such inclusion of humans, we are permitted to share in God's fellowship and life, while at the same time God participates in our fellowship and lives. It is the Spirit who engages this communion of lives divine and human. The Spirit provides a bridge or nexus that "relates all creation to the Trinitarian history without succumbing to pantheism or the hierarchical dualism that sharply separates the divine from the creaturely."[26] And it is precisely at

---

22. See George S. Hendry, *God the Creator: The Hastie Lectures in the University of Glasgow, 1935* (London: Cokesbury, 1938), 78–79.

23. Later in this chapter we will return to the doctrine of the image of God in humans and its implications for God's people.

24. Marshall, "Participating in the Life of God," 150.

25. Migliore, "The Missionary God," 18.

26. Marshall, "Participating in the Life of God," 147.

this nexus where the church must live—in the presence of God's Spirit and power. The church continues God's outreach to the other by making room for those most unlike them and calling them to join the dance of God along with us in the community of faith. Hence, the missionary work of the church is precisely that of an invitation to experience and be encountered by the God of the Scriptures, the God of Abraham, Isaac, and Jacob—indeed, the God of our Lord Jesus Christ.

The Life of the Triune God as a Paradigm for the Church

The pattern of the inner trinitarian life of God provides a paradigm with which believers may begin to reflect God's own nature in their lives. While we are certainly not God and will never possess the capacity to be and do in the same way what God is and does, as new creatures in Christ who are empowered by the Spirit, we can *begin* to reflect God's character in our interpersonal relations with people in the local community of faith and the world. As Miroslav Volf has rightly cautioned, "Our notions of the triune God are not the triune God, even if God is accessible to us only in these notions."[27] Indeed, there are limits to the correspondence between God's inner being and our relational being in the community of faith. Nonetheless, there is also some foundation for using the nature of the Triune God as a paradigm for our relations with each other in the body of Christ.

Before engaging this idea more specifically, we need to consider some significant challenges to using the Trinity as a paradigm. George Vandervelde, a Reformed theologian, has noted some important hurdles to overcome in this regard. First, he proposes that there are no biblical passages that speak with clarity about the inner relations of the Trinity.[28] Hence, he views *any* reflection on the life of the Triune God as outside of the purview of humans and therefore impossible to use as a paradigm of communal life. He states, "When, on the basis of these revealed economic relations, theologians draw conclusions regarding immanent triune relations, these conclusions need to be regarded as human speculation, interesting, perhaps, but no more than the imaginative labour of the human mind."[29] And with one wave of the hand, books and projects of trinitarian theologians of the past fifty years (not to mention some of the profound thoughts of the early church) are set aside! What is accurate about this charge is that such attempts can be very specula-

27. Volf, *After Our Likeness*, 198.
28. George Vandervelde, "The Challenge of Evangelical Ecclesiology," *Evangelical Review of Theology* 27, no. 1 (2003): 4–26, here 22–23.
29. Vandervelde, "The Challenge of Evangelical Ecclesiology," 23.

tive *if* one approaches the task without the logic of God's self-revelation in Christ to tether one down.[30]

Second, Vandervelde suggests that John 17, where Jesus prays that the disciples may be one as the Father and Son are one, is inapplicable for the purpose of understanding inner-trinitarian relations. "At most, it refers to a bi-unity, the relation of Father and Son."[31] Vandervelde interprets John 17 as applicable to the Father-Son relation only *in terms of mission*, not the inner life of God. This seems too restrictive in several ways. Much of the New Testament expresses a binity or bi-unity of Father and Son; the understanding of how the Spirit relates to the Father and Son remains mostly inchoate. However, John 14–16 (the section just prior to John 17) contains some of the richest language in all the New Testament about who the Spirit is and what the Spirit is to do. Why can this unity of Father and Son not point to the inner life of God as something paralleled by the outward missions of Word and Spirit? Isn't it reasonable that early church believers used these Johannine passages of John 17 and also John 14–16 to develop some understanding of the relationship between the three persons?

Third, Vandervelde urges that we know "precious little about the inner being and interior relations of the triune God."[32] This seems to be his main challenge all along. He states, "The most sophisticated theological elaborations of the eternal, inner relations of three persons within God's triune existence are still no more than that, *our* elaborations, our limited theories about the transcendent infinite being of God."[33] Since God is incomprehensible, attempting such theological investigation is "transmuting theology into conjury."[34] Evangelical theology, he recommends, should stay clear of the "metaphysical minefield" that so easily devolves into a maze that is impossible to decipher.[35]

These are serious challenges to the entire endeavor we are proposing. However, I do not think they are as serious as they first appear. There are plenty of biblical examples that open up the life and thought of the Triune God for us. Since the nature of God is revealed in Scripture as faithful, true, and righteous altogether, cannot we infer, with the logic of this revelation, that the God of revelation (economic Trinity) is at least as parallel to God as God is

---

30. I use this imagery in a way similar to how Karl Barth speaks of the development of his christological centrality in *CD* II/2:3–5.

31. Vandervelde, "The Challenge of Evangelical Ecclesiology," 23.

32. Vandervelde, "The Challenge of Evangelical Ecclesiology," 24.

33. Vandervelde, "The Challenge of Evangelical Ecclesiology," 24 (his emphasis).

34. Vandervelde, "The Challenge of Evangelical Ecclesiology," 24.

35. Vandervelde, "The Challenge of Evangelical Ecclesiology," 24.

to Godself (immanent Trinity)? Moreover, God reveals something of Godself in every encounter with humans that is recorded in Scripture, whether clearly stated or unstated. Furthermore, since the fullness of the Godhead dwells in Christ in bodily form, we have a perfect record of who this God is in the person and work of Christ. Cannot we infer from the revelation of God *in Jesus Christ* that we understand something of the nature of this God as God is to Godself? We also have numerous testimonies from Christ's own mouth related to the character of the inner nature of God the Father and the Son (John 5, 8, 10, 14, and 17). Because John 14–16 comes just prior to John 17, it seems to bring that passage into a broader interpretive scheme than one that accounts for just Father and Son.[36]

In recent years a German theologian named Heribert Mühlen has underscored the idea that in Johannine literature there exists an "inner-trinitarian 'we'" in several texts. Mühlen notes that when Jesus says, "I and the Father are one" (NIV) in John 10:30, the phrase more literally should be rendered, "I and the Father, *we* are one" (ἕν ἐσμεν | *hen esmen*).[37] From this and other texts, Mühlen crafts a "we" theology of inner-trinitarian life. These "we" accounts provide "access to God's innermost life and 'being' which we post-biblically label 'trinitarian.'"[38]

Vandervelde's "metaphysical minefield" metaphor misses the point entirely. God has revealed Godself to us in Jesus Christ. It is the task of theology to probe into the nature of who our God is by investigating the *logic of God's revelation* to us, unraveling the various clues from God's own self-revelation in Jesus Christ. Such unraveling is not speculative conjuring as long as it has its basis in the *logic* of the revelation itself, thereby legitimately showing us an understanding of the God who is behind the veil. It is *God's* movement toward us in revelation that gives us assurance to postulate what God may be like beyond that specific revelation to us. Further, the God who confronts us in revelation is not one who can be comprehended by our human words

---

36. Almost all scholars today hold that when Jesus speaks of the comforter, "who proceeds from the Father" (John 15:26 KJV), he means the *sending* of the Spirit in this historical, economic realm not some inner "procession" within the inner life of the immanent Trinity. I grant that Vandervelde has a point: *a part* of John 14–17 deals with the earthly mission and work of the Trinity. However, John 17 seems to speak to an ontological unity between Father and Son, thereby refuting much of Vandervelde's claim that none of this material deals with the inner life of the Trinity. Also, his comment that what can be described is at best a "bi-nity," not Trinity, seems to ignore how this Gospel speaks of the Spirit as being in lockstep union with Father and Son.

37. Heribert Mühlen, "Epilogue: 'We as We Ourselves Are with You': The Fundamental Promise of the New Covenant," in Wolfgang Vondey, *Heribert Mühlen: His Theology and Praxis—a New Profile of the Church* (Lanham, MD: University Press of America, 2004), 321–22.

38. Mühlen, "Epilogue," 311.

or "in any of the categories of our finite thought."[39] The Scottish theologian Donald Baillie has placed the right emphasis on the relation between the mystery of God and the revelation of God to humans: "God can be known only in a direct personal relationship, an 'I-and-Thou' intercourse, in which He addresses us and we respond to Him."[40] The result, Baillie suggests, is that we end up with a theology that has elements of paradox. Since we must theologize and must use words and concepts about God in worship,[41] we must be keenly aware that our attempts at harnessing God within our linguistic bridles will always fail. God cannot be harnessed by anyone or anything, even the best-intended theologies. However, as humans who think in linguistic modes, we need to theologize and worship with language that is true to the revelation of God in Scripture and (primarily) in Jesus Christ. Therefore, the task of theology is to search out language that reflects God's self-revelation as closely as possible; further, theology must then examine the "distinctive talk about God" in the Christian church.[42]

My point in examining this line of thought is twofold: (1) the nature of the God who confronts us directly is one whose very presence is transformative; and (2) the nature of this God becomes, by the power of the Spirit, the nature of God's people, even in this life to some extent. That is the basic thesis of this book. The task of theology is deciphering and organizing the signals we get from Scripture and from reasoning out the logic of this revelation into human constructs. These are not useless metaphysical speculations about some obscure theological footnote but are disciplined inquiries into the being of God as revealed to us; on this basis, the life of the Trinity (even if understood only within limited, finite thinking) may become a paradigm for our own relations of love within the Christian community and the world. Unlike some metaphysical speculation, this theology has practical implications for the life of the church.

Allow me to illustrate how the doctrine of the Trinity can be used as a paradigm by offering several examples of God's relational character, which should also become our character as we live together. As will be noted, some of these come from Miroslav Volf's detailed trinitarian ecclesiology.

---

39. Donald M. Baillie, *God Was in Christ: An Essay on Incarnation and Atonement* (London: Faber & Faber, 1961), 108. Baillie makes a crucial point that paradox, therefore, remains a fundamental aspect of the Christian faith. We do not know everything about God because we are on different levels. Also, God cannot be studied like some object among other objects, as Karl Barth reminded us frequently: "God is not God if He is considered and conceived as one in a series of like objects." See *CD* II/1:15.

40. Baillie, *God Was in Christ*, 108.

41. Baillie, *God Was in Christ*, 108.

42. *CD* I/1:12 (2nd ed.).

Within the Triune Godhead, there is no principle of hierarchy. The perichoretic dance is one where no one is ahead of the other: no person of the Trinity takes the lead simply because that person is always in charge. To be clear, there are differences in function, but there is unity of purpose. There are differences of work but sameness of essence. Father, Son, and Spirit are equally God, but through the eternal wisdom possessed by this Triune God, they operate with distinct functions. For example, the Son, not the Father or the Spirit, became a human being. It was the planned function from eternity for the Son to take on human flesh. It was the Father's task to orchestrate the entire plan of redemption and to send the Son and Spirit to humans for our sakes and our salvation. It was the Spirit's task to empower the Son while in human flesh so that he could overcome the enemy and do the Father's will; it is still the Spirit's task to empower believers in our flesh so that we can also overcome and do the Father's will. Yet within this differentiation of function, there is no principle of hierarchy in relation to their Godness, their essence as deity. While the functions may reveal the Son as submitted to the Father for the purpose of accomplishing an agreed-upon task, none of the persons is diminished in deity thereby. Because all three persons share equally the divine nature or substance, one is not more God than the other. The three persons are all united as the One God in their relations and in their unity.

With regard to the church, this paradigm of the inner-trinitarian life could clarify every functional role within our communities of faith by reminding us that we all were made in God's image and that we all contain this image without variation of its quantity or diminution of its quality. Therefore, we are all equal in our essence, in the "stuff" that makes us human. While we may not live up to that ideal due to sin, at the very least the community of Christ should witness to the entire world that no one of its members is more valued in terms of their essential being than other humans within their own community *and* beyond it. While humans may put a high value on *function*, God places a higher value on *essence*. *What we do* in the community of faith should be in grateful response to the grace that God has showered on our lives; *who we are* in the community of faith is the basis for equal treatment by God. God's own manner of assessing humans is initially based on who they are rather than what they do; this must be the starting point for all of our own interactions both inside and outside the Christian community. For God is no respecter of persons: God simply does not play favorites (Acts 10:34). All humanity is the object of God's love. Just as there is no principle of hierarchy in the Trinity, there must be no principle of hierarchy in the body of Christ— other than this: Christ is the head of the church, and we are the members of his body. Pastors cannot say to janitors that pastors are esteemed by God as more valuable because of their function, can they? Church treasurers cannot say to nursery workers that the tending of church monies is deemed more valuable to God than that of tending babies, can they? If what we *do* for God is anything other than a loving response to God's gracious initiative toward us in Jesus Christ, then what we do will go up in smoke on the last day. Who we *are* is something we are born with (on the one hand): we are created in God's image, born, and worthy of equal standing before God as his special creation. Who we *are* is also something we may have done to us: we are born anew from sin by God's Spirit, re-created in the image of Christ. What we *do* for God is in response to that gracious re-creation so that we put off our old selves and put on the garments of righteousness (Col. 3:10–12). Within Christian churches, as within all human groups, there will certainly be differences of function, but when it comes to our essential natures, we are equal before God and each other.

Miroslav Volf has suggested a term to describe this divine equality of persons in the Trinity: polycentric.[43] If I understand his proposal correctly, this term overcomes the problems associated with a "monarchy of the Father" as well as any central focus on one person of the Trinity. "Polycentric" refers to the three at the center of the life of God, which is not and cannot by definition be monocentric or bicentric or even tritheistic. Volf's proposal points to the life of the church in very profound ways. As I have noted in *Serving the People of God's Presence*, the "monarchy" of pastor within the life of the church is not God's intention for the people of God; church leadership is usually plural in the New Testament. Moreover, the body of Christ is meant to operate with a full array of spiritual gifts offered by a variety of God's people gathered together. If a Christian community is not open for God's presence and does not make space within its worship and life for people to share their gifts, then that community will become less and less relevant to the world in which it sits. Finding ways to make the life of the church more of a shared commitment is one of the transformations most necessary in the church today. This polycentric aspect of God's life carries us a long way in that direction.

With regard to the church, another dimension of God's inner trinitarian life is vital: the doctrine of *perichōrēsis*—the mutual reciprocity of the persons that flows in a rich fellowship of movement with and around each other in the Trinity, thereby making room for each other. The church *can reflect* God's perichoretic, other-centered life by its own demonstration of unity in movement together, where others are respected and deemed better

43. Volf, *After Our Likeness*, 217.

than oneself (Phil. 2:4). Obviously, humans cannot coinhere with each other as persons, so in some sense we can never fully reflect this perichoretic reality of God. Nonetheless, the power and presence of God works its way into our own natures, prompting us to reflect—within our own limited sphere of existence—this triune lifestyle of mutuality and reciprocity.

Over fifty references to "one another" appear in the New Testament, and each has a specific verb that precedes the object (one another). Several times Jesus says to "love one another" (John 13:34; 15:12). Paul's writings admonish us to "be devoted to one another in love" (Rom. 12:10), "accept one another" (15:7), "instruct one another" (15:14), "serve one another humbly in love" (Gal. 5:13), "be kind and compassionate to one another" (Eph. 4:32), "forgiv[e] each other" (4:32), "value others above" ourselves (Phil. 2:3), and "encourage one another" (1 Thess. 4:18). In twenty-one of the twenty-seven books of the New Testament, the phrase "one another" is used. The sheer quantity of "one another" passages points to the importance of other-centered living within the community of faith. Yet a closer look at the quality of *how* we are to deal with "one another" reveals an intensive quality of relationship within the body of Christ. The verbs used in these passages press us to action—to admonish, instruct, bear with, forgive, encourage, offer hospitality, live in harmony with, serve, submit to, and love one another. While not precisely the trinitarian life of *perichōrēsis*, this style of church life points us analogously toward a human perichoretic style of life together.

The Spirit of God is the One who binds us together and orchestrates the music of the perichoretic dance; it is the Spirit who teaches us *how to dance* in divine rhythm with one another like the Trinity dances. However, since humans cannot and do not "exist in one another" or possess the capacity for mutual reciprocity, *we* cannot be fully perichoretic with other humans. If that is the case with us, then what is the point of speaking of humans reflecting God's inner perichoretic nature here in the church? Since the same Spirit of God is God's presence in believers in the church, we can expect something of this relational, perichoretic nature of God to be instilled in us. If the other-regarding nature of *perichōrēsis* is one of the prominent ways that the Triune God displays love for each person of the Trinity, then when the Spirit "pours out" God's love in our hearts (Rom. 5:5), we experience love within the framework of such other-regarding focus. Indeed, this is one reason why Paul can expect human believers to relate to others in a spirit of mutual humility and other-regarding love, valuing "others above yourselves, not looking to your own interests but each of you to the interests of the others" (Phil. 2:3b–4). Hence, the Spirit who is "present in all

Christians 'opens' each of them to all others."[44] It is the Spirit of God who causes us to move with each other in some imitative choreography of the Trinity that we may not fully understand at the moment it is happening, melding our lives together for God's purpose. Because of who we are, this dance can never occur as fully as it does in the life of the Trinity, but the Spirit brings glimpses of such unity and diversity of movement to us here and now as we fellowship, worship, live, and work together, enriching and being enriched by the reciprocal giving of each part of the body of Christ. "It is not the mutual *perichoresis* of human beings, but rather the indwelling of the Spirit common to everyone that makes the church into a communion corresponding to the Trinity, a communion in which personhood and sociality are equiprimal."[45]

Volf uses a phrase to encompass this dimension of trinitarian life that can be mirrored in our ecclesial life: "symmetrical reciprocity."[46] Corresponding to the divine multiplicity in God, we humans have various gifts and diverse abilities in the body of Christ. Closely akin to the *perichōrēsis* of the Trinity, in which movement of persons is perfectly balanced and "in sync," there is a symmetrical give-and-take in the body of Christ whereby individual believers are recognized for their worth and gifts. Consequently, the entire body is benefited by the encouragement of sharing what God has given to them all.

With regard to the church, God's inner trinitarian life of overflow to others is a pattern for our own mission in this world. From the richness of life in the Spirit as we live together in the local community of Christ, we rise to confront the world with a message of reconciliation. We reach out to the other—those unlike us and those who may even frighten us due to their difference—in order to invite them into the circle of our lives, indeed, into the circle of God's trinitarian life. These are several ways that the inner life of the Trinity relates to the doctrine of the church. In this regard, Daniel Migliore strikes an accurate image of God and the church in the following statement:

> If we seek an analogy to the Spirit-empowered and Spirit-guided community of Christ, our reference must be to the triune life of God in whom personhood is profoundly communal and in whom equality allows for difference and difference does not subvert equality. The community of Jesus Christ in the power of the Spirit is *imago trinitatis*, a community of love and service in which each person expends self and receives self in continuous reciprocity, thus reflecting

44. Volf, *After Our Likeness*, 189.
45. Volf, *After Our Likeness*, 213.
46. Volf, *After Our Likeness*, 217, 219.

in creaturely community the perichoretic or mutually indwelling love of the persons of the Trinity.[47]

It is the Triune God who invites us to fellowship and union with him; it is God who invites us to the party, to join in the dance of trinitarian life. This is the God whom we experience, the God who calls us to commune with him. The people of God who have experienced this ecstatic life of the Trinity are being transformed by it. We join the dance and in some way create an "echo of trinitarian life" on earth.[48] Since the nature of God is joyous, overflowing communion, should not the nature of the people of God reflect that communion and union? In doing so, the church will become a "finite echo or bodying forth of the divine personal dynamics."[49] This is the implication of *beginning* with the nature of God when attempting to present a doctrine of the church. There need be no disjunction between God and his people since God has touched us directly by pouring out his love on us by the Holy Spirit (Rom. 5:5). Perhaps it was something of this reflective communion between God and humans that caused Charles Wesley to write that believers are "Mystically one with Thee, / Transcript of the Trinity, / Thee let all our nature own, / One in Three, and Three in One."[50]

Catherine LaCugna may overstate the point, yet she underscores an important idea: the Trinity is not just about God but about our life *in God*. She states, "The doctrine of the Trinity is not ultimately a teaching about 'God' but a teaching about *God's life with us and our life with each other*. It is the life of communion and indwelling, God in us, we in God, all of us in each other. This is the 'perichoresis,' the mutual interdependence that Jesus speaks of in the Gospel of John (John 17:20–21)."[51] As believers directly experience this triune, social God, they become transformed into humans who may increasingly reflect God's perichoretic image. In other words, they become the *people of God* because they have been encountered by this God. As a people created anew in the image of Christ Jesus, we are to put off ourselves and put on Christ (Col. 3:10). The nature of God is to be reflected in the nature of God's people.

47. Migliore, "The Missionary God," 22.
48. Pinnock, *Flame of Love*, 47.
49. Gunton, *The Promise of Trinitarian Theology*, 74.
50. Charles Wesley, "Transcript of the Trinity," in *Hymns and Sacred Poems* (1740), 188, part 1:1, stanza 1. This information is from S. T. Kimbrough Jr., *Partakers of the Life Divine: Participation in the Divine Nature in the Writings of Charles Wesley* (Eugene, OR: Cascade, 2016), 66–67. Also, compare the hymn by C. Wesley, "Sinners Turn, Why Will Ye Die?," in *The United Methodist Hymnal* (Nashville: United Methodist Publishing House, 1989), #34, where the fifth stanza reads, "You, whom he ordained, to be the transcript of the Trinity . . ."
51. LaCugna, *God for Us*, 228 (her emphasis).

If we are encountering God directly, what does this mean? Who is the God who confronts us in this encounter? Leonard Hodgson, a British theologian, offered insight into the nature of this experience in a series of lectures given in 1943 at Edinburgh.[52] He established an approach that took full advantage of the scriptural narrative and the religious experience of those bound within it, as well as the experience of those gripped by it in the present. His thesis is succinct and compelling: "The Christian life is life 'in the Spirit,' and as such reproduces in each Christian the same way of life as was that of Christ on earth. As He sought, found and did the Father's will through the Spirit, so does the Christian. He seeks to find and do the will of the Father with the companionship of the Son through the guidance and strength of the Spirit."[53] It is clear from this that just as Jesus Christ relied on the Father and Spirit while here on earth, so too must the believer. The God whom the believer experiences is the Triune God. Reproducing Christ's life is not a matter of merely copying Christ's pattern but is "made possible by an initial act of God 'adopting' the Christian to share in the sonship of Christ."[54] Just as Jesus shared a relationship with the Father and Spirit, so does the believer. As Hodgson concludes his point, he makes the issue clear with regard to experiencing God: "The Blessed Trinity is not some incomprehensible mystery which we dimly worship from without; it is the revealed nature of God 'in whom we live and move and have our being,' as well-known and familiar to the Christian, and as often unnoticed as the air he breathes."[55]

It is the expected experience of believers who follow the New Testament to reproduce the life of Christ—to be "little Christs," as it were. It should also be the expectation of believers today to experience the same God of our Lord Jesus Christ and immediately find a connection between Father, Son, and Spirit similar to what Jesus himself experienced. If the Spirit lives in us and God's love has been poured out into our lives by the Holy Spirit, and if, indeed, we must have the Spirit of Christ in us in order to belong to Christ at all (Rom. 8:9), then we should expect there to be some experience of the Spirit's reality commensurate with the Spirit's person. In other words, Christians do not merely experience Jesus. When Christians accept Jesus as Lord and Savior, they do so because the Father has lifted him up and drawn

---

52. Some have considered Hodgson the stimulus for a renewal in trinitarian thought, especially under the rubric of "social Trinity." In this lecture, I find his model and method a perfect paradigm for the model of the church understood in terms of the Trinity. More will be developed on this theme later.

53. Hodgson, *The Doctrine of the Trinity*, 49–50.

54. Hodgson, *The Doctrine of the Trinity*, 50.

55. Hodgson, *The Doctrine of the Trinity*, 50.

them to the Son and because the Holy Spirit has wooed and convinced them of the Son's efficacious work for them. Therefore, Christians enter the world of relationship with Christ, which brings them into immediate contact with God the Father and God the Spirit. This is the expectation and promise of the New Testament. It need not be diminished in today's preaching or living of the gospel. Through this Spirit we cry, "Abba, Father" (Rom. 8:15). It is through the Spirit that the reality of being children of God is made concrete and discernable. However, this reality brings us into contact with the Trinity, not with some ethereal, other-worldly being who cannot be known or experienced or even described, but with the God of our Lord Jesus Christ. It is the Spirit who makes known to our hearts the truth of Jesus's life, death, and resurrection, sealing us until the day of redemption (Eph. 1:13–14).

The Relational Nature of the People of God

As set forth at the beginning of this chapter, the doctrine of the church relies on the doctrine of the Triune God for its foundation. However, we also noted that this was only one side of the equation (albeit the larger side); the doctrine of the church also requires a robust understanding of theological anthropology in order to complete the picture of who God's people are called to be in this world. It is to the doctrine of humanity that we now turn for insight into what it means to be a human being and therefore what it means to be a *people* of God.

Who are the people of God? They are humans who have responded positively to God's encounter with them in the person of the risen Christ, whose presence has been revealed to them through the work of the Spirit. Further, they are also immediately incorporated into the community of believers by the Spirit's power. As shown earlier in this chapter, the nature of God needs to be reflected in the nature of God's people; this is what it means to belong to God, to be a people of his own possession (1 Pet. 2:9–10). God intends his people to be like him in some sense. Yet at the same time, the people of God are *people*—that is, humans who are physical/spiritual creatures made in God's image. They are not immaterial, independent, or infinite beings who create worlds. Therefore, in what sense can humans realistically reflect God's nature if they are not God? How can we be *like* God when we seem to be nothing like God at all? The remainder of this chapter will attempt to provide answers to these questions by reflecting on what it means to be a human being who has been made in God's image and likeness, yet also a creature encountered by the Creator God.

The Human as Creature

Foundational for understanding human beings is recognizing that they are *dependent creatures*. Despite a tendency for abnormal self-regard and even a penchant for playing God, humans are not God. Humans are created beings. In this respect, we share our creatureliness with other animals of the created order. We exist on the plane of dependency and contingency, as does all creation. The world of matter is not simply an extension of God. God is not us, and we are not God. As Karl Barth says, "God never and nowhere becomes the world. The world never and nowhere becomes God. God and world remain over against [*bei dem Gegenüber*] each other."[56] This fact separates us from the Creator in two important ways: (1) God is not dependent on anyone or anything and therefore is not a contingent being, whereas humans are entirely dependent and contingent; and (2) the world is not an extension of God's own being or nature and therefore is not "divinized" or infused with God's own life. Without the Creator, we would not exist; without the Creator's maintenance of all that is dependent on him, we would not continue to exist. Thus, all creatures are contingent and dependent beings.[57] Humans experience existence and death, as do all beings that exist on the "field of creatureliness."[58]

In the scriptural framework, on the other hand, humans are not just creatures. Humans are unique in the creation narrative of Genesis 1 in that they are the only creatures who are said to be made in God's image and likeness. They are also the only created beings for whom God holds a special counsel with Godself before creating them. "Let us make humankind in our image, according to our likeness" (Gen. 1:26 NRSV). Previously, God had spoken things into existence: "Let there be light" or "Let there be a dome in the midst of the waters" (1:3, 6 NRSV). But that is not how humans were made. They were crafted with great intentionality and, as Genesis 2 tells us, with the very hands and breath of God molding and invigorating Adam (and eventually Eve) from the dust of the ground. No other creature received this kind of attention in the creation narrative.

While we cannot deny our existence as creatures ("It is he [God] that hath made us, and not we ourselves," Ps. 100:3 KJV), we must also affirm from a

---

56. Karl Barth, *Credo*, trans. J. S. McNab (Eugene, OR: Wipf & Stock, 2005), 34; cf. Barth, *Credo: Die Hauptprobleme der Dogmatik dargestellt im Anschluß an das Apostolische Glaubensbekenntnis, 16 Vorlesungen, gehalten an der Universität Utrecht im Februar und März 1935*, 3rd ed. (Munich: Kaiser, 1935), 34.

57. Ray S. Anderson, *On Being Human: Essays in Theological Anthropology* (Pasadena, CA: Fuller Seminary Press, 1982), 21.

58. Anderson, *On Being Human*, 22. This is Anderson's phrase for the arena of commonality between humans and other creatures.

theological perspective that humans are *more* than creatures. Our creatureliness does not entirely define our humanity.

The Human Created in God's Image and Likeness

From a theological perspective, then, one of the unique aspects of human beings is their reflection of the image of God (*imago Dei*). Numerous questions arise from this concept: What is the image of God in humans? Is it something that inheres in human nature throughout all time? Is it a capacity to reason? Is it a part of our substance (e.g., located within the soul and not the body)? Is it our freedom of choice?[59] What happens to this image of God *after* the fall of Adam and Eve (Gen. 3)? Is it lost entirely and retrieved only when the Spirit re-creates believers, or is it merely damaged and in need of slight repair? How does sin affect the image of God? Does the image of God in humans provide Christian ethics today a basis from which to argue for human dignity and worth?

A frustrating dimension of any theological attempt to interpret the *imago Dei* in its biblical context and for theology is that there is precious little offered either in the text or in the context to assist us in figuring out what the image of God is supposed to mean. It has become a theological umbrella phrase under which a great deal of moral and theological value has been placed, yet the specific nature of its meaning seems to remain shrouded in the text itself.[60]

Let us turn to the text to see what might be useful for our purposes. Perhaps we could begin by recognizing that Genesis 1:26–27 identifies the image of God in the relationship of male and female: "Then God said, 'Let us make humankind in our image, according to our likeness; and let them have dominion over the fish of the sea and over the birds of the air, and over the cattle, and over all the wild animals of the earth, and over every creeping thing that creeps upon the earth.' So God created humankind in his image, in the image of God he created them; male and female he created them" (Gen. 1:26–27

---

59. For a generalized portrayal of various options over the history of Christian thought, see Paul K. Jewett, *Man as Male and Female* (Grand Rapids: Eerdmans, 1975). For five proposals as to the meaning of *imago Dei*, see Gordon J. Wenham, *Genesis 1–15*, ed. John D. W. Watts, Word Biblical Commentary, ed. David A. Hubbard and Glenn W. Baker (Grand Rapids: Zondervan, 1987), 29–31. The five proposals are these: (1) the image and likeness are distinct from each other; (2) the image refers to mental/spiritual faculties that humans share with their Creator; (3) the image consists of a physical resemblance; (4) the image grants the human being dominion on earth as God's representative; and (5) the image is a capacity to relate to God.

60. This is one reason why a recent theologian handling theological anthropology, David Kelsey, has refused to take it up as a central idea within his recent two-volume work. See *Eccentric Existence: A Theological Anthropology* (Louisville: Westminster John Knox, 2009), esp. 2:1008–51, the chapter "Coda: Eccentric Existence as Imaging the Image of God."

The *Imago Dei* throughout History

Paul Jewett identifies three major schools of thought regarding the image of God: (1) the Greek fathers (the androgynous approach), who viewed the human being in Genesis 1 as without gender or sexuality—the androgynous person, combining both sexes within it—and the human being of Genesis 2 as distinct in gender, male and female; (2) Augustine, Calvin, and others (the traditional approach), who viewed the image somewhere *within* humans; and (3) Karl Barth and trinitarian theologians (the relational approach).[a]

There are major difficulties with this rather simplified categorization of a very complex discussion in theology. For example, to speak of the Greek fathers as having one approach (the androgynous one) is too broad a claim. There is huge variation between Irenaeus, the Alexandrian school (Clement, Origen, and even Athanasius), the Cappadocians, and the Antiochene school (John Chrysostom and Theodore of Mopsuestia). What Jewett has described as the Greek approach is really more the single approach of Gregory of Nyssa and not all the Greek fathers. Further, the nuances of Augustine's use of "image of God" in his *De Trinitate* is unique among all approaches. Calvin and Luther have distinct approaches to understanding what it means to be created in God's image, as well as clear lines of demarcation for what happens to that image after the fall. My point is that a careful study of these sources will reveal great variety on this important topic—such variety, in fact, that generalizing categorizations do not really help us understand the topic better.

a. Paul K. Jewett, *Man as Male and Female* (Grand Rapids: Eerdmans, 1975).

NRSV). As Victor Hamilton has commented concerning this passage, "It is clear that verse 26 is not interested in defining what is the image of God in [humans]. The verse simply states the fact, which is repeated in the following verse."[61] What we can see in this text, however, is a form of Hebrew parallelism: the juxtaposition of the word "image" in verse 27 with the words "male and female" in the same verse. Beyond a literary identification, this parallelism is used by some to help clarify and expand the meaning of "image."[62] In this verse we see that the "image of God" is explained further by the synonymous phrase "male and female." In other words, whatever the image of God may

61. Victor P. Hamilton, *The Book of Genesis, Chapters 1–17*, New International Commentary on the Old Testament, ed. R. K. Harrison and Robert L. Hubbard Jr. (Grand Rapids: Eerdmans, 1990), 137.
62. Wenham, *Genesis 1–15*, 32–33.

be in terms of content, there is at least something of it to be found in the male and female distinctions of gender within the species of *homo sapiens*.[63] Does this mean there is sexual distinction within God? Do humans in their sexuality reflect some gender differences in the Godhead?

Partially out of fear of envisioning sexuality in the Godhead, theologians have sidestepped this rather obvious interpretation.[64] To be sure, God is not a physical being but rather spirit. There is no materiality in God's essence, no physicality. Hence, there cannot be sexuality in God. So then, what can this parallelism mean? How is God reflected in the fact that the human race was made in two distinct genders, male and female?

Karl Barth was a proponent of analyzing this aspect of the *imago Dei* more carefully to find some clue about God's nature that is reflected in humans. Barth proposed that in human gender distinction, there is a relationship of an "I and a Thou" confronting each other in their similarity and difference.[65] Just as there is distinction within unity in the Trinity, there is some reflection of this nature in the distinction within unity of the human race (in terms of gender differences). Both genders are human, but within this species, there are two dimensions that are different—similar in their humanity yet distinct in their gender differences. The male meets "the other" in the female, and the female meets "the other" in the male. Such relationship reflects something of the relationship within the Trinity. Barth calls this *analogia relationis* (analogy of relation).[66] In some manner, there is a relationship between the different genders that reflects God's inner relationship and yet is not identical with it. Hence, it is only analogous.[67]

Do humans reflect something of our God's nature through our own existence as male and female? Is this what the *imago Dei* means? Frankly, I am uncertain that any one aspect of human nature or relationships can completely fulfill what it means to be created in the image of God. As I have conceded earlier, there could be multiple ways such reflection takes place. I do think the text provides a hint that leads us toward what Barth suggests, but Barth's proposal seems to rely heavily on the text itself giving us certitude

---

63. It also means that the image of God belongs to *both* male and female.

64. Ray Anderson calls this "fear of anthropomorphism." See Anderson, *On Being Human*, 71.

65. *CD* III/1:196; also 149. While I recognize the potential weaknesses of Barth's interpretation here, especially as it relates to gender issues, I think the essential point about relationality and the other still remains a solid theological understanding from the text.

66. See Gary W. Deddo, *Karl Barth's Theology of Relations: Trinitarian, Christological, and Human; Towards an Ethic of the Family*, Issues in Systematic Theology 4, ed. Paul D. Molnar (New York: Peter Lang, 1999), 43, 112, 138.

67. Karl Barth, *The Doctrine of Creation*, trans. Harold Knight et al., in *CD* III/2:220. Barth states that Jesus Christ is *the* image of God and is plainly the *analogia relationis* (221).

for understanding the image of God. In many ways, the Bible does not seem prone to define what the image means.

However, for our purposes in this section, let us broaden the issue of gender distinction itself (male and female) into a depiction of *relationship between an I and Thou*. It appears that God's intent in making humans was to have *relationship* with them. Perhaps a concomitant result of this relational creature was the innate need for relationships with other humans. Hence, humans were made in God's likeness so that God could connect with them in communication and fellowship and they could reciprocate with God and other humans to some degree. Without the image of God in humans, it seems that the distance between God and the human creature would be so broad that communication—let alone relationship—would be impossible. Therefore, God established something like himself in humans so that they could reflect God's own nature in witness to their Creator. Humans are relational beings because God designed them for relationships with God's own being and with other human beings, who could respond to their personhood accordingly.

So, what can be said regarding the theological value of the *imago Dei*? Without entering a fully orbed discussion of the *imago Dei*, I propose that there may be multiple ways in which human beings reflect their Creator. Whatever this collection of attributes or dimensions looks like, the unique yet incomplete ramifications may be gleaned from several parts of the text in Genesis:

1. Humans can relate to or interact with God (3:8–11).
2. Humans can relate to or interact with each other (2:20; 3:6–7).
3. Humans can "rule over" the created order like loving rulers (1:28).
4. Humans deserve respect and dignity (cf. 9:6, where humans are warned not to kill other humans because they are made in the image of God).

What do these brief summary results tell us about human beings? Without defining the *imago Dei* itself, we can infer from these points that they demonstrate the uniqueness of humanity. Humans were created for the Other (God) and by the Other in order to be with the Other. God created humans to live in relationship with the Other (God) and with others (humans primarily, but perhaps also animals and all life-forms). In other words, humans were created to reflect God's nature by being in relationship with others. Humans are not meant to be solitary beings, dwelling in isolation from each other; rather, humans are made *for* and *to* the other. Fundamentally, humans are social beings because their Creator, the Triune God, is a social being. Yet more than being social beings, humans are designed by their Creator to be shaped and formed by communal groups of other humans. This capacity for relationality is surely one aspect of our reflection of the Creator's nature. The myth of sole individuals climbing up against the forces of life in order to succeed on their own is just that—a myth.

We have previously established in this chapter that the Triune God is communal. Relationship among Father, Son, and Spirit is so rich that it spills over into God's gracious actions outward (both in creation and redemption). God made humans "wired" for relationships because the very essence of the Triune God is relational. God made humans so that God could encounter them and engage them as an "I" confronting a "Thou." It was Martin Buber, a twentieth-century Jewish philosopher, who initially taught theologians about the importance of what "I" and "Thou" mean in relationship.[68] When treating humans as "objects" to be used or manipulated, Buber suggested that this reflects an I-It relationship. This style of relationship is one of the ways humans relate to others—and the most common one at that.[69] The second style is the I-You (I-Thou) relationship. These are the two styles of relationship among humans based on the two foundational words (*die Grundworte*).[70] What is the basic difference between these two attitudes of humanity? "Whoever says You does not have something for his object; . . . where You is said, there is no something [*hat kein Etwas zum Gegenstand*]."[71] It is because the You places us in the world of relation (*Beziehung*), not the world as experience (*als Erfahrung*).[72] A human being becomes an I through a You.[73] Within the I-It world, the I appears as an ego who becomes conscious of itself as a subject. However, within the I-You world, the I appears as a *person* who is conscious of itself as subjectivity—that is, a person in relation.[74] As Buber brilliantly explains this difference, "Egos [*Eigenwesen*] appear by setting themselves apart from other egos [*Eigenwesen*]. Persons [*Personen*] appear by entering into relation to other persons [*zu anderen Personen*]."[75] With these remarks

68. Martin Buber, *I and Thou*, trans. Walter Kaufmann (New York: Simon & Schuster, 1970).
69. Buber, *I and Thou*, 54.
70. Martin Buber, *Das dialogische Prinzip: Ich und Du; Zwiesprache; Die Frage an den Einzelnen Elemente des Zwischenmenschlichen* (Heidelberg: Schneider, 1965), 7. This work has several of Buber's writings in it; I have used it to examine the German behind Kaufmann's translation of *I and Thou*.
71. Buber, *I and Thou*, 55; Buber, *Ich und Du*, 8.
72. Buber, *I and Thou*, 56; Buber, *Ich und Du*, 10.
73. Buber, *I and Thou*, 80; Buber, *Ich und Du*, 20.
74. Buber, *I and Thou*, 111–12.
75. Buber, *I and Thou*, 112; Buber, *Ich und Du*, 65.

on the *imago Dei* and Buber's foundation about I-Thou relations, we are ready to move forward to a consideration of the significance of this for the people of God.

Persons-in-Relation

Within much of our modern Western society, a human being is viewed as an independent self with only tangential connections to other humans or creatures. Indeed, the modern self is noted for its isolation and even its loneliness.[76] Loneliness is different from being alone. Loneliness can stem from a sense of "not being a part of anything, of being cut off."[77] This is not the way God intended humans to flourish and live.

Humans have been created as persons-in-relation, not as persons-in-isolation. In other words, the intention of God for humans is that they live in relatedness. Martin Buber points us to understanding this intention of God as he describes the human condition: "Inscrutably involved, we live in the currents of universal reciprocity."[78] Humans were made relational beings by God. Yet how do we know God's intention here?

At least a part of this knowledge of God's intention can be deduced from the distortion of relatedness, first with God and then with other humans. Alienation, self-centeredness, and the resultant loneliness shape the contours of human lives and mar the cycles of our attempted relationships. Isolation marks the beat of so many lives, even amid thousands of people in urban settings. If sin is a description of life the way it was *not* supposed to be, and if alienation in relationships is one of the major results of sin among humans, then it can be deduced that health and flourishing in relationships was God's original intention for human beings.[79]

76. While this idea has been around a long time (I point to the 1936 film written and directed by Charlie Chaplin, *Modern Times*, which highlights the modern human caught in the alienation of an increasingly mechanized world), only recently has the situation reached the attention of health professionals. A former surgeon general for the United States, Dr. Vivek H. Murthy, noted in 2017 that loneliness had reached epidemic proportions in terms of public health. He compared the reduction in one's life span due to loneliness to that caused by smoking fifteen cigarettes a day! See Jena McGregor, "This Former Surgeon General Says There's a 'Loneliness Epidemic' and Work Is Partly to Blame," *Washington Post*, Oct. 4, 2017; also, Eric Klinenberg, "Is Loneliness a Health Epidemic?," *New York Times*, Feb. 9, 2018.

77. Jean Vanier, *Becoming Human* (New York: Paulist Press, 1998), 33.

78. Martin Buber, *I and Thou*, 67; Buber, *Ich und Du*, 20. The German reads almost poetically here: "*Unerforschlich einbegriffen leben wir in der strömenden All-Gegenseitigkeit.*"

79. Cornelius Plantinga Jr., *Not the Way It's Supposed to Be: A Breviary of Sin* (Grand Rapids: Eerdmans, 1995), 10–12. Plantinga reminds us that shalom is the way God intended things to be, where all is "universal flourishing, wholeness and delight" (10); sin, however, is the "vandalism" or disturbance of shalom (12).

This perspective on the uniqueness of humans has been underscored by an emphasis from various philosophers in the past century regarding what it means to be a "person" or a "self." Some of their insights will take us a long way toward grasping the significance of our communal existence within the body of Christ and toward minimizing the cultural onslaught of individualism.

Personalism has roots in the nineteenth century but comes to the fore in the early twentieth century with the likes of Edmund Husserl, Emmanuel Mounier, Jacques Maritain, Gabriel Marcel, Emmanuel Levinas, and Pope John Paul II. Personalism influenced and was influenced by existentialism, especially in France. In Germany, it was connected with phenomenology, especially with Husserl. Some of the main characteristics of personalism are these: (1) Humans are unique in their person, being different from other creatures. (2) Humans cannot be reduced to either a material essence or spiritual one. (3) Human persons are granted dignity by their existence as humans. (4) There is concern for the "self" of a person and (5) an emphasis on the intersubjective, relational nature of persons. While I will be referring to several different philosophers who may fall into the category of personalism, this does not mean that I accept all the accompanying philosophical frameworks of each thinker. For our purposes, I am merely trying to show from the various perspectives of personalism that humans are made for relationships with others and that their dignity is affirmed by their existence.[80]

According to this view of personalism, humans are most fully "persons" when they are *in relation with* "the other"—that is, some other human being who stands opposite them. Hence, to conceive of a person as an individual who acts as an independent self is to misunderstand the nature of being human. John Macmurray, a twentieth-century Scottish philosopher, has noted that "the self is constituted by its relation to the Other."[81] Consequently, holding on to a concept of the "self," which is isolated and alone like a "spectator of all time and all existence," is a mere idea, not a living entity that acts.[82] Humans are neither autonomous nor independent, regardless of the modern Western

80. Thomas D. Williams and Jan Olof Bengtsson, "Personalism," in *The Stanford Encyclopedia of Philosophy* (Summer 2018 ed.), ed. Edward N. Zalta, https://plato.stanford.edu/archives/sum2018/entries/personalism/.

81. See John Macmurray, *Persons in Relation*, Gifford Lectures, 1953–54 (Amherst, NY: Humanity Books, 1991; orig. ed., 1961), 17, 113. Philosophers to whom I refer will be using "Other" (with a capital O) in reference to a human being who encounters a person with a potential for relating to them. From what I can discern, the "Other" in this context is capitalized to distinguish it from an "other," which is simply an *object* to be used by the self instead of a legitimate "I" as a counterpart standing before me. The capitalization seems to be a way of marking the respect and attention needed for the other who calls for my attention.

82. Macmurray, *Persons in Relation*, 17.

rhetoric that preaches to the contrary. "The idea of an autonomous and self-constituting person is an illusion. It neglects the role community has in identity formation. Relation with others is primary, not secondary."[83] Unfortunately, Western societies have too long laid claim to a "rugged individualism" that heralds the single hero who rises to the top on her own strength and wit, without any reliance on others. The work of Robert Bellah and others has shown that such individualism is "peculiarly powerful in American culture"[84] and may be overcome only through reeducating ourselves with regard to communal existence.[85] To posit each human as an independent, self-sustaining individual essentially ignores "our embedding in webs of interlocution."[86] We come to know who we are through interactions and communication with others. Hence, only when the self is in "dynamic relation with the Other" can there be a claim to the self's existence.[87] "The individual becomes a person only in the presence of others."[88]

A contemporary Canadian philosopher, Charles Taylor, has named these connections in human relationships "frameworks," by which he means "a crucial set of qualitative distinctions" that help to shape a "sense" within us that some action or way of living or even feeling has a "higher" value for connecting us to "the good" than do other actions or ways of living.[89] Such frameworks structure people's lives, providing "the background, explicit or implicit, for our moral judgments, intuitions, or reactions" in the various dimensions of life.[90] Consequently, living without such frameworks is "utterly impossible for us."[91] For Taylor, such a view of frameworks necessary to undergird life indicates something transcendent in human beings—a craving that not even the most virulent naturalist reductionism can dampen.

In this context Taylor carves out an anti-individualistic agenda. A self cannot be a self on its own: "I am a self only in relation to certain interlocutors."[92]

---

83. Thomas E. Reynolds, *Vulnerable Communion: A Theology of Disability and Hospitality* (Grand Rapids: Brazos, 2008), 83.

84. This turn of phrase describing Bellah's work is from Charles Taylor, *Sources of the Self: The Making of the Modern Identity* (Cambridge, MA: Harvard University Press, 1989), 39.

85. Robert N. Bellah, Richard Madsen, William M. Sullivan, Ann Swidler, and Steven M. Tipton, *Habits of the Heart: Individualism and Commitment in American Life* (Berkeley: University of California Press, 2008; orig. ed., 1985), esp. 55–65, which deals with North American ideals of "self-reliance" and the concept of "leaving home" in order to blaze one's own trail in life.

86. Taylor, *Sources of the Self*, 39.

87. Macmurray, *Persons in Relation*, 17.

88. Reynolds, *Vulnerable Communion*, 83.

89. Taylor, *Sources of the Self*, 19–20.

90. Taylor, *Sources of the Self*, 26.

91. Taylor, *Sources of the Self*, 27.

92. Taylor, *Sources of the Self*, 36.

In answer to the perennial and persistent human question "Who am I?," we find our self-definition not by looking inward to our isolated mental states but by turning to the community around us, among the "interchange of speakers"[93] or a "web of interlocutors."[94] Defining who I am can only arise from the position out of which I speak—"in the family tree, in social space, in the geography of social statuses and functions, in my intimate relations to the ones I love, and also crucially in the space of moral and spiritual orientation within which my most important defining relations are lived out."[95] This militates against the common perception of the self as an individual who carves a sculpture of the self in their autonomous mental life and then lives it out in the reality of their own existence. In such solipsistic reality, other humans are either "objects" against which we may bump now and then by accident or are "objects" that we choose to manipulate to further our own egoistical sketch of reality. The obvious weakness of this view should be apparent to anyone who reflects on their own human existence and personal identity. As the theologian Thomas Reynolds states, "Human beings do not simply come forward as self-sufficient and complete individuals from a place outside of a social world. The individual becomes a person only in the presence of others."[96]

What is the upshot of this perspective of human interdependence for our doctrine of the church? This will become clearer as we move forward to discuss the way humans develop within a social context of relatedness to others. However, it should already be obvious that God made us for communion and community with God and other humans. This purpose for our creation underscores the divine plan that humans should not live alone. Precisely how this living together might look will be developed in this next section.

The Presence of the Other

If the self is defined only in the presence of others, then who is this Other, and what is my responsibility with respect to the Other? From the work of Emmanuel Levinas, a twentieth-century Jewish philosopher, we can begin our sketch of what the Other might look like and how that impinges directly upon our understanding both of humanity and of the people of God, the church.

93. Taylor, *Sources of the Self*, 35.
94. Taylor, *Sources of the Self*, 36.
95. Taylor, *Sources of the Self*, 35.
96. Reynolds, *Vulnerable Communion*, 83. For the moment, we shall bypass the question of whether God can be this "Other," but we shall return to it later.

As early as 1953, Levinas proposed that the idea of the "Other" (*Autrui*) is best understood by using the idea of the "face."[97] It is in the naked face—unadorned by covering, mask, or clothing—that humans begin to recognize that there is an Other who stands opposite them as a person who exists in and for itself (or as Levinas uses Plato's terms, *kath' heauto* | καθ' ἑαυτό).[98] However, in order to understand Levinas here, we need to place his concept of "the face" within its setting of his broader philosophical endeavor. In Levinas's view, all previous philosophy had focused on a *totality*—that is, an "encompassing whole in which each part has intelligibility solely through its place within the whole."[99] This tended to make each part of the whole the same—or at least related to the same whole. However, for Levinas, the "face" stood over against a person as something or someone who was not the same as us, not open to being stuffed into our own understanding of totality and its relations. The face of the Other confronts us like an epiphany; it cannot be "surmounted, enveloped, dominated," but rather is "independent of us."[100] Hence, the face does not submit to a reduction as another being who is the same as I am—or even as a similar part of a common whole, the "totality." Levinas suggests, "The way in which the Other presents himself, exceeding *the idea of the other in me*, we here name face."[101] In other words, the excess or overflow of finite thought by its content is what we experience in the encounter with the Other; therefore instead of fitting as a part to a whole (totality), Levinas sees the face as *exceeding* the whole and thereby resisting possession of it or control over it by me (infinity). He also calls the face of the Other a *transcendence*, because we are brought to the face as a "pure experience"[102] whereby we encounter a presence that "breaks up the system."[103] Such a transcendent presence is truly Other and therefore "when face to face, I can no longer negate the other."[104] When encountering the Other, we should

97. Emmanuel Levinas, "Freedom and Command" (1953), in *Collected Philosophical Papers*, trans. Alphonso Lingis, Phaenomenologica (Dordrecht: Martinus Nijhoff, 1987), 19.

98. Levinas, "Freedom and Command," 20.

99. Gary Gutting, *French Philosophy in the Twentieth Century* (Cambridge: Cambridge University Press, 2001), 355.

100. Emmanuel Levinas, *Totality and Infinity: An Essay on Exteriority*, trans. Alphonso Lingis (Pittsburgh: Duquesne University Press, 1969; orig. French ed., 1961), 89. Levinas repeatedly uses the concept of the face as "epiphany." See *Totality and Infinity*, 199; also see Emmanuel Levinas, "Philosophy and the Idea of Infinity" (1957), in *Collected Philosophical Papers*, 55.

101. Levinas, *Totality and Infinity*, 50 (his emphasis).

102. Levinas, "Philosophy and the Idea of Infinity," 59.

103. Emmanuel Levinas, "The Ego and the Totality" (1954), in *Collected Philosophical Papers*, 43.

104. Levinas, "The Ego and the Totality," 43.

not think of parts or totality but rather of the excess—"infinity," as Levinas defines it. "Transcendence designates a relation with a reality infinitely distant from my own reality, yet without this distance destroying this relation and without this relation destroying this distance."[105]

The Other cannot be subjected to our sameness of categories within the totality. The Other calls to us from its "face," asking us to turn to its summons and respond. Thus the "epiphany of the face" is a "moral summons" proceeding from the Other.[106] Encountering the Other demands my respect of the Other as someone I cannot control or dominate. Hence, I am "obligated" by the face of the Other because I am placed in relation with the being of the Other.[107] Such an encounter cannot be reduced to interiority where I absorb the Other into myself as an object who is similar to me and therefore one that I can control. Confronted by the face of the Other, I may choose to ignore it or choose to engage it, but I cannot deny that this Other comes to me as a human being "from the outside, a separated—or holy—face."[108] Levinas calls the room between two persons that opens the possibility for a relational encounter the "curvature of the intersubjective space."[109] Relations between human beings occur in this "curvature of space."

It is true, then, that we live "before the faces of others."[110] The Other comes to us from outside of us, summoning us to recognize the Other's uniqueness and otherness. As human beings we may choose to ignore the Other or even absorb the presence of the Other within our own solipsistic sphere. Yet if we carefully reflect on the Other, we can begin to see our need for the Other in order to reverse our tendency toward egocentricity. The French philosopher Gabriel Marcel offered a great word to describe this centripetal moral force: "egolatry," the idolatry of the self.[111] Marcel proposed

---

105. Levinas, *Totality and Infinity*, 41.

106. Levinas, *Totality and Infinity*, 196.

107. Levinas, *Totality and Infinity*, 201, 212.

108. Levinas, *Totality and Infinity*, 291.

109. Levinas, *Totality and Infinity*, 291. This idea sounds very similar to another one we will confront later in this chapter: the concept of an "in-between zone" or a "space of reciprocity, of giving and receiving" or an "intersubjectivity." These are all part of the philosophy of relations put forward by the twentieth-century French philosopher Gabriel Marcel. See Gabriel Marcel, "On the Ontological Mystery," in *The Philosophy of Existentialism*, trans. Manya Harari (New York: Citadel, 1956), 36–40; see also Marcel, *The Mystery of Being*, vol. 1, *Reflection and Mystery*, Gifford Lectures (1949–50), trans. G. S. Fraser (South Bend, IN: St. Augustine's Press, 1950), 207.

110. David F. Ford, *Self and Salvation: Being Transformed*, Cambridge Studies in Christian Doctrine 1, ed. Colin E. Gunton and Daniel W. Hardy (Cambridge: Cambridge University Press, 1999), 17.

111. Gabriel Marcel, "The Ego and Its Relation to Others," in *Homo Viator: Introduction to a Metaphysic of Hope*, trans. Emma Crauford (New York: Harper & Brothers, 1962), 20.

that if humans were to *exist with* (*coesse*) others, then they would need to start by "exorcizing the egocentric spirit."[112] Indeed, he devised another term to place opposite egocentric: "heterocentric," or other-centered.[113] What good is the Other to a self-centered person? Something must reverse the inner focus and force in order for the self-centered person to see the Other and respond.

While Levinas placed an accent on the "face" (*la visage*) of the Other, Gabriel Marcel revolved his approach toward the Other around a concept of "presence." For Marcel, presence is something that "infinitely transcends all possible verification."[114] Presence is "more than the object" because it "exceeds the object on every side."[115] It exists in an "immediacy beyond all conceivable mediation."[116] Indeed, presence is a *mystery*. When one encounters a presence as a mystery, one is involved in an event, which cannot "become objectified as an acquisition or property because it transcends every conceivable technique of mastery."[117] Therefore, when I encounter another's presence, I cannot control or manipulate it, as I might be able to do with an "object." Presence, then, "involves a reciprocity which is excluded from any relation of subject to object or of subject to subject-object."[118]

In several helpful passages, Marcel further explains what he means by presence through an example.[119] Someone may be in the same room with us but may not make her *presence* felt to us. Although we may even converse, we still do not engage in anything more than communication, a simple back-and-forth of chatter. "I" am not engaged by the presence of the "Other" because "I" am not drawn into a participation in the "Other's" being or—just as importantly—"I" do not draw the "Other" into my own being. This type of

---

112. Gabriel Marcel, *The Mystery of Being*, vol. 2, *Faith and Reality*, Gifford Lectures (1949–50), trans. G. S. Fraser (South Bend, IN: St. Augustine's Press, 1950), 7. Marcel used the Latin term *coesse* to describe this concept of "being with." It is a compound infinitive formed by adding a prefix meaning "with" (*com* or *cum*, shortened to *co-*) to the verb *esse*, or "to be." See Marcel, "The Ontological Mystery," 39.

113. Marcel, *Mystery of Being*, 2:8. Egocentrism poses a "barrier between me and others." Heterocentrism understands we are *together with others* or *in relation with* others. "The fact is that we can understand ourselves by starting from the other, or from others, and only by starting from them" (Marcel, *Mystery of Being*, 2:7–8).

114. Marcel, "The Ontological Mystery," 15.

115. Marcel, "The Ontological Mystery," 36–37.

116. Marcel, "The Ontological Mystery," 36–37.

117. These are Thomas Reynolds's words, explaining Marcel's point from "The Ontological Mystery," 19–21; see Reynolds, *Vulnerable Communion*, 120.

118. Marcel, "The Ontological Mystery," 40.

119. Marcel shares this example in the first part of his Gifford Lectures from 1949. See *Mystery of Being*, 1:204–5. It is also offered from a slightly different angle in "The Ontological Mystery," 39–40.

nonengagement would be communication, not communion, not an encounter with a presence. Such a person "gives me nothing" and "cannot make room for me in himself."[120] Presence, therefore, requires *availability*—an openness to give and receive from and to the Other. Such reciprocity breaks down the "egocentric topography" of our lives.[121] With regard to this Other who is more like an object than an Other, Marcel says, "He understands what I say to him, but he does not understand *me*: I may even have the extremely disagreeable feeling that my own words, as he repeats them to me, as he reflects them back at me, have become unrecognizable. By a very singular phenomenon indeed, this stranger interposes himself between me and my own reality, he makes me in some sense also a stranger to myself; I am not really myself while I am with him."[122] Placed in the framework of Martin Buber's I-Thou versus I-It, this engagement would be the latter—a communication in which the "I" does not experience the Other (Thou) as being fully a person in the Other's own right, but rather as an object (It) to be either used or ignored.[123] We might say in common parlance that such engagement is "shallow."

On the other hand, we could be in a room with another person and clearly recognize their "presence" with us. A person who is a "presence" with us is one who "is at my disposal" when I am in need, someone who is "capable of being with me with the whole of himself."[124] By comparison, the person who is not available, not at my disposal, "seems merely to offer me a temporary loan raised on his resources."[125] Marcel concludes, "For the one I am a presence; for the other I am an object."[126] Presence is a mystery within the intersubjectivity that "is more comprehensive than the fact of just being there."[127] Presence becomes "manifest" to each Other.[128] When some being is "granted to me as a presence," it means "that I am unable to treat him as if he were merely placed in front of me; between him and me arises a relationship which, in a sense, surpasses my awareness of him; he is not only before me, he is also within me—or, rather, these categories are transcended."[129] At this point, it may be best to let Marcel describe this event in his own words:

120. Marcel, "The Ontological Mystery," 40.
121. Marcel, "The Ontological Mystery," 41.
122. Marcel, *Mystery of Being*, 1:205 (his emphasis).
123. Buber, *I and Thou*, 80. "It" is an "object of detached perception and experience."
124. Marcel, "The Ontological Mystery," 40.
125. Marcel, "The Ontological Mystery," 40.
126. Marcel, "The Ontological Mystery," 40.
127. Marcel, "The Ego and Its Relation to Others," 15.
128. Marcel, *Mystery of Being*, 1:207.
129. Marcel, "The Ontological Mystery," 38.

When somebody's presence does really make itself felt, it can refresh my inner being; it reveals me to myself, it makes me more fully myself than I should be if I were not exposed to its impact. All this, of course, though nobody would attempt to deny that we do have such experiences, is very difficult to express in words; and we should ask ourselves why. The fact is that the notion of *object*, as such, is linked in our minds with a whole set of possible practical operations . . . that can be taught and that can thus be regarded generally communicable. But these considerations do not apply, in any sense at all, to the notion of *presence*, as such.[130]

This rather lengthy detour through the land of twentieth-century personalism was not just a Sunday drive for the scenery. All along there are key points where the reader could see our own previous discussion about God's presence among us reflected in this discussion. The very way that the *presence* of the *Other* is *manifested* or is *granted* to us provides potential insight into the encounter between God and humans (considered further in chap. 3).

However, what was the purpose of this detour for our current analysis of theological anthropology for the doctrine of the church? It is the fruit of this discussion, which we shall harvest in the next segment.

Implications of Persons-in-Relation for the People of God

Even if some dimension of what it means to be created in the image of God can be seen in the fact that humans are communal, relational beings, then why is it that not every "face" or every "Other" is taken as a gift of "presence" and treated as if their worth is as valuable as one's own? In other words, why is it that the portrait of human intersubjectivity depicted by both Levinas and Marcel appears more like abstract modern art than the realism of a Rembrandt? Why is it that we do not recognize the Other and provide a reciprocity of giving and receiving with them? In some ways, the view of the Other among these personalists seems to lack a place in our reality—perhaps vividly occurring on occasion for some rare few but passing by most of us without notice. To be sure, both Levinas and Marcel attempt to craft why this may be the case, pointing especially to the noncontrolling factor in the Other; the presence of the Other comes to us as a gift. It comes from beyond as something transcendent or mysterious. For Levinas, there seems to be little that we can do to improve our chances of recognizing the transcendent that exists in the absolutely naked face of another. Yet somehow we are seized by it—it affects us not in the indicative but in the

130. Marcel, *Mystery of Being*, 1:205 (his emphasis).

imperative.[131] Since the Other comes to us without mediation, "he signifies by himself"—that is, he is a "signifyingness of its own."[132] Hence, we are *obligated* by the Other, cast into an ethical relationship because the Other's presence is a "summons to answer."[133] For Marcel, however, there is a clear path to assist us in discovering the presence of the Other. We must exorcize the "ego-centric spirit."[134] In so doing, we begin to see others less as *objects* to be used by our self-centered egos and more as *Others* who come to us as a gracious gift. In several places, Marcel calls this approach *pure charity*, or *availability* (*disponibilité*).[135] In other words, a disposition of love is necessary to open one's eyes to see Others as a genuine presence instead of an object. By starting with the Other (and not ourselves), we can begin to understand ourselves.[136]

However, there remains the concern expressed in the above paragraph: Why do such experiences of the Other not fill our existence as human beings? Allow me to suggest that, from a theological perspective, one reason is sin. Since the fall, humans have lived in alienation from God and others—indeed, alienation from themselves. Perhaps Levinas and especially Marcel are pointing to a reality of intersubjectivity as God intended it for us when God made us in his image. At present, however, the reality of relationality among all humans is hit or miss. There may remain enough evidence of its existence that we may postulate that this was the way God intended us to live, but now we cannot see it in its fullness. We must be satisfied with glimpses of such mysterious, transcendent experiences.

What does this mean for our present consideration of human beings and the church? Here I shall make a bold claim, one that will undoubtedly call for qualification. While all humans currently live with a damaged image of God and thereby cannot reflect the fullness of God's healthy relationality in their own interactions with God or humanity, believers who have been encountered by this God and are being transformed by the Spirit are created anew in the *image of Christ* and thereby should increasingly reflect the nature of Christ in their human relationships (Col. 1:15).

Here I could be accused of being out of touch with reality. Surely I appear to be crafting a form of "triumphalism" that confuses the eschaton with

131. Levinas, "Freedom and Command," 21.
132. Emmanuel Levinas, "Meaning and Sense," in *Basic Philosophical Writings*, ed. Adriaan T. Peperzak, Simon Critchley, and Robert Bernasconi, Studies in Continental Philosophy, ed. John Sallis (Bloomington: Indiana University Press, 1996), 53.
133. Levinas, "Meaning and Sense," 54.
134. Marcel, *Mystery of Being*, 2:7.
135. Marcel, "The Ontological Mystery," 39; "Ego and Its Relation to Others," 23.
136. Marcel, *Mystery of Being*, 2:8. We shall return to "availability" shortly.

the present. We cannot reflect the nature of God in this world, can we? To suggest that we should do so is unrealistic; it denies the power of sin in our natures and the strength of mortality dragging us down into living within our sphere of time and space. Really? Is not this precisely a perennial problem with the church, that it does not live out what it claims—or more exactly, that it assumes that the claims of Scripture that speak triumphantly about the superabundant power of the Spirit over the power of the flesh and this age are not really meant for us today. If we do not assume that we can begin in our finite world to live freed from the bondage of sin, then we probably should not preach from Paul's letters. Paul's optimism seems unbounded by such fleshly, "realistic" concerns. Compared with the power of the Spirit, our flesh and the principalities and powers of this age are no match. If someone should aver that such optimism about the Spirit might have worked for Paul, it was only because Paul was someone special—an apostle, a saint. We cannot expect such optimism about overcoming real human challenges.

While I am fully aware of the weight of this argument and the fact that our human flesh weighs us down, keeping us from living a perfect life in this world, at the same time I am also fully aware that to deny the Spirit's power to transform us daily into the image of Christ is to surrender the gospel of Jesus Christ to the hopelessness of living this life under our own power. If this is triumphalism, so be it.[137] I would rather the church preach the realistic optimism of the gospel of Christ than the realistic pessimism of life without God. If the church is not offering—at least in one aspect of its message—a gospel whereby humans can experience the transforming power of God, then what difference will we provide from any social club in human affairs?

137. In a recent German monograph, Giovanni Maltese has analyzed some of the theological writings of Amos Yong and myself, finding within both of our works a "latent triumphalism" (*ein latenter Triumphalismus*). See Giovanni Maltese, *Geisterfahrer zwischen Transzendenz und Immanenz: Die Erfahrungsbegriffe in den pfingstlich-charismatischen Theologien von Terry L. Cross und Amos Yong im Vergleich* (Göttingen: V & R Unipress, 2013), 18, 209–10. While Maltese recognizes that neither Yong nor I succumb to the depth of some in the charismatic movement in this regard, he seems to believe that there remains an underlying triumphalism due to our Pentecostal backgrounds and contexts. I think this charge is unwarranted for both Yong and myself. Further, Maltese never clearly defines what he means by "triumphalism," so it is difficult to know how he arrived at this conclusion. My understanding of a charismatic-Pentecostal triumphalism would be exemplified by the Word of Faith movement, the health-and-wealth theology, and in general an over-realized eschatology where the kingdom of God is fully here and now. In these parts of the movement, there seems to be lacking the "already/not yet" motif from the New Testament. Typically, classical Pentecostals have distanced themselves from such triumphalism, although they have been more silent than they should have been about its excesses and fundamental errors. For an approach toward this problem, see Terry L. Cross, "The Doctrine of Healing," in *Transformed Power: Dimensions of the Gospel*, ed. Yung Chul Han (Cleveland, TN: Pathway, 2001), 177–231.

Loving God and Neighbor: Availability

It is among the community of believers that humans gradually discover how to make room for God in their worship and lives together. In this way, they learn how to love God with all their heart, soul, and mind, which is the primary command (Matt. 22:37–38). It is by loving God that humans begin to learn to love other believers and eventually the neighbor as themselves—the secondary command (22:39).

If we take seriously Marcel's idea about availability as a form of "pure charity," then we "make room in ourselves" for the Other. This is an act of pure love. It is the manner of love that is displayed in the relationality of Father, Son, and Spirit in the Triune Godhead. What does such love as availability look like among humans? Marcel suggests that it is an "aptitude to give oneself to anything which offers, and to being oneself by the gift."[138] Thus, availability as love is an openness to the Other, engaging the Other in a reciprocal relationship of wholly giving my person to the Other and wholly receiving the Other into my person. It is, as Marcel says, "making room in oneself" for the Other.[139] In this way I come to *know* the Other as well as know something about myself. Yet Marcel insists that this knowledge of an individual "cannot be separated from the act of love or charity by which this being is accepted in all which makes him a unique creature, or, if you like, the image of God."[140]

Love contains such other-regard that it welcomes the presence of the Other, even the stranger.[141] In this way, it traces the paradigm of the love of the Triune God. The Trinity contains "self-giving and other-receiving love"[142] among Father, Son, and Spirit. Hence, there are "two movements" in the life of the Trinity. This seems to be exactly what Marcel means by reciprocity: a self-giving and other-receiving love. Yet this trinitarian love does not remain internal to the Godhead. There is another aspect of God's love—namely, the creation of "space in himself to receive estranged humanity."[143] Prior to this redemptive "making room," the Triune God also made room for the Other in terms of creation. In both creation and redemption, we see God's "withdrawal of himself" (*Zurücknahme seiner selbst*)—that is, his "self-limitation" (*Gott*

---

138. Marcel, "Ego and Its Relation to Others," 23.

139. Marcel, "The Ontological Mystery," 40.

140. Marcel, "Ego and Its Relation to Others," 24.

141. Levinas has written provocatively about "the stranger" as the Other. See Levinas, *Totality and Infinity*, 213, where he says, "The poor one, the stranger, presents himself as an equal."

142. Miroslav Volf, *Exclusion and Embrace: A Theological Exploration of Identity, Otherness, and Reconciliation* (Nashville: Abingdon, 1996), 127.

143. Volf, *Exclusion and Embrace*, 126. While this language refers to the passion of Christ, Volf carries it through to the life of the Trinity on the next page.

Selbstbeschränkung) in opening space for the existence of creation[144]—and his forgiveness in opening his arms as a "sign of a space in God's self and an invitation for the enemy to come in."[145]

Love and Hospitality

The love of the Triune God in its self-giving and other-receiving nature is to be replicated in the love of the people of God for the Other/s. Such a love never handles the Other as an object, as an *I-It* relation. Instead, it makes room in the self for the Other, regarding them as a gift from God and treating them with the honor and dignity due to those made in God's image. Further, we "set a table" for them—we offer hospitality to the Other. As Volf notes, having "been embraced by God, we must make space for others in ourselves and invite them in—even our enemies."[146] Such a theology has immediate consequences for the current challenge concerning immigration in the United States and the refugee migration across Europe. Christians are those who "make room for others" within our own lives. In so doing, we reflect the prior action of God's hospitality of grace toward us—even "while we were still sinners" (Rom. 5:8).

The divine hospitality given to us as believers is a gift. Our own hospitality must reflect that gift. My colleague Daniela Augustine has fleshed out this concept and its implications for the church very well with her comments about the Spirit's "divine embrace" on the day of Pentecost: "The Spirit invites all humanity to make its habitat in the inter-sociality of the Trinity. This invitation implies the host's self-giving (or surrender) to the other and not their colonization. It is an initiation of dialogue by re-spacing oneself and creating conditions for conversational inclusion of the other. It is a gesture of welcoming all foreigners, aliens, and strangers, literally in their own terms."[147]

---

144. Jürgen Moltmann, *The Trinity and the Kingdom*, trans. Margaret Kohl (San Francisco: Harper & Row, 1981), 59; cf. Moltmann, *Trinität und Reich Gottes: Zur Gotteslehre* (Munich: Kaiser, 1980), 75. Moltmann constructs this idea with great eloquence and precision: "With the creation of a world which is not God, but which none the less corresponds to him, *God's self-humiliation* begins—the self-limitation of the One who is omnipresent, and the suffering of the eternal love" (Moltmann, *Trinität*, 75). Further, he says, "For God, creation means self-limitation, the withdrawal of himself, that is to say self-humiliation. Creative love [*Schöpferische Liebe*] is always suffering love [*leidende Liebe*] as well." Moltmann, *Trinity*, 59; Moltmann, *Trinität*, 75.

145. Volf, *Exclusion and Embrace*, 126.

146. Volf, *Exclusion and Embrace*, 129.

147. Daniela Augustine, *Pentecost, Hospitality, and Transfiguration: Toward a Spirit-Inspired Vision of Social Transformation* (Cleveland, TN: Centre for Pentecostal Theology, 2012), 65.

Regardless of one's *political* leanings on the issue of borders and immigration, Christians should be marked as those who reflect God's loving embrace through their own welcoming hospitality. How can Christians mistreat or disrespect the immigrant or refugee, who may actually be "one of the least of these" (Matt. 25:45)? How can such Christians expect to receive entrance into Christ's kingdom if they refuse entrance into their own homes of these ones in whom Christ is somehow present? As Christine Pohl ably demonstrates, "Hospitality is not optional for Christians, nor is it limited to those who are specially gifted for it. It is, instead, a necessary practice in the community of faith."[148] Further, the Greek word for "hospitality" (*philoxenia* | φιλοξενία) joins the word *phileō* (to like/love) with *xenos* (stranger), making a connection between hospitality and showing love to strangers.[149] Christians are marked by showing welcome to strangers in contrast to the world's way of dealing with strangers: *xenophobia* (fear of strangers). Thomas Reynolds perfectly describes the work of God in believers' lives in this regard: "The Spirit turns xenophobia into *philoxenia*, the fear of the stranger into a love of the stranger."[150]

Emmanuel Levinas captured the term "hospitality" as the only reasonable response to the presence of the Other. When one welcomes a face, one turns to it with hospitality and opens one's life to inviting the Other in. The subject serves as a "host."[151] How does one welcome the Other? "I welcome the Other who presents himself in my home by opening my home to him."[152] In such a welcome there is obviously a risk, but hospitality opens the door without condition. In a farewell discourse to Levinas, Jacques Derrida engages Levinas's concept of hospitality, noting that a central feature of it is the "interruption of the self by the self."[153] Seen in this phrase is a form of self-limitation of the self for the sake of the Other—something that, as we have already noted, occurs in God's dealings with humans.[154]

I find in this approach of unconditional hospitality something of the divine hospitality that opens itself to the Other, despite what we might, in some

---

148. Christine D. Pohl, *Making Room: Recovering Hospitality as a Christian Tradition* (Grand Rapids: Eerdmans, 1999), 31.

149. Pohl, *Making Room*, 31.

150. Reynolds, *Vulnerable Communion*, 242.

151. Levinas, *Totality and Infinity*, 299.

152. Levinas, *Totality and Infinity*, 171.

153. Jacques Derrida, *Adieu to Emmanuel Levinas*, trans. Pascale-Anne Brault and Michael Naas (Stanford, CA: Stanford University Press, 1999), 53.

154. While both Levinas and Derrida are speaking primarily of a point in phenomenology when the phenomenological task itself ceases (and the self is interrupted), I am using the phrase more in line with its rather commonsense notion—that is, a pause in one's own life for the sake of the Other. In effect, that is where Levinas was heading, but he sketched it more clearly in his own philosophical phenomenology than I have chosen to do here.

sense, call the risk. God's own initiative to open up the divine life to and for the Other—the human creature made in his image—is demonstrative of a similar love demanded of us as Christians. We make room for the Other—even the wayfarer and stranger, and amazingly, the enemy—because the love of God has been "shed abroad" in our hearts by the Holy Spirit (Rom. 5:5 KJV). The "unconditional" nature of this interruption of the self in hospitality also parallels the divine hospitality. A concomitant *vulnerability* lays open the subject to wounding.[155] This means that unconditional hospitality opens the self to exposure, to risk and vulnerability. Indeed, this is what it means to love: to give oneself over for the sake of the Other and to receive from them what they offer. Again, we see that love has two poles: giving and receiving.[156] Thomas Reynolds has described this aspect with great clarity: "Love signals the fact that I have become involved and invested, vulnerable to another, drawn into a relation by the proximity of an 'other' who stands before me. But there is more at stake than another just being there. I am rendered unable to remain indifferent, a neutral onlooker or dispassionate observer."[157] Within the curvature of space where relations occur between two people, love "involves welcoming another into a space of mutual vulnerability."[158]

Why have I been discussing openness and vulnerability? It is because the basis of loving human relationships rests on these two characteristics. Without openness, how can we welcome the Other? Without vulnerability, how can we engage the Other at any depth that is worthy of someone made in the image of God? If God opens Godself up to being wounded, how can God's people expect to operate within the walls of a sanctuary in safety? Without the ability to be vulnerable to the Other and also to be safe in their hands, how can love move beyond the chitchat greeting so often experienced in church foyers these days? "By being subject to the other's vulnerability, I am brought to my own vulnerability, not as a sterile form of self-contemplation but in a posture of vulnerability to the other. I am disposed toward and made 'response-able' to the other, brought into a relation that changes me."[159] The well-known

---

155. Vanghelis Bistoris drew the connection between vulnerability and unconditional hospitality for me. He is the compiler of the notes for Derrida's *Adieu*. See Derrida, *Adieu to Emmanuel Levinas*, 141n51. Bistoris points to a philosophical text by Levinas called "No Identity," in which Levinas explains "openness" as a "denuding of the skin exposed to wounds and outrage. This openness is the vulnerability of a skin exposed, in wounds and outrage, beyond all that can show itself." Emmanuel Levinas, "No Identity," in *Collected Philosophical Papers*, trans. Alphonso Lingis (Dordrecht: Martinus Nijhoff, 1987), 146.

156. Reynolds, *Vulnerable Communion*, 119.

157. Reynolds, *Vulnerable Communion*, 119.

158. Reynolds, *Vulnerable Communion*, 119.

159. Reynolds, *Vulnerable Communion*, 121.

founder of L'Arche (The Ark), Jean Vanier, established a house in France where people who were having difficulty due to intellectual disabilities could come and receive love. This concept has grown, and now there are similar houses all over the world. He has described this love thus: "You are not just being generous, you are entering into a relationship, which will change your life. You are no longer in control. You have become vulnerable; you have come to love that person."[160]

In the openness and vulnerability of loving the Other, we are brought into a *communion* with them. What is this communion? It is a "mutual trust, mutual belonging, it is the to-and-fro movement of love between two people where each one gives and each one receives."[161] Such communion is not static but dynamic. It opens us up to being vulnerable. "It means accepting the presence of another inside oneself, as well as accepting the reciprocal call to enter into another."[162]

It is to this loving, open, vulnerable communion with God and others that we are called as the people of God. The relational God desires a relational people, not simply for the sake of relationships but also as a witness to the character of the God who has encountered and transformed them. The relational God made humans in such a way that they flourish primarily in the community of other humans. This is what it means to be human yet also called to be among the people of God.

The New Humanity and New Community

Through the work of Jesus Christ and the powerful application of that work by the Spirit to the lives of individuals, God has called believers out of their isolated and fractured existence into a new humanity—a new community (Eph. 2:15).[163] The "old" humanity was characterized by a division between gentile and Jew; the "new" humanity is characterized by its union. Now there is only *one* humanity without division or hostility. "For he [Jesus] is our peace; in his flesh he has made both groups into one and has broken down the dividing wall, that is, the hostility between us. He has abolished the law with its commandments and ordinances, that he might create in himself one new humanity in the place of the two, thus making peace, and

---

160. Jean Vanier, *Encountering "the Other"* (Dublin: Veritas Publications, 2005), 12. This was also cited in Reynolds, *Vulnerable Communion*, 121.

161. Vanier, *Becoming Human*, 28.

162. Vanier, *Becoming Human*, 28–29.

163. Daniel L. Migliore, *Faith Seeking Understanding: An Introduction to Christian Theology*, 3rd ed. (Grand Rapids: Eerdmans, 2014), 262. Migliore's entire chapter on the church has influenced much of what I have written here.

might reconcile both groups to God in one body through the cross, thus putting to death that hostility through it" (Eph. 2:14–16 NRSV). This new humanity is "called out" from the world; it is the *ekklēsia* of God. Humans have been called into this new community from the high barriers that divide them and into the spacious, barrier-free fields of God's grace. Thus, what might separate people in the world—things like race, gender, age, interests, political directions—loses its centrifugal force in the new community of grace. Such a new community becomes increasingly characterized by God's own other-centered life.

> The triune God is a God that communicates the goodness of the dynamic go-round of God's own life outward in love for what is not God. The whole point of God's dealings with us as creator, covenant partner, and redeemer in Christ is to bring the good of God's very life into our own. Our lives participate in that divine mission and thereby realize the shape of God's own economy by giving that follows the same principle: self-sharing for the good of others.[164]

Competition, which has been the way of life in the common social enterprise of the world, is exchanged for an economy of grace, one without strings.[165] Thomas Reynolds notes that societies operate on an "economy of exchange"—that is, a "system of reciprocity that regulates interactions in a community."[166] Whatever a community values becomes the common currency for exchange. Reynolds points to this exchange as one that in current Western societies is driven by healthy, powerful bodies that do not deviate from the "cult of normalcy."[167] In such an exchange economy, people are valuable according to what they can contribute to the society as a whole. This style of exchange is directly opposed to God's "economy of grace." In the latter, value is placed not on one's ability to give something back to God or even to contribute to the whole but on a person's worth as created in the image of God and on the fact that God loves people without expectation of anything in return. Playing favorites, which has plagued the interactions of human relationships since the entrance of sin into the world, is exchanged for the equal value of all people in which God is no respecter of persons. Stingy self-centeredness, which has fettered human life in the world, is exchanged for extravagant generosity.

164. Kathryn Tanner, *Economy of Grace* (Minneapolis: Fortress, 2005), 85.
165. Anthony Thiselton, *Interpreting God and the Postmodern Self: On Meaning, Manipulation and Promise* (Grand Rapids: Eerdmans, 1995), 163. As Thiselton notes, "'Grace' means love 'without strings.'"
166. Reynolds, *Vulnerable Communion*, 56.
167. Reynolds, *Vulnerable Communion*, 57–60.

To be sure, such a lifestyle of reversal from the tug of the world toward our own centers is not something usually remedied in an instant, especially if we are speaking of the community as a whole. Like the sirens to Ulysses, the lure of self-centeredness will call even believers for as long as we are in this life. Indeed, to *become* a Christian may take a mere instant, a moment of faith in Christ; to *live* as a Christian takes a lifetime. Such growth into living as a Christ-follower requires a community of fellow believers who "speak . . . the truth in love" and who exercise their own roles in the body of Christ, encouraging me to exercise my own role (Eph. 4:15–16). Yet this is the goal toward which we as the church of Jesus Christ march, becoming more and more like the One we serve and worship.

As we conclude this chapter, it should be clear that the one, new humanity in Jesus Christ follows a different path from that of the world. Respecting others as created in the image of God, the new community reflects (here and now) the shalom of life in God's presence. Thus, given all the points made in this chapter regarding both the nature of God and the nature of God's people, what are the implications for the church? I offer six points that may assist us in summarizing and also setting the stage for future discussion on the task of the people of God.[168] Each of the six points is described by the same adjective: "radical." By using this term, I mean to point to the twofold way that this term is used in English: (1) descriptive of the new or different way of doing something; and (2) descriptive of something that *goes to the root* (*radix*). Both senses are meant in the following points.

1. *Radical shalom.* The people of God gathered in community are meant to reflect the life of God's presence both here and in the future eschaton. A biblical term that demonstrates this life in God is the Hebrew word "shalom." While it is most commonly understood as meaning "peace," it has a depth of meaning beyond this surface understanding. Shalom is the flourishing of life where all beings glorify God by being all that they were created to be without any hindrance of sin or distraction. Shalom is not only this flourishing of life but also a harmonious life with others. Such harmony demands honor, respect, and equity for everyone in this society. Therefore, shalom produces justice—a harmony of right living and equitable distribution of goods. And already I can hear the reader thinking, "Yeah, right!" This is precisely why the shalom required of

---

168. It will be obvious that points 2–5 are drawn conceptually from Thomas Reynolds, *Vulnerable Communion*, 242–46. While I have made them my own in relation to this project, I have found his ideas about the church in relation to our summary such that I cannot easily determine where or what I have gleaned from him.

Christian communities of God's people *points to* this perfect life of the future, but also why we see glimpses of it here in the present among us. God's Spirit alone can produce such harmonious life along with such other-regarding respect, all within the community where justice prevails. As I contend throughout this book, it is to this goal that the church must struggle, bringing the picture of God's redeeming love and justice to a world that lives in anything but that. This is why God's shalom among God's people is radical: it provokes us to become more than we currently are, and in so doing, it provides us a way back to our "roots" as a people who reflect the nature of God.

2. *Radical openness.* As we have seen above, Ephesians 2 provides us with a portrait of a "new humanity" in Christ (2:15), and yet there are other terms used to describe God's people there. One is "the household of God" (2:19 NRSV). We have been made a part of God's family, members of God's house. Such a people have richly received from the bounty of God's grace and therefore have a desire to offer of their bounty to others. Hence, God's house is not open only to some and closed to others. Like the parable that Jesus told concerning the great banquet, the invitation extends now to everyone—the poor, crippled, blind, and lame (Luke 14:15–24). Indeed, "Strangers—people who are despised, poor, unclean, sick, or have disabilities—are invited into the household of God."[169] The nature of God's love that is extended to people in the world excludes no one! As the people of God, we are invited to extend this love to the world through our own hands, inviting all who will come to join us for the banquet of life that God has prepared for us. Such openness is indeed radical.

3. *Radical hospitality.* While we have said a good deal about hospitality already, it needs to be stated clearly that the people of God are *open* to others, but this openness is not simply attitudinal. The people of God are hospitable, welcoming. More than merely opening the door to strangers, they set a banquet for them. For the early Christians, "hospitality meant extending to strangers a quality of kindness usually reserved for friends and family. The focus, however, was on strangers in need, the 'lowly and abject,' those who, on first appearance, seemed to have little to offer."[170] The people of God make others feel "at home" in the household of God, even if—or perhaps especially if—others have no way of returning the hospitality. The motivation for this risky business

169. Reynolds, *Vulnerable Communion*, 244.
170. Pohl, *Making Room*, 19.

of hospitality is clear: God loved us in Jesus Christ when we were strangers, aliens to the covenant of God (Eph. 2:12). "Being a follower of Christ then means to be taken up into the circle of God's hospitality, which spills outward in the Spirit toward others in the shape of a radically welcoming and inclusive community symbolized by an open table fellowship."[171] The people of God place themselves in the way of strangers, thereby making themselves *available* for others according to their needs. The church's welcome door of hospitality is a radical stance toward our neighbor in need, acting out the love of God in the purest and most practical form.

4. *Radical decentering*. One way to conceive of the sinful nature of human beings is to trace the way that love as God intended it to be—other-regarding—warped into an abnormal love for oneself. This is most clearly depicted by Luther's phrase *homo incurvatus in se*, "a person curved inward upon himself/herself."[172] Salvation is intended to begin to redirect our affections toward God and others. Sanctification surely is intended to continue that turn in direction toward God and others by extending our love toward the Other. However, this "decentering" is not merely personal or individual. While sin affects our inner personal lives, thereby warping our sense of reality away from God's perspective, it also affects our communal, social lives, warping the direction of groups and cultures away from God's perspective toward one's own desires. Hence, "decentering" here is meant to be a sanctifying of both one's personal life *and* corporate lives together. While sin may still hold believers in its grip on occasion, it does not command us. While principalities and powers of this age may still appear to reign over the flow of human existence on this earth, we recognize that their "end is sure." God alone can "decenter" our personal lives, causing us to revolve around God and others; God alone can help us "decenter" our corporate lives, living according to Christ's new order—an "order of love."[173] Thus, the decentering is radical.

5. *Radical reciprocity*. As we have noted above, there is a fundamental characteristic of personalism that also extends very nicely to Christianity: the idea of reciprocity. Love is not merely a one-directional gift

171. Reynolds, *Vulnerable Communion*, 244.
172. Martin Luther, *Luthers Vorlesung über den Römerbrief, 1515/1516, Die Glosse*, ed. Johannes Ficker (Leipzig: Dieterich'sche Verlagsbuchhandlung, Theodor Weicher, 1908), "Corollarium on Romans 8:3," 184, line 18. Cf. Luther, *Lectures on Romans*, Ichthus ed., trans. and ed. Wilhelm Pauck, Library of Christian Classics 15, (Philadelphia: Westminster, 1961), 218–19.
173. Reynolds, *Vulnerable Communion*, 249.

to the Other. The love that God gives also receives from the Other. Love is reciprocal. In the Christian community there is a temptation for people of similar likes, dislikes, and even social status to come together and "love" each other. However, the gathered people of God is not a collection of similar people who give and receive love to and from *only* each other. This type of reciprocal love is nothing more than a stagnant pond that has some movement bubbling around here and there but has no fresh water coming in or going out. When one closes the circle of love to include only those who are like oneself and to exclude those who are different (Other), then such love shuts off the entrance and exit of fresh water, thereby killing itself in stagnancy. Love requires movement—a give-and-take, a to-and-fro. God's love moves toward the Other in an ever-expanding circle of openness, ready to give *and* receive from the Other—even the radically Other who is different from God. In the recent past, much of the church's evangelism has been earmarked by treating people (sinners) as objects—targets of our attention for the purpose of winning them to Christ, not for helping them feel loved and accepted as human beings in their own right. While bringing someone to Christ is a valid task, I am unsure that we have handled others as we might like to be handled in such situations. If we are unready (or unwilling) to receive from others as well as to give to them, then others become mere objects of our attention. In other words, if I treat unbelievers as "things" rather than as living, human beings who were made in the image of God, then I have lost the appreciation for what I might *receive* from them in such an encounter. When evangelism understands itself as receiving the gift of the Other's presence as well as giving them something, then I believe that it is displaying the genuine love of God to them. Such love is radically reciprocal.

6. *Radical eccentricity.* We will examine the word "eccentric" more carefully in a later chapter, but its basic idea has already been part of this chapter. A primary meaning for the term refers to odd, unconventional, or irregular people. However, it is also a mathematical term that refers to a deviation from a circular path; an example of this is an elliptical orbit. In physics, it refers to a disk (or wheel) having its axis of revolution displaced from its center, thereby allowing it to provide reciprocating motion. Used figuratively, it can point to a movement that elongates from the center outward. Later I shall use it to describe God's character in terms of mission—a love that reaches out from his center of being toward the Other (humans) in order to save them. Here I use it to refer to

the *other-centered* nature of the people of God. Just as God is eccentric (reaching outward to the Other), so too God's people are eccentric.

The people of God are created anew in Christ Jesus in order to reflect the relational, loving nature of the Triune God. How does this come about? It is to an explanation of the encounter with the presence of God that we turn in the next chapter.

3

The Encounter
between God and Humans

The Nature and Problem of Religious Experience

Since so much of the argument about the people of God in the previous chapters revolves around the *direct* encounter between God and humans, it is important to establish more precisely what this may mean. Christian mystics have claimed that they have experienced the "immediate or direct presence of God."[1] In a similar yet different manner, it has been asserted by many within the free-church or believers' church tradition that they had "unmediated access to God, apart from human-made prerequisites such as special ministry, sacraments or liturgies."[2] These related yet different assertions form a two-pronged approach to the question of direct experiences with God and direct access to God. In this way, they help to clarify what I have been suggesting all along: believers have experienced God directly and therefore have unmediated

---

1. Bernard McGinn, *The Presence of God: A History of Western Christian Mysticism*, vol. 1, *The Foundations of Mysticism: Origins to the Fifth Century* (New York: Crossroads, 1991), xvii.

2. This description is offered by Veli-Matti Kärkkäinen, *An Introduction to Ecclesiology: Ecumenical, Historical and Global Perspectives* (Downers Grove, IL: InterVarsity, 2002), 62. While the mystics and free-church tradition may be saying similar things, the result of the latter group's claim is to highlight the immediate *access* to God (usually individually considered) and thereby to downplay any need for mediation. Our thesis in this book clearly picks up both the mystical and free-church traditions in this regard, but it also attempts to clarify the nature of the encounter between God and humans as well as to amplify the work of the Holy Spirit to bring about a community within which God's presence lives and operates.

access to God either beyond or within the instruments used by God in the encounter (even the church). However, these claims hold very little acceptance among many Christian thinkers today. The claims of mystics are met with a rather sneering arrogance among some academicians, as if their experiences were the result of some subjective fantasy. The claim of the believers' church tradition is met with stunned disbelief that some within their group would dare call themselves a Christian church without professional "clergy" to mediate for them or to perform the sacraments; indeed, some strands of that tradition do not celebrate the sacraments at all. In today's theological landscape, some deny the possibility for an *immediate* or *direct* experience of God's presence, or at least the possibility of describing it. Instead, God's presence is viewed as always mediated through some form, sign, or symbol that is more accessible to humans. The result of this thinking is that humans may say they have encountered God, but in reality, this has been an encounter with some "thing" that God has used in order to mediate God's presence to them according to their limited ability to comprehend. While I agree that God accommodates to our finite level in order to meet us in something other than his bare, naked majesty, I remain uncomfortable with the notion that humans can never claim to have been encountered *directly* by the presence of God. Therefore, in this chapter, I intend to show the reasoning behind the claim for a *direct* encounter with God's *immediate* presence by

1. considering philosophical and hermeneutical concerns regarding it;
2. reflecting on the events of divine presence from the Scriptures; and
3. offering a theology of divine-human encounter.

The second prong of concern related to *direct access*, then, becomes clearer in the companion volume, *Serving the People of God's Presence*. For now, I turn to the more pressing issue of what it means to speak of having a *direct encounter* with God.

Philosophical and Hermeneutical Concerns with Religious Experience

"It is a fundamental insight of Christian theology, encapsulated in the central tenets of Christology, that there is no unmediated access to or awareness of God. We can discern neither God's presence nor its true character without mediation: it is a hidden presence, for both soteriological and epistemological reasons."[3]

---

3. Ingolf U. Dalferth, "Representing God's Presence," *International Journal of Systematic Theology* 3, no. 3 (November 2001): 237–56, here 240. We will engage this article more extensively later in the chapter.

This statement by German theologian Ingolf U. Dalferth appears to run counter to our proposed thesis but in line with many theological assessments of religious experience. To be sure, Dalferth is not alone among contemporary theologians in this understanding that God's presence is only mediated to humans. Thinkers as diverse as John Hick, John Baillie, Jürgen Moltmann, and Amos Yong (to name only a few) could be placed alongside Dalferth. Why is this the case? Why is there such universal denial of humans experiencing God's presence *directly* and *immediately*? In this section, I will engage the challenges to a direct experience of God from various sectors. Within each challenge, a proposed response to it will be offered. In this way, we may arrive at a clearer grasp of the problems involved in both denying this thesis and proposing it.

The Finite Cannot Contain the Infinite

Theologians seem to agree that the infinite cannot connect with the finite in a direct way. Put simply, this connection must always be mediated by forms or something other than God. The distance between God and humans is too great. One way to open up this understanding is to review the argument against a direct encounter as another form of the old Lutheran-Reformed eucharistic and christological debate on the ubiquity of the body of the risen Christ. Lutherans argued that the "finite is capable of holding the infinite" (*finitum capax infiniti*). They considered that in the human Jesus the fullness of the Godhead dwelled in bodily form; therefore, the human nature of Jesus shared in the majestic attributes of God. Hence, for Luther, the body and blood of the risen Christ can really be present everywhere across the world and on every eucharistic table because *both* the divine nature and human nature of Jesus Christ share the attribute of omnipresence.[4] The Reformed thinkers responded with Calvin's assertion that the idea of the ubiquity of Christ's risen body was absurd. Calvin argued that instead of sharing the infinite attributes of God with the finite flesh of Christ, the Word of God became flesh but was not "confined within the narrow prison of an earthly body."[5] With respect to the presence of the risen Christ in the Eucharist, Calvin understood this presence to be spiritual not a literal distribution of some omnipresent resurrected body of the Lord. Thus, *finitum non capax infiniti*: the finite was incapable

---

4. Luther's standard statement on the ubiquity of the risen Christ's body comes in the context of his discussion of the Eucharist. See Martin Luther, *That These Words of Christ, "This Is My Body," etc., Still Stand Firm against the Fanatics* (1527), in *The Annotated Luther*, ed. Hans J. Hillerbrand, Kirsi I. Stjerna, and Timothy J. Wengert, vol. 3, *Church and Sacraments*, ed. Paul W. Robinson (Minneapolis: Fortress, 2016), 163–273, esp. 209–30.

5. *Inst.* 1.13.4 (481).

of holding the infinite. The Word was present in the human Jesus and active "beyond the flesh of Christ himself."[6] This "beyond" aspect was mocked by the Lutheran camp as an "extra" added by Calvin; they called this the *extra Calvinisticum*.[7] For Lutherans, the finite could contain the infinite because it did so in the God-Human, Jesus Christ; for the Reformed, the finite could not contain the infinite because the infinite aspect of God's being overflows beyond the humanity. To suggest otherwise is to limit Christ's divinity by a finite, physical body.[8]

Following Dietrich Bonhoeffer, I see problems with both views.[9] In *Christ the Center*, Bonhoeffer says, "The finite is *capable* of taking up the infinite, not through itself, but through the infinite" (*finitum* capax *infiniti, non per se sed per infinitum*).[10] This seems to take seriously the fact that God in Christ entered human flesh—a miracle that in some way overcomes the previous chasm between the infinite and finite. Bonhoeffer's point is that humans cannot bridge the chasm from our finite side or by our finite power; only the Infinite One can cross this divide and does so in such a way that the One who was not us becomes one of us, living with us in every aspect of finite human existence. In some sense, then, perhaps the old Lutheran-Reformed argument is unhelpful for our discussion because it lays aside the potential for bridging the gap between infinite and finite as revealed through the incarnation.

The incarnation shows us that God can and did overcome the chasm between the finite and infinite. Yet some might still see the incarnation as just one more example of *indirect* mediation. God does not reveal Godself to us in all God's glory but "hides" in the form of a human being to communicate better with us. Such "divine incognito" requires eyes of faith to see the reality of God behind (or in) the flesh.[11] Perhaps God's true nature is disguised in

---

6. *Inst.* 1.13.4 (481).

7. E. David Willis, *Calvin's Catholic Christology* (Leiden: Brill, 1966). This remains the definitive discussion on the *extra Calvinisticum*.

8. For a fuller discussion of this, see Terry L. Cross, "The Divine-Human Encounter: Towards a Pentecostal Theology of Experience," *PNEUMA: The Journal of the Society for Pentecostal Studies* 31, no. 1 (2009): 3–34, here 10–20.

9. See Dietrich Bonhoeffer, *Act and Being: Transcendental Philosophy and Ontology in Systematic Theology*, ed. Wayne Whitson Floyd Jr., trans. H. Martin Rumscheidt, Dietrich Bonhoeffer Works (Minneapolis: Fortress, 1996), 2:84, 126.

10. Dietrich Bonhoeffer, *Christ the Center*, trans. Edwin H. Robertson (San Francisco: Harper & Row, 1978), 93 (his emphasis).

11. Kierkegaard made famous this idea, expressing his understanding of the absolute contradiction of the incarnation. See Søren Kierkegaard, *Practice in Christianity*, ed. and trans. Howard V. Hong and Edna V. Hong, Kierkegaard's Writings (Princeton: Princeton University Press, 1991), 20:127–28. "What is unrecognizability? Unrecognizability is not to be in the character of what one essentially is—for example, when a policeman is in plain clothes. And thus it

Jesus Christ. At the very least it seems that the revelation of God in Christ is *indirect*. Nonetheless, for our purposes we can see that God uses a form of mediation (the humanity of Jesus) in order to come to us. God does not appear in the sky as a brilliant glowing apparition; he comes as one of us and in this sense takes on human form as a disguise to the eyes of sense yet revealed to the eyes of faith. (We shall return to this under the biblical considerations of presence below.)

With regard to the challenge that the infinite cannot connect with the finite in a direct way, the incarnation illustrates rather than refutes my point. It is true that the incarnate flesh of Jesus Christ is finite, but it is also true that *in that flesh* God was in Christ, reconciling the world to himself (2 Cor. 5:19). We have already established that as a rule God uses some medium in order to reveal Godself. The medium itself is not the point of the revelation; God's presence within the medium encounters humans—that is the point. What was true of the incarnation remains true today when God uses media to connect with humans. While the medium may appear to make the entire encounter between God and humans indirect or once removed (so to speak), I argue that even in media or secondary means, God's presence is located within that "thing" so that God *directly* engages the human being by the Spirit. Even in the use of media, God's presence remains a direct encounter with humans. Hence, the incarnation itself and any use of media by God today operate under the rubric of paradox: somehow God is located within the medium, thereby making the experience of God both direct and indirect. This is why some have chosen to call this mystery a "mediated immediacy."[12] I shall examine this phrase more closely below.

---

is unrecognizability, the absolute unrecognizability, when one is God, then to be an individual human . . . is the greatest possible distance, the infinitely qualitative distance, from being God, and therefore it is the most profound incognito."

12. Tracing this phrase, I have only been able to go back to John Baillie in his 1939 book, *The Knowledge of God* (New York: Charles Scribner's Sons, 1959), 181. Baillie states that it was not through any self-awareness or even some "voice from the skies" that he came to an awareness that he was "not his own" but under authority and yet ought to be something he was not; it was through the "spiritual climate of the home into which I was born" (182). Eric C. Rust uses the phrase as well in *Religion, Revelation and Reason* (Macon, GA: Mercer University Press, 1981), 49–75. However, Rust does not, as far as I can discern, precisely define what he means by this. He comes closest to such a definition when he speaks of "revelation as a mediated disclosure" (51), or when he describes "all dimensions of experience" as mediating a divine disclosure (74). Amos Yong suggested that Balthasar should have used such a phrase to describe his idea of "radical unmediatedness," and thereby qualify it so as not to imply any directness in knowing God. See Amos Yong, *Spirit-Word-Community: Theological Hermeneutics in Trinitarian Perspective*, ed. David Jasper et al., Ashgate New Critical Thinking in Religion, Theology and Biblical Studies (Burlington, VT: Ashgate, 2002), 229. I shall consider Balthasar's claim below and assess Yong's evaluation of it there.

The Finite Cannot Comprehend the Infinite

Another argument against a direct encounter between God and humans assumes that humans cannot "grasp" the Infinite One and therefore humans cannot truly "know" God. Those who argue that the finite cannot comprehend the infinite challenge any *direct* grasp of who God is with two concerns. First, they assert that humans have "no cognitive access to God *per se* but only to God as he *discloses himself to us* by accommodating himself to our particular limitations and circumstances."[13] We cannot know anything about God unless God presents Godself to us. On our own, then, humans cannot grasp any reality that is God. Second, they point to the fact that humans cannot ever know God *exhaustively*. Our finite attempts to understand the Infinite One fall short of anything like a comprehensive knowledge. We may "know" the media or forms through which God encounters us but not really the God who is using them to encounter us. These challenges have some weight to them, especially the first one. I agree it is a truism in Christian theology that whatever we come to know about God must be revealed to humans by God. However, this challenge does not seem to be hitting the target of concern, that those who adhere to a *direct encounter* with God believe they have some knowledge of this God. The point is that they still may believe God initiated the encounter and provided the content of the knowledge about Godself to humans.

It is the second challenge that underscores the perceived problem with humans knowing something about God through a direct encounter with God—namely, that humans cannot know God (the Infinite One) exhaustively or comprehensively while in this finite sphere. However, such a challenge seems to derogate the very concept of "knowing God" itself, since from the outset it is assumed that in order to claim they know anything about God, such knowledge must be comprehensive. Hence, knowing God in this way is simply beyond the limits of our finitude. Not only would God be out of reach for our exhaustive understanding but even other more mundane objects would not be known, if this definition were held. Do we ever know anything exhaustively (as the thing is in itself, to use Kant's language)? I want to argue that God gives Godself to humans in such a way that the content of the divine encounter with humans entails some informational content about who this God is. It seems reasonable to suggest that within the limitations of human finitude, we can know something *true* about God (not necessarily *exhaustive*) only as this God reveals Godself to us.[14]

13. Dalferth, "Representing God's Presence," 243 (his emphasis).
14. In developing a "theology of the divine-human encounter" below, I shall need to expand the sketch that is offered here.

It is because God wants to reveal himself to humans that we are allowed to experience anything of who this God is at all. As Barth makes clear, God is not an object in a series of similar objects that humans may analyze (*CD* II/1:15).[15] This God is Subject, who for our sakes accommodates to our perceptual and intellectual abilities and then reveals himself through some medium. As the Sovereign Lord, God presents Godself to every human, allowing himself to become an "object" of revelation for our sakes, yet all the while remaining Subject. Only Father, Son, and Spirit are immediately objective to Godself. With us humans, the Triune God is only mediately objective—and this because of God's grace in the revelatory event to grant it. Humans cannot perceive God as an object, unless God desires it to be so. "[God] meets us under the sign and veil of other objects" (*CD* II/1:16). In the encounter, "this piece of his environment" is a creaturely reality and so not identical with God, "but it represents God. That is to say, it represents God in so far as it is determined, made and used by God as His clothing, temple, or sign; in so far as it is peculiarly a work of God, which above and beyond its own existence (which is also God's work, of course) may and must serve to attest the objectivity of God and therefore to make the knowledge of God possible and necessary" (*CD* II/1:17).

In this way, Barth suggests, God remains sovereign over this revelatory event, controlling its delivery and reception. Barth maintains the sovereignty and transcendence of God in revelation by keeping the revelation of God to humans as indirect or "objectively mediate" (*CD* II/1:16). Yet within this revelatory event,

> God is known, not simply because He is God in Himself, but because He reveals Himself as such; not simply because His work is there, but because He is active in His work. Biblical knowledge of God is always based on encounters of man with God; encounters in which God exercises in one way or another His lordship over man, and in which He is acknowledged as sovereign Lord and therefore known as God. They are encounters which are always initiated by God, and which for man always have in them something unforeseen, surprising and new. They may be preceded by a whole history of man's relationship to God. (*CD* II/1:23)

Returning to the challenge that the finite cannot comprehend the infinite and that we therefore cannot speak of a *direct encounter* with God, I argue that the truth that we can never know God exhaustively does not mean that God cannot be known truthfully—in part. Further, Barth seems quite correct

15. Here Barth says, "God is not God if He is considered and conceived as one in a series of like objects."

in his assertion that only the Triune God is objectively immediate to Godself, yet that does not mean humans lack any knowledge of God whatsoever due to their finitude. God's revelation is just as much a gracious act as creation and redemption. Humans cannot perceive God *on their own* or *through their own finite perceptual/conceptual apparatus*. This means that no human can claim to "know" God without first having been given some knowledge about God by God. As Barth concludes, "At bottom, knowledge of God in faith is always this indirect knowledge of God, knowledge of God in His works, and in these particular works—in the determining and using of certain creaturely realities to bear witness to the divine objectivity" (*CD* II/1:17).

Agreeing with the majority of Barth's description here, I remain concerned that someone will ask how to tell the difference between a human imagination that conceives of God versus a real revelation from God. For Barth, such questions would not really matter since faith is its own surest foundation. For me, however, I see a way toward my own thesis without denying the important points Barth has claimed here in order to keep human hands from encompassing and holding on to God. Where could this be? Barth claims that God is known to us because God wants to reveal Godself to us "as such." We can say that God has revealed Godself to us because God has crafted some medium to represent himself within our finite sphere. Yet this alone is not enough: it is "not simply because His work is there, but because He is *active in His work*" (*CD* II/1:23).[16] Immediately, Barth goes on to discuss "biblical knowledge" of the God who encounters humans in revelation, pressing his point that it is not simply the medium that reveals something about God to humans, but *encounters of humans with God* whereby God takes the initiative and then exercises sovereignty over these humans. Surprising and unforeseen things happen at such encounters! Why? It is because God is *active in his work*. Within the medium that God has chosen to represent himself, there is God operating the medium for God's own purposes with the human recipient of revelation. It is my contention that God's Spirit engages the human spirit at some prereflective level so that in the revelatory event, God may be said truly to encounter the human being *directly* and *immediately*.

All Experience of Objects Involves Interpretation

Another challenge to our thesis suggests that human perception and knowledge of all life experiences are always one step removed from the experience itself. Therefore, we cannot speak of any experience as *direct* but only as

16. My emphasis.

indirect. How can this be? An explanation in support of this challenge suggests that we may experience an event, but as soon as we turn to *interpret* or *reflect on* that event, it becomes absorbed in a web of our mental constructs; we shape the world in which we live by interpreting it through a variety of previous experiences or ways of understanding. The idea of this way of viewing and knowing the world stems primarily from Immanuel Kant. Humans can never grasp (know) things *as they are in themselves* (the *Ding-an-sich* of the noumenal world) but only things *as they appear to us* in the realm of media (the phenomenal world). Hence, humans are always one step removed from every *direct* encounter or from knowledge of that direct encounter by the necessary limitation of our humanity. Some have suggested that all experience of the world involves interpretation.[17] Hence, what we have been calling "direct experience" of God is impossible, since even that experience is not "pure experience" but a cognitive reflection on the perceived event within a web of interpretation.

The philosopher of religion William P. Alston agrees that "normal perceptual experience is shot through with 'interpretation'" but argues that the conceptualization involved with sense perception is not the only way we know objects. Alston argues for a *direct awareness* of objects that *present themselves* to one's consciousness.[18] *Perceiving* an object, Alston proposes, suggests something more than thinking about or remembering the object. Using something as simple as a house to illustrate this, he suggests that a house is "presented to consciousness" and therefore is "something of which I am *directly aware.*"[19] This awareness is different from conceptualization, belief, or any interpretation. So, when we perceive a house, we are not interpreting our experience "as manifesting a house," but a house is directly presented to our experience. "And any sort of interpretation is something over and above that."[20] Since this line of thinking is crucial for our thesis, I want to interact with it further.[21]

17. Dalferth, "Representing God's Presence," 245–46n27. Dalferth explains his disagreement with William Alston on this point. Dalferth asserts, "We have access to reality, but in and through interpretation, not apart from it."

18. William P. Alston, *Perceiving God: The Epistemology of Religious Experience* (Ithaca, NY: Cornell University Press, 1991), 27. In the direct context of Alston's explanation here, he challenges a proposal by John Hick that suggests all experience involves interpretation. See John Hick, *Faith and Knowledge,* 2nd ed. (Ithaca, NY: Cornell University Press, 1966), esp. chap. 5, "The Nature of Faith," 95–119.

19. Alston, *Perceiving God,* 27 (his emphasis).

20. Alston, *Perceiving God,* 28.

21. Using only a part of Alston's proposal here can be risky. Alston wants to demonstrate by the end of his book that "putative direct awareness of God can provide justification for certain kinds of beliefs about God." *Perceiving God,* 9. Yet the basis of his complex and rigorous

Alston then applies this approach to our experiences of God. When we say that we are "perceiving" God directly, we are saying that God presented Godself to us or appeared to us. This "theory of appearing" is what Alston means by "perception."[22] "What distinguishes perception from abstract thought is that the object is *directly presented* or *immediately present* to the subject so that 'indirect presentation' would be a contradiction in terms."[23] It is here that Alston provides my thesis with support by likening such direct awareness of God's presence to that of the mystical tradition in Christianity. Mystics speak of a direct apprehension of God in a manner that parallels my own proposal of a direct awareness of God's presence. While certain mystics have ended up with some extreme views whereby the distinction between God and the human mystic is transcended in some form of encounter, I do not propose such a union of essences. However, what is similar is the idea that God "acts immediately upon the soul in order to communicate Himself to [a person]; and it is God, not an image of God, not the illusion of God, that the soul perceives and attains to."[24]

Therefore, to say that believers have been encountered *directly* by God may mean something like this: that God the Spirit has connected with their embodied spirits—indeed, through their spirits to their entire beings—to communicate Godself with humans through an experience that is prereflective and perhaps, we might even say, precognitive. God connects directly with humans who are made in God's image, thereby producing an *unmediated awareness of God's presence in them.* I call such direct experiences of God *primordial events*, by which I mean experiences prior to interpretation and reflection. In this sense, it is something like what Amos Yong calls "pure experience," which in his estimation is "unavailable for reflection."[25] I will argue (below) in my presentation of a theology of divine-human encounter that this

---

demonstration of this thesis lies in his first chapter, "The Experience of God." It seems appropriate to use this in a stand-alone fashion as we have done here because it is a whole argument in its own right. Not only does Alston's proposal provide us with terminology for our own concerns regarding a direct experience with God, but it also agrees with our basic point that humans may experience God directly. Further, Alston points to Immanuel Kant's ideas as the root of the approach to reality as entirely interpretation. Specifically, he cites the pragmatism of the twentieth century and the idealism of the nineteenth century as purveyors of such views that have gained a strong foothold in contemporary thought. According to Alston, these groups were convinced that there "could be no form of cognition that is not mediated by general concepts and judgment, a view that seems to me a baseless prejudice." See Alston, *Perceiving God*, 37–38.

22. Alston, *Perceiving God*, 16. Alston calls this style of perception "putative direct awareness of God" (9).

23. Alston, *Perceiving God*, 20 (his emphasis).

24. Alston, *Perceiving God*, 23.

25. Yong, *Spirit-Word-Community*, 247.

primordial event is a direct experience that is transformative (because it is the very presence *of God*) and as such has ramifications for our Christian walk. Further, given appropriate understanding of the limitations involved, this primordial experience is made available for reflection so that humans may share their experiences with each other in the community of faith, thereby supporting and correcting each other as they continue to be led by the Spirit of God. In other words, I disagree with Yong that a "pure experience" of God is "unavailable for reflection." Such an experience is the very basis of what constitutes humans as sons and daughters of God.

In response to the challenge "all experience of objects involves interpretation," I would say that this is true of most experiences but not necessarily all. As Alston has argued, there may be experiences that cast their presence on humans in such a way that they are experienced in preinterpretive manners. Further, God is not an object in a series of objects. God is unique as an object of our experience and awareness. More fully developed arguments against this challenge will be offered in the theology of encounter below.

What I have argued to this point is that God confronts the human directly through the Spirit, even if media are used to accommodate to our finite level of perception. This pure experience or primordial event presents God directly to our awareness and as such is prior to reflection, interpretation, or theologizing. Nonetheless, it is impactful on our human lives because it is the very presence of the living God, not just some "object" among a series of objects in the world. Such encounters by God's Spirit carry the potential for transforming our lives into the very nature of Christ. However, since these experiences are difficult to describe in words through cognitive means, I need to develop a theology of this experience so that its importance for the doctrine of the church can be clarified. Before moving to that task, I begin with a rehearsal of manifestations of God's presence throughout the Bible in order to determine if they can offer us something toward our theology of encounter.

Biblical Narratives concerning God's Presence

Manifestations of God's Presence in the First Covenant

God in the Cloud

The God of the Scriptures is one who wants to be with humans and wants humans to be with him. It is within this broad frame of understanding who God is and what God wants that the God of the covenant confronts his people. The presence of God frequently manifests itself to the people of Israel through various forms—theophanies, in theological jargon. Since the covenant God, YHWH, was not visible to them, this God would appear in some manner so they would "see" something representing him but not "see" God per se. The most common form in which God appeared was that of a cloud. God's presence was recognized when "the cloud" (as it was frequently termed) descended over the tabernacle in the wilderness (and eventually the temple in Jerusalem), over the ark of the covenant in the holy of holies, or in front of the "tent of meeting."

Even with this *indirect* manifestation of the cloud, God's presence was obvious to all the people. It signaled to them that God was not absent but *indirectly* present through visible manifestations. Yet while the people observed at a distance, Moses talked more directly with God: face-to-face, as one talks with a friend (Exod. 33:11; Num. 12:6–8). What could this mean? Was it still an *indirect* encounter but less so than the cloud? What did Moses "see" in this encounter? Did he "see" God in some manner? If God is spirit, then how could Moses see anything of God with his physical eyes? So was Moses simply standing in a cloudy mist with a voice bellowing forth from it? We do not have precise answers to these questions. However, I want to inquire what we can learn from these manifestations about God's presence *in them* through the way people *around them* reacted.

First, the people recognized the presence of God in the cloud and/or pillar of fire. Within the visible form itself was something that transcended the form. God manifested himself to the Israelites as the One who is transcendent and at the same time immanent, the One who is above all the earth and yet simultaneously in the midst of his people.[26] YHWH is so great that the heavens cannot contain him, yet so desirous to be with his people that he chooses to dwell in a tent in the midst of their camp. When the cloud descended on the tent of meeting, "all the people would rise up and worship, each at his tent door" (Exod. 33:10b ESV). What were they worshiping? Certainly not the cloud, a thing of nature. How did they know that their God was in the cloud? Was not their object of worship the invisible God whose presence they (somehow) recognized *in* the cloud (or beyond it or behind it)? As Gregory Polan suggests, "The people here assume a position of adoration before the theophanic manifestation of the cloud, and Moses, without intermediary, in conversation with God."[27]

Second, the reality of the invisible God *in* the cloud over the tent of meeting had also been part of their previous experience in the wilderness. God

26. Gregory J. Polan, "Divine Presence: A Biblical Perspective," *Liturgical Ministry* 3 (Winter 1994): 13–21, here 15.
27. Polan, "Divine Presence," 15n11.

was *in* a pillar of a cloud by day and *in* a pillar of fire by night to lead them (Exod. 13:21–22). God's presence was directly connected with the cloud/fire. Along with this, some messenger or angel of God moved behind the camp to protect them from the camp of the Egyptians, and the cloud moved with that messenger (14:19). This angel also went before the Israelites to guard them and keep them going in the right direction (23:20–23).[28]

God's Glory Shown to Moses

In what is perhaps the most vivid revelation of God to any human in the old covenant, God shows himself to Moses. In response to Moses's request for God to "show me your glory" (Exod. 33:18), God allowed Moses to stand beside him while God's "goodness"—or perhaps better, God's beauty (*tûb*)— passed before him and while God proclaimed the name of the covenant God (YHWH).[29] God warned Moses, however, that Moses could not see God's face, "for no one may see me and live" (33:20). God would allow Moses to see his back but not his face. The Lord "came down in the cloud and stood there with him" (34:5). As God "passed by" Moses, God proclaimed his name, YHWH, describing himself as "compassionate and gracious, slow to anger, abounding in love and faithfulness" (34:6). So God covered Moses with his hand while Moses stood on a rock, and the glory of YHWH passed by him. Moses's response to this was to bow to the ground in worship (34:8).

There is so much in this story that remains mysterious to us. What does it mean that God showed Moses his "back" yet not his face? Does this imply that God has body parts? What does it mean that God's presence is described as God's *glory* that passes by in front of Moses? How does God *stand* there with Moses (Exod. 34:5)? Why does God pronounce his name, YHWH, and then offer a list of attributes that give concrete expression to the character of God? I do not have answers to these questions, only conjectures. For our purposes, however, the point I want to make here is this: God presented Godself to Moses in some *indirect* yet *direct* manner (perhaps similar to the

28. Some see this angel as YHWH himself since "my Name is in him" (Exod. 23:21). See Walter A. Maier, "The Divine Presence within the Cloud," *Concordia Theological Quarterly* 79 (2015): 79–102, here 80.

29. Hans Urs von Balthasar notes this variation of the Hebrew word, *tûb*, as "beauty." God causes all his beauty to pass before Moses. "The beauty of God, which is really seen even though his essence (his face) is not seen: *beauty* as a word for a knowledge which, even in its concealment, is nonetheless disclosed and laid bare, a word for an intimacy such as Jesus must have meant when he reproaches the Jews: 'His voice you have never heard, his form [*eidos*] you have never seen; and you do not have his word abiding in you' (John 5:37[–38])." See Balthasar, *The Glory of the Lord: A Theological Aesthetics*, vol. 6, *Theology: The Old Covenant*, trans. Brian McNeil and Erasmo Leiva-Merikakis, ed. John Riches (San Francisco: Ignatius, 1991), 38.

mediated immediacy?). Within the medium of some form, which God called his "back," Moses "saw" God; yet this form itself was not God but something provided by God so that Moses could rightfully say he had "seen" God in some sense. However, this "seeing" was not a view of God's face, for anyone who looks God in the face (directly?) shall die. Because this revelation was *indirect* (God's back) instead of *direct* (God's face), does this mean that Moses was not *directly encountered* by God? Or does it mean that Moses was not *directly aware* of God's real presence? I think not on both questions. As I have been arguing, this seems to be a case where God's very being (presence) exists *within* the medium (in some sense) so that what Moses saw was once removed from the reality of God's essence. Moses saw the form, the indirect medium fashioned by God for the purpose of revealing Godself to Moses. However, within the medium itself is an *immediacy*, a *directness* of God's presence that is not equated with the medium itself. God himself was present to Moses so that Moses had a direct awareness of God's presence in that moment. God accommodated himself to Moses's finitude but also was really present to Moses via the instrumentality of the visual form of God's back. The result was that Moses had a direct encounter with God, even though it was processed through a medium that God prepared. As we discover within this narrative itself, God cannot be seen directly in this earthly life, or the finite human will die. Therefore, God uses media to bring about a connection with humans. Yet my point is that we are not communing with a thing—a medium, a form crafted for such connection. Through the Spirit, God in God's nature encounters us through the medium.

One more point seems important before moving to other examples. There was a *verbal pronouncement* by God. Again, the fact that a voice was heard by Moses points to the fact that this was a medium used by God to communicate in Moses's language. However, the Lord here gives Moses information about himself that provides some content about the character of the God who confronted him. While I am not suggesting that all encounters with God match this as if it were a paradigm for divine-human encounters, I am saying that there usually is a purpose for such encounters. Thus, these events sometimes provide *content* to assist our understanding or knowledge about God (or even about ourselves). Nevertheless, the direct presence of God offers a potential for a transforming moment.

God Meets and Greets the People of Israel

Within the narrative of the giving of the covenant (esp. the Ten Commandments), God desired to speak directly to Moses and be overheard by the people of Israel (Exod. 19:9). So God settled in a "dense cloud" filled with darkness on Mount Sinai (19:9). On the third day, after preparations, God descended on the mountain with thunder, lightning, and a thick cloud; the sound of a trumpet bellowed through the smoke. All of the people of Israel trembled (19:16). "Then Moses led the people out of the camp to meet with God" as he had been instructed (19:17). "Mount Sinai was covered in smoke, because the LORD descended on it in fire. The smoke billowed up from it like smoke from a furnace, and the whole mountain trembled violently. As the sound of the trumpet grew louder and louder, Moses spoke and the voice of God answered him" (19:18–19). Elohim was in the "thick darkness" (*'ărāpel*, 20:21) on the mountaintop, and that is precisely where Moses went.[30] By walking into the dark cloud where Elohim was dwelling, Moses "came into the immediate presence of the Godhead, but he, like the people, saw nothing other than 'the mask of Yahweh.'"[31] The coming of the Holy One of Israel is marked with a powerful demonstration of the elements of earth. "There is now set loose sources of energy, power, and authority so enormous and so fearful that the intended 'containers' of God's presence are unable to contain."[32]

After delivering the Ten Commandments to Moses on Mount Sinai (perhaps loudly enough so the people assembled at the foot of the mountain could "overhear"), God sends Moses down to tell the people what God requires of them (Exod. 19:25; 20:1).[33] Apparently the loud pyrotechnic display surrounding the presence of God on the mountain continued: thundering, lightning flashes, the sound of a trumpet blast, fire smoldering on the mountaintop, and smoke

30. Samuel Terrien notes that this thick darkness "points to the mythology of the storm god," but refers specifically to the thunderhead. It may have overtones of both divine presence and divine hiddenness. See Terrien, *The Elusive Presence: Toward a New Biblical Theology* (San Francisco: Harper & Row, 1978), 128.

31. Terrien, *The Elusive Presence*, 128.

32. Walter Brueggemann, *Exodus: Introduction, Commentary, and Reflections*, New Interpreter's Bible, ed. Leander Keck et al. (Nashville: Abingdon, 1994), 1:836.

33. The narrative of these events remains a little unclear. Does Exod. 20:1–17, which begins with "and God spoke all these words" and then offers the Ten Commandments through the next sixteen verses, refer to God speaking with Moses on Sinai? In other words, did the people assembled below actually hear God's loud voice give out the Ten Commandments? It seems so, but I suggest there is some lack of clarity in the narrative since Moses speaks out to God (19:19b) and God responds to him by voice (19:19c). Then God asks Moses to go up on the mountain in 19:20, and God tells him to go back down to tell the people specific instructions in 19:21. Moses is said to have gone back down the mountain in 19:25, and then the Ten Commandments are given in the narrative. Clearly the people heard God speak to Moses on the mountain (since that seemed to be one way God chose to connect with the people of Israel that day), but did the speaking forth of the commandments occur when Moses was on the mountain and the people overheard, or did it occur after Moses had come down? The narrative afterward (20:18–21) does not assist us in resolving the issue.

coming forth from the mountain. The result was (again) great fear covering the people (20:18). Perhaps this is the closest the community of Israel ever got to being confronted directly by the covenant God, YHWH. The people "trembled and stood afar off" when they saw it (20:18 NKJV). They begged Moses to be a mediator between this God of the mountain and them. They said not to let God speak with them "or we will die" (20:19). God had desired a covenant people who would be a special treasure to him, "a kingdom of priests and a holy nation" (19:5–6). There was no desire for a go-between on God's part; indeed, God desired people to speak directly with him, like priests who intercede for others. Moses could talk with God *in the cloud* and even face-to-face, but the people of God feared to do this, lest they die. And so, the people of God removed themselves from God's awesome presence by standing afar off.[34] Concerning this result, Walter Brueggemann states with remarkable acuity, "Israel will not again be exposed to the direct presence of God."[35]

In this instance, the people's fear of the media got in the way of their rightful position in God's direct presence. Yet the narrative clearly illustrates that God was *in* the media. I do not believe that thunder and lightning, smoke and fire, produced such fear in God's people alone. There must have been a clear demonstration of God's *direct presence within the fire and smoke, lightning and thunder*. Indeed, they heard God's voice—another medium, to be sure, but one that was tailored to the nature of this Almighty One who spoke from Sinai.[36] When God is said to come to the mountain, a cloud settles over it (Exod. 19:9, 18–20; 20:21; 24:15). God's glory was said to be there *in the cloud* (24:16). "The sight of the glory of the Lord was like a consuming fire on the top of the mountain in the eyes of the children of Israel" (24:17 NKJV), yet they saw Moses going into the middle of the cloud to talk with God! God presented himself *indirectly* to the people through marvelous, awe-inspiring signs and wonders. However, God's own presence was *in* the signs and wonders, making God directly present to their awareness. When this event was described later, in Deuteronomy 5:23–24, what happened on this previous occasion was still described similarly: "When you heard the voice out of the darkness, while the mountain was ablaze with fire, all the leaders of your tribes and your elders came to me. And you said, 'The Lord our God

---

34. In *Serving the People of God's Presence*, I point to this event as the beginning of a priestly caste that mediated between God and humans in the first covenant—something that is abrogated in the second covenant.

35. Brueggemann, *Exodus*, 854.

36. Of course, it is possible that God foreknew this response; as the narrator says through Moses in Exod. 20:20, God may have done this to place reverential fear of God before them so that they "may not sin" (NKJV).

has shown us his glory and his majesty, and we have heard his voice from the fire. Today we have seen that a person can live even if God speaks with them.'" They had heard God speaking out of the fire and had lived. Yet they felt it was too much for them: "But now, why should we die? This great fire will consume us, and we will die if we hear the voice of the LORD our God any longer. For what mortal has ever heard the voice of the living God speaking out of fire, as we have, and survived?" (Deut. 5:25–26). This God of Israel is utterly free—"untamed and undomesticated"—demanding a reorientation of the people's lives.[37] It was this that they feared more than the pyrotechnic show that accompanied God speaking with them directly.

God Seals the Covenant with the Elders at a Meal

In one of the most unusual narratives in Exodus, in which God provides a covenant with the Israelites and asks them to vow their obedience, God meets Moses, Aaron, Nadab, Abihu, and seventy elders on the mountain to seal the covenant with a table meal.[38] The description is stark yet vivid: "[They] saw the God of Israel" (Exod. 24:10a). What can this mean? The narrative continues: "Under his feet was something like a pavement made of lapis lazuli, as bright blue as the sky" (24:10b–11). Here again we find people described as seeing God. This is clearly not a *direct* vision like what we will experience in eternity, but nonetheless a vision of what God wanted them to see. While the nature of the form used by God is not fully described here, there is a hint of it in the phrase "under his feet." Apparently, God presented Godself to this representative group of Israelites through something like human form, even participating in the covenantal meal.[39] How, then, did they realize it was God? Again, I propose that there was the presence of God within the medium of presentation that made the Israelites *directly aware of God*. It is a form of "mediated immediacy."[40]

---

37. Brueggemann, *Exodus*, 838.

38. Samuel Terrien states curtly: "Such a story is without parallel in the Hebrew tradition." Terrien, *The Elusive Presence*, 135.

39. Terence E. Fretheim, *Exodus*, ed. James L. Mays and Patrick D. Miller, Interpretation: A Bible Commentary for Teaching and Preaching (Louisville: Westminster John Knox, 1991), 260. Fretheim further comments, "The exact nature of the divine participation in this meal is ambiguous, but God was certainly fully present in the midst of the people during the eating and drinking. It is a communal activity, in which both God and people participate" (260).

40. We could rehearse other narratives in the first covenant that would follow a similar line of analysis. For example, how did Abraham recognize that the three visitors were really the Lord? How did Moses grasp that the strange phenomenon of a bush that was burning with fire and yet not consumed was really God? Was it because it talked to him? I think not. It seems more likely that Moses grasped with some type of direct awareness that the encounter with this bush held the real presence of the living God.

God's Presence and Glory Fills the Temple of Solomon

Another example from the first covenant that we shall consider is the presence of God descending into the temple of Solomon when it was dedicated (1 Kings 8:10–11; 2 Chron. 5:13–14; 7:1–3).[41] Frequently the thick cloud that surrounded God's presence in the wilderness tabernacle and the more permanent temple was connected with the "glory" of God. Ezekiel speaks of the glory of God as a blazing fire with a radiant glow (Ezek. 1:4; 8:2). So while the whole earth is filled with God's glory (Isa. 6:3), there are times in Israel's history when the presence of God's glory is seen and felt. The Hebrew noun for "glory" (*kābôd* | כָּבוֹד) is what God possesses because of who he is. The *kābôd* of God entered the holy of holies, sanctifying the tent of God (Exod. 29:43). The root idea behind this word is "heaviness" or "weight."[42] If someone or something is "heavy," it is powerful or important.[43] In the ancient world, things were frequently valued by their weight. For example, coinage was usually labeled and measured according to its weight. When one considers the covenant Lord of Israel, his worth is "heavy"—that is, beyond our ability to control or "lift." The glory of God, then, is the full sum of God's attributes. The glory of God is God's life, God's power, God's activity, God's fullness, God's grace.[44] To refer to the presence of YHWH as the glory of God is to refer to God's power, splendor, or honor; it may even have some connotation of the quantity—the weight—of God.[45] Frequently the glory of God is connected with the cloud or the presence in the sanctuary.

On some occasions in Israel's history, the *presence of God's glory* is seen and felt by observers. Several of these occasions with the Israelites in the wilderness have already been considered. However, in Exodus 40:34–38, we have an event where when Moses completed the building of the tabernacle, "the cloud covered the tent of meeting, and the glory of the LORD filled the tabernacle. Moses could not enter the tent of meeting because the cloud had settled on it, and the glory of the LORD filled the tabernacle" (Exod. 40:34–35). While the cloud and the glory of the Lord had both been described and encountered previously in the sojourn in the desert, the depiction here is unusual in that

---

41. It is interesting to note that in 1 Kings 8:10–11 and the parallel passage in 2 Chron. 5:13–14, the cloud of God's glory fills the temple *after* the ark of the covenant is placed in its permanent position in the holy of holies; in 2 Chron. 7:1–3, the cloud of God's glory fills the temple *after* Solomon prays and dedicates the temple.

42. S.v. "*kābôd* | כָּבוֹד," *BDB*, 457–58.

43. M. Weinfeld, "כָּבוֹד | *kābôd*," *TDOT* 7:23, 25.

44. Paul S. Minear, *Horizons of Christian Community* (St. Louis: Bethany, 1959), 29.

45. Joseph R. Greene, "The Spirit in the Temple: Bridging the Gap between Old Testament Absence and New Testament Assumption," *Journal of the Evangelical Theological Society* 55, no. 4 (2012): 717–42, here 723.

the cloud settles over the tent of meeting and the glory of the Lord fills the tabernacle, apparently settling and filling two different places in the camp of the Israelites. Further, the narration tells us that Moses could not enter the tent of meeting because the glory of the Lord filled the tabernacle, something that had not been described in any previous encounter. In whatever way we are supposed to understand what was happening in the camp, it came at the completion of the work on the tabernacle. "And so Moses finished the work" (40:33). Then the cloud and glory appeared.

At the completion of the temple of Solomon, a similar event occurs. Solomon had completed his prayer and "fire came down from heaven and consumed the burnt offering and the sacrifices, and the glory [*kābôd*] of the LORD filled the temple. The priests could not enter the temple of the LORD because the glory of the LORD filled it. When all the Israelites saw the fire coming down and the glory of the LORD above the temple, they knelt on the pavement with their faces to the ground, and they worshiped and gave thanks to the LORD, saying, 'He is good; his love endures forever'" (2 Chron. 7:1–3). Again we are told that God's glory with and in the cloud was such that humans could not fulfill their duties. The presence of God was felt; it was something experienced by Moses and the priests in Solomon's day that caused them not to enter the tent or tabernacle, places that had been opened to them officially. Something they sensed stopped them on this occasion yet not on other occasions when the cloud and glory of God were said to be present.[46] On occasion, then, it seems the presence of God's glory becomes so overwhelming in the midst of his people that they feel the heaviness or weightiness of their God in rather palpable form. The priests could not enter the temple and perform their service there because of "the glory of the LORD" filling the building.

The Shekinah of God

For years, I thought that "Shekinah" was a biblical term for God's presence because it was used so frequently in our church movement to describe the presence of God in our meetings. However, the term is not in the Hebrew

---

46. Usually Israel saw God in the theophanic cloud, protecting them from looking at the deity. In Lev. 9:23, however, at the consecration of the tabernacle, the glory of the Lord appeared to all the people and "fire came out from the presence of the LORD and consumed the burnt offering and the fat portions on the altar. And when all the people saw it, they shouted for joy and fell facedown" (9:24). This seems similar to the events on Mount Sinai when God revealed himself in some way, yet it is not entirely clear if the people actually saw God's naked glory (like Moses did) or if the flames from God's presence were assumed by them to be God's glory. The narrative is less than clear as to what they saw that caused them to identify this as the glory of God. See Weinfeld, "כָּבוֹד | *kābôd*," *TDOT* 7:31.

Bible, but it does develop from a Hebrew verb meaning "to dwell" or "to rest."[47] During the postexilic and rabbinic periods of Israel's history, which are several hundred years before and after the birth of Christ, the word "Shekinah" was used to describe the presence of God dwelling on earth.[48]

Since God clearly dwelled in the temple, where did God's presence go when the exile occurred? Some Jewish scholars in the postexilic period saw God's presence as remaining with the people in their captivity and suffering.[49] Others found it necessary to provide a way of speaking of the all-glorious, transcendent Lord, who was also immanent (in some sense), choosing to occupy particular places (like the tabernacle). God was not a body and therefore could not "occupy" space; yet God is described as "dwelling" in the tabernacle among his people in the desert and in the temple of Solomon. In an attempt to work through this transcendence/immanence issue, the word "Shekinah" began to fill the role of how God could dwell in a physical location. For these postexilic thinkers, whose language was Aramaic,[50] the Shekinah came to be almost a personification of God's presence in the way the God who cannot be contained by the heavens themselves can somehow fit into the little temple of Solomon in Jerusalem (1 Kings 8:27). In such a setting, "The *Shekinah* was God's Presence and yet not God."[51] The Shekinah was not a divine attribute but somehow the very presence of God "present at a particular place and at a particular time."[52] In this way, Shekinah was seen as the "earthly, temporal and spatial presence of God," yet also in some way as distinct from God.[53]

During the rabbinic period of Judaism, the rabbis proposed various ways of understanding the Shekinah. Some rabbis thought that God's Shekinah rested only on the people of Israel or only when Israel gathered in large numbers; others thought that ten students gathered to study the Torah was enough

47. Polan, "Divine Presence," 19.

48. In such cases, it usually appears in the Targums (Aramaic translations of the Torah) commenting on many of the Exodus passages we have just considered, often using the word (or its derivatives) "Shekinah." The term also appears in the Midrash of the rabbis. See George F. Moore, "Intermediaries in Jewish Theology: Memra, Shekinah, Metatron," *Harvard Theological Review* 15, no. 1 (1922): 41–85, here 55. While this source is old, some of the details concerning etymology remain up-to-date.

49. For a description of these sources, see Jürgen Moltmann, *Spirit of Life: A Universal Affirmation*, trans. Margaret Kohl (Minneapolis: Fortress, 1992), 47–51.

50. Aramaic was a Semitic language that looked a great deal like Hebrew. Its origin was in Syria, but its use became pervasive all over the ancient Near East, being especially prominent as the common language among Jews in the first few centuries before and after Christ. Jesus spoke a Galilean dialect of Aramaic.

51. Leonard S. Kravitz, "*Shekinah* as God's Spirit and Presence," *The Living Pulpit* (January–March 1996): 22–23, here 22.

52. Moltmann, *Spirit of Life*, 48.

53. Moltmann, *Spirit of Life*, 48.

to bring about the presence of Shekinah; still others thought the minimum number of students gathered for Torah study should be two.[54] Later rabbinic scholars conceived of the Shekinah as having an almost independent existence, serving like an intermediary or even a divine emanation for this world.[55]

While I recognize that Judaism did not entirely sanction the concept of Shekinah, the very fact that there was discussion about this tension between the transcendence of God and the immanence of God demonstrates a concern that remains in both Judaism and Christianity today. How do we (Jews and Christians) confess the one God when we also confess this God is impassible and unchangeable? Christians can see this tension even without the background of the Shekinah. A Jewish professor of the Midrash, Leonard Kravitz, has suggested that Christians might view their understanding of the Holy Spirit "in some ways analogous to the *Shekinah*."[56] Since the Holy Spirit is viewed as God and yet distinct from the Father and Son, the Spirit is like the Shekinah in that God chooses to become immanent with humans, first in the presence of Jesus Christ and next in the ongoing presence of the Holy Spirit in the lives of believers.

The Spirit of God, like the Jewish Shekinah, is more than an attribute of God. The Spirit is the presence of the Triune God among and in we who believe. Jürgen Moltmann points out that the idea of Shekinah posits three clues to our understanding of the Spirit of God. First, the Spirit is the "presence of God in person." Second, the Spirit indwells humans and this earth, especially among those who are wandering and suffering (as did Israel in its exile and journeys). Third, the Spirit of God "renounces his impassibility and becomes able to suffer because he is willing to love." Moltmann calls this last feature "the kenosis of the Spirit."[57]

What is the upshot of all this? The infinite, transcendent God has entered our finite, mundane existence in ways that show his glory among us. This much is clear from the descriptions of his theophanies in the Hebrew Bible.

---

54. Kravitz, "*Shekinah* as God's Spirit and Presence," 22. The language of this last rabbi's admonishment sounds quite similar to Jesus's words: "When two sit down together to study Torah, the Shekinah is in their midst" (as quoted in Moltmann, *Spirit of Life*, 48; from the Mishnah, in 'Abot 3.2); and Jesus in Matt. 18:20: "For where two or three gather in my name, there am I with them."

55. Kravitz, "*Shekinah* as God's Spirit and Presence," 22; Moltmann, *Spirit of Life*, 48.

56. Kravitz, "*Shekinah* as God's Spirit and Presence," 23.

57. Moltmann, *Spirit of Life*, 51. All three of his points appear on this page. In his final point, reference is made by Moltmann to his doctoral student's dissertation on this topic: Lyle Dabney, *Die Kenosis des Geistes: Kontinuität zwischen Schöpfung und Erlösung im Werk des Heiligen Geistes*, ed. Wolfgang Huber et al., Neukirchener Beiträge zur Systematischen Theologie 18 (Neukirchen-Vluyn: Neukirchener Verlag, 1997).

Yet we have seen difficulty among Jewish thinkers attempting to resolve the tension that is clearly posed to us by the *divine presence* in the midst of *human existence*. How can the true God be immanent and with us while at the same time transcendent and above all else? The New Testament will offer some further reflection on the glory and presence of God on earth.

The Manifestation of God's Presence in the Second Covenant

The explicit understanding of the New Testament is that the glory of God, which presented itself to the Israelites, rests entirely on and in the God-Human, Jesus the Christ. One of the crucial ways this is explained is by John's Gospel. While some of the Aramaic Targums that I mentioned above were written after the first century CE, Raymond Brown believes that the "theology of the *shekinah* was known at that time."[58] He further speculates that John's prologue may actually reflect something of the Shekinah theology with its use of "dwelling" language. Exodus 25:8 records God's command to Moses for the people to make a sanctuary so that God could "dwell among them" (Exod. 25:8). In the Septuagint (LXX), the Greek translation of the Hebrew Scriptures that was the "Bible" for the New Testament church, the noun for "tabernacle," where God will dwell, is the Greek word *skēnē* | σκηνή. John uses the verb form of this noun in John 1:14: "The Word became flesh and made his dwelling among us. We have seen his glory, the glory of the one and only Son, who came from the Father, full of grace and truth." The Word *made his dwelling* (ἐσκήνωσεν | *eskēnōsen*) among us. One could even translate this as "The Word *tabernacled* or *pitched his tent* among us."[59] God dwelled in the tabernacle (*skēnē*) in the wilderness, where the presence of God hovered over it like a cloud and the glory of God shone in it. Now, however, God has tabernacled (*eskēnōsen*) among us in the man Jesus Christ. The fact that John continues immediately to discuss the place of God's glory now in the Son shows us that he may have had the tabernacle presence of God in mind—or perhaps even the Shekinah presence. Then John concludes the section with words that take us back directly to Exodus: "No one has ever seen God, but the one and only Son, who is himself God and is in closest relationship with the Father, has made him known" (John 1:18). Moses may have "seen" God in some sense, but not in his fullness. If he had seen God fully, he would have

---

58. Raymond E. Brown, *The Gospel according to John*, Anchor Bible 29 (Garden City, NY: Doubleday, 1966), 32.

59. This is an aorist (past) tense, so there is an "ἐ" placed on the front of the stem, but one can see the root part of the verb in the *skēn-*, which is connected with the noun form for "tabernacle" (*skēnē*).

died immediately. However, John testifies that the only Son has seen God and, as God, has been in closest relationship with the Father. This Son has made known the Father to us. His glory, which we have seen, is the same as the glory of the Father. "If you really know me," Jesus says, "you will know my Father as well. From now on, you do know him and have seen him" (14:7). Then John's record of Jesus's words continues: "Anyone who has seen me has seen the Father" (14:9b). Jesus the Christ is the glory of God in human form, visible in a way that was less mysterious and fear-producing than the cloud and fire, thunder and lightning, but he is still God in all his glory nonetheless (Heb. 12:22–28). The Aramaic Targum of Exodus 25:8 reads, "I shall cause my *shekinah* to reside among them."[60] For John's Gospel, this is most fully brought about through the incarnation of the Word.

Paul continues the theme of the glory of God in Jesus Christ. It is clear for Paul that the fullness of God dwelled in Christ in bodily form (Col. 2:9). All of God's glory was present within the body of Jesus Christ, the image of the invisible God (1:15). It is the god of this age that has blinded the minds of unbelievers, causing them to be blind to the light of the gospel "that displays the glory of Christ, who is the image of God" (2 Cor. 4:4). God, who created light out of darkness, "made his light shine in our hearts to give us the light of the knowledge of God's glory displayed in the face of Christ" (4:6b). How else did we receive this "light in our hearts" so that we could recognize God in the face of Christ if not through a direct encounter with God's Spirit?

Why is the "face of Christ" the locus for detecting God's glory? We need to return to the previous chapter of 2 Corinthians (3:14–18), where Paul addresses Exodus 34 and Moses's face that glowed with the radiance from being in God's glory. Unaware that his face was radiant when he came down the mountain, Moses shared God's commands to the Israelites with his face uncovered. Later he covered his face with a veil; when he returned to speak with God, he removed the veil (Exod. 34:29–35). Paul points to this veiling and unveiling as a demonstration that the law with its covenant and glory was already passing away in Moses's day. Hence, the glorious covenant with Israel was transient.[61] When people hear the old covenant read, there is a veil over their eyes, so they cannot see Christ (2 Cor. 3:14–15). When people turn to

60. As quoted in Polan, "Divine Presence," 19.

61. There are a number of different ways to understand 2 Cor. 3:13, but this seems the least problematic. See Murray J. Harris, *The Second Epistle to the Corinthians: A Commentary on the Greek Text*, New International Greek Testament Commentary, ed. I. Howard Marshall and Donald A. Hagner (Grand Rapids: Eerdmans, 2005), 298–99. Harris gives about seven different views of commentators and then offers his own, an interpretation close to the one I have given here.

Christ, the veil is removed. The Lord who is the Spirit is the One who brings such freedom of understanding (3:16–17). Then Paul concludes: "We all, who with unveiled faces contemplate [or "reflect"] the Lord's glory, are being transformed into his image with ever-increasing glory, which comes from the Lord, who is the Spirit" (3:18). Gordon Fee aptly summarizes the Spirit's role as described by Paul in this passage: "The Spirit of the living God not only gives us the life of God, but serves for us as God's presence and enables us to behold God's glory so that we are being transformed into his likeness. That is 'glory' indeed!"[62]

There are several key points to make concerning this pericope. As we noted in the introduction to this book, the Greek of this sentence emphasizes the *corporate nature* of the people of God gathered before the Lord's glory. *We all, with a single unveiled face*, "continually reflect (as in a mirror) the glory of the Lord."[63] No longer does Moses, the mediator of the covenant whose face glowed with the presence and glory of God, stand alone face-to-face with God. It is all of us who stand without a veil and with the full knowledge of Jesus Christ. We no longer need Moses or another human as a go-between for us.[64] We enter God's presence and live. *Together* we shine with ever-increasing radiance as we reflect the glory that is the Lord's alone or, in this instance, a radiant glory that comes from the Lord, who is the Spirit.

As we have already described, God's intention for his people was clarified in Exodus 19:5–6, where God promises Israel that they will be a "treasured possession," as well as a "kingdom of priests and a holy nation." It seems that God desired to encounter his people *directly*, even face-to-face, as with Moses. A few days later, God descended with thunder, lightning, a thick cloud, fire, and trumpet blasts (Exod. 19:16–18). God's voice was heard (19:19). The people's response was to back away from the presence of God. In the person of Jesus Christ, however, we have a *direct* encounter with the living God that does not involve reverence-inducing pyrotechnics. The glory of God rests in the Son of God on earth. *In the face of Christ*, the knowledge of God's glory is fully displayed. While we reflect that glory of Christ's face as in a mirror

---

62. Gordon Fee, *God's Empowering Presence: The Holy Spirit in the Letters of Paul* (Peabody, MA: Hendrickson, 1994), 309–10.

63. "*We all* with *a single unveiled face* reflect the glory of the Lord." The word "face" is in the singular, describing how we all together (plural) are to reflect (or contemplate) God's glory. The Greek of 2 Cor. 3:18 reads thus: ἡμεῖς δὲ πάντες ἀνακεκαλυμμένῳ προσώπῳ τὴν δόξαν κυρίου κατοπτριζόμενοι τὴν αὐτὴν εἰκόνα μεταμορφούμεθα ἀπὸ δόξης εἰς δόξαν καθάπερ ἀπὸ κυρίου πνεύματος.

64. Harris nicely comments on this: "With regard to access to God, *pantes* | πάντες [all] eliminates all distinction between God's messengers and those to whom they are sent. The one and the many of Exodus 34 (Moses and the Israelites) have become the 'all' of 2 Corinthians 3." See Harris, *The Second Epistle to the Corinthians*, 313.

now (and therefore, somewhat indirectly), it does not mean believers lack a direct or true encounter with that glory here and now. Indirect does not mean untrue. Within the limited, finite ability of human frailty, we are given the task of collectively focusing upon the glory of God as with one face in the community of Christ. We may not perceive God's glory fully here in this life, but we may reflect it appropriately, given our limitation. Since the glory of God is now located for us in the face of Christ, not a thunderous cloud of mystery, we must realize that this particular face radiates God's glory as the Crucified–Risen One, who became flesh for our sakes, who suffered with humans by sharing in their humanity, being made like them, "fully human in every way" (Heb. 2:17). The glory of our God is not resident only in God's splendor and majesty as the omnipotent Creator but also in God's humiliation and self-limitation by becoming human and obedient to death, even death on a cross (Phil. 2:5–8). When we gaze on the face of Christ as a gathered community, we reflect God's glory only to the extent that we witness to this One who loves humans to the point of emptying himself for their sakes.

In this life, then, the body of Christ honors the One who died for them by reflecting the radiance of his glorious suffering and powerful resurrection on our behalf. However, this is not the end of our grasp of God's glory in Christ. John, who gave us a clear understanding of the glory of God resident in the Word made flesh, has also pointed to a future day when the dwelling of God will permanently become a habitation with humans. The "Holy City" will descend from heaven, and the curse will no longer exist (Rev. 21:2; 22:3a). The servants of the Lamb of God "will serve him" (22:3b). Then John describes an event where the desire of God in Exodus comes full circle: "They [the servants] will see his face, and his name will be on their foreheads" (22:4). The daughters and sons of God will *see his face*. This will not be a reflection of God's glory in the face of Christ, as if in a mirror, but a *direct vision* of the glory of God face-to-face with Christ, the Lamb slain—without any kind of media or indirect form. Grant Macaskill has noted that the language of Revelation 22:4–5 reflects the experience of Moses in Exodus as well as the covenant language of Exodus 19:6. He states, "This allusion to Moses' vision of the divine face—an experience now enjoyed by all of God's servants—is developed by a reference to the eternal reign of the servants in [Rev. 22:5], which is linked by the use of βασιλεύσουσιν ["they will reign"] to 5:10 and 20:6, both of which explicitly use the covenant language of Exodus 19:6, of God's people as a royal priesthood."[65] And so in the future eschaton, God's

---

65. Grant Macaskill, *Union with Christ in the New Testament* (Oxford: Oxford University Press, 2013), 190. In addition to these references to Rev. 5:10 ("You have made them to be a

desire for face-to-face communion with his people comes to pass. As John says elsewhere, "Dear friends, now we are children of God, and what we will be has not yet been made known. But we know that when Christ appears, we shall be like him for we shall see him as he is" (1 John 3:2).

Toward a Theology of Divine-Human Encounter

The Presence of God within Believers

Indwelling

To this point in our examination of encounter, we have not considered an aspect of God's presence that is available to the children of God. Therefore, before moving to examine the nature of the direct encounter with God, we need to consider what it means to be indwelt by God as described in the New Testament. While I have been addressing the issue of encounters with God and humans as something that may sound almost "occasionalistic," there is a deeper, more enduring description of God's presence in relation to believers in the New Testament. It is that of "indwelling" or "living in." What is this mystical language of union, and how does it relate to our discussion of encountering God's presence?

The concept of "dwelling with" or "indwelling" was already promised by Jesus before his death. "Those who love me will keep my word, and my Father will love them, and we will come to them and make our home with them" (John 14:23 NRSV). Believers will be indwelt by the Father and Son by means of the Holy Spirit. As the Russian theologian Sergius Bulgakov has stated, "This abode is the Holy Spirit, Who by His coming makes us an abode of the Son and, with Him, of the Father. That is, He makes us an abode of the Holy Trinity."[66] After the resurrection of Jesus Christ and the descent of the gift of the Spirit at Pentecost, the Spirit has direct access to believers by means of indwelling them. Not only is God the Spirit directly present in them, but God the Spirit is present in a more permanent manner than seemed to be available previously under the first covenant. Whatever may have been required in terms of distance between God and humans before Pentecost is no longer mandated for all encounters with God. Barriers have been removed; the veil

---

kingdom and priests to serve our God, and they will reign on the earth") and 20:6 ("The second death has no power over them, but they will be priests of God and of Christ and will reign with him for a thousand years"), I add 1:5–6, "To him who . . . has made us to be a kingdom and priests to serve his God and Father."

66. Sergius Bulgakov, *The Comforter*, trans. Boris Jakim (Grand Rapids: Eerdmans, 2004), 304.

has been torn asunder. We have direct access to God through Jesus Christ, and we have the immediate presence of God indwelling us through the Holy Spirit. Living within us is the down payment of the Spirit, which grants us a foretaste of the full, face-to-face presence of God on the day of redemption.

How can we speak about Christ living *in us* by means of the Spirit without somehow understanding this to refer to God *directly indwelling* us with his presence? The love of God "has been poured out into our hearts through the Holy Spirit" (Rom. 5:5). However, in this pouring out, God is not simply giving us a gift of love but giving the Holy Spirit, who is the very love of the selfsame Triune God. The result, as Moltmann says, is that "God himself is 'in us' and we ourselves are 'in God.'"[67] In this way, we experience the Spirit as the "reciprocal perichoresis of God and ourselves."[68] The *reciprocal* nature of this perichoretic indwelling, suggests Moltmann, is the fact that "God participates in our transitory life, and we participate in the eternal life of God."[69] In the New Testament, what is the meaning of the indwelling of the Spirit if not some new, direct, and even intimate relationship with God that cannot be reduced to sheer human enthusiasm?[70]

Participation (*koinōnia*)

Another concept in the New Testament that offers insight into the indwelling presence of God the Spirit is found in the word *koinōnia* | κοινωνία, which can mean "fellowship" or "participation" or "holding things in common." As Paul tells us in 2 Corinthians 13:13, *koinōnia* is the particular sphere in which

67. Moltmann, *Spirit of Life*, 195.
68. Moltmann, *Spirit of Life*, 195.
69. Moltmann, *Spirit of Life*, 196 (his emphasis).
70. While much of the language of being "in Christ" or of Christ being "in us" has been taken over in today's churches by a twisted form of pietistic individualism, the descriptive mark of God's presence in Christ through the power of the Spirit is *plural*, not singular. In a plethora of instances, the phrases "Christ in us" or "we in Christ" are used in the New Testament: We are created *in Christ* to do good works (Eph. 2:10a). "*All of us* who were baptized *into Christ* were baptized into his death" (Rom. 6:3). It is because of God that *you all* (pl.) are *in Christ Jesus* (1 Cor. 1:30a). It is God who makes both us and you stand firm in Christ (2 Cor. 1:21). God the Father has blessed *us in Christ* with every spiritual blessing (Eph. 1:3). *Christ in you* (pl.) is the hope of glory (Col. 1:27). To say that there is a mystical union of the believer and Christ is not an entirely accurate statement. According to Scripture, it is more precise to speak of the union between Christ and *believers* (pl.) since most of the occasions in the text speak in either the second-person plural (you all) or first-person plural (we/us). While I do not deny the personal relationship established by the Spirit between Jesus Christ and individual believers, we must never allow individualism to blur the point made by Scripture: Christ is within the group of believers gathered in his name. The Spirit deals with each of us individually, to be sure, yet also propels us outward to other people who are in Christ so that we might move even further outward to people who do not know Christ.

the Holy Spirit operates. Believers are brought into a living communion with God, a relationship characterized by the very nature of the Holy Spirit. The Spirit brings us into fellowship with Christ so that this union can be characterized as being "in Christ." The Spirit brings us into fellowship with the Triune God so that our participation in the divine nature is one that sweeps us into the life of God. "If it is characteristic of the divine Spirit not merely to communicate this or that particular thing, but actually to enter into fellowship with believing men and women—if indeed he himself becomes their fellowship—then 'fellowship' cannot merely be a 'gift' of the Spirit. It must be the eternal, essential nature of the Spirit himself."[71]

First John 1:3 develops a two-dimensional shape to *koinōnia*: "We declare to you what we have seen and heard so that you also may have fellowship [κοινωνίαν] with us; and truly our fellowship [κοινωνία] is with the Father and with his Son Jesus Christ" (NRSV). We have *horizontal koinōnia* ("fellowship with us") and *vertical koinōnia* ("fellowship with the Father and Son").[72] As Thomas Smail notes, it is the preaching of the gospel that helps to create these two dimensions. "The Holy Spirit is the Spirit of relationship: as he opens us up to the Father and the Son, he opens us up to one another as well."[73]

In 2 Peter 1:3–4 we find the locus classicus for texts relating to sharing in God's divine nature: "His divine power has given us everything we need for a godly life through our knowledge of him who called us by his own glory and goodness. Through these he has given us his very great and precious promises, so that through them you may participate in the divine nature [γένησθε θείας κοινωνοὶ φύσεως | *genēsthe theias koinōnoi physeōs*], having escaped the corruption in the world caused by evil desires." More literally, these things have been given us by Christ so that "you may become sharers/participants or partners of the divine nature."[74] What can this important text mean? While it may be difficult to know precisely, clues from the context indicate that becoming partners in God's covenant allows us to partake in his divine action. In particular, Christ's divine power has given us everything for godly life; therefore we can *share* in that power *by participating in* Christ's moral nature. To do so, we need to make every effort to add to our faith the

---

71. Moltmann, *Spirit of Life*, 218.

72. Thomas A. Smail, *The Giving Gift: The Holy Spirit in Person* (Eugene, OR: Wipf & Stock, 1994), 182–83.

73. Smail, *The Giving Gift*, 184.

74. Two sources provide us with the terms "sharers/participants" and "partners." The first grouping is from James M. Starr, *Sharers in the Divine Nature: 2 Peter 1:4 in Its Hellenistic Context*, Coniectanea Biblica New Testament Series 33, ed. Birger Olsson and Kari Syreeni (Stockholm: Almqvist & Wisell, 2000), 47. The second term (partners) is from Macaskill, *Union with Christ in the New Testament*, 281.

virtues outlined by Peter in the next few verses (1:5–11). These are divine virtues of Christ. We can become virtuous in some sense by participating or partnering in Christ's moral excellence and righteousness. Such sharing probably does not mean deification in the sense that Athanasius would take it three hundred years later. Rather, "Christ believers are thus envisioned as sharing in divine nature not in the sense that they are deified, but in the sense that they come to share qualities found supremely in Christ's nature."[75]

Yet, how is it that these qualities are *shared*? It is through the indwelling presence of the risen Christ by means of the work of the Holy Spirit. There is something of an indicative/imperative scheme operating here in the text. In verse 3, believers have already been given everything they need for living life in this world with godliness. That is the indicative, the declarative statement of fact. Based on that "given," we are commanded to "make every effort to add to your faith . . ." (1:5). That is the imperative, the command to do something that cooperates with the prior act of God in one's life. In sum, "what this means is that 2 Peter 1:4 portrays believers not as sharing in the divine essence—either in terms of absorption into God or in a Platonic sense—but rather as those who are in covenant with God, constituting his people and actively cooperating with his will and intentions for the world."[76]

The Temple of the Spirit

The Spirit dwelling in every Christian is like the presence of God in the cloud that entered the tabernacle or temple of the former covenant. In the new covenant, however, the temple is not a building but the people of God. The Spirit of God fills us individually *and* corporately, giving us a taste of God's own nature by the Spirit's presence in us and among us. As the presence of YHWH with Israel distinguished them from every other nation on the earth, so the presence of the Spirit with God's people marks them as God's own possession.

Paul addresses this concept several times: 1 Corinthians 3:16; 6:19; Ephesians 2:21–22; and 2 Corinthians 6:16–7:1. I will examine the three listed Corinthians passages for their insight into the indwelling of God's Spirit. First, Paul admonishes the Corinthians, "Don't you know that you yourselves are God's temple [ναός | *naos*] and that God's Spirit lives in you?" (NCV). What may not be obvious in the English translation is that the verbs and pronouns are *plural*; that is, "Don't *all of you* know that *you all* are the sanctuary of God and that the Spirit of God dwells in *you all*?" Collectively, the new

---

75. Starr, *Sharers in Divine Nature*, 45.
76. Macaskill, *Union with Christ in the New Testament*, 282.

people of God are the new temple of God. The deity dwells in a sanctuary, and that is precisely where God is now located—in and among God's people. The use of the plural and the clearly corporate aspect of Paul's words here is unmistakable. As Gordon Fee comments, "It is difficult to overemphasize the significance of this text for Paul's understanding of the church—as primarily a people of the Spirit."[77] God intends to live in our midst, dwelling in our communal lives as surely as in the tabernacle and temple of Israel.

Second, Paul moves on to discuss the body as the temple of the Spirit, but this time he speaks in the singular. In the context of a discussion on sexual immorality and the importance of caring for one's body since our bodies are "members of Christ himself" (1 Cor. 6:15), Paul states, "Do you not know that your body is the temple of the Holy Spirit who is in you, whom you have received from God?" (1 Cor. 6:19 NKJV). In this passage, the second-person plural remains in the verbs and pronouns (as in 1 Cor. 3:16), but each time the word "body" is used, it is singular, not plural. "Don't all of you [pl.] know that the body [sg.] of you all [pl.] is a temple [sg.] of the Holy Spirit, who is in you all [pl.], whom you all [pl.] have from God?" (my trans.). Perhaps this could be interpreted as speaking about the gathered body of Christ, but there are hints that Paul is addressing individual bodies. Previously, Paul had noted that an individual who unites his body with a prostitute is joining Christ to that prostitute through his body. "Do you not know that your bodies [pl.] are members of Christ himself?" (1 Cor. 6:15a). It seems clear that the context focuses on the potential hazard of how individual bodies may be misused. Further, the use of the singular in verse 19 may be a Semitic device called a "distributive singular."[78] The point Paul is making here is that each person's body is a temple of the Spirit. This is different from the previous passage, where the emphasis was on *all* the people of God in Corinth as the location of God's dwelling. Here, however, each individual believer has God's presence within their temple-like structure of the body. Hence, the previous passage reminded them that *together* they are God's habitation; this passage reminds them that *individually* they carry around God's Spirit in their body. Against the wisdom clique of Corinth and groups who tended to despise the body and focus their theology on *spiritual* existence, Paul reminds the Corinthians that the Spirit who indwells them does not despise the body but revels in it to the extent that he makes his home there. Indeed, the "presence of the Spirit in their bodily existence is God's affirmation of the body."[79]

77. Fee, *God's Empowering Presence*, 115.
78. Fee, *God's Empowering Presence*, 134n179.
79. Fee, *God's Empowering Presence*, 136.

The third passage of temple language comes from 2 Corinthians 6:15b–16: "What does a believer have in common with an unbeliever? What agreement is there between the temple of God and idols? For we are the temple of the living God. As God has said, 'I will live with them / and walk among them, / and I will be their God, / and they will be my people.'"[80] Here Paul returns to the plural language of the first passage we examined, yet not the second-person plural (you all) but the first-person plural (we). The point is significant: all together, *we* are the habitation of the living God, who lives in us and with us. Yet to live with his people, God requires cleansing from the pollution of the flesh and spirit (2 Cor. 7:1). The promise from the former covenant is clearly applied to the new people of God. God dwells in and among us because we are now the temple of the living God. Why would anyone who has experienced the indwelling of the Spirit ever want to visit or participate in pagan rituals and temples (cf. 1 Cor. 10:14–22)?

Concluding Points on Indwelling

This brief excursus into the realm of the New Testament concept of the Spirit indwelling believers was meant to direct our attention to the fact that Christians are those who have already experienced God's presence in their own temples (their bodies) and in their communal lives together (the gathered church). It is this presence in our midst that Christians bring with them wherever they gather in Christ's name. While our focus throughout the book thus far has been on the nature of the encounters between God and human beings, we cannot ignore the fact that God is living with and in us. This fact has transformative potential as we grow in Christ with each other.

It might legitimately be asked whether we need to talk about encounters with God's Spirit *outside* of the initial encounters that brought us to a relationship with Christ. If we have the Spirit in us, why do we need encounters? In the last section of this chapter, I attempt to show how God's Spirit continues to work with us through indwelling us as well as through transformative encounters in the corporate gathering that shape us more and more into the image of God in Christ.

Theologies of Indirect Encounters with God

As the reader may already have noticed, I like to sharpen my own theological points on the whetstone of other theologians so that I might glean something in the give-and-take of the enterprise. This is especially true when

---

80. The quotation comes from Lev. 26:11–12.

developing a theology of the divine-human encounter. In this section, I consider Karl Barth's discussion of indirect encounters with God and then move on to the useful concept of *mediated immediacy* with the help of John Baillie, Hans Urs von Balthasar, and Amos Yong. After engaging these theologians, I will offer my own proposal for a theology of encounter with God.

Barth and Indirect Encounters with God

As noted earlier in this chapter, Karl Barth offers much helpful insight on the concept of revelation and the notion of an encounter with God. God gives himself to humans in revelation, not as God is to Godself but as an object suited to human understanding. The resultant knowledge from this secondary form of revelation is a limited knowledge, one that requires faith (*CD* II/1:40). Hence, the encounter is always *indirect*. Referring to God's revelation to Israel in the wilderness, Barth uses the events to underscore his point about the indirect nature of the encounter: "[God] really stands before them; He really speaks to them; they really hear Him. But all this takes place, not in a direct, but in an indirect encounter. What directly confronts them are the historical events, forms and relationships which are His Work" (*CD* II/1:19).

Following the notions of John Calvin, Barth contends that God can never be experienced *directly*.[81] Humans can only have an experience of God's "work and sign" (*CD* II/1:57). In this way, Barth's view of indirect knowledge of God is similar to Calvin's understanding of sacramental presence. For Barth, it seems to be an attempt to guard the utter subjectivity of God so that humans cannot boast that they have "grasped" the infinite God as

---

81. For Calvin, God's essential nature remains hidden, even to the faithful. God's character is revealed, but his essence concealed. See Edward A. Dowey Jr., *The Knowledge of God in Calvin's Theology*, expanded ed. (Grand Rapids: Eerdmans, 1994), 12. As Calvin states, "For who even of slight intelligence does not understand that, as nurses commonly do with infants, God is wont in a measure to 'lisp' in speaking to us? Thus such forms of speaking do not so much express clearly what God is like (*qualis sit Deus*) as accommodate the knowledge of him to our slight capacity. To do this he must descend far beneath his loftiness" (*Inst.* 1.13.1 [121]). Therefore, the essence of God cannot be the subject matter of theology, but rather God as he accommodates himself to our lowly status. Since God's essence is truly hidden and his character is revealed in such a manner that we have some knowledge of the true God, Calvin considered theophanies (appearances of God) in Scripture to be similar to sacraments. They possess the same "revelatory function" (Dowey, *The Knowledge of God in Calvin's Theology*, 13). Humans do not receive a direct encounter with the essence of God but a masked encounter with the God who accommodates himself to our abilities. Humans cannot encounter God's "substance" but can only indirectly experience God as in a theophany or some sacramental medium. Even the greatest theophany, the incarnation of Jesus Christ, was not a revelation of God's essence but only the manner in which God "mirrored" himself to humankind (Dowey, *The Knowledge of God in Calvin's Theology*, 14–16).

they might any other object. God is beyond our concepts of him; God is beyond our knowing him.[82] Moreover, we do know him in some legitimate sense because of his grace in revelation, but even here it is not knowledge of the experiential type that we have been describing but a secondary, mediated knowledge with which God has stooped to grace us. And yet Barth can say that God encounters us in the mode of a "coming presence" by the Spirit (*CD* I/2:95). Nonetheless, this presence still requires faith, not the scientific calculations of an empiricist. It is a presence that is not like any other presence that can be measured.

The Concept of Mediated Immediacy

Several theologians use the phrase "mediated immediacy" yet do not entirely clarify their meaning of it. We will interact with the thoughts of John Baillie, Hans Urs von Balthasar, and Amos Yong in order to develop our own theological insights on this important phrase. Allow me to offer my understanding of it and then interact with the three theologians who discuss it. First, God's presence is embedded within the media (instruments) that God chooses in order to accommodate the encounter with us at a level that is more suitable for humans. Some theologians speak of this as a mediated immediacy—that is, that God's presence always comes to us through some means that arises from the world of creation.

Therefore, the phrase "mediated immediacy" implies what we have already conceded (for the most part)—namely, that God does not usually confront humans without media, since several consequences would follow: (1) we would die (no one has seen God—at least not the naked reality of the Infinite One—and lived); (2) when we shall see God with some level of immediacy in the future eschaton, we "shall be like him, for we shall see him as he is" (1 John 3:2). What I think this means is that humans will need to be transformed in order for us to see God as God is (or at least as much as will be possible for humans to "see" God on that day in eternity).

Second, the phrase "mediated immediacy" has been used by Baillie, Rust, and Yong in ways that tend to explain the *mediated* aspect yet leave the *immediacy* dimension without clarification. Perhaps this is due to their understanding that such directness cannot yield cognitive benefits, and so the experience of the encounter with God can only be discussed as a second-order event (something subject to the interpretive web of human reflection, language,

82. For further discussion on the limits of human knowledge of God in Barth, see Terry L. Cross, *Dialectic in Karl Barth's Doctrine of God*, Issues in Systematic Theology 7, ed. Paul D. Molnar (New York: Peter Lang, 2001), esp. 156–70.

and knowledge). It is this aspect of the divine presence—the directness or immediacy—that I wish to address more specifically in the theology of encounter that is offered below.

Scottish theologian John Baillie was one of the first to use the phrase "mediated immediacy" to refer to the way God's presence encounters us. God is "directly known in His approach to the human soul," and thus the "immediacy of God's presence to our souls is a mediated immediacy."[83] For Baillie, the "mediated" part of the phrase refers primarily to "the fact that God reveals Himself to me only through others who went before, yet in so doing reveals Himself to me now."[84] Baillie admits that this phrase sounds "self-contradictory" but then further explains that the mediated feature describes his parents' home, where he learned about God and various ways of approaching God through his family's modeling; yet the experience of God revealing Godself to his own soul was "immediate," or direct. In this way, God used the media of Baillie's home, village, and culture in order to connect with him directly—hence, mediated immediacy.[85]

This approach comes close to what I have been describing in this chapter as a way that God uses media to connect with humans on their level, somehow directly connecting with them nonetheless. However, Baillie's claim that God reveals Godself "only through others who went before" seems to limit the field of media that God could use. Further, Baillie's depiction of the immediacy of God's presence lacks clarity.

In laying the foundation for his approach, Baillie refers to two medieval theologians: Thomas Aquinas and Bonaventura. Aquinas proposed that humans had no knowledge of God per se, but only through God's effects in the world of nature.[86] Bonaventura held that humans have "*some* direct knowledge of God" within the soul; such knowledge is prior to any attempt to offer an argument for God's existence.[87] Further, Bonaventura notes in his *Sentences* that God is present to the soul itself.[88] While God is knowable through God's creatures by the concept of similitude (*per similitudinem*), God is more truly

---

83. John Baillie, *Our Knowledge of God* (New York: Charles Scribner's Sons, 1959; orig. ed., 1939), 126, 181. Earlier in this chapter, I noted that Baillie's use of "mediated immediacy" was the first that I could find.

84. Baillie, *Our Knowledge of God*, 185.

85. Baillie, *Our Knowledge of God*, 184–85.

86. Baillie, *Our Knowledge of God*, 132.

87. Baillie, *Our Knowledge of God*, 170 (his emphasis).

88. Baillie, *Our Knowledge of God*, 132. Also, see Bonaventura, *Sententiarum*, lib. I, dist. iii, part 1, ques. 1, in *Opera Omnia*, Tomus Primus, ed. A. C. Peltier (Paris: Ludovicus Vives, Bibliopola Editor, 1864), 66. The Latin reads, "sed Deus est ipsi animae unitus per praesentiam" (But God is united through presence to the soul itself).

known (*Deus verius cognoscitur*) through presence (*per praesentiam*).[89] There is an immediacy of the mind's experience of God, since the image of God is formed by God's truth and not mediated by some intelligence (as philosophers in Augustine's day had suggested).[90] For Bonaventura, this means that the human being "is joined with God without mediation."[91] As Augustine had said, in the future day of the Lord, "God will be seen clearly [*expresse*], at which time God will be all in all."[92] Until that time, says Bonaventura, while we are people on the journey (*viatorum*), we know God only "half-fully" (*semiplene*), but when that time comes, we will comprehend God perfectly (*perfecte*).[93]

Baillie's approach through the lens of Bonaventura seems to offer us something for my own proposal. God is present to the soul itself. Hence, "there is no reality which more directly confronts us than the reality of God."[94] While our senses may provide a more obvious connection to "reality" for humans, God's reality is "the more intimate, touching us as it does so much nearer to the core of our being."[95] It is here that I wish to build on Baillie's thought in order to extend his ideas nearer my own. How can the reality of God's presence be perceived by humans as a reality that is nearer to us than the realities of our senses? Baillie does not say precisely, but he hints at an answer: "Not all our thinking can be discursive; it must contain some element of immediacy."[96] Almost every thinker that I have studied in this area would disagree with that statement.[97] As already noted above, once reflection on any event begins, interpretation takes over, and something other than immediacy or directness is engaged by the mind.

89. Bonaventura, *Sententiarum*, lib. I, dist. iii, part 1, ques. I, 66.

90. Bonaventura, *Sententiarum*, lib. I, dist. iii, part 1, ques. II, Conclusio, 68–69.

91. Bonaventura, *Sententiarum*, lib. I, dist. iii, part 1, ques. II, Conclusio, 69. The Latin reads, "*et Deo immediate conjungitur.*" I decided to translate *immediate* (the adverb) as "without mediation," because to use the word "immediately" has more of a time orientation than is meant here.

92. As quoted by Bonaventura, *Sententiarum*, lib. I, dist. iii, part 1, ques. III, Conclusio, 70. This comes from Augustine, *De civitate Dei* 22.30. The quoted statement above from Augustine by Bonaventura is not precisely stated this way in Augustine's writings. It is a fair summary for the first part of the quote, however.

93. Bonaventura, *Sententiarium*, lib. I, dist. iii, part 1, ques. III, Conclusio, 70. Cf. Baillie's comments on this in *Our Knowledge of God*, 172–74.

94. Baillie, *Our Knowledge of God*, 155.

95. Baillie, *Our Knowledge of God*, 155.

96. Baillie, *Our Knowledge of God*, 148.

97. While engaging Balthasar's discussion of "unmediated" connection between the human spirit and the divine Spirit, Amos Yong summarizes the general belief well: "Undoubtedly, in our time, many cringe at even that denial of mediation to human experience." See Yong, *Spirit-Word-Community*, 227.

However, taking Baillie's points here, I suggest a further possibility. If the reality of God confronts us directly and is closer to us than any other reality, and if not all thinking is discursive but contains some element of immediacy, then perhaps the presence of God confronts humans directly (the Spirit of God to the spirit of the human), connecting an awareness of God's own presence in the "core of our being" (as Baillie suggests). This "core" of our being is the center of what makes you, you. Also, if God confronts us in the core of who we are, it is mostly in a precognitive, prereflective realm, prior to much mental engagement or interpretation on our part. In a very real way, our thinking is shaped by this precognitive element within the human being. Perhaps it is in this way that an encounter with God's presence connects with our core being so as to cause our interpretive mental network to respond, attempting to reflect on the encounter in such a way as to explain it to ourselves. Yet within the encounter itself, I submit that there is something unique about God's presence so that as this God confronts us, some "content" of who this God is comes across to us in a quasi-cognitive manner. It seems feasible that in this way some type of "thinking" could contain elements of immediacy. If God were not present in the medium, then we would simply have interaction with an object. Yet God's presence is unlike other presences in that it controls the effect that it has on humans and in that it is always the subject that graciously makes itself into an object of our observation for our sakes. God wants to commune and communicate with humans to such a degree that God willingly lowers Godself to our level of interaction.

So one aspect of my theology of encounter is that God is immediately present to the soul—to the core of our being—so that in this life humans can perceive God's presence directly, yet incompletely. The implication of this reality is that God is nearer to us than anyone or anything else is. The power that exists in God's presence is perceived directly at a level below or prior to our conscious thought. Yet even in the reflective cognition of the event of encounter, some of the "afterglow" of the immediacy remains, thereby affecting our interpretation of the event as well.

Another point raised by Baillie and Bonaventura recalls Paul's statement that we "know in part" (1 Cor. 13:12). We perceive God's presence directly, but this does not mean we know God exhaustively. However, Baillie has struck the right tone, it seems to me, by saying, "Even in our earthly communion with God there is something more than an earnest, a fragmentary foretaste of that which is to come, yet it too is in its measure an enjoyment of the real presence of God."[98] This seems to be precisely what Bonaventura was think-

---

98. Baillie, *Our Knowledge of God*, 172.

ing with the term *semiplene* (half-fully). The direct vision of God's face will have to wait for the final day, to be sure, but the direct encounter with God's presence can be truly experienced here and now as a foretaste of what is to come, even if it is experienced only in a portion of its fullness. I submit that such a down payment of the Spirit is a true experience of the reality of God in this life—not a full one but one brimming with the eternal life of God's nature. It is the encounter with *this God* that brings a new heart and results in a new life. The core of our being is affected, and we are changed by the presence of God. As Jürgen Moltmann says, "In the experience of the Spirit the spring of life begins to flow in us again" so that a "charismatic quickening of one's own body is already experienced even now."[99] The result is that in this present life, the experience of the Spirit "is the experience of the divine life which makes our human life something truly living."[100]

It is this *eschatological* aspect of our lives as Christians that frequently seems missing in the discussions of encountering the Spirit. While we anticipate the future eschaton and the fullness of God's presence, our lives as Christians are not simply in the future out there somewhere. The future has overlapped into the present by the Spirit's coming at Pentecost, creating a life for Christians that exists between the two ages as "already/not yet." This tension fills the New Testament. Christians live with a taste of the future eschaton here and now in this world. Eternity has entered our hearts, and the powers of the age to come have been siphoned back upon us who live in this present age. Hence, by the power and work of the Holy Spirit, Christians achieve something of a foretaste of that future in the here and now.

Perhaps theologians who deny either direct access to God or direct experiences with God have not taken into account the eschatological feature of the Christian faith and life. This is a crucial gap in the creation of a theology of direct encounters. When God's presence is among us, something of the realm of eternity meets us here and now. Yet within the limitations of our finitude, how do we describe this eternal life within us or the eternal Spirit who confronts us in our experience? While yet in this life, Christians must admit with Paul that we "see through a glass, darkly [ἐν αἰνίγματι | *en ainigmati*]," or dimly, as in a reflection of a dark glass (1 Cor. 13:12 KJV). In contrast, the reality on the final day will be seeing God "face-to-face." The Spirit, then, is a *foretaste, deposit, down payment, an advance on future payment in full* (ἀρραβῶν | *arrabōn*) (Eph. 1:14). This means the taste is not complete or perhaps not even "clear" as to what it is, yet its flavor is unmistakable. It is God

99. Moltmann, *Spirit of Life*, 95.
100. Moltmann, *Spirit of Life*, 278.

himself, not simply a mediation of our previous ideas about God. It is the Spirit himself bearing witness with our spirits that we are the children of God (Rom. 8:14–15). How does this happen with such certitude? It is because the Spirit connects with us *directly*, I suggest, so that beyond the usual cognitive categories of assessing propositional claims about things in which we might believe, the Spirit assures us by the Spirit's own person that we have been taken into the family of God. Such certitude cannot come from our debatable notions about God or what it means to be in a relationship with this God; prior to our cognitive reflection on this event through our web of knowing, we experience God the Spirit *directly*, perceiving (yet still within our limitations) God as God really is. It is this directness of which I speak when I say I have been directly encountered by God. A foretaste is not a comprehensive knowledge of the entirety of God's being; it is not an exhaustive understanding of the nature of the Triune God. In our finitude, such knowledge is beyond our ability—even a graced ability! Yet at some core level of our being, believers have experienced the Spirit of God.

Moreover, this foretaste is not simply *outside* of us, confronting us in an encounter. Christians have been given the Holy Spirit as a down payment of future redemption in eternity—a guarantee that the promises of God about our future will surely occur. We need such a guarantee *inside* of us because the external evidence battering our faith from the horrific challenges of death, suffering, and pain in this life all militate against what God has promised us in Christ Jesus. It is the Spirit of God within us who guarantees for us the reality of eternal life *in the future* because the Spirit fosters a *foretaste* of that eternal life *in the present*. Just as the Spirit cries within us, "Abba, Father," and lets us know we are the children of God, so too the Spirit's presence within us assures us that the age to come will bring us into the fullness of God's eternal life.

Let us move on from discussion of John Baillie's understanding of *mediated immediacy* to the contribution of the Swiss theologian Hans Urs von Balthasar.[101] While Balthasar does not use the full phrase "mediated immediacy," he does address the second concept as "unmediated." In a discussion of death, Balthasar notes that humans have a spirit: "For all its subspiritual dimension, the fundamental substructure of the spirit is penetrated by spirit."[102] Hence, the human's being is "directly from God and is directly oriented to God."[103]

---

101. Through reading the work of Amos Yong on Balthasar, I came to consider this Swiss theologian's views more carefully. The interaction with both Yong and Balthasar that will be evidenced below has helped me shape my own ideas on immediacy.

102. Hans Urs von Balthasar, *Explorations in Theology,* vol. 3, *Creator Spirit,* trans. Brian McNeil (San Francisco: Ignatius, 1993), 20.

103. Balthasar, *Explorations in Theology,* 3:20.

It is the eternal Spirit who relates to the human's own spirit. Balthasar could describe the human spirit as providing "an immediate orientation to God."[104] What does this mean? Amos Yong understood this to refer to the relationship between the human spirit and divine spirit as "unmediated," but that word does not occur here.[105] What seems to be described by Balthasar is a *direct orientation* to God that is established by the Spirit with human spirits. There is no real discussion of religious experience or unmediated access or immediacy of God's presence.

Where Balthasar uses the concept most clearly is later in the same work, *Creator Spirit*, where he speaks of "seeing" God and what this means. God the Spirit is the One through whom humans "see" (*sehen*). Humans hold within their inner experience of the Spirit precisely what it means to speak of God's essence as love. Because of this indwelling of the Spirit, "the question of whether there is something like an (objective) beholding of God [*wie eine (gegenständliche) Anschauung Gottes*] is superfluous [*müßig*]."[106] The answer to this question, says Balthasar, can be yes and no. Since the following words are critical for our discussion, I will provide them in my translation (which is slightly different from that of the printed ET).

> The One through whom we "behold" [*anschauen*] God is the Spirit, the non-objective mystery [*ungegenständliche Geheimnis*], which eternally breathes beyond all objectivizing [*jenseits aller Objektivierung*], in whose light, however, everything that is capable of being illuminated becomes clear and transparent. But this light essentially clarifies for us the form of the world, the highest of all, the God-Man, to whom church, humanity, and cosmos are joined [*angegliedert sind*]. *In him* we shall behold [*anschauen*] God(-Man), who reflects God to us and points out to us who the Father is. And since we shall look at him with eyes and hearts that are made like God's by the Spirit, we cannot say that this "show" [*Schau*] will only be "mediated," indirect [*vermittelte, indirekte*]. We shall "see" [*sehen*] God to the extent that God is seeable [*sehbar*] at all. God's mystery will be the light by which we shall look at his light, which is dimming/dawning in mystery.[107]

This rather dense passage from Balthasar needs careful examination. What is he saying here? In Amos Yong's view, this passage portrays the "pneumatic overcoming of the subject-object dualism" that hinders much of our modern

---

104. Balthasar, *Explorations in Theology*, 3:20.
105. Yong, *Spirit-Word-Community*, 227.
106. Balthasar, *Explorations in Theology*, 3:112. For the original German text, see Balthasar, *Spiritus Creator*, in Skizzen zur Theologie 3 (Einsiedeln: Johannes Verlag, 1967), 101.
107. Balthasar, *Spiritus Creator*, 101 (his emphasis, my trans.).

thinking.[108] Perhaps this is true, but I am not sure that this is all the passage is doing. The tradition of "seeing" God hearkens back to the ancient Christian thinkers (esp. Augustine) who speak of the "blessed vision" or "beatific vision" of seeing God face-to-face. Some theologians and mystics of the Middle Ages thought that an ecstatic visionary experience of God was possible in this life as the highest form of capturing some sight of God on this side of eternity. Is that what Balthasar is attempting to show here—a mystical beatific vision? No, it seems there is something more going on in his approach, although the beatific vision is certainly a part of the background for his statements.

Here is how I summarize the high points of this quote and their significance. First, the Spirit of God is the means by which humans "see" God—to some degree in this life but in fullness of sight in the next life. Second, the Spirit of God is the "nonobjective mystery" who in his eternal spiration is "beyond all objectivizing." I take this to mean that the Spirit cannot be an object (in the usual sense of that term) for Balthasar. Instead, the Spirit is the ontic basis on which all experience of subjects and objects operates. It is this that I think Yong points to in understanding that Balthasar is attempting to overcome the dualism between subject and object. Third, only in the life of the Spirit can anything be seen clearly, since it is the Spirit who makes everything clear. Yet this light only seems to clarify things that already have the "form of the world" (*das Weltförme*), such as the church, humankind, and the whole cosmos joined in the God-Man. Fourth, it is through this God-Man that we see a *reflection* of who God is.

At this point in the statement, however, the tense of the verbs turns entirely to the future: we *shall see* God with divinized eyes and hearts; we *shall see* God to the extent that God is seeable at all. Balthasar has turned his attention to the eschaton, when we will have eyes that are able to see God directly. Therefore, in the eschaton our vision of God cannot be described as "mediated, indirect." It can only be immediate and direct.

So it seems that the Spirit assists humans in this life to "behold" God in some sense here and now. This vision is not the direct one of the future, but rather mediated and indirect in the present. Neither the Triune God nor the Spirit of God can be "seen" in this life because the Spirit is "beyond all objectivizing"—that is, beyond our attempts to lasso the Spirit into the categories of our own understanding. God is not an object of our minds and will not be made into such. God is bigger than our minds' ability to make God into an object. However, Balthasar suggests that the clarifying power of the Spirit's light is to illumine things that are objects in this life—in par-

108. Yong, *Spirit-Word-Community*, 228.

ticular, the God-Man. Since everything is incorporated into the God-Man, when that One is clarified by the Spirit, then all things in the form of the world are illumined. Only the future will hold a directness of sight without mediation.

Amos Yong interprets Balthasar here as yielding too much to finite human minds with his notion of "radical 'unmediatedness.'"[109] Finite minds cannot access the infinite God.[110] Therefore, Yong concludes, "Von Balthasar's radical 'unmediatedness' should therefore be qualified as a 'mediated immediacy.'"[111] Yet without further explanation about why this fits Balthasar's meaning in this passage, Yong simply points to the fact that humans know "in the Spirit" and "by and through the Spirit."[112] Which of these aspects is mediated, and which is immediate?[113]

This brings us to a further examination of Yong on the question of mediated immediacy. For our purposes, we will consider the question that Yong provides related to our proposal: Is there a "direct experience of the divine apart from our experiences of and with each other and the world?"[114] In response to this question, Yong examines the "explicit theological mediations" of the incarnation and Pentecost.[115] Are these cases direct experiences of God by humans?

With regard to the incarnation, Yong believes that even with the Son of God in the flesh, there is no direct experience with God. If one responds that surely there is a face-to-face experience with those alive at the time of Christ, Yong offers the rejoinder that Peter's confession that Jesus is the Messiah (Matt. 16:17) was *revealed* to him, not arrived at through the usual cognitive methods. Hence, "the encounter with the divine through Jesus of Nazareth

109. This is Yong's term for Balthasar's approach. Yong, *Spirit-Word-Community*, 229.

110. Yong reads Balthasar here as attempting to exalt the human imagination as an "autonomous faculty." He thinks Balthasar has made humans into creatures who have the capacity to engage God directly. Yong seems to fault him for not acknowledging the contingency of creatureliness and for not noting the need for the Spirit's work in knowing God. Yong, *Spirit-Word-Community*, 229. I do not think that this was what Balthasar was doing in this section, but I fully admit that he used rather obtuse language—I am uncertain what much of what he says here may mean. (E.g., how can God's mystery be the light by which we shall see his light in the twilight of mystery, or as I try to make sense of it in my translation, ". . . his light, which is dawning [or dimming?] in mystery"?)

111. Yong, *Spirit-Word-Community*, 229.

112. Yong, *Spirit-Word-Community*, 229.

113. A further question is which aspect of Balthasar's statement refers to "beholding" *in this life* (and therefore, presumably a mediated vision) and "beholding" *in the next life* (and therefore a direct, immediate vision). It does not seem that Yong has noted these differences in "beholding" from Balthasar's own text.

114. Yong, *Spirit-Word-Community*, 207.

115. Yong, *Spirit-Word-Community*, 207.

is therefore unavoidably semiotic," which means that the flesh of the Son of God in Jesus was a "sign" that could be used to interpret perceptions and facts.[116] Only the Spirit of God could give someone the inspiration that Jesus was the Messiah, the Son of God. In one cogent passage, Yong explains his answer to the question of whether or not there is a direct religious experience of God through the Spirit.

> Put epistemically, all knowledge is semiotically mediated and therefore at least one step (or sign) removed from the richness of experience. Put experientially, the first Christians experienced the Spirit through the violent rushing wind, through the tongues of fire which alighted on each of them, through stammering lips and strange tongues, all of which were interpreted or understood, at least in part, through the sacred writings. . . . Put theologically, Christians experience Jesus through the pneumatically constituted body of Christ.[117]

So, is there a direct experience of God through the Spirit? Yong suggests that from the standpoint of knowledge (epistemically), it must be answered no, since all knowledge is *mediated* and therefore indirect. Reflection on the experience, then, is always one step removed from the experience itself. From the standpoint of experience (experientially), even here the Spirit on the day of Pentecost is experienced *through* the mediated signs of rushing wind, tongues of fire, and speaking in tongues, and so the question must again be answered no. As Yong says elsewhere, "pure experiences" are not available for reflection.[118] From the standpoint of theology (theologically), the experience of Jesus Christ comes through the community of believers.[119]

Are there direct experiences of the divine for Yong? This is very difficult to discern because Yong's focus is on the role of the Spirit, Word, and community in "continuous interplay" to provide theological interpretation of our experiences.[120] Therefore, Yong provides a theology of interpretation of experience within the religious realm, but he has very little to say about the experience with God itself. This is only appropriate for one who believes that "pure experiences

---

116. Yong, *Spirit-Word-Community*, 208.

117. Yong, *Spirit-Word-Community*, 208.

118. Yong, *Spirit-Word-Community*, 247.

119. While Yong's entire book is an effort to bring the normative character of these experiences into the purview of the community of believers, at this point he does not explain how he understands the "pneumatically constituted body of Christ" to operate theologically in helping Christians to perceive this experience of Jesus Christ. A more general way that the role of discernment operates in the community with regard to experiences is offered later, but this still does not elucidate how the community helps "Christians experience Jesus." See Yong, *Spirit-Word-Community*, 252–53.

120. Yong, *Spirit-Word-Community*, 245.

are unavailable for reflection."[121] However, throughout the text Yong seems to imply that experiences with the divine are the basis for our second-order interpretations. The difficulty seems to be that we cannot say anything about these experiences themselves, only the interpretation of them (which is always one step removed from the experience itself). Even Scripture, he suggests, is "interpreted experience," so we cannot interpret Scripture directly but are "at least twice removed from the reality described by what has been understood as the primary (biblical and traditional) sources of theology."[122]

Are there direct experiences of the divine for Yong? Yong's basic thesis is to "argue that the Christian experience of God, whether breaking upon the believer as radically other or mediated liturgically, ritually, mystically, or otherwise, is fundamental to the data of theological interpretation."[123] From this statement and others like it, Yong seems to be open to such experiences of God as "radically other" and therefore unmediated, but in reality, he does not explain what this means or what it might look like. His focus has remained on the second-order reflection of experience, which is actually the only *theologically and epistemically* relevant avenue for discussion.

Thus, the answer for Yong with regard to direct experiences of the divine seems to be this: yes, we may have them, but we cannot really talk about them. We can only experience them, and then our reflective interpretation takes over.[124] The effect of this approach is essentially to nullify the experience with God for use in normative ethics and for theological reflection. I propose that we need to examine the experience with God more carefully and try to come to an understanding of the impact that such an experience can have on human beings. Admittedly, this will require some discursive reflection on an event that may push such reflection to its outer rim, but I contend that inferences can be made regarding this event. These inferences can help to shape a theology of encounter with the divine.

A Proposal for a Theology of Encounter

In all that has been examined above in this chapter, there has been some clarity offered on the issue of mediation of God's presence. However, what

121. Yong, *Spirit-Word-Community*, 247.
122. Yong, *Spirit-Word-Community*, 247.
123. Yong, *Spirit-Word-Community*, 252.
124. Yong's trialectic of Spirit, Word, and community is a powerful model for interpretation and reflection on experience. My own preference is to say more about the direct experiences with God so that what confronts us is God's presence, which is transformative at a core level of our being. At that point, the epistemic reflection on the experience with God can follow Yong's plan quite well.

seems missing in all of these accounts is the meaning of the *immediacy* of God's presence in the divine-human encounter. My proposal for a theology of encounter attempts to develop this dimension and delineate ramifications for the people of God's presence.

Allow me to state up front my theological conclusion of this section. I believe that God's Spirit encounters humans at a core level of their being (namely, the human spirit) in a primordial event that causes "pure experiences" of God's presence. Such a primordial encounter with God exists at a prereflective, preinterpretive level, creating an impact on humans that may (or may not) bring about a personal relationship between God and the person. Our experiences of these encounters may be said to be "direct"—that is, unmediated—even though they may come to us through mediated forms. We may call this direct yet mediated encounter a *mediated immediacy.* God's presence directly encounters our own lives in ways that command our attention and require our response (the initial potentially salvific encounter); further encounters with God's Spirit within the context of the people of God (the church) help to make us aware of the indwelling of the Spirit so that we all may be shaped into the image of Christ. Essentially, initial encounters with God may lead toward salvation, a relationship with God; further encounters, both individually and corporately, may bring about transformation so that the nature of God becomes the nature of believers.

I believe that pure experiences with God *are available* for reflection but are not available like other objects that humans encounter in this world and therefore may not be examined or discussed in the same way as one describes experiences of other things. When we begin to reflect on these encounters, we stumble over how to express what happened. Storytelling, narrative, or testimony are the more appropriate ways of engaging these encounters; that is, they are more suited to the object of their inquiry. However, since they are not discursive in the sense that the core of the event is precognitive or prereflective, they are not easily explained in usual theological language.

What follows is a theology of encounter revolving around three aspects: firsthand encounters, secondhand reflections, and witnessing to the encounters. Using the material already provided in this chapter, I shall offer an explanation for the meaning of each of these aspects.

Firsthand Encounters

By "encounters experienced firsthand," I refer to the direct, unmediated experience that I have previously called a "primordial event." God's presence through the Holy Spirit confronts the human spirit directly. By pointing to the human spirit as the point of connection with God's Spirit, I am *not* arguing that the more important part of the human being is spirit; neither am I arguing for some Platonic division of body and soul. I am proposing that God *connects* with humans through the spiritual dimension of their creaturehood; from there, God's presence radiates throughout the body as well, bringing the whole human being into the encounter. However one might wish to describe it, I submit that the image of God in which humans were created was for the purpose of communication and connection between God and humans. To no other creature was this gift of the *imago Dei* given.

Following Paul's logic as portrayed in 1 Corinthians 2:9–16, it is the Spirit of God who "searches all things, even the deep things of God" (2:10b). Paul provides something like an "analogy of the Spirit," stating that a person's own thoughts are known by the spirit of the person. "In the same way no one knows the thoughts of God except the Spirit of God" (2:11b). The analogy here is strongly suggestive: our spirits come to know God's Spirit by the spiritual connection between them. James Loder suggests, "We know the Holy Spirit as such only through the self as spirit; we know the Spirit only in his own medium, so to say."[125]

So the divine-human encounter probably takes place between the divine Spirit and the human spirit. What can be said about this encounter from the divine side? We have already seen that theologians and philosophers of religion suggest that it is impossible to think or provide discourse about this encounter with God's presence since it is prereflective. If this is granted, then there is precious little—if anything!—that we can say about who or what has encountered us, only our inchoate impressions or beliefs about it. If we only allow for the encounter to be meaningful for humans on the basis of *cognitive reflection*, then we will always be one step removed from the experience itself.

Throughout this book I have argued for a *direct* encounter with God's presence that brings about transformation. By this I do not simply mean that such transformation occurs only upon theological reflection on the primordial event. Somehow within the event of encounter with God, the true and living God confronts us, Spirit to spirit. Landing in the core of our being at a point that is precognitive, the Spirit of God, who searches the heart of God and knows the very center of God's essence, encounters us by entering our own hearts (core of our being) and exposes us to this numinous presence and power. Hence, before the human mind engages in interpretation or questioning about who or what the encounter was, the presence of the Spirit

125. James E. Loder, *The Transforming Moment*, 2nd ed. (Colorado Springs: Helmers & Howard, 1989), 93.

has connected with us in order to bring within us an awareness of God's direct presence.

God, then, confronts us with a directness that is genuine yet not complete in its eschatological fullness. What does this mean for the human side of the encounter? In the last century, much has been written concerning the role of prereflective or precognitive experiences. At this point in human understanding of the way experience and reality interact with our brains, we may not be able to offer a detailed analysis of these realities but only pointers to a possibility for how this occurs. After all, if something is precognitive, then by definition it seems to be out of bounds to describe, discuss, or even place into language what we have experienced. Or is it?

I submit that these precognitive experiences help to shape our understanding of the world, especially how we may live in it (or how we are oriented to function in it). Said another way, these primordial experiences shape our basic orientation to the world (and to God). Instead of ignoring such experiences as trivial in the overall framework of human life, philosophers and theologians of the last century have been raising questions and proposing answers concerning the ramifications elicited by them. Some of their proposals help to provide a foundation for my theology of divine-human encounter.

First, what do I mean by "precognitive experience"? The presence of the Spirit of God engages the human spirit below (or above) the level of cognitive awareness, sparking an experience in human beings that makes them aware that God is present to them. As noted earlier in this chapter, William Alston suggested something like this when he spoke of a house that "is presented" to our consciousness, and therefore something of which I am *directly aware*. Such direct awareness is different, he suggests, from conceptualizing, believing, or interpreting the house. A house presents itself to our experience, and we are directly aware of it. It seems reasonable to suggest that not all human experiences of objects demand conceptualization through sense perception. Could not God present himself to us *directly*, causing an awareness of God's presence that is similar to the awareness of the house?[126]

Is it not feasible that the God who created human beings knows how best to contact them at a deep level of their being, communicating God's own presence to their awareness even before they have an ability to reflect on it?

If this sounds too fantastical, allow me to sketch some ideas about precognitive experiences that have arisen in recent years. First, Eleonore Stump, a professor of philosophy, has recently provided an astounding attempt to

126. Alston, *Perceiving God*, 20–23.

Compulsion and God's Direct Presence

A word needs to be said here about the potentially compelling power of a direct encounter with the divine presence. If God were to present himself to humans directly without any "buffer," would that alone not compel humans so encountered to fall to their knees, proclaiming the lordship of this God? I believe so. Those who see salvation more in Calvin's terms of God's election have it simpler here; they can say that God directly confronts only those predestined to become sons and daughters. Since I do not hold to such a form of predestination, how do I explain that God's presence could confront us directly and engage our core without producing (almost automatically) a confession of faith?

Here my response is nuanced. First, our finitude and sin limit the human experience. Humans may distort genuine experiences with God or even twist them into something idolatrous. The human heart can be deceitful (Jer. 17:9). Second, the compelling power of God's presence leads to a confession that Jesus Christ is Lord by everyone only in the eschaton (Phil. 2:10–11), when every knee will bow and every tongue confess. So, the face-to-face vision of God in the eternal realm is *the* compelling presence. However, in our present situation, we must walk by faith, not sight. In other words, the Spirit-to-spirit encounter is not "fixed" so that the human recipient is compelled to say yes to God. Even in the most overwhelming and direct encounters with God's presence, enough hiddenness remains that the heart must come to *believe* that the divine presence engaging it is truly the God who raised Jesus Christ from the dead by the Spirit's power.

What do these encounters mean when experienced in the church by God's people? In this chapter's last section, I offer my understanding for salvific encounters in contrast with ongoing encounters. At this point, however, I am concerned mainly with the initial encounters by the Spirit that move one toward confessing Jesus Christ as Savior.

respond to the problem of suffering. Her book *Wandering in Darkness*[127] has much to commend it, but for our purposes I highlight a segment early in her effort to lay out the way human beings know. Using a broad typology, which she admits has weaknesses but is useful for sketching differences, Stump sketches two distinct ways of knowing as portrayed by two medieval monks, Dominic and Francis. She calls the two different ways of knowing "Dominican" and

127. Eleonore Stump, *Wandering in Darkness: Narrative and the Problem of Suffering* (Oxford: Clarendon, 2010).

"Franciscan." Dominican knowledge, as forged by Thomas Aquinas and many others, is knowledge *that* something is true or can be portrayed in propositional form. Knowledge *that* is the usual form of capturing objects within propositional language. It is the knowledge of a more "ordinary philosophical kind."[128] Franciscan knowledge suggests a knowledge that "cannot be reduced to knowledge *that*."[129] Knowing colors may be one such type of knowledge that cannot be reduced to knowing *that*.

How does this relate to our proposal? From this general approach to epistemology, Stump proceeds to engage in a specific type of knowing: the knowledge of persons. Is it possible that some dimensions of knowing people can be more than propositional, more than knowledge *that*?

Stump affirms that this is the case and leads us through a variety of convincing examples. However, it is her reflection on mirror neurons and the deficits that autism brings to social cognition that draws my attention. Prelinguistic infants are able to differentiate people from things. This type of social cognition is necessary for language development and other cognitive tasks. Yet, as Stump notes, this type of knowledge (that a prelinguistic infant can tell the difference between people and things) cannot be knowledge *that*, because such an infant is not capable of knowledge *about* people. This infant *can* know her mother and even know some of her mother's mental states, but not in any way that we could now call propositional or knowledge *that*.[130] From the research she presents, Stump notes that some autistic children have this aspect of "direct knowledge of persons and their mental states" impaired and therefore cannot recognize the same signs that a child without autism might readily experience.[131] Direct knowledge of persons and their mental states is very different from knowledge *that*. What if a precognitive encounter with God at the core of our being is analogous to a prelinguistic infant's direct knowledge of persons and their mental states?

Stump moves on to establish her points about Franciscan knowledge even more. Shifting to a discussion of the philosophy of art, Stump calls on Dominic McIver Lopes to analyze the aspects of knowledge gleaned from a painting. Lopes speaks of three types of knowledge arising from studying art: knowledge *about*, knowledge *through*, and knowledge *in*.[132] Observing

---

128. Stump, *Wandering in Darkness*, 51.
129. Stump, *Wandering in Darkness*, 51 (her emphasis).
130. Stump, *Wandering in Darkness*, 66.
131. Stump, *Wandering in Darkness*, 66.
132. Dominic McIver Lopes, *Sight and Sensibility: Evaluating Pictures* (Oxford: Clarendon, 2005), 133–34. Stump examines only knowledge *about* and knowledge *in*. See Stump, *Wandering in Darkness*, 72.

a painting (like Rembrandt's *Belshazzar's Feast*), one may learn *about* the painting—that it was by Rembrandt, that it was painted with oils, that it depicted God's handwriting on the wall. These speak to the picture's properties, information *about* the picture and therefore knowledge *about*. In addition to this type of knowledge, we may infer from paintings facts about their makers and the historical settings. This is what Lopes calls "knowledge *through*" the picture. For example, one may learn that Rembrandt had some sense of the Hebrew language in order to write the letters on the wall or that the biblical figures were portrayed in the dress of the Dutch from the 1600s. Finally, there is a knowledge *in* the picture: the moral or lesson of the portraiture. This is gained by "seeing into" the picture.[133] Lopes argues that these three forms of knowledge are different because "they have different kinds of contents."[134]

Lopes concludes that knowledge *in* is not "propositional knowledge amenable to analysis by the standard, triadic account of knowledge. It is a different creature entirely."[135] What is this type of direct knowledge *in*? Stump suggests it is "analogous to the knowledge of persons, not only in the sense that it is not reducible to knowledge *that*, but also in the sense that it is immediate, intuitive, and difficult to articulate in language."[136] There exists a knowledge that does not resolve into grammatical syntax or linguistic propositions; it is a knowledge that is more direct and immediate, like the knowledge of persons. What if our encounters with God were along these lines, pointing to the depth of our beings with a truth that is experiential yet not expressible in ways to which our languages are accustomed? Indeed, perhaps it is something of this amazing overflow of direct experience of God that occurred on the day of Pentecost, causing men and women to bypass the usual hemispheres of the brain where linguistic control is located and speak in languages not their own. Perhaps.

Akin to the views of Stump and Lopes concerning knowledge, the direction of philosopher James K. A. Smith is most instructive. While Smith is after something a bit different from the others, he still provides a possible way to view what may be shaping our precognitive experiences, which in turn may shape our knowledge of things. Smith makes the point that as embodied creatures, humans are affected by their dispositions or "adaptive unconscious" at a level that is noncognitive.[137] While attempting to argue for worldviews

---

133. Stump, *Wandering in Darkness*, 72.

134. Lopes, *Sight and Sensibility*, 134.

135. Lopes, *Sight and Sensibility*, 144.

136. Stump, *Wandering in Darkness*, 72.

137. James K. A. Smith, *Desiring the Kingdom: Worship, Worldview, and Cultural Formation*, Cultural Liturgies 1 (Grand Rapids: Baker Academic, 2009), 58. He brilliantly summarizes his point about embodiment: "We are not conscious minds or souls 'housed' in meaty containers;

that help to shape our desire, Smith notes that frequently we have thought of worldview-making as an entirely cognitive endeavor, influenced by theory not praxis. Using the insights gleaned from Martin Heidegger and Charles Taylor, Smith carefully exposes the flaw of focusing solely on the cognitive realm without considering the "affective" realm (composed of "cares, concerns, motivations, and desires").[138] In another context, Smith talks of "fundamental beliefs" whereby we hold to beliefs that are "pretheoretical," yet are often not "consciously, rationally reflect[ed] on."[139] Such "control beliefs" operate "subterraneously."[140]

While we do not need to dive deeply into Heidegger to grasp the significance of his phenomenalistic approach to human knowing, we do need to connect the lines from his thinking to Smith's concept of the pretheoretical (and from there to Charles Taylor's social imaginary). This will help to establish the case for dispositional, noncognitive experiences that affect our everyday orientation to God and the world.

Within Heidegger's phenomenological approach to existence, we find the age-old question, What is being?[141] His answer sidestepped the usual response, which portrayed "being" as some type of substance, preferring instead to investigate the everydayness (*Alltäglichkeit*) of human existence.[142] What Heidegger proposed is that "being" is not a substance or entity but rather a "being-in-the-world" or a "being-there" (*Da-sein*). This word, *Dasein*, describes the type of being that human beings have.[143] *Dasein* is human existence itself, not properties that can be investigated like objects but rather the *possibility* of being in a variety of ways.[144] *Dasein* is not a "what," but the real "thereness" of something.[145]

---

we are selves who *are* our bodies; thus the training of desire requires bodily practices in which a particular *telos* is embedded" (Smith, *Desiring the Kingdom*, 62 [his emphasis]).

138. Smith, *Desiring the Kingdom*, 64, esp. the chart.

139. James K. A. Smith, *Thinking in Tongues: Pentecostal Contributions to Christian Philosophy*, Pentecostal Manifestos, ed. James K. A. Smith and Amos Yong (Grand Rapids: Eerdmans, 2010), 28.

140. Smith, *Thinking in Tongues*, 28.

141. Martin Heidegger, *Being and Time*, trans. Joan Stambaugh and Dennis J. Schmidt, SUNY Series in Contemporary Continental Philosophy, ed. Dennis J. Schmidt (Albany: State University of New York Press, 2010), §1, 2–4. Cf. Martin Heidegger, *Sein und Zeit*, 7th ed. (Tübingen: Max Niemeyer, 1953; orig. ed., 1927), §1, 2–4.

142. Heidegger, *Being and Time*, §5, 16–17; Heidegger, *Sein und Zeit*, §5, 16–17.

143. Heidegger, *Being and Time*, §6, 21–22; Heidegger, *Sein und Zeit*, §6, 15–17.

144. Heidegger, *Being and Time*, §9, 42; Heidegger, *Sein und Zeit*, §9, 42.

145. Magda King, *Heidegger's Philosophy: A Guide to His Basic Thought* (New York: Macmillan, 1964), 67. For a full discussion of *Dasein* and its meaning for Heidegger, see Stephen Mulhall, *Routledge Philosophy Guidebook to Heidegger and "Being and Time"* (London: Routledge, 1996), 12–15.

How does Heidegger's philosophy relate to our discussion of direct experiences of God? The relation arises from his proposal concerning *understanding* (*Verstehen*). The process of understanding does not refer to an intellectual exercise, as one might assume from the term. Instead, understanding refers to how *Dasein* operates at the "ground level" of human existence.[146] Understanding is "the preconceptual extension of human being throughout the world-extensive field of possibility."[147] What this means for Heidegger is that there is something at work in the way humans exist in the world that provides them with a preconceptual grasp of what will be interpreted. Understanding is *not* an interpretive grasp (that would require intellectual reflection) of what is "given" beforehand. Instead, it is the "primordial occurrence of what is to be interpreted, occurrence that bears toward us and in this bearing-toward first grants the possibility of our comprehending it."[148] This is how humans exist in the world—through understanding as an "occurrence of being" that "bears-toward" us, yet without "any subjective coloring or illumination of that which is pregiven."[149] Thus, preceding any particular presence is some type of presentment of that presence.

To put this in more straightforward language, the human way of being-in-the-world is through understanding. "This unique character of man, that he exists understandingly, is not confined merely to his thinking or cognitive activities, but a priori determines all the ways in which he can be."[150] Described in this way, understanding is different from theoretical cognition; it involves *pre*conceptuality. What does this mean? "No interpretation of an object could conceivably be free of preconceptions, because without some preliminary orientation, however primitive, it would be impossible to grasp the object at all: we would have no sense of what it was we were attempting to interpret."[151] Yet this does not imply that subjectivism or prejudice is involved in all interpretation. An example frequently given is this: How do we humans grasp the significance or meaning of a hammer? If one did not know in general what a *tool* was, it would be difficult, if not impossible, to understand the meaning of a hammer. Such *understanding* is shaped with some cognitive input, to be sure, but the point is that prior to this cognition there must be a foundation upon which it is based, a type of locating of the

---

146. Robert P. Orr, *The Meaning of Transcendence: A Heideggerian Reflection*, AAR Dissertation Series 35, ed. Wendell Dietrich (Chico, CA: Scholars Press, 1981), 71.

147. Orr, *The Meaning of Transcendence*, 71.

148. Orr, *The Meaning of Transcendence*, 72.

149. Orr, *The Meaning of Transcendence*, 73.

150. King, *Heidegger's Philosophy*, 27.

151. Mulhall, *Routledge Philosophy Guidebook to Heidegger*, 88.

Heidegger's Three Structures of Human Existence

For Heidegger, there are basic structures in human existence, three of which produce a disclosing of being: (1) attunement (*Befindlichkeit*); (2) understanding (*Verstehen*); and (3) speech (*Rede*).[a] Only the first two aspects connect with our thesis. We have discussed *Verstehen* in the main text, but some aspects of *Befindlichkeit*, or "attunement," may be beneficial.

Attunement is a process of disclosing one's moods or feelings. Coming from the German verb *befinden*, it points toward how one may be *feeling*. The moods (*Stimmung*) of humans reveal something about the way a human being exists—a way of being. Heidegger suggests that moods can be very important because they show what a person "factually" is. A mode of awareness is termed "mood" by Heidegger, coming from the German word *Stimme* (voice) and the verb *stimmen* (to tune or be in tune with).[b] Such "moods" are not the equivalent of interior feelings: a mood "names the affective state of being attuned to something."[c] Moods come about from humans' "thrownness" into the universe, the fact that a human finds herself already here and can never "get behind this already."[d]

hammer within the broader "genre" of instrument. Whatever is "foregoing" (*vorgängig*), experience takes it by the hand, as it were, and leads it. It is a priori and preconceptual in this sense.

Heidegger posits that *understanding* (*Verstehen*) is relegated to the preconceptual realm; it does not lodge in the cognitive region but in "the more affective region, which is 'closer' to the body."[152] Therefore, understanding is quite different from *knowing* or *knowledge* (*Wissen*). Knowledge is relegated to the cognitive realm, to the mind or brain of a human. It grasps an object with the intellect, thereby producing propositional and theoretical statements/ideas about the object. In this respect, *Wissen* (knowledge) is similar to Stump's description of "knowing *that*" or Lopes's "knowing *about*." *Verstehen* (understanding) is similar to Stump's Franciscan knowledge or "direct knowledge of persons" that cannot be reduced to knowing *that*; it also has features similar to Lopes's "knowing *in*."

As Jamie Smith elaborates, "Understanding" (*Verstehen*) may be an "inarticulate understanding of our whole situation" and thereby provide a "back-

152. Smith, *Desiring the Kingdom*, 65.

Yet moods do not disclose the world by themselves; understanding must help. The understanding (*Verstehen*) of humans is not "theoretical cognition" but preconceptual.[e] Yet in attempting to offer a more conceptual analysis of *Verstehen*, Heidegger points to the idea of interpretation (*Auslegung*). He states, "In interpreting, we do not, so to speak, throw a 'signification' over some naked thing which is present-at-hand [*zuhanden*], we do not stick a value on it; but when something within-the-world is encountered as such, the thing in question already has an involvement which is disclosed in our understanding of the world, and this involvement is one which gets laid out by the interpretation."[f] When humans interpret an object in the world, they have this object "in advance" of their interpretations.[g]

a. See King, *Heidegger's Philosophy*, 76.
b. See Orr, *The Meaning of Transcendence*, 94.
c. Orr, *The Meaning of Transcendence*, 94.
d. Orr, *The Meaning of Transcendence*, 78.
e. See Michael Inwood, *Heidegger: A Very Short Introduction* (Oxford: Oxford University Press, 1997), 44.
f. Heidegger, *Being and Time*, §32, 150; Heidegger, *Sein und Zeit*, §32, 149–50.
g. Heidegger names three "advance" aspects: *Vorhabe* (fore-having), *Vorsicht* (fore-sight), and *Vorgriff* (fore-conception). See Heidegger, *Being and Time*, §32, 150; *Sein und Zeit*, §32, 150.

ground" to the more theoretical knowledge (*Wissen*).[153] This does not mean that our precognitive understanding is the only way to knowledge but that both *Verstehen* and *Wissen* are necessary in our world in order to understand how we are oriented to navigate it. Hence, for our proposal, adding something like *Verstehen* to the process does not propel it forward as an anti-intellectual approach to God or knowing God. Rather, it suggests that adding this dimension of understanding that is prereflective and inarticulate "displaces a *fixation* on the rational or cognitive, emphasizing that even 'knowledge' is situated by desire/love."[154]

153. Smith, *Desiring the Kingdom*, 65–66. Smith is quoting Charles Taylor, *Modern Social Imaginaries* (Durham, NC: Duke University Press, 2004), 25. Similar discussion is found in Charles Taylor, *A Secular Age* (Cambridge, MA: Harvard University Press, 2007), esp. 172–73.
154. Smith, *Desiring the Kingdom*, 64, from the text of the chart (his emphasis). For his purposes, Smith is drawn more toward the communal, social aspect of Taylor's *social imaginary*. I have chosen to focus more on the description of Heidegger's *Verstehen*, which is the basis for Taylor's social imaginary. It seems feasible, however, that Amos Yong's proposal for a "pneumatological imagination" is also along these lines, as Smith himself admits. See Smith, *Thinking in Tongues*, 30. Also see Yong, *Spirit-Word-Community*, 119–21, for a general description

Given the discussion to this point, we have some reasons to suggest that at least a few aspects of human understanding may be influenced at a noncognitive and prereflective depth. In this proposal for a theology of the divine-human encounter, I am suggesting that the firsthand encounter with God is formative at some core level of the embodied creature (the human). Theologically speaking, the locus of God's encounter with humans seems to occur in the "heart." This biblical term expresses a sense of the core level of the human being without making the human into a soul sealed within a "meaty container" (as Smith has described such views)[155] and without losing the importance of the bodily senses for obtaining knowledge of God. While the heart can be "devious above all else" and "perverse" (Jer. 17:9 NRSV), the Bible also describes it as the metaphorical location for what is essential in the human being. Not everything that encounters the heart can be put in propositional language. Not everything the heart believes can be proved by the empirical sciences. There is more to the divine-human encounter than can be encompassed by reason alone! Humans are quite a bit more than "brains on a stick," as one of my bright students expressed it.

To say that God the Spirit encounters humans directly and immediately at the core of their being is to say that there is more to the Christian faith than intellectual assent. Having been encountered by the Spirit of God with the truth about Christ and the gospel, humans become convinced of their standing before God as one of sinfulness, thereby creating a crisis of decision. Will I agree with God's assessment and repent? Will I agree with God's assessment and not repent? Will I disagree with God's assessment or even admit that God confronted me?

If I repent, the Spirit brings me into a new relationship with the risen Christ, whom he presents to me as if two thousand years had not passed. The impression left upon me in that encounter moves me to act. The person of Christ, as conveyed by the Spirit's power to the inner core of my being, begins to transform my life, a transformation that will continue through my earthly existence, shaping me more and more into the contours of Christ. It is the identity of God that confronts us, resulting in an experience that is transformative.[156]

Therefore, if God is truly present to all of us (even though not all of us are aware of this presence), then "we all have first-hand apprehensions of God and not merely second-hand beliefs about him. We know God not only by

of the section titled "The Pneumatological Imagination"; and 133–41 for development of his ideas in particular.

155. Smith, *Desiring the Kingdom*, 62.

156. Henry H. Knight III, *The Presence of God in the Christian Life: John Wesley and the Means of Grace*, Pietist and Wesleyan Studies 3 (Lanham, MD: Scarecrow, 1992), 129.

hearsay, but because God is at work in our lives, whether we are aware of it or not."[157] Knowing only *about* God is not adequate for a personal relationship with God. As Dalferth asserts, "We must have first-hand knowledge of [God's] presence to our own life and not merely second-hand knowledge about his presence to some other life."[158] Hence, firsthand experiential knowledge is vitally important for the Christian faith.

However, if the firsthand encounter is noncognitive, how can I use language and propositions to describe it? Isn't such an encounter beyond describing with propositional (knowing *that*) language? Is there any *content* from the revelatory encounter that can be carried over into reflection? It is my belief that this personal revelation engages the entirety of our human essence and existence, causing us to turn our attention to a different goal in life. We experience a reorientation of our core values and especially a shift in the things we desire. To say there is no "content" in such an experience is to lock our thinking into a propositionalist-only world in which experience does not count for truth. Entire theological enterprises still remain in twenty-first-century Christianity that latch onto propositionalism as if any experience with God were sordid subjectivism lacking the dignity of the faith. Yet it seems that such enterprises remain unable to answer a simple question: If Jesus is "the way and the truth and the life" (John 14:6), then doesn't that mean, at least in some sense, that truth is found in a person? To cleave the personal from the propositional damages the integrity of Christianity. I argue that at the core of evangelical experience of the gospel of Jesus Christ is an encounter that must be had with the risen Lord through the agency of the Spirit. Without such an encounter, I no longer have an existential, experiential framework for my Christian faith.

Here is where the radical nature of my proposal lands hard. Without humans experiencing a firsthand encounter with the Triune God in something like what I have described above as a primordial event, I have serious reservations that such humans can become committed followers of Jesus Christ. In turn, this affects the nature and composition of the church, the collected "people of God."

For now, however, I will turn to the question of what happens with such encounters once thinking and reflection engage the mind.

Secondhand Reflection

The second level of consideration in a theology of encounter is that of the secondhand or second-order reflection on the primary experience with God.

---

157. Dalferth, "Representing God's Presence," 253.
158. Dalferth, "Representing God's Presence," 254.

For the next few paragraphs, I will sketch what this may look like for an individual; later I will outline its meaning for the gathered people of God. As Amos Yong has noted, experience is "both phenomenologically and logically prior to reflection and the second-order activity of theologizing."[159] The primordial event that we have described in the firsthand encounter with God is an experience that seems to operate at nonconceptual levels.[160] How might we come to understand more about this raw experience with God? As we have already noted, the process of thinking or reflecting moves us into an interpretive mode that seems to be one step removed from the prior mode of pure experience. There are some obvious limitations to this second-order step, one of which is that humans reflect on experience but cannot encompass the whole of their experiences. In other words, humans have slices of experiences that we concentrate on, but our finitude limits how much of those experiences we can consider—or even better expressed, humans can never grasp the whole of experience at once. Our reflections "do not engage the entirety of our experiences."[161] Another limitation may be the difficulty in discerning the accuracy of our interpretations/reflections on the primal experiences. As mentioned earlier, Amos Yong argues that "pure experiences" are "unavailable for reflection."[162] While I am not entirely clear what he might mean by this, I argue that pure experiences with God (what I have called primordial events) *are* available for reflection.[163] To be sure, thinking involves interpretation, but this does not demand that we surrender to the host of influences on our interpretive webs and give up any feasible way to secure some theological reflection that is congruent with the experience of God. In this secondhand experience, then, the human mind reflects on who or what has been experienced in the encounter with the divine presence. To be sure,

159. Yong, *Spirit-Word-Community*, 246.

160. Paul S. Fiddes, *Participating in God: A Pastoral Doctrine of the Trinity* (Louisville: Westminster John Knox, 2000), 272. Fiddes is citing John V. Taylor's *The Go-Between God: The Holy Spirit and Christian Mission*, 2nd ed. (London: SCM, 2004; orig. ed., 1972).

161. Yong, *Spirit-Word-Community*, 246.

162. Yong, *Spirit-Word-Community*, 247.

163. What Yong may mean is that since some experiences "emerge as objects for theological reflection precisely as interpretations from the beginning," then sometimes our theological reflections are based not on pure, nonconceptual experience but on thinking, "which involves interpretation all the way down." In this regard, Yong sees Scripture as interpreted experience. Therefore, we "do not interpret either Scripture or tradition directly, but rather interpret our experience of reading Scripture and tradition" (Yong, *Spirit-Word-Community*, 247). Added to this is the complex weave of experiences of the self and the self-in-community. If I grasp what Yong is trying to say, I agree to an extent with his approach to interpretation. However, removing "pure experience" from theological reflection or assuming that *all* theological reflection is based on one's interpretation of an experience of reading Scripture or tradition seems to deny the possibility of God's inbreaking into our lives through the power of the Spirit (this latter being something Yong claims to want to preserve).

openness or closedness to this presence may depend on a number of factors, such as the impact of religion on one's thinking, the way one's society thinks about such encounters, or even a crisis that sets the stage for openness to receive something higher than one's self. Just as our common experiences function as "objects for theological interpretation," so our thinking "grasps by way of abstractions our experiences which are continuous and dynamic."[164] Shouldn't what is true of our *common experiences* also be true of our *pure experiences*, especially if this experience is of the living God, who in some manner controls and guides the entire process from experience to reflection? In my proposal for a theology of the divine-human encounter, the Spirit of God is unique among all our experiences, even our experiences of the transcendent. The Spirit of God guides our thinking and reflecting on the primordial event, pushing us to come to a decision about who and what we have experienced. Unlike other objects that we perceive, God is the Subject who becomes an Object for our sakes, yet remains in control of the encounter.

What does such second-order reflection look like? Ingolf Dalferth has offered a description that provides clarity. Second-order reflection involves two aspects: interpretation and re-presentation.[165] Dalferth says that humans "apprehend something *as something*," by which he means that we "re-present to ourselves what is presented to us *in a specific way*."[166] This re-presentation to ourselves is done through the use of concepts. The result of this process of abstraction and reflection is the building of mental constructs to help us understand what has presented itself to us. In our discussion, I have maintained that God is the One who encounters humans at the core level of their being. The purpose of this primordial encounter is to develop a personal relationship with humans. Yet personal relationships are "symmetrical"; that is, they require the initiative of both partners to establish and maintain them.[167] Simply being aware of God's presence does not result in a personal relationship with God. Humans who have been encountered by the presence of God must freely choose to engage the personal relationship with God. Such a choice brings the human into the realm of faith.

Theological reflection on the encounter with God assists humans to become aware of the presence of God and then to clarify what has happened. To be sure, it is difficult to use language and concepts in order to grasp what has occurred in the encounter, but theology can assist in that process. For

---

164. Yong, *Spirit-Word-Community*, 246.

165. Dalferth, "Representing God's Presence," 245. The hyphen in "re-presentation" is important here.

166. Dalferth, "Representing God's Presence," 245–46 (his emphasis).

167. Dalferth, "Representing God's Presence," 248.

example, theology can provide language and concepts that may assist us in characterizing our experiences with God without feeling a need to squeeze the totality of our encounter into one particular conceptual box.

The "pure experiences" of God on which humans reflect in this second-order level are not created solely by our expectations of who God is or linguistic representations of one's religion. I submit that these primordial experiences engage us in ways that provide "background knowledge," or a deep orientation, for our conscious lives as Christians. As such, they may be difficult to explain, especially in the primary linguistic mode of theology (namely, discursive), but perhaps there is more to human action and thinking than pure linguistic discourse that must fit into someone's propositionalist category in order to demonstrate truth.[168]

Here Amos Yong's analysis and proposal are most fitting and important. Yong speaks of the Spirit inspiring and guiding the process of theological interpretation.[169] The very One who encounters humans also oversees the reception and eventual understanding of that event. However, because humans are fallible—even, or perhaps especially, with regard to grasping divine encounters—the Spirit of God uses the Word (Scripture) and the community of believers to help individuals come to some discernment of their experiences with God. Such theological work, then, is a "continuous interplay of Spirit, Word, and community."[170] Individuals on their own are not meant to achieve some type of unique meaning of their own individual encounter with God but are meant to discern such encounters within the context of the "self-in-community."[171] It has been my contention that this precognitive encounter with God's Spirit is both *transformative* of our human natures and *informative* for our theological understanding. As Yong puts it, "My purpose so far has been to argue that the Christian experience of God, whether breaking upon the believer as radically other or mediated liturgically, ritually, mystically, or otherwise, is fundamental to the data of theological interpretation."[172]

At this point the Christian reader may rightly ask, "What about the preacher? What about the *human* instrument in sharing the gospel?" As I noted previously when discussing Romans 10, faith does come by hearing the Word of God; that has never been in question and will be made abundantly

---

168. John Baillie makes such a suggestion (but does not expand on it): not "all thinking can be discursive." See Baillie, *Our Knowledge of God*, 148.

169. Yong, *Spirit-Word-Community*, 242.

170. Yong, *Spirit-Word-Community*, 245.

171. Yong, *Spirit-Word-Community*, 253.

172. Yong, *Spirit-Word-Community*, 252.

clear in a future chapter on proclamation. Here, however, I am suggesting that through the instruments of preaching, teaching, reading Scripture, and sharing a testimony about God's love, God's Spirit engages a human being with a powerful divine presence, making a connection with the human spirit that "testifies" to them that what they are hearing, reading, or seeing is really the truth about God. It is this underlying, hidden encounter with the Spirit of God that engages the human spirit (and thereby the whole being) and makes the preached Word, the written text, or the human narrative come to life. Without the *direct encounter* of the Spirit of God, the words are lifeless. However, with the Spirit's direct presence, the words become a wellspring of insight, removing the caked-on mud of sin and self-deceit so that we can see, truly see, God's purposes and our own shame.

What is important to understand about secondhand reflection is that it cannot adequately contain or communicate our firsthand experiences with God. Since discursive language is not helpful at this point, the language of narrative becomes the basis on which to build a theology of encounter. If we cannot communicate the nature of the primordial encounter itself, we can communicate how God has encountered us through storytelling. Thus, the point of theology in service of the church at this juncture is to help the community of believers coordinate our firsthand experiences of God with our secondhand reflection about this God to others. By doing this, we can help people to draw their attention to God's presence.

Can Knowledge Come from Divine Encounters?

There remains an important question to ask within this second-order reflection. Is any knowledge possible from a direct encounter with God, especially if that encounter is at a level of precognition? In other words, can we know anything about God through the experience of God in encounters with God?

Karl Barth insisted that although God is truly known, this knowledge arises only "from outside" (*CD* II/1:57). God is the eternal "I" who is always Subject and is Object only to himself. He "leases" his subjectivity to all other subjects and objects so that they have a sense of "I"-ness. God stoops to our benefit when the eternal Subject becomes an object of sorts; God becomes not only an "I" but also a Thou in relation to others. While possessing an "eternal and irrevocable subjectivity," God is known as a Thou and a he (*CD* II/1:57). God is known only "from outside, for in an incomprehensible way there is an outside in relation to God" (*CD* II/1:57). From this distance, humans can know God in a participation that is true and real, although God operates with an "indirect participation" (*CD* II/1:59). We receive revelation of the knowledge of God, but this revelation cannot be had apart from God's gracious accommodation to us on the one hand, and fellowship with God on the other. "Knowledge of God, in Barth's theology, is essentially a form of *koinonia*. The key word is again 'participation.'"[173] However, this participation is at a distance. It makes humans more like spectators than participants. Surely fans in the stands participate in a football game in some sense, but not in the same way as the twenty-two people on the field. There is still a great barrier to our full knowledge of God as God is in Godself (and perhaps some remnants of Kant remain in Barth's approach here). In addition, the focus of the result of participation is *knowledge* in revelation, not *transformation* of character. I believe that I have participated so closely with the very nature of God's presence that I am transformed by the event. While my participation may be more personal and relational than ontic, it nonetheless is real and substantial.[174] I do not just walk away from this encounter having seen God from a distance, but I have been "in the game," to push the football analogy further. I have interacted with Father, Son, and Spirit. I have joined in the dance—indeed the very life—of the perichoretic Godhead. It is my argument that the experience of communion and participation with God through the Spirit helps to provide some type of knowledge *about* this God, but even more than this, it provides a knowledge *in*.

A concept proposed by the eighteenth-century British Anglican John Wesley may help my point here. Wesley spoke of a realm in a person that he called the "affections" or "tempers." These are aspects of human nature that shape the direction of our energies, toward which love may head. Therefore, they can be holy or unholy. In a sermon from 1781, Wesley describes the interior life of a Christian where love sits on the throne (love for God and neighbor), yet "near the throne are all *holy tempers*: long-suffering, gentleness, meekness, goodness, fidelity, temperance—and if any other is comprised in 'the mind which was in Christ Jesus.'"[175] These tempers or affections are "motivating factors" located in the heart of a person—at the core level of being.[176] Such

---

173. George Hunsinger, "The Mediator of Communion: Karl Barth's Doctrine of the Holy Spirit," in *Disruptive Grace: Studies in the Theology of Karl Barth* (Grand Rapids: Eerdmans, 2000), 170. Cf. also *CD* II/1:182.

174. Clark Pinnock, *Flame of Love: A Theology of the Holy Spirit* (Downers Grove, IL: InterVarsity, 1996), 181. "Let me reiterate: union with God is not pantheism—creatures never cease to be creatures. This is not ontological unification. Instead we are caught up into the relationship of triune love" (181–82).

175. *Sermons*, 3:313 (his emphasis).

176. The phrase "motivating factors" comes from Wesley scholar Kenneth J. Collins, *The Theology of John Wesley: Holy Love and the Shape of Grace* (Nashville: Abingdon, 2007), 228. It seems to be a precise modern fit for Wesley's eighteenth-century language of "tempers."

affections are "abiding dispositions which dispose the person toward God and the neighbor in ways appropriate to their source and goal in God."[177] Any "works" that are acceptable to God after salvation must "spring from *holy tempers*."[178]

In the new birth of regeneration, Wesley saw the work of the Holy Spirit, who is the transforming love of God. The Spirit prepares us "for his inward kingdom"[179] by pouring the love of God into our hearts. The effect of this outpouring of love is the transforming work on our human nature, creating in us a qualitative change.[180] The presence of the Spirit is "the immediate cause of holiness in us,"[181] because the Spirit is the same life force that raised Jesus Christ from the dead. As Kenneth Collins states, "Wesley maintained that the work of the Spirit in adjusting the dispositions of the heart to their proper end results in the habituation of holy tempers, over time, that are not only long-lived but also not easily shaken."[182] The terms "tempers" or "affections" are eighteenth-century language for the dispositions or settings of the heart that can be changed through the Spirit's presence. These were more than feeling or sheer emotions; they were like dispositions or mind-sets in which a human being's love is fixed on God, the object of its affections. Wesley pointed to the Spirit's presence *in us* as the transformative agent of our own affections so that we now may demonstrate our love for God. The Spirit transforms our affections so that our dispositions are set on God and not on things as the centerpiece of life.[183]

Why have I raised John Wesley's thought here? As I have been attempting to show throughout this chapter, I believe that God's presence confronts humans directly. When that encounter results in salvation, there is a qualitative change of one's orientation that occurs. I have suggested that in the firsthand encounter, there is a transformative moment when God's Spirit moves in us in ways that are difficult to describe cognitively or discursively. However, I have also suggested that such an encounter brings a transformation of one's basic orientation to God and life; as such, it is a necessary determinant for a personal relationship with Christ. What if God's presence encountering us through the Spirit engages humans at a precognitive level of being—at the

177. Steven J. Land, *Pentecostal Spirituality: A Passion for the Kingdom*, 2nd ed. (Cleveland, TN: CPT, 2010), 132.

178. *Sermons*, 3:320 (his emphasis).

179. "Satan's Devices," in *Sermons*, 4:34.

180. This is the language of Collins, *The Theology of John Wesley*, 125.

181. John Wesley, "A Letter to a Roman Catholic," in *The Works of John Wesley*, ed. Thomas Jackson (Grand Rapids: Baker, 1978), 10:82.

182. Collins, *The Theology of John Wesley*, 127.

183. Knight, *The Presence of God*, 72.

core or heart of who we are—and "adjusts the dispositions of the heart" so that our orientation to life is redirected? For Wesley, the "affections" are not entirely cognitive, although they may be influenced by knowledge. Further, the cognitive level of humans is not the "core" of who we are as humans. It is important but is not the final arbiter of what orients us toward a relationship with God. In his final sermon at Oxford University, he underscored this point: "Without love all learning is but splendid ignorance, pompous folly, vexation of spirit."[184] Love is the core of the Christian faith; it is this love *of God* that invades and overflows our hearts, thereby creating a "sanctuary" for God's presence to dwell in us continually. Because of God's love poured into us by the Holy Spirit, our love *for God* spills over toward both God and the neighbor. Through a continual habituation of our affections, we fix our eyes on the lodestar of our love (God), who then requires us to turn our attention to the focal point of his love (humans).

Therefore, the question is less "What can I *know* from this firsthand experience with God?" and more "How are my loves and my self reoriented at the core of my being?" In other words, the encounter with God is not solely for the purpose of "knowing" per se but is also for the purpose of "being." Transformation of our nature is accomplished by God at a level so deep in our human core of existence that we have difficulty describing precisely what happened in the encounter with the Spirit. We sense a transformation, a reorientation of our entire lives, but we cannot seem to depict the experience, as if we were external observers to an experiment happening outside of us. It is because we are *not* external onlookers but are the object of God's presence, and something far below (or beyond) the level of cognition and mental capabilities encounters us there.

What is required of us in this second-order, theological reflection? Allow me to suggest several summary points for consideration.

First, while we need to process the experiences with God in our own selves, we cannot be so individualistic here as to think we alone have experienced God this way. Therefore, we must engage and be engaged by fellow pilgrims in the community of faith—in other words, with the people of God's presence.

Second, to understand what has happened to me as an individual in the encounter with God, I need to find language and concepts to reflect it as accurately as can be done. Here is where theology should provide a service to the church. How can I speak of my experiences with God? Encountering the presence of God is not the same as other everyday experiences (al-

---

184. *Sermons*, 1:176. Also quoted in Collins, *The Theology of John Wesley*, 125.

though the presence of God may indeed come to us *through* such experiences). Given the nature of God's use of media to encounter humans, theology must help believers to become aware of the presence of the Spirit in all avenues of life.

Third, one task of the community is to clarify belief about the God who encounters us. God, who met us in experience and began a transformation of our inner beings, is also the One who plants us among his people. We are people who not only have heard *about* God from Scripture but have also had some experience *with* God. We do not merely "know *that*" but we also "know *in*." Because God has become present to us and we are aware of that presence, we begin a process of interpretation as a self-in-community.[185] Yet it is the community's task to proclaim the gospel of Jesus Christ, declaring that the one true God is the One who has both connected with humans directly *and* has revealed himself most clearly in Jesus Christ. "Christian faith is a *response* to the word of the messianic gospel, and the *resonance* of that word in the hearts and lives of men and women."[186]

Fourth, the church cannot "communicate God's presence to others" but can only give witness to the way we have grasped it.[187] As Ingolf Dalferth states, "We can hope to create a sense of the presence of God in others, but not make God present to them."[188] Here is where theology can help the church. Theology can assist selves-in-community to examine their beliefs and belief-system in order to help coordinate their firsthand encounters and beliefs in God with a secondhand communication of God's presence to others.

Fifth, the people of God's presence gather to provide religious instruction through God's previous revelation in Scripture and in Jesus Christ. Reading Scripture within a communal context of God's people may help to stave off any self-advantageous elements of our understanding of an encounter with God and drive us toward a greater grasp of who the God of Scripture truly is so that the God of our encounter can be coordinated with this.

Sixth, believers gather as a community to engage in Christian practices that make space for God's continual presence among them. As I will show in the final section of this chapter, the gathered people of God's presence may continue to experience God's presence among them in corporate worship and service. Indeed, it may be one of the more significant tasks of the leadership of our churches to find and implement ever-increasing ways of opening our gathered congregations to the presence of God among us.

185. Yong, *Spirit-Word-Community*, 245.
186. Moltmann, *Spirit of Life*, 68.
187. Dalferth, "Representing God's Presence," 255.
188. Dalferth, "Representing God's Presence," 255.

All of these steps taken by the community together help to prepare for the next level of engagement: witness to the encounters.

Witness to the Encounters

Given the difficulty of communicating our experiences with God, how can I speak of bearing witness to such encounters? As we have seen above, perhaps the genre of narrative or storytelling is better for reflecting something about our encounters with God than the genre of discursive thought. Further, the telling of our encounter stories is not for the purpose of generating religious experiences like ours in the lives of our hearers; the fact that I share my own testimony of how God encounters me should provide a platform for others to find a clearer awareness of the presence of God in their own lives.

So, in this third level, we come to discern and clarify our experiences with God in relation to God's prior revelation in Scripture and Jesus Christ within the midst of God's people. It is important that such witness begins in the context of the community of believers so that we may better discern what we have experienced through the help of brothers and sisters in Christ. Once the divine encounter occurs and reflection on the experience has been guided by the Spirit and discerned by the community, we reach a level of confession or witness, first to ourselves and then to others. This tertiary event, so to speak, is where the continual role of the community comes to the fore in the Christian faith.

From the days of Jesus, witness has always been an important dimension of Christian faith. People were encountered by Christ and frequently told stories of that encounter to others. The story of the woman at the well is paradigmatic for this witness: "Come, see a man who told me all that I ever did. Can this be the Christ?" (John 4:29 ESV). The result was that the townspeople went out to Jesus at the well. "Many Samaritans from that town believed in him because of the woman's testimony [διὰ τὸν λόγον τῆς γυναικὸς μαρτυρούσης | dia ton logon tēs gynaikos martyrousēs], 'He told me all that I ever did'" (4:39 ESV). Literally, it was "through the word of the woman's witness" that many came to believe. Her experience with Christ transformed her thinking and orientation for life. Yet one may legitimately argue that such a response seems only appropriate since it was the *real* Jesus of two thousand years ago who confronted her with such direct knowledge about her own life. Why should we expect such a transformation or a response of witness today when it seems impossible to be contemporary with Christ?

Here a hermeneutical principle that has arisen over the past several hundred years may be helpful. A recent Baptist theologian, James McClendon, has argued that there is a particular "baptistic vision" concerning the text of Scripture. He uses the small letter *b* in order to distinguish it from a denominational Baptist vision. What is this vision? It is simply that what one reads in Scripture is the same experience that can be had today. He calls it a "this-is-that" hermeneutic, recalling the sermon of Peter on the day of Pentecost (Acts 2:16).[189] In other words, what has happened to us today is the same thing that happened in the first century CE. If God confronted humans directly during the days of Jesus's life, then God through the Spirit brings the risen Jesus Christ directly to humans today in order to have an encounter with them. In this sense, the Spirit makes us a "contemporary" with Christ.[190] Therefore, the natural response of sharing the life-changing results of such an encounter with the living Christ is just as likely for humans today as it was for the woman at the well. Indeed, the Great Commission of Matthew 28:19–20 is not simply an apostolic commission—that is, one fitting only for the first-century apostles—but is applicable to *all believers* today. Using a this-is-that hermeneutic, Christians today who engage in witness believe that they are fulfilling this command of Jesus. It was meant for us today as much as for the first-century believer.[191] For this reason Elton Trueblood's comment rings true for many today: "In short, a person cannot be a Christian and avoid being an evangelist."[192]

What does it mean to bear witness to the encounter? Just as the French philosopher Gabriel Marcel assisted us in a previous chapter on persons in relationship, so he can provide us some interesting insight on witness. What does witness mean? For Marcel it begins with *conversion* or, to use our own language, an encounter that transforms one's orientation. Marcel states, "Conversion is the act by which man is called to become a witness. This presupposes, however, that something has actually happened in which he will have to discern the action of the living God, or again a recognizable call which he will have to answer."[193] Based upon the event of encounter with God, the human being is summoned to testify—to bear witness of the event and the God who initiated it. In Marcel's terms, a witness is more than

189. James W. McClendon Jr., *Systematic Theology*, vol. 1, *Ethics* (Nashville: Abingdon, 1986), 33–34.

190. Søren Kierkegaard establishes this idea of contemporaneity with Christ most clearly. See his *Practice in Christianity*, 62–64.

191. James W. McClendon Jr., *Systematic Theology*, vol. 3, *Witness* (Nashville: Abingdon, 2000), 349.

192. Elton Trueblood, *The Company of the Committed* (New York: Harper & Brothers, 1961), 55.

193. Gabriel Marcel, "Testimony," in *The Mystery of Being*, vol. 2, *Faith and Reality*, trans. G. S. Fraser (South Bend, IN: St. Augustine's Press, 2001), 133.

an observer who shares a story. "The witness, of course, is not just he who observes or makes a statement; that is not what he really is, but he is one who testifies and his testimony is not a mere echo, it is a participation and a confirmation; to bear witness is to contribute to the growth or coming of that for which one testifies."[194] Thus a witness is different from an on-looker, an observer.[195] How is this so? It is because a witness operates with a level of commitment to the object of the testimony. "To be a witness is to act as a guarantor. Every testimony is based on a commitment and to be incapable of committing oneself is to be incapable of bearing witness."[196] What does Marcel mean by "commitment"? When a witness testifies, the testimony itself "bears on something independent from me and objectively real; it has therefore an essentially objective end. At the same time it com-mits my entire being as a person who is answerable for my assertions and for myself."[197]

This seems to me to be precisely what witness means from a biblical stand-point as well. It is not a mere rehearsal of data regarding the encounter, not a spewing of information *about* the encounter. Rather, it is a commitment of my entire being as one who is answerable for my testimony. It is in this context, then, that Marcel's words have a potent caution for theology—especially a theology of the church: "A theology which is not based on testimony must be looked at with suspicion."[198]

The church—the people of God's presence—bears witness to the encounter the people have had with God. This makes the church into a "storytelling fellowship."[199] The people of God's presence "narrate the story of Christ, and its own story with that story, because its own existence, fellowship and ac-tivity spring from that story of liberation."[200] The fellowship of God's people should have the greatest storytellers in the world, especially since they have the "greatest story ever told" (to use Fulton Oursler's book title).[201] Since narra-tive is the most appropriate way to engage the encounter with God, it should

194. Gabriel Marcel, "Rilke: A Witness to the Spirit: Part I," in Homo Viator: *Introduction to a Metaphysic of Hope*, trans. Emma Craufurd (New York: Harper & Brothers, 1962), 213.

195. Marcel, "Testimony and Existentialism," in *The Philosophy of Existentialism*, trans. Manya Harari (New York: Citadel, 1956), 96.

196. Marcel, "Testimony and Existentialism," 93.

197. Marcel, "Testimony and Existentialism," 95.

198. Marcel, "Testimony," in *Mystery of Being*, 2:139.

199. Jürgen Moltmann, *The Church in the Power of the Spirit: A Contribution to Messianic Ecclesiology*, trans. Margaret Kohl (Minneapolis: Fortress, 1993), 225.

200. Moltmann, *The Church in the Power of the Spirit*, 225.

201. Fulton Oursler, *The Greatest Story Ever Told* (New York: Doubleday, 1989; orig. ed., 1949).

come to the fore in all of our discussions about the mission of the church. As Trueblood reminds us, "It was the vocation of Christ to bear witness to the *truth*; it is our vocation to bear witness to Him."[202]

Karl Barth essentially defines the Christian community by this task of witness.[203] Like the finger of John the Baptist in Barth's favorite painting by Matthias Grünewald, the task of the community is to point—to direct the attention of the world to Jesus Christ. However, the finger-pointing work is not offered solely in silence. Even in this painting from the early 1500s, in which John the Baptist's long finger points to Christ on the cross, the *words* of John the Baptist are painted below in Latin: "Behold, the Lamb of God, who takes away the sin of the world!" (John 1:29 ESV). Such finger-pointing and verbal focus become the task of the people of God's presence.

How is this the case for the church? Christ has called us into union with him, so as to engage us in *his* prophetic office and work. Barth refashions the threefold offices of Christ (priest, king, and in particular, the prophetic office) to such a degree that the prophetic ministry of Christ continues through the Christian community to the world today.[204] It is my contention that a basis for this prophetic ministry of the people of God's presence is the very encounter that initiates their salvation. As we gather for worship and the Word, we have further encounters in the corporate setting that will move us toward our work in the world today.

Direct Encounters among the People of God Gathered

The gospel of Jesus Christ comes down to us in story form. By entering the story of Jesus, we come to God and believe that we can experience today what humans experienced in the first century. Through the means of the Holy Spirit, the gospel story of the text brings us to awareness of the reality of Jesus Christ and our true position before him. This encounter can occur in a variety of ways. James McClendon notes this variation: "Followers come to the Master each in his or her own way, and those ways differ sharply. One may hear the gospel story at church; another may hear it outside. One may read Scripture and be persuaded; another's persuasion may come from the

202. Trueblood, *The Company of the Committed*, 67.
203. Joseph L. Mangina, *Karl Barth: Theologian of Christian Witness* (Louisville: Westminster John Knox, 2004), 143.
204. John Webster analyzes this so well in relation to Calvin's introduction of the threefold offices of Christ. See John Webster, "'Eloquent and Radiant': The Prophetic Office of Christ and the Mission of the Church," in *Barth's Moral Theology: Human Action in Barth's Thought* (Grand Rapids: Eerdmans, 1998), 125–50, esp. 128–32. We will discuss Barth's concept of witness more thoroughly in the chapters on the mission of the church.

example of a saintly friend—or stranger."[205] However, approaching the gospel is quite different from continuing to follow the gospel. "'Virtual reality' is not enough; we live by having a share in this truth."[206]

While the divine-human encounters I have been describing may or may not occur within a church setting, their goal is to bring us into a relationship with Christ through the *re*-presentation of the risen Lord by the power of the Holy Spirit. While the Spirit may *approach* humans in a variety of ways to confront us with the risen Christ, the Spirit has assigned the community of believers to be the context for learning how to *follow* Christ. With this in mind, the Spirit's work is focused not only on our relationship with God but also on our relationships with others. Within the body of Christ, we continue to experience encounters with God that augment our understanding of God as well as clarify the Scriptures as we gather today to listen for the Spirit's guidance. This does not mean that we have one person tell us each week what we are to think about the Scriptures or what the Spirit is saying to the church. It is clear that spiritual gifts are meant to operate in a plurality among God's gathered people so that all may be used and all may be benefited.

Therefore, we gather to focus our attention on God in worship, lifting our eyes from our current situations so that we may communally draw our attention to the God who sits enthroned above the circle of the earth. In so doing, the people of God's presence may actually experience God's presence again and again together in such worship settings. As we will describe in the next chapter, worshiping God lifts us into God's presence even in the midst of our mundane existence. When we do this together, the presence of the risen Christ is among us through the work of the Spirit in order to bring glory to God the Father. So while the Spirit mediates our initial encounter with the reality of the risen Christ, the Spirit also brings about continual encounters with this reality in our midst. In many ways, then, our church gatherings should *make room* for the Spirit through our different practices of worship. The encounter with God in the gathering of God's people transforms our lives by connecting with our core level of being. Steven Land points this out precisely, especially in relation to our dispositions or affections: "Christian beliefs and practices shape and express these affections. Christian affections require for their proper genesis and ongoing expression a relationship with God, the church, and the world."[207]

The Christian community of believers, then, is a community of God's presence. This means that a primary task of our gathering together is to

205. McClendon, *Systematic Theology*, 3:356.
206. McClendon, *Systematic Theology*, 3:357.
207. Steven J. Land, *Pentecostal Spirituality*, 131.

create space for the Spirit to come among us and do what is necessary for life and witness together. As Moltmann suggests, this community "grows in the sphere of the Holy Spirit into a charismatic community, where potentialities and capabilities are brought to life."[208] Instead of thinking it odd that various people in a congregation experience gifts of the Spirit for the purpose of sharing these with the local body of Christ, such experiences should be the norm for a people of God's presence. If we are engaging in daily communion with Christ by the Spirit, then when we enter a common space together to worship God, should we be surprised if God "shows up"?

A final word may be needed at this point. Am I suggesting that the foundation of Christian faith is experience? Yes and no. I am saying that we do not need to feel something/someone in order to activate faith in God, yet the Christian life is brought to us by the miracle of revelation in which God encounters us. This encounter still demands faith to believe and obey, but it is the basis of the transformation in salvation. For the sake of our continued growth in Christ, we need continual encounters with God, not necessarily experiences. What I mean by this is that God engages us; therefore, we do not need to "have" more experiences with God so we can feel better or get another spiritual high to last the week. We simply encounter the living Lord on a continual basis among God's people. Do we experience something in that encounter? Absolutely! However, on its own this experience is not enough to sustain our Christian faith or maintain our devotion for God. Such communal encounters provide motivation and direction for our individual and corporate growth; they also provide motivation and direction for the community's mission. It is to that mission we now turn.

208. Moltmann, *Spirit of Life*, 69.

4

The Tasks of the People of God
in Gathered Community

As we have proposed in the previous chapter, we become the people of God through a direct encounter with God. The power of God's personal presence has a transforming effect on our lives so that the relationship begun in the encounter may grow to the extent that we naturally reflect in our actions the very nature and actions of our God, who encounters us. *Who we are* as God's people should shape *what we do*; and *what we do* as the people of God should flow out of *who we are* in God's presence. Our mission is based on the mission of God, our character on his character. As I will show, this character development and performance of our mission require being together with other believers. Therefore, the people of God are gathered in a local place by the guidance of the Spirit, cemented together by the loving bond of the Spirit, and clothed by the same Spirit with the power of the coming age to live in this present world in a manner that reflects the age to come. In this way the church becomes the people of God's immediate presence who live in the difficult moment of tension between the times of this age and the age to come; we are God's people, whose work and relationships reflect the work and relationships of the Triune God. In other words, the church is an eschatological, missionary fellowship on this earth that reflects through character and actions the nature of the God we have encountered.

While we have already considered the role of the nature of God and its function as a paradigm for God's people, we now turn to ask what we should do in the context of the fact that the future has somehow folded over on or invaded us in the present. What are the actions, the tasks, of the people of God in this setting?

The Church "between the Times"

Before engaging in a discussion of the specific tasks of God's people, we need to consider the context in which such tasks are performed. In other words, we need to examine further the eschatological dimension of the church and how that affects its function in the world today. What is the reason for speaking of eschatology at the beginning of mission? Is it simply the *context* of our work in mission? There is more than just context at work here. The fact that the future age (the "age to come" in biblical terms) has broken into our present age as evidenced by the resurrecting power of the Spirit, demonstrated both in raising Jesus from the dead *and* in raising sinners from death to life, means that the church is a people of God's power, which comes to us from the future (or however one can describe the dimension of eternity in relation to the present). The cross-resurrection event of Jesus the Christ inaugurates a chain of events that spells the end of sin, death, and even the devil. Yet the reality of the fullness of God's kingdom remains a future hope. In this age, we are still plagued with evil—suffering, sickness, injustice, oppression, and death. This present age is opposed to everything that the age to come will bring, primarily because "the god of this age [ὁ θεὸς τοῦ αἰῶνος τούτου | *ho theos tou aiōnos toutou*] has blinded the minds of unbelievers, so that they cannot see the light of the gospel that displays the glory of Christ, who is the image of God" (2 Cor. 4:4). Believers, however, experience a foretaste of the future day when we shall see God face-to-face; therefore, we reflect here and now something of the glory of God in the face of Christ (4:6).

Believers are the ones on whom the "ends [consummation] of the ages has come" (1 Cor. 10:11). The word "ends" or "consummation" of the ages (τὰ τέλη τῶν αἰώνων | *ta telē tōn aiōnōn*) possibly hints that the two ages *overlap*. This word, *telē*, can be used to designate "the ends of the two lines"—namely, the end of the old age and the beginning of the new age.[1] As a people of God's presence, we have in our human bodies something of eternity here and now—this "treasure in jars of clay to show that this all-surpassing power is from God and not from us" (2 Cor. 4:7). This is the paradox for Christians: our bodies live under the rule of this present age, subject to pain and decay,

---

1. George E. Ladd, *A Theology of the New Testament* (Grand Rapids: Eerdmans, 1974), 371.

but our bodies also sense a power within us that creates buoyancy in resisting the pressures of this external world. "Therefore we do not lose heart. Though outwardly we are wasting away, yet inwardly we are being renewed day by day" (4:16). In this sense, we live with feet planted firmly on this earth and in this age but also with our hearts anchored in the invisible but very real realm of the life to come. We are given God himself, the very Spirit of God, as a down payment or deposit (ὁ ἀρραβών | *ho arrabōn*) "guaranteeing our inheritance until the redemption of those who are God's possession" (Eph. 1:14; cf. 2 Cor. 1:22; 5:5). The *arrabōn* is "a promise" and also a "realization" of the promise; it is "deposited money that both promises the full payment in the future and gives a partial payment in the present."[2] The promise we have been given is God himself—not a *thing* but a *presence* who *empowers us with the life of the age to come here in this present world.*

In one sense, the kingdom of God has already come to earth with the mission and work of Christ; in another sense, it is yet to come in fullness at the coming of Christ. When considering the tasks of God's people gathered together, it is paramount that we understand the power by which we are able to perform these tasks. Such power does not arise from our effort but primarily from the Spirit of God, who brings the "powers of the coming age" and rests them on us and in us here and now (Heb. 6:5). Without understanding this eschatological dimension of the Christian life, working for God will become filled with our own efforts. The result will be that the church's work appears more like well-intended human activities than the spiritual mission that can only be accomplished in the Spirit's power.

So while eschatology is the context of our work, it is not the only reason eschatology is important for the church. Through the Spirit's presence, the eschatological future is opened up into the present, thereby making God's people the locus for his presence and power in this present age. The reason that we have the audacity to do the works of God as the body of Christ is that we have the power of God from another realm to perform them. The kingdom has already come, so we work while there is still daylight. The key to the church's *mission* is to recognize this fact: the kingdom of God has come and is present now in the world (albeit not in fullness as it will be in the eschaton). Therefore, we are a people with two citizenships—this world and the world to come—with primary citizenship in the kingdom of God.

What, then, does it mean for the people of God to say that we are eschatologically determined? It means that the eternal God draws us toward the

2. Ladd, *A Theology of the New Testament*, 371.

future and that through the cross-resurrection event, time and space have been invaded by the world to come. The presence of the Spirit in us here and now gives us hope for the future in God.

> Anyone who experiences the Spirit of the new creation in fellowship with the risen Christ already experiences here and now something of the "life given" [*Lebendigmachung*] to his mortal, sick and repressed [*unterdrückten*] body. If hope looks forward to the final spring-time of the whole creation, then in the Spirit the charismatic quickening [*die charismatische Belebung*] of one's own body is already experienced even now. In the experience of the Spirit, the spring of life [*die Quelle des Lebens*] begins to flow in us again.[3]

We are the people of God's immediate presence now, but our experience of that presence is muted by our finite existence in this cursed world. We were created to enjoy fellowship with the eternal God. Only by the grace of God's Spirit do we experience God's presence on this earth; until we live in God's presence without the shadow of the curse, we shall make this journey with the Spirit by our side and with the people of God's presence walking along with us, helping to make the load bearable.

The Church in Mission

Introduction to the Mission of God and the Church

Not only is the church determined by the eschatological future, but it is also commissioned with several tasks to perform while here on earth. The mission of the church arises from the prior and continuing work of the *missio Dei*—the mission of the Triune God. In other words, the church does not *have* a mission as the add-on program amid other programs; the church *is* the continuing mission of Jesus the Christ on this earth, which in turn was and is the mission of God from eternity. As David Bosch, a recent missiologist, has rightly said, "Mission is not primarily an activity of the church, but an attribute of God. God is a missionary God."[4] Mission is seen in God's movement toward the world, which predates the existence of the church and gives the church its primary reason for existence. Jürgen Moltmann has said, "It is not the church that has a mission of salvation to fulfil in the world; it

---

3. Jürgen Moltmann, *The Spirit of Life: A Universal Affirmation*, trans. Margaret Kohl (Minneapolis: Fortress, 1992), 95; Moltmann, *Der Geist des Lebens: Eine ganzheitliche Pneumatologie*, Werke 7 (Gütersloh: Gütersloher Verlagshaus, 2016; orig. ed., 1991), 107.

4. David J. Bosch, *Transforming Mission: Paradigm Shifts in Theology of Mission*, 20th anniv. ed. (Maryknoll, NY: Orbis, 2011), 400.

is the mission of the Son and the Spirit through the Father that includes the church, creating a church as it goes on its way."[5]

Organizing and performing the task of the mission of God in our human, culture-laden congregations is the challenge of the church's self-understanding today. In one sense, the mission of the church is simple, a continuation of the mission of God to the people of this earth. In another sense, the mission of the church is a complex challenge, a determination of how best to accomplish this mission within an increasingly hostile environment and how to motivate and organize the people of God to perform what God has requested of us. How are we to be witnesses to people around us as well as to the farthest reaches of the world (Acts 1:8)? How are we to go into the world preaching the gospel, baptizing and teaching disciples (Matt. 28:20)? Where do we start to fulfill this mission?

In this chapter and the next, I provide some direction that may assist the people of God in continuing the *missio Dei* on earth as the *missio ecclesiae* (mission of the church). From the introduction of this book I have maintained that the crisis for the church in Western societies today cannot be solved by throwing another program or ad campaign at the challenge. The crisis of the church needs a *theological* response grounded in the Scripture and in the divine purpose for the church itself. In previous chapters I have argued for a basis of the theological grounding for the *nature* of the church in the nature of the Triune God. In this chapter and the next, I will propose a theological grounding for the *mission* of the church. Returning to such theological inquiry is an essential move if the people of God are to remain relevant to the needs of the world, but even more importantly, if we are to remain connected to the purpose for which God called us out of darkness into his marvelous light.

One further note is required before considering the specifics of the tasks to which the people of God are called. The people of God assemble to perform the will of God *collectively*. We who have experienced the presence of God and have been transformed by that encounter—and are continuing to be transformed by it and by the continual encounters we have with God and his people—operate out of that experience and transformation. The mission of the church calls for God's people to work *together*, bringing the presence of Christ to the world through the power of the Holy Spirit for the glory of God the Father.

---

5. Jürgen Moltmann, *The Church in the Power of the Spirit: A Contribution to Messianic Ecclesiology*, trans. Margaret Kohl (Minneapolis: Fortress, 1993), 64. In chap. 5 we will consider how the nature of God influences our mission and more precisely what that mission entails.

Perhaps the most insidious hindrance to the church performing the tasks assigned to it by God is *individualism*. Earlier I mentioned that this book would attempt to build something like a dialectical tension between the person and the corporate body; we need to remind ourselves here as well that individualism becomes the millstone around the neck of the church in terms of a hindrance to doing the work of God *together*. Individualism has become part of the warp and woof of modern society in Western culture. The individual self is the focal point of one's attention. Participation in a group is agreed to only if it benefits the individual in some way. Daniel Migliore describes this view of life well: "The self of the individual is thought to be complete in itself and has no essential need of others. This individualistic view of human life seems singularly out of touch with an age that yearns for genuine community and is increasingly aware of the connectedness of life. Moreover, modern individualism is utterly at odds with the biblical witness."[6] In contrast to this prevailing individualistic sentiment in modern culture, Christian theology asserts that humans were created by God for community, reflecting the society that exists in the Trinity.

It may seem that much of the discussion up to this point in previous chapters has been following an individualistic pattern. We are a people of God's direct presence. This can be taken to mean that we exist as individuals who experience God in our solitary selves, without any need for others. And "now it's Jesus and me," as an old popular gospel song goes.[7] Such a view of the church is not only harmful but, as Migliore has said, also militates against the biblical witness.

The problem can be highlighted through the following approach: If being a Christian is all about me being in the presence of God, then why do I need the church, those other persons who have been encountered and transformed? While an easy answer lies in the biblical witness, the more complex response lies in the nature of God. In the biblical witness, God ordains humans to be in community, requiring his people to exist in a community of faith. The nature of God, however, is triune—social and communal. If God were not such a relational being within his very core, then there would be no urgency for believers to join in a society of fellow believers—or perhaps the better way to say this is that the Spirit of God would have had little reason to bind us together by his presence if God himself were not relational. However, since God is this One who is communal in the core of his essence and reality of

6. Daniel Migliore, "The Missionary God and the Missionary Church," *Princeton Seminary Bulletin*, NS, 19, no. 1 (1998): 14–25, here 15.

7. Written by Ira Stamphill, it is titled "Jesus and Me."

his existence, he desires the rich communion that exists within the members of the Trinity to be reflected in the communion that should exist within the members of his church on earth.

This has been the clear direction we have been moving in the previous chapters, attempting to provide a rationale for why individuals who have been encountered by God are also placed by God in a *communio sanctorum*, a communion of saints. Now, however, such a communal nature in God's being can assist us to see the reason for why we celebrate and assemble *together*: we gather to celebrate the nature of the Triune God who calls us his people and to reflect the nature of this God in our lives and relationships with each other. We have been created "for community with God and with each other."[8] Further, our meetings create occasions for God's presence to be manifest among us in a corporate sense. Just as the Triune God "makes room for the other" in the divine dance of *perichōrēsis*, we are drawn up into that dance *with other human beings*, and thereby we learn how to "make room for others" in our communal lives. For this reason, we should not abandon assembling together, especially as we see the day drawing closer (Heb. 10:25).

Beyond this assembling for the purpose of reflecting the nature of the Triune God and for creating occasions for God's presence among us, God has asked us to assemble in order to continue the *missio Dei*. Fulfillment of God's own mission (which now is the mission charged to the church) requires the people of God to perform certain tasks. While the specific answer to *what* the mission of the church is will be offered in the next chapter, a response to *why and how* the church engages in continuing God's mission is considered in this chapter. As human beings, believers need to understand why they are doing certain activities on behalf of God. Therefore, I offer a theological basis for action as seen in several tasks. To these tasks we now turn.

A Theological Basis for Action

The Westminster Shorter Catechism (1647) opens its instruction with a question and answer: "What is the chief end of man? Man's chief end is to glorify God and to enjoy him forever."[9] I have always considered this question and answer a wonderful clue to the meaning of life *for an individual person*. I am unsure if the divines who wrote this in 1647 were intending it for an

8. Daniel Migliore, *The Power of God*, Library of Living Faith, ed. John M. Mulder (Philadelphia: Westminster, 1983), 88.
9. "Westminster Shorter Catechism," in *Creeds of Christendom*, vol. 3, *The Creeds of the Evangelical Protestant Churches*, ed. Philip Schaff, 1977 ed. (Grand Rapids: Baker, 1977), 676.

individual, for the church as a corporate body, or both. Nonetheless, I take it as the starting point for the task of the church assembled. The people of God, who have experienced the presence of God, should glorify God and enjoy God whenever they assemble together. Clearly, there will be more to do as God's people, but I contend that if this is our mantra, reminding us of the reason for our life and work together, then we may be more God-centered and other-centered than self-centered in our tasks at hand. I propose that from the loving fellowship and reciprocal relationships that occur when the people of God gather—be it in homes, on the street, at coffee shops, or a church building—the church moves forward to do God's mission in the world. In other words, glorifying God and enjoying him *together* builds a community of believers who are exponentially more powerful than a single individual alone doing God's bidding. The work of God begins with us understanding what it means to glorify God.

To Glorify God

Worshiping Together, We Glorify God

When the people of God's presence gather, their chief purpose is to glorify God in all they do and say. What is the meaning of this rather religious phrase "to glorify God"? The glory of God refers to the weight or heaviness of God—essentially meaning the value of God, if such a thing could be measured out on scales. God is greater and heavier than all beings that have ever existed. The combined set of attributes joins to make God's value "off the scales," as it were.[10] When we acknowledge this glory of God, we offer words to God that ascribe "the honor and blessing appropriate to God's holiness and to the mystery of God's being."[11] How do we do this task together? Based on God's gifts and his initiative toward humans, believers *respond* to God's presence by directing their worship to him. In a very real way, God is both the Subject and Object of our worship: he initiates the movement toward us, and we respond by ascribing him the worth that he is due.[12] It is not that God needs this from us—he is, after all, self-sustaining and never dependent on anything from us—yet when God asks us to worship, it pleases him to see us joined together to recognize the One who made all things: "When you open

10. We will say more about what it means to "glorify God" below.

11. Don E. Saliers, *Worship as Theology: Foretaste of Glory Divine* (Nashville: Abingdon, 1994), 85.

12. I am taking the idea of God as Subject and Object of worship from Marva J. Dawn, *Reaching Out without Dumbing Down: A Theology of Worship for This Urgent Time* (Grand Rapids: Eerdmans, 1995), 76–82.

your hand, they [creatures] are filled with good things" (Ps. 104:28 ESV). All opportunities for corporate worship are occasions for God to encounter us in ways that transform us, empowering us with his presence to accomplish the tasks he gives us.

Unfortunately, many churches have meetings where human need and misery, rather than the transcendent God, are a primary focus. As pastoral theologian Paul Waitman Hoon said decades ago: "God is the first reality in worship, not [humans]; the soul feeds on the life God gives, not on itself; and the test of worship is not our subjective reaction but whether Christ in his truth and grace is authentically proclaimed."[13] Worship must focus our attention on God, not on us. Here the Psalms remind us of this truth: "Not to us, LORD, not to us / but to your name be the glory, / because of your love and faithfulness" (Ps. 115:1). In this task of transferring our attention from the natural inclination toward the self to the God who is worthy, it is the *presence of God*, the Holy Spirit in our midst, that helps us to lift up our hearts to the Lord and recenter our attention upward from the daily grind of our lives to the One who gave us life—and indeed, continually gives us *new* life. Worship that does not lift us toward God will simply bring us back to ourselves. True worship lifts our gaze from the field of everyday life with its turmoil and trouble, focusing our attention on the God of grace and glory, whose presence encounters us in the midst of this life. The presence of God does this for us, but *we* must "make room" for his presence among us. Worship engages our minds and spirits and bodies—our whole being—without denying the harshness of human reality that we may have left behind at the doors of our meetinghouses, yet it does so also without allowing us to give in to that harshness as permanent or, worse yet, eternal.

One of the ways the people of God show their love for God is by gathering together for worship. In our English language, we often use the phrase "worship service" to describe our times of gathered adoration of God. The Germans commonly use the phrase *Gottesdienst* to describe the same thing. Literally, it means "service of God." The word *Dienst* (service) is joined with *Gottes* (of God) to form this compound word. Expanding on the idea of *Gottesdienst*, Karl Barth has provided important insight into the centrality of worship for the people of God. The true Christian community begins its work as it comes together (*congregatio*) and "gives itself to be known as such before God and His angels and the world and not least itself and its individual members" (*CD* IV/2:638; *KD* IV/2:722). To serve God by gathering together

---

13. Paul Waitman Hoon, *The Integrity of Worship: Ecumenical and Pastoral Studies in Liturgical Theology* (Nashville: Abingdon, 1971), 104.

in worship is the community's "common work" (*CD* IV/2:638; *KD* IV/2:722). In this way, the church is edified by God and edifies itself. It is *Gottesdienst* that separates the Christian community from an "appearance of a mere idea" (*CD* IV/2:639; *KD* IV/2:722). Worship makes the community a "concrete event at a specific time and place" (*CD* IV/2:639; *KD* IV/2:722). Christian worship, then, is the "action of God, of Jesus, and of the community itself for the community, and therefore the upbuilding of the community" (*CD* IV/2:639; *KD* IV/2:722–23). It is from this "center" (*Mitte*) of worship of God that the community spreads out into the "wider circle of the everyday life of Christians and their individual relationships" (*CD* IV/2:639; *KD* IV/2:723). In this way, their daily activities and attitudes "become a wider and transformed worship" (*ein erweiterer und transformierter Gottesdienst zu werden*) (*CD* IV/2:639; *KD* IV/2:723).

As Barth points out a little further on, worship and the everyday living of Christians belong together like two concentric circles, "of which worship is the inner which gives to the outer its content and character" (*CD* IV/2:640; *KD* IV/2:723). Serving God in worship produces a life of witness in one's everyday living. Worship produces a wider and transformed worship by infusing spiritual significance into the mundane activities of Christians in their day-to-day living. As a result, this provides a common witness. "Assembling for divine worship is self-evidently the centre and presupposition of the whole Christian life, the atmosphere in which it is lived. It hardly needs to be specifically emphasized or described" (*CD* IV/2:640; *KD* IV/2:724).

I have carefully reproduced the thoughts from two pages of Barth's writing about worship because it is the foundation for my understanding of the relation of worship to mission. As will be clear in this chapter, mission is given its impetus when the people of God are gathered in God's presence and experience the living God encountering them through the focused act of worship. The work of *mission* (out there in the world) begins with the work of *worship* (in the gathered community). By making room together for God's presence among us in worship, we become prepared to make room for the presence of those who are radically other than us, both inside and outside of the community of believers.

Geoffrey Wainwright has offered a definition of worship that may appear strange to some at first but is quite fitting for our purposes. He states, "Worship is better seen as the point of concentration at which the whole of the Christian life comes to ritual focus."[14] Typically, some who would describe

14. Geoffrey Wainwright, *Doxology: The Praise of God in Worship, Doctrine and Life: A Systematic Theology* (New York: Oxford University Press, 1980), 8.

themselves as a people of God's presence are uncomfortable speaking about ritual. However, Wainwright clarifies the use of ritual by removing its more pejorative sense of meaningless repetition of religious act and by suggesting that it describes "regular patterns of behavior invested with symbolic significance and efficacy."[15] In its broadest sense, worship refers to every act we do as humans. "Whatever you do, whether in word or deed, do it all in the name of the Lord Jesus, giving thanks to God the Father through him" (Col. 3:17). Therefore, we may worship God even in the most mundane acts of life. Yet in the particular sense that we are considering—namely, where and when the people of God are *assembled*—worship brings our entire Christian life to focus in our corporate rituals. Even churches that do not believe they have rituals or liturgies (and would decry those who do) actually do possess them. It is simply that these churches name certain actions as ritualistic and therefore color them with negative hues because of the haunting concern that mere performance of a religious action will produce a corresponding response of grace, thereby making the entire religious event a matter of mechanical performance for receiving grace from God. To color all use of the word "ritual" or "liturgy" with such a pejorative sense is entirely unnecessary and in many cases uncharitable to our brothers and sisters in Christ. As with any religious act, what lies unseen in the heart is the important aspect of its function and efficacy. Only God sees the heart.

God-ward Worship: Making Room for God's Presence

When we worship in sincerity together before our God, we gather to focus our attention on him and to give honor that belongs to him alone. While many cultures and groups may have different ways of worshiping God, one thread runs through all genuine worship: it "magnifies" God in the midst of his people. We declare God's greatness to and with the people. We do whatever "makes God bigger" and greater in the eyes of his people. However, we do this while entirely aware that this magnification of God is offered in simple adoration *God-ward*, because God is the focus of this gathering, because God is the One to whom all praise is due.

Genuine worship, then, *directs its attention to God by making room for God in our midst*. Worship brings us into God's very presence *together*. Here is the interesting point about such regular and repeated action of God's people when they worship God and magnify him by making room for him in their midst: the *God-ward* direction of their praise returns to them in the

15. Wainwright, *Doxology*, 8.

human-ward direction of God's presence. God dwells in the praises of his people (Ps. 22:3 KJV); by faith we understand that God *is present* when we make room for him. How do we do this? We make room for God when we focus on God, acknowledging his presence and his worthiness to receive all glory and honor. We discipline our minds to focus on God *in the midst of others gathered to worship*; we focus not on others in our midst but on our God. Somehow the Spirit of God takes our meager attempts to waft praise his direction and comes to us in ways we may not be able to express with our intellects but cannot deny with our hearts. When the community of believers makes room for God's presence, God shows up! I say this not tritely or carelessly but with amazement. It is not that we humans control God's movements but rather that our God is so desirous to commune with us humans—his people—that he comes to us running, much like the father in the story of the prodigal son (Luke 15:11–32). And so making room for God's presence must become the sole initial direction of our gathering together to magnify him. God's love for us responds with him running to us by the power of his Spirit. Worship in God's presence, then, lifts us to look higher than ourselves for help (Ps. 121:1).

The point here is this: God is so bent toward loving humans and communing with them that he will move all barriers to reach them, including the barrier between the infinite Creator and finite creature. God loves humans to such a degree that he became one himself in order to understand them from the inside of their existence *and* to overcome the enmity between God and humans so as to reconcile the broken relationship. The initiative is God's; the solution to the problem is God's. The power for humans to live in right relationship with God is poured into us by the Spirit. Therefore, why should believers find it odd that God *wants* to be present to his people? While we do not force God's hand to "show up" just by gathering or saying the right words, we can surely expect God's presence to be with us because our God wants to be with us when we gather to glorify his name together. God's presence will be with us because God intensely desires to be intimate with us as we gather in one place. God is bent toward loving us—this is God's grace directed toward people.

Humans tend to think that we have to *do* something to be worthy of such love, but the God of the Scriptures always initiates action *on the basis of his own character* never *on the basis of our action*. "God demonstrates his own love for us in this: while we were still sinners, Christ died for us" (Rom. 5:8). God is ready—anxious—to be with us.

Worship may come in many forms: a responsive reading, spontaneous declarations of praise, silent or vocal moments of prayer, songs, hymns, or even dance. The people of God are those who "declare the praises of him who called [us] out of darkness into his wonderful light" (1 Pet. 2:9). Our words—even kinetic actions—express praise to God. Our rituals performed together before God create occasions for God's presence in our midst.

Therefore, worship ushers God's people into a level of participation in God's very nature that cannot be ushered in the same way when one is alone. As a communal God, he draws us into community together to share in the trinitarian dance of God's life. "In worship we are drawn beyond ourselves. Our lives are redirected and our imaginations are renewed."[16] When we gather and focus on God's glory, we make room for God to dance with us and even to teach us to dance with him. Someone might aver, "But I get distracted in worship with others." I admit it may be easier at first to worship in my own basement alone, but that level of worship can only go so far. It is effective and necessary but not the goal. God desires us to be with other human beings in community, raising our voices and hearts to him as the One who longs to be with us forever. Distractions and perturbations will come to all of us in times of worshiping together, but God himself loves to draw his people into his life through the community of believers, where the Spirit binds our hearts in true fellowship and unity, first with the Triune God and then with each other.

Directing our thoughts and intentions toward God, we never lose sight of this life and its troubles (indeed, petitions are part of the worship itself), but our primary focus—even when asking God for help—is God directed, giving praise and adoration due to him. God joins us in our meetings in order to encounter us corporately and individually through his Spirit, lifting us up to participate in the divine nature while at the same time transforming us more and more into his likeness. This mysterious process of participation in God (as Wainwright calls it) is central to the Christian life. Why is this the case? It culminates in a "Christian vision" that "aims at a change for the better, or rather for the best of all. The change from sin to saintliness means death and resurrection. Christian identity is achieved only dialectically, through a self-surrender which becomes a reception of the self from the Other. That is to participate in God."[17] The church assembled experiences the possibility for a transforming encounter with God *together*, thereby making our meetings a vital aspect of what it means to live the Christian life by making room for *the Other* (God) while we are *with others* (fellow believers). In so doing, we glorify our God through worship.

16. Migliore, *The Power of God*, 99.
17. Wainwright, *Doxology*, 12.

A Biblical Sense of Worship—Is It Possible?

The Hebrew Bible. Having been privileged to worship in a variety of cultures and contexts both in the United States and overseas, I find it a truism to say that worship is wrapped up in the cultural and historical contexts within which it functions. Preference for hymns over choruses fractured many churches in the 1970s and 1980s (and perhaps still does today). Musical tastes differ about as much as tastes in flavors of ice cream. Styles of prayer range from a chorus of everyone praying at once (called "concert prayer" in Pentecostal circles) to a single priest praying to God on behalf of the people assembled. Some people like structure so that every word pronounced is written and said when it is supposed to be spoken; other people like freedom from restraint in their worship and therefore move about in their seats, pews, and aisles without fear that an usher will rein them in. Worship is different wherever one may go. But these cultural differences and preferences are not fundamental to the meaning of true worship. What lies at the core of worship? Let's examine several key points from Scripture to retrieve a better sense of some fundamentals of worship as found there.

Yet I must offer a word of caution even here. Simply to transfer the exact manner of singing, chanting, or other engagement that we find in Scripture is to replace our own culture for one that remains very distant in the past (and in many ways irretrievable). We may have some clarity as to how the Israelites worshiped God, but we are not Hebrews. We have even less clarity as to how the first-century Christians worshiped, but our goal here is not to mine the ancient past deeply in order to retrieve a biblical form of worship. My point is that we are not searching for a *form* of worship at all, since that may be entirely culturally laden. We are searching Scripture for what lies at the core of worship. While I cannot promise that everyone will agree with the principles I will set forward, I can suggest from my experience and study that these dimensions of worship do not appear like cultural trappings but more like foundations for the meaning of true worship of God. They may come in cultural form (after all, humans wear culture something like their skin, unnoticed but rather important to keep one's innards together), but behind them is something that applies to all cultures of the people of God in worship.

Let us focus our attention on the Psalms, the language of God's people in worship for millennia now. Walter Brueggemann divides the Psalms into three groups: psalms of hymns (or orientation: pure praise), psalms of lament (or disorientation: a crisis or trouble that causes enough concern to cry out to God), and psalms of thanksgiving (or reorientation: the return to praise for what God has done).[18] Clearly these psalms were set in some type of cultural and historical context when they were written, but some of that is lost to us (e.g., what the word "Selah" means—who knows?—and what tunes were meant by the heading "for the chief musician"—who knows?). I suggest, however, that beneath the historical contexts of the Psalms there lies a language of praise that can be translated into all cultures and times. For example, the language of praise is Hebrew (a cultural expression in itself), but praise does not need to be sung or said in Hebrew and may be transferred easily into every human cultural expression in some manner. A closer examination of the words used for worship and praise in the Psalms will give us a better sense of some rudiments for true worship transferred to our own day and culture.

The Psalms are chock-full of richly textured words for worshiping God. I will enumerate and illustrate some of them in groups, giving a few examples from the Psalms in context. Then we will consider the principles that may arise from them.

First, there are words that express *bodily prostration* or *knee bending* in worship. The most prominent word for this is *šāḥâ* | שָׁחָה, which means "to depress, prostrate, bow down, crouch, or fall down."[19] This is the most commonly used word for worship in the Hebrew Bible. Another similar word, *kāra'* | כָּרַע, clearly expresses the idea of "bowing down."[20] Further, a third word, *bārak* | בָּרַךְ, continues the idea of paying homage to someone by "kneeling" before them, but it can also mean "to bless."[21] These three words all occur together in one verse in Psalm 95:6: "Come, let us *bow down* [*kāra'*] in *worship* [*šāḥâ*], / let us *kneel* [*bārak*] before the LORD our Maker" (my emphasis).[22] This threefold dimension of worship demonstrates the importance of our

18. Walter Brueggemann, *The Message of the Psalms* (Minneapolis: Augsburg, 1984). Also, a shortened version of this book, Brueggemann, *The Spirituality of the Psalms* (Minneapolis: Augsburg Fortress, 2002).

19. S.v. "*šāḥâ* | שָׁחָה," BDB, 1005.

20. BDB, 502.

21. BDB, 138. It is unclear precisely how it can mean "kneel" and "bless," but perhaps the image of someone bowing down before another to receive a blessing is the imagery in the background. As noted in *TWOT* 1:132, its roots and derivatives occur 415 times in the Hebrew Bible: 214 times it appears in the Piel stem, which is always translated "to bless." In the Qal passive participle, it is used 61 times and means "blessed." However, its meaning "to kneel" arises only 3 times (twice in the Qal, 2 Chron. 6:13 and Ps. 95:6; and once in the Hiphil, Gen. 24:11). "On this basis some argue that *bārak* 'to kneel' is a denominative verb from *berek* 'knee' and is unrelated to *bārak* 'to bless.' However, there may have been a felt association between kneeling and the receiving of a blessing." See "285 *bārak* | בָּרַךְ," *TWOT* 1:132.

22. In the following pages, I have italicized these verbs or nouns as they are used in the psalms being quoted. This may help to clarify which words represent the Hebrew being used and explained in any given passage.

bodily position, which would reflect one's *inner attitude* of humility or bearing homage to One who is superior to humans. Indeed, such a humble stance is the proper posture for worship.

Second, a certain group of words describe how *the voice* or *sound* is used in worship. One of the most prominent words is also one that comes into our English language in a rather consistent form: Hallelujah! (literally, "Praise Yah"). The word by itself is *hālal* | הָלַל, which as a verb can mean "to be boastful" or "to praise" or even "to glory in."[23] Psalm 150:1 has a well-known use of this word: "*Praise* the LORD. / *Praise* God in his sanctuary" (my emphasis). We can also find "singing of hallals" in the Psalms (22:3; 40:3). This group of *hallal* words, then, prods us to consider precisely how we can rave about God in his presence and before others. How can we rehearse God's faithfulness and blessings to us? How can we sing out praise for who God is in his majesty? This is the challenge of true worship: understanding more about our God so that we can better express ourselves in his presence among us. Further, we are told to "*sing* unto the Lord *with thanksgiving*" (147:7a NRSV), which thereby encourages us to pay attention to God by singing to God. The word here, *'ānâ* | עָנָה, means "to sing" or "to chant." Words of "thanksgiving" are being repeated to God as if in a singsong chant, perhaps like a refrain. The word "thanksgiving" here renders into English a difficult word in Hebrew. It is *tôdâ* | תּוֹדָה, which stems from its root, *yādâ* | יָדָה. Essentially, *yādâ* is an "acknowledgment" of something and therefore a spoken expression of that recognition. It can refer to confession of sins or to confession of praise in recognition of the attributes of God.[24] In certain tenses it can refer to throwing or casting something, so perhaps at its core is the idea of casting up appreciation to God in the form of praise or thanks. From this verb, then, comes the noun *tôdâ*, translated as "thanksgiving" in 147:7a by the NRSV. This expression of praise acknowledges (confesses) God and abandons sin.[25]

In addition to these words that deal with the voice or sound, there are numerous others that seem to home in on some specific aspect of vocal sound. We are told to "*shout* to the LORD with *loud songs of joy*" (Ps. 47:1 NRSV). Here the word phrase combines the word for "shout" (*rinnâ* | רִנָּה)[26] with "loud songs of joy" (*qôl* | קוֹל) or "shoutings of joy";[27] the first word refers to a resounding or ringing cry while the second word connotes a loud sound or voice. The idea, then, is to cry out with one's voice to God (here not in

23. *BDB*, 237.
24. *BDB*, 392. Also, cf. *TWOT* 1:364–65.
25. *BDB*, 392, points to Ezra 10:11 as an example of this dual dimension.
26. *BDB*, 943.
27. *BDB*, 876–77.

supplication, however, but in praise, as the context shows). Related terms in the Psalms encourage us to "*shout for joy* to the LORD" (*rîʿih* | רִיעָה; 100:1),[28] or as another translation puts it, "*Make a joyful noise* to the LORD" (NRSV). The same word is used in 98:4, where we are commanded to shout aloud for joy to the Lord, making a noise that is loud enough to hear. And in verse 7: "Let the sea *roar* and all that fills it; the world, and those who live in it" (NRSV). Here we learn that the inhabitants of the world are invited to "roar" or "make the sound of thunder" (*rāʿam* | רָעַם) with their praise, just like the roaring sea. David speaks of his deliverance from his enemies and says that God will lift his head up above them, and "at his sacred tent I will sacrifice *with shouts of joy*" (27:6, my emphasis). The phrase "shouts of joy" comes from another word that actually addresses a loud noise for alarm, like a trumpet sounding the charge in battle. This is a specific kind of shouting, one that urges a commencement for battle or a warning over the airwaves (*tərûʿâ* | תְּרוּעָה). However, here with the word "sacrifice," it is clear that David is willing to stretch the battle cry or bugler's reveille, which is loud enough for all in the surrounding environs to hear, into a priest-like function of offering these joyous shouts to God.

The principle that seems to resonate from these "sound" words is that humans are encouraged to speak, sing, or shout out loud with great joy because of their God. There should be uproar in our midst when we praise God. I realize that this sounds contrary to our Western notions of church worship services being done "decently and in order" (1 Cor. 14:40), but the time has come to remember to whom we are giving such loud praise and not to be so concerned about others who frown at our revelry in God's presence.

Third, another word grouping calls for *movement*—either with one's *legs* as in dancing or one's *hands* as in clapping. "*Clap your hands*, all you peoples" (Ps. 47:1 NRSV). The word for "clap" here is *tāqaʿ* | תָּקַע, which is also used metaphorically to address rivers to clap their hands (98:8). Unlike modern associations of clapping hands for the purpose of honoring a performance or praising an individual's speech, this clapping of hands is usually directed to God so that we make a natural sound of slapping the hands together. Whereas the previous group focused on the sound of our voices to express joy in our God, this group uses the sound of bodily movement or the movement itself to express such joy. Often the two are joined—singing and dancing, for example, or clapping our hands to God and making a joyful noise to him. Again David speaks of bodily movement in Psalm 143:6: "I *stretch out my hands* to you" (NRSV). While this context may be read as one where David is

---

28. *BDB*, 929.

literally reaching out to God in desperation, the word itself contains the idea of "spreading out" one's hands to God in worship. The verb *pāraś* | פָּרַשׂ can mean spreading out one's wings or a net, scattering items, or more specifically, spreading out the hands in a posture of prayer.[29] So perhaps both a desperate stretching to God and a prayer-filled spreading of the hands to worship were intended here.

From David's own life story we find a clear example of movement called dance. In an expression of great joy at the return of the ark of the covenant to Jerusalem, David was "leaping and whirling" in the presence of God and the people—much to his wife's chagrin (2 Sam. 6:16 NKJV). David was springing about wildly for joy (1 Chron. 15:29). It should not surprise us that such dancing and whirling as an expression of joy is a part of the Psalms. "But let all who take refuge in you rejoice; / let them ever sing for joy, / and spread your protection over them, / that those who love your name may *exult* [*ʿālaṣ* | עָלַץ] in you" (Ps. 5:11 ESV). This word *ʿālaṣ* refers to an emotional response, which is clear in the old English word "exult." It means to be ecstatic, elated, even causing one to jump for joy.[30] The reason for such an ecstatic, gushing response that spills over from one's inner well of joy onto the body is that the people of God place their trust in him and love his name. This is reason to jump up and down for joy! Indeed, the "[LORD has] turned for me my mourning into *dancing* [*māḥôl* | מָחוֹל], [he has] loosed my sackcloth and clothed me with gladness" (30:11 ESV). The dancing here is a matter of overwhelming joy that expresses itself in bodily movement. And this isn't just for one's basement: "Praise the LORD. / Sing to the LORD a new song, / his praise in the assembly of his faithful people. / Let Israel rejoice in their Maker; / let the people of Zion be glad in their King. / Let them praise his name with *dancing* [*māḥôl* | מָחוֹל] / and make music to him with timbrel and harp" (149:1–3). Again in 150:4 it is repeated: "Praise him with timbrel and *dancing*." The assembled people of God *dance for joy before their God.*

One final word of movement, which is more appropriate for a field of battle than the temple, is used quite clearly in worship: "May we shout for joy over your salvation, / and in the name of our God *set up our banners* [*degel* | דֶּגֶל]!" (Ps. 20:5 ESV, my emphasis). Here the term for the battlefield is transferred to the temple, where figurative flags of the Lord's triumph over his enemies could provide a colorful and visible reminder of the Lord's saving hand. This psalm continues in verse 7: "Some trust in chariots and some in horses, / but we trust in the name of the LORD." Our God is One who wars for us and

29. *BDB*, 831.
30. *BDB*, 763; also *TWOT* 2:613.

who delivers us. Surely that is worth raising a banner, hoisting the victory flag, lifting up the name of our Lord along with colorful fabric waving in the wind. Shout with the voice of triumph and wave the Lord's banner flags.

So what is the principle involved in this third group of words? The principle seems to ask us to join in the celebration of our God with great joy—joy that is almost impossible to contain within one's own body and that therefore gushes out into bodily movements like dancing, whirling, or jumping for joy in our God.

Finally, there is a word grouping that I might call "other." These obviously relate to worship in the Psalms and are quite commonly used. These words seem to handle the more technical issue of *how* to worship God. In English, the following words will sound familiar to anyone who has read the Psalter: to magnify, to extol/exalt, and to glorify. Let's consider these one by one in the context of the Psalms.

Blessing God. We have already seen the word *bārak* | בָּרַךְ, which speaks of a posture of kneeling before God, but it also holds the connotation of "to bless." In the Hebrew Bible, the meaning of blessing someone (usually from one greater to one lesser, as father to son) is "to endue with power for success, prosperity, fecundity, longevity,"[31] and so on. Its opposite, "to curse," is seen as esteeming someone lightly. However, how can this relate to humans blessing God? When we bless someone, we *proclaim that good things might come their way*, so that they would "be blessed." This word may hold a rather reciprocal relationship between what God does for humans by blessing them and what humans do by blessing God in response. In archaic English, the phrase "Blessed be God" speaks to this assignment of human blessing on God. So the psalmist exclaims, "*Blessed be* the LORD! / For he has heard the voice of my pleas for mercy" (Ps. 28:6 ESV, my emphasis).[32] The psalmist addresses his own being to "*Bless* the LORD, O my soul, / and all that is within me, / bless his holy name!" (103:1 ESV, my emphasis). In a very real sense, humans cannot bless God—if by blessing we simply mean bestowing on God something that he does not have; however, we may view it more like a sincere wish for God to continue to be God. Perhaps it could be rendered something like this: "May the One who blesses us always live in blessing!" Yet we must also remember its connection to the bowed knee.

Blessing God seems to have behind it this posture of kneeling before One who is greater than us. The irony is that God, who blesses living things, is

---

31. *TWOT* 1:132.

32. A phrase identical or very similar to this continues through the Psalms: 31:21; 41:13; 72:18; 89:52; 106:48; 119:12; 124:6; 135:21; 144:1. *BDB*, 138.

blessed by humans, who cannot really bless him with anything that he does not already possess in himself. This fact alone should cause reverence, a literal bowing of the knee to One in whose presence we are unworthy to stand. Such blessing on our part is filled with an honest assessment of the glory of the One whom we are honoring, contrariwise of the unworthiness of the one offering a blessing in response. And so on bended knee (in our hearts and minds, if not also in our bodies), we bless God by adoring him. In this context, then, the angels are told, "*Bless* the Lord, O you his angels, / you mighty ones who do his word, / obeying the voice of his word!" (Ps. 103:20 ESV, my emphasis). The blessing of God by angels here seems to be connected with their action of obeying God's voice. "All you heavenly forces, / *bless* the Lord! / All you who serve him and do his will, / *bless* him!" (103:21 CEB, my emphasis). The armies of heaven are called upon to bless the Lord. How do *they* do this? They bless God by serving him and performing his will. "*Bless* the Lord, all his works, / in all places of his dominion" (103:22a ESV, my emphasis). Whatever God has made and wherever God rules, let all things in this category bless the One who made them. And finally, returning to the beginning of Psalm 103, the psalmist urges his own being to "*Bless* the Lord, O my soul!" (103:22b ESV, my emphasis). Blessing is clearly more than thanking God; it requires an attitude of the heart that is filled with gratitude for what God has done to bless us. As the hymn goes, "Thou art giving and forgiving, ever-blessing, ever-blest."[33] Here is the reciprocity: we bless the One who blesses us. Here is the irony: we cannot really bless God, so we respond on bended knee *and* live in ways that hearken to his voice and obey his commands. We bless God with our speech *and* our actions—both of which are *responses to God's gracious nature of giving*. While such action can be—even should be—an individual response to God's goodness, it is often in the context of the assembly of God's people that the Psalms remind us to sing his praises and bless his name.

Magnifying God. "Oh, *magnify* [*gādal* | גָּדַל] the Lord with me, / and let us exalt his name together!" (Ps. 34:3 ESV, my emphasis). This word *gādal* has as its root idea the concept of growing up or becoming great.[34] Whereas humans may be "poor and needy," we cry out, "Great is the Lord!" (40:16–17 ESV). Therefore, even if the psalmist is "afflicted and in pain," he will "praise the name of God with a song; / I will *magnify* him with thanksgiving" (69:29–30 ESV, my emphasis). For our God is great, unlike others who are called gods and are merely the work of human hands. How do humans "make God great"

---

33. "Joyful, Joyful, We Adore Thee," words by Henry Van Dyke. This is frequently sung in the United States to the tune of Beethoven's "Ode to Joy."
34. *BDB*, 152.

or "magnify God"? Once again we have something of a paradox: God is God because he is the greatest of all beings and therefore by definition cannot need anything, being dependent on no one for anything. Yet we are told to make God great in our worship together. "Magnify the Lord *with me*. Let us *exalt his name together*." How do we do this? The phrase just before this verse is "My soul makes its boast in the Lord" (34:2 ESV). Perhaps one part of an answer lies in the manner by which we are to make God great (or greater)— namely, by *boasting* about God both before God and before others. As Moses and the Israelites sang after the parting of the Red Sea, "Who among the gods / is like you, Lord? / Who is like you— / majestic in holiness, / awesome in glory, / working wonders?" (Exod. 15:11). This boast becomes a way of *exalting* our God, of lifting him up before others as the One beyond compare. "With whom, then, will you compare God?" (Isa. 40:18).

Perhaps another part of the answer in Psalm 34 for how we make God great lies in being *together* to magnify God. Gathered as God's people, humans can both speak and hear the praises of God from their own mouths and from those of the community. They can make God greater *in each other's eyes* by proclaiming God's greatness in the assembly. We rehearse God's greatness of his being—his nature and *who* he is. We recount our own history when God intervened in our lives, and we interlace these stories with praise for our great God. Much like Psalm 136, we are to "Give thanks to the Lord, for he is good. / His love endures forever" (136:1). In that psalm, every deed of creation, deliverance, and guidance is recounted in God's presence before others. We tell of his goodness to us, much as Psalms 106 and 107 tell the story of God's enduring love to Israel by recounting their history when God showed up and led them forward. So, "let the redeemed of the Lord tell their story— / those he redeemed from the hand of the foe, / those he gathered from the lands, / from east and west, from north and south" (107:2–3). After all, "Who can proclaim the mighty acts of the Lord / or fully declare his praise?" (106:2). God made his power known through drying up the Red Sea and leading Israel through the desert wilderness. Psalm 106 becomes a litany of Israel's stubborn sin *and* a litany of the Lord's stubborn love. We magnify our faithful God, then, when we tell of his mighty acts and great deeds to us, despite our unfaithfulness to his covenant.

Exalting God. Related to the idea of magnifying God is the word *rûm* | רוּם, which is also used in Psalm 34: "Oh, magnify the Lord with me, / and let us *exalt [rûm]* his name together!" (34:3 ESV, my emphasis). Indeed, this word "exalt" or "extol" may be seen as a synonym of "magnify." However, the root idea behind *rûm* is the connotation of "lifting up." So perhaps a distinction might be made between "making bigger or greater" and "lifting higher or raising high." Thus, to "exalt" the name of the Lord is to lift it high among the nations. David places God in an exalted state because God has lifted him up: "I will *exalt* you, LORD, / for you lifted me out of the depths" (30:1, my emphasis). I will lift you high because you have lifted me out. God is exalted by us when he has the position of preeminence in our lives.

Glorifying God. At the very beginning of this section, I suggested that worship is a subset of actions that comes under our rubric "to glorify God." While I only hinted at what this "glorifying God" might mean there, we will examine it further here within the context of the Psalms and worship. In Psalm 22, the psalmist declares, "I will tell of your name to my brothers; / in the midst of the congregation I will praise you: / You who fear the LORD, praise him! / All you offspring of Jacob, *glorify* him, / and stand in awe of him, all you offspring of Israel!" (22:22–23 ESV, my emphasis). Clearly the word "to glorify" (*kābēd* | כָּבֵד) is placed here in the context of corporate worship of the assembled people of God. In this respect, it operates within a Hebraic parallelism with the words "praise" and "stand in awe of him." This means that these could be seen as synonyms of what it means to glorify someone or something. However, since the root idea behind this word is "heaviness" or "weight,"[35] it seems more likely that there is an evaluation of something or someone's worth. Hence, to glorify is to "say that someone is deserving of respect, attention, obedience."[36] So David sings, "Great is the LORD and most worthy of praise; / his greatness no one can fathom. / One generation commends your works to another; / they tell of your mighty acts. / They speak of the *glorious* splendor [*kābēd* | כָּבֵד][37] of your majesty— / and I will meditate on your wonderful works" (Ps. 145:3–5). Here the glory of the Lord is connected with his majesty (*hôd* | הוֹד) or splendor, which carries connotations of both dignity and authority of a ruler. Again, the context is one of the *greatness* of the Lord and *rehearsing God's mighty deeds*. It is this greatness and these deeds that generations tell from one era to another, thereby enhancing each new group's grasp of just how majestic God's glory is. God is a "weighty" God, whose worth is beyond measuring or comparing.

Most of us have seen monarchs come to their coronation robed in resplendent clothing and dazzling jewels. These accoutrements of royalty come to create a sense of majesty. However, the psalmist is quite clear that such majesty cannot compare to God's glory. "LORD my God, you are very great; / you are

---

35. *BDB*, 457–58.
36. *TWOT* 1:427.
37. More literally, this reads "the honor of the glory."

clothed with splendor and majesty. / The Lord wraps himself in light as with a garment; / he stretches out the heavens like a tent / and lays the beams of his upper chambers on the waters. / He makes the clouds his chariot / and rides on the wings of the wind" (Ps. 104:1–3). Can any earthly monarch compete with such a One? This One is the true God, the King of kings and Lord of lords. "Among the gods there is none like you, Lord; / no deeds can compare with yours. / All the nations you have made / will come and worship before you, Lord; / they will bring *glory* [*kābēd* | כָּבֵד] to your name. / For you are great and do marvelous deeds; / you alone are God" (86:8–10).

When we glorify God, we testify to his worth—especially to his incomparability. Indeed, the noun "glory" (*kābôd* | כָּבוֹד) is what God possesses because of who he is. It was the *kābôd* of God that entered the holy of holies, sanctifying the tent of God (Exod. 29:43). It was the *kābôd* of God that Moses asked to see, and God granted a portion of that request by saying, "I will cause all my goodness to pass in front of you, and I will proclaim my name, the Lord, in your presence" (33:19). This is expanded in the report of the event: God "came down in the cloud and stood there with [Moses] and proclaimed his name, the Lord. And he passed in front of Moses, proclaiming, 'The Lord, the Lord, the compassionate and gracious God, slow to anger, abounding in love and faithfulness, maintaining love to thousands, and forgiving wickedness, rebellion and sin'" (34:5–7). This is the *glory*— the weight or worth—that Moses asked to see. It consists of the attributes of God's nature, beginning with his covenant love (the name "Lord") and continuing with central characteristics that spiral out from the center core of love (compassionate, gracious, slow to anger, loving thousands, forgiving sin). It is this glory of which Moses caught a glimpse.

"The whole earth is full of [the Lord's] *glory*" (Isa. 6:3). Yet on some occasions, the *presence of God's glory* is seen and felt by observers. At the completion of the temple, after Solomon finished his prayer, "fire came down from heaven and consumed the burnt offering and the sacrifices, and the *glory* [*kābôd*] of the Lord filled the temple. The priests could not enter the temple of the Lord because the *glory* of the Lord filled it. When all the Israelites saw the fire coming down and the *glory* of the Lord above the temple, they knelt on the pavement with their faces to the ground, and they worshiped and gave thanks to the Lord, saying, 'He is good; his love endures forever'" (2 Chron. 7:1–3). While the glory of the Lord fills the whole earth, it seems that such a recognition is not always clear (visible?). It is a reality to those with eyes of faith, but on occasion it seems that the presence of God's glory becomes so overwhelming in the midst of his people that we feel the heaviness or weightiness of our God in rather palpable form. The priests could not enter the temple and perform their service there because of the glory of the Lord filling the building.

While we may or may not experience such an event today, as Christians we have come to understand that the Son of God himself came to earth as a human being in order to show us God's glory. It was this Word made flesh, who pitched his tent among humans, that teaches us who God is in his fullest array of attributes. John says, "We have seen his glory, the glory of the one and only Son, who came from the Father, full of grace and truth" (John 1:14b). When the Spirit reveals to us more about who Christ is, we are seeing the glory of God in his manifest presence; when we acknowledge the lordship of Christ and his divinity, we experience the glory of God while still on this earth. This time, however, the glory of God is not reserved for a few—like Moses or Solomon or the Israelites—but rather for all to see. "Behold, the Lamb of God, who takes away the sin of the world!" (John 1:29 ESV). God's presence came into our flesh and dwelled among us. Now through the power of the Spirit, we may still sense God's presence among us in the person of the risen Lord. This is the glory of our God, the full array of his attributes revealed perfectly in human flesh.

The New Testament and Worship

The basis for New Testament worship is the centrality of the person of Christ and, in particular, his once-for-all sacrifice (Heb. 7:27c). Christian worship centers on Christ but not to the exclusion of God the Father or God the Spirit. It is always trinitarian worship, even when it has its focus on one of the persons of the Trinity.

In the New Testament, worship continues its Hebraic direction but removes the cult of sacrifice that required the taking of a life. In the old covenant these sacrificial offerings dealt with sin, which erected a barrier between God and humans. In the new covenant, the sacrifice of Christ on the cross and his resurrection from the dead inaugurate a new era—one that no longer needs the performance of certain details of Hebraic worship but sees Christ's death as the sacrifice to end all sacrifices.[38] The only sacrifice remaining in the new covenant is that of giving one's life to God in praise and service.

Romans 12: worship is living and serving. What, then, does it look like to bring such sacrifices to God in the Christian cultus? "The gifts which Christians bring, and whose acceptance by God is guaranteed by Christ, are no

---

38. For a balanced discussion of the atonement and the fact that the cross ended all need for sacrifice, see an excellent work by Mark Heim, *Saved from Sacrifice: A Theology of the Cross* (Grand Rapids: Eerdmans, 2006).

longer cultic offerings in the true sense. They are spiritual offerings. That is, they have the nature of the Spirit of God who works in Christians. A life which is received from God is offered back to God."[39] Christians worship God by bringing all of themselves to lay on the altar—a sacrifice of their *body*, which remains alive to serve (Rom. 12:1). True worship begins precisely at this point: we acknowledge that we have received everything from God (life, gifts, talents, goods), so we respond by giving back everything to God on an altar appropriate for such an offering. What is this altar in the new covenant? It is any place where we hand over everything that we think is ours and remind ourselves that it is all God's; it is any spot where we no longer need to substitute an animal's life for our own but indeed where we give our own lives as if a *living sacrifice*, presenting our very bodies to God's care so that he can do with them as he alone chooses. Let us repeat Johannes Behm's succinct and powerful statement in this regard: "A life which is received from God is offered back to God."[40] This, then, is the foundation for Christian worship. It is not simply a moment in time when we enter God's sanctuary in praise or sacrificial offering of some type. It is not about what we can receive in worship, but rather what we can give back to God in response to his mercy that moves so potently in our lives. Christians live their worship! This holy living is what pleases God. "Therefore, I urge you, brothers and sisters, in view of God's mercy, to offer your bodies as a living sacrifice holy and pleasing to God—this is your true and proper worship" (12:1–2).[41]

From the sacrifice of worship that infuses our very lives, we see that Paul encourages us to view this sacrifice as a "true and proper worship" (τὴν λογικὴν λατρείαν | *tēn logikēn latreian*). The word here for "worship" (λατρείαν | *latreian*) is used about ninety times in the Septuagint (LXX) to describe what the Levites did in their service at the temple.[42] In the New Testament, probably influenced by the Septuagint, the word always refers to sacred service, never "human relations" or "secular services."[43] The English word "liturgy" derives from the Greek verb λατρεύω | *latreuō*, which means "to render religious service" or "to worship." At its root, it connotes the idea of *service*. And so translators find it particularly difficult to know whether to translate it in some

39. Johannes Behm, "θύω, θυσία, θυσιαστήριον," *TDNT* 3:185.

40. Behm, "θύω," *TDNT* 3:185.

41. The key Greek lines of this passage read as follows: παραστῆσαι τὰ σώματα ὑμῶν θυσίαν ζῶσαν | *parastēsai ta sōmata hymōn thysian zōsan*, "to offer the bodies of you all a living sacrifice."

42. Hermann Strathman, "λατρεύω," *TDNT* 4:60. Strathman notes that *latreuō* in the LXX usually translates the Hebrew word עָבַד | *ʿānad*. It is usually connected with sacrificial work or temple service.

43. Strathman, "λατρεύω," *TDNT* 4:62.

passages with the English word "service" or "worship." Since its original use contained a sense of "work" or "service," especially a work that is done by God's people on behalf of God, it would be most beneficial to find English words to fit this idea.[44] This is especially true in today's era, when worship tends to be considered a mental exercise engaging one in a particular building at a particular time during the week. An example of a worship service that exemplifies the connotation of *latreuō* would be the work of the Levites performing their duties in the temple.

In the New Testament, this word is offered as a description of the worshipful service of the people of God in the new covenant. Romans 12:1 is a particularly obvious example: we are to offer our bodies as a living sacrifice, which is our "reasonable service" (KJV), our "spiritual service of worship" (NASB), our "spiritual worship" (ESV; HCSB; NRSV), "our true and proper worship" (NIV), our "appropriate priestly service" (CEB), our "act of intelligent worship" (Phillips), or "the worship of your head and heart" (NEB). These English translations are attempting to render the rather odd Greek phrase τὴν λογικὴν λατρείαν | *tēn logikēn latreian*, which combines something of *logic* (from the first word) with some form of *worshipful service* in the second term.[45] This latter term, *latreia*, is generally a religious term used to describe cultic rites performed by a priest.[46] This, then, becomes the linguistic basis (etymology) for our English word "liturgy." It is used five times in the noun form in the New Testament and twenty-one times in a verbal form. For believers in the new covenant, this is *our* Levitical service: to offer ourselves entirely to God, worshiping him by *what we do*. But note that this *doing* is entirely a *response to God's prior doing*! Believers are to consider the mercies of God and then offer themselves up with this spiritual form of intelligent worship. "Life is a sacrifice—the direct opposite of the offering of the life of another in cultic sacrifice."[47]

Hebrews 13:15–16: worship is praising and sharing. What else do we offer as sacrifices in the New Testament? Prior to this point we have discussed gathering together in order to praise and worship God with our lips and verbal expressions as well as with our bodily movements in the assembly of God's people. However, it is clear that worship in the New Testament begins with this sacrifice of our own selves, this ultimate handing over of our wills and

---

44. Wainwright, *Doxology*, 8.

45. Strathman suggests this phrase was from the philosophy of Paul's day and describes a "service of God which corresponds to human reason" and has divine reason at work. Strathman, "λατρεύω," *TDNT* 4:65.

46. Walter Bauer, "λατρεία," BDAG, 468.

47. Behm, "θύω," *TDNT* 3:185.

dreams so that God's will may be completed in us (Rom. 12:2). In the act of self-giving through what we do, we become priests of the new covenant (cf. Heb. 13:15–17). Therefore our liturgy is not just a matter of repetitious, empty words spoken at a meeting together but the sacrificial work of the people of God in this world whereby we lay down our lives on the altar for God's use. Wainwright summarizes this well: "Into the liturgy the people bring their entire existence so that it may be gathered up in praise. From the liturgy the people depart with a renewed vision of the value-patterns of God's kingdom, by the more effective practice of which they intend to glorify God in their whole life."[48] So liturgy is a way of life-worship not purely lip-worship.

Too easily is one's life from Monday through Saturday separated from one's worship on Sunday. The people of God's presence experience and encounter God through the week, offering their lives on the altar of his will. When they come together to celebrate the mystery and magnificence of God on Sunday, it is not without the works that they have performed in Jesus's name during the week. All of this is scooped up into the presence of God during the "liturgy," since all of believers' lives are "liturgy." On Sundays, however, we join with others who have encountered God and give glory to him with our lips *and* our lives.

"Through Jesus, therefore, let us continually offer to God a sacrifice of praise—the fruit of lips that openly profess his name. And do not forget to do good and to share with others, for with such sacrifices God is pleased" (Heb. 13:15–16). These (and the sacrificial imagery of one's body in Rom. 12:1) are the only cultic sacrifices for Christians in the new covenant. Notice that these "sacrifices" pleasing to God are not bloody or even similar to the sacrifices required in the Levitical cultus. They do not even require a priestly caste to perform them. All believers are expected to do these priestly functions. They come in three parts:

1. a sacrifice of praise (θυσίαν αἰνέσεως | *thysian aineseōs*);
2. a sacrifice of doing good acts (τῆς εὐποιΐας | *tēs eupoiias*); and
3. a sacrifice of sharing (κοινωνίας | *koinōnias*).

The offering of praise seems to be the one carryover in worship from the old covenant to the new. All of the praise ideas that applied in the old covenant (many of which we covered above) make their way into the worship pattern of the new covenant. Also, the writer to Hebrews explains that this sacrifice of praise is "the fruit of lips that openly profess his name." The

48. Wainwright, *Doxology*, 8.

fruit of the field or of the flocks is no longer required by God, only the fruit of lips that confess or publicly acknowledge their allegiance to the name of Jesus Christ, the One who offered up his own life outside the gate of Jerusalem (Heb. 13:11–12). It is there, outside the gate, where we must come to join our crucified Lord, bearing the "reproach he endured" (13:13 ESV). In this context, then, the name of Christ is the one we must acknowledge on our lips, praising the One who died for us.[49]

The sacrifice of "doing good acts" refers to the deeds that the readers/ hearers were previously admonished to do with and for each other. "And let us consider how we may spur one another on toward love and good deeds [καλῶν ἔργων | kalōn ergōn], not giving up meeting together, as some are in the habit of doing, but encouraging [παρακαλοῦντες | parakalountes] one another—and all the more as you see the Day approaching" (Heb. 10:24–25). And further on the author says, "Sometimes you were publicly exposed to insult and persecution; at other times you stood side by side with those who were so treated. You suffered along with those in prison and joyfully accepted the confiscation of your property, because you knew that you yourselves had better and lasting possessions. So do not throw away your confidence; it will be richly rewarded" (10:33–35). Doing "good works" is precisely what is required of us. What are these good deeds? The nature of what is "good" in these actions will be defined by what the motivation and the goal of the action might be. However, it is very clear that these "good works" are not simply well-wishing, but they are actions that bind one together in solidarity with other believers (in this case, those who were under intense persecution). In order to perform these good actions, believers must know the true situation in which other believers live. How can I help others or assist them in any way if I am not aware of their circumstances? These good works require believers to know the recipients of their actions and then search out ways to meet their needs. These are not works that *earn* salvation, to be sure, but are works that *follow* salvation. They fall in line with Paul's admonition to the Galatians that circumcision or uncircumcision has no value. "The only thing that counts is faith expressing itself through love" (Gal. 5:6b). This is a sacrifice that is pleasing to God—one we are told not to forget.

The last sacrifice (of sharing) may be attached to the previous one as an explanation of what "good deeds" are. It is the sacrifice of "sharing," or literally, "fellowship." This word has a basic meaning of "association, com-

---

49. The context of the entire treatise of Hebrews shows that the author is trying to rally the discouraged and persecuted believers toward a goal of not going back into previous religious commitments but instead maintaining the strength to persevere in the way of Christ.

munion, fellowship, or close relationship."[50] It can speak of the intimacy of marriage or of the church body, whom the Spirit draws together in fellowship (2 Cor. 13:13). It can also speak of "participation" with someone or "sharing" something with others.[51] Paul mentions the *koinōnia* that the Corinthians offered for the purpose of relieving fellow believers' suffering by giving money (2 Cor. 8:4). Paul also says that we "[participate] in the blood of Christ" when taking communion (1 Cor. 10:16). We "share in" the sufferings of Christ (Phil. 3:10 NCV). The essential idea of *koinōnia* in classical Greek reveals a close connection or bond, a *sharing* of things where people hold something together in common.[52] There can also be religious tones in this sense of fellowship—a participation with the deity. Both usages are found in the New Testament, but here in Hebrews 13:16 it appears in the context of sharing resources with someone. Our fellowship with the Triune God connects us in fellowship with other believers. When one of them stands in need, we are to "share" or participate in their lives by sharing what we have as ours together. With such sharing of goods, God is well pleased. Clearly, this type of worship cannot be done alone since others are to be the recipients of our sharing. We should do good actions and share out of the substance of what we have, as if what we possess belonged to them.

The meaning of all of this for Christians is both fundamental and monumental. The basis of how and why we perform sacred worship is no longer established on the Levitical priesthood or the old covenantal system of sacrifice. The entire priestly order of Aaronic and Levitical ministers has been swept away, and the whole people of God are now priests before God and each other (1 Pet. 2:9). From each believer individually and as we gather corporately, worship arises to God the Father, through the Son, by the power of the Spirit.

Allow me to share a very personal story about the value of corporate worship. My family attends a church that has about one thousand people worshiping God every Sunday. Although the worship is spirited, it is never overly exuberant or disorderly. People usually stand for about twenty minutes in order to sing worship songs that are mostly centered on God and Christ's work for us. Due to a severe neck injury and subsequent surgery a decade ago, I usually cannot stand in one place for that length of time. Moreover, I can't raise my right hand or arm, but I am grateful that I still have some limited use of it. As a point of fact, I am somewhat stooped now in my posture due to this injury. Sometimes when I come to worship God with this local body of

---

50. BDAG, 439.
51. BDAG, 440.
52. Friedrich Hauck, "κοινός, κοινωνέω, κοινωνία," *TDNT* 3:798.

Christ, my heart becomes so full of gratitude that I wish I could stand beyond ten minutes or raise my hands to God in celebratory joy of worship. Now I need to state clearly that I am not overcome by this urge very often—indeed, I'm a rather dry, unenthusiastic worshiper who probably needs a great deal of improvement in this respect. (The study that produced the material above on the kinetic worship found in the Psalms has made me feel particularly lacking!) However, now that I cannot seem to do physical things like stand in worship or raise my hands, I find that I miss that bodily movement that is so vital in worship. I could bow on my knees in the seats, but there isn't really room to do that appropriately.

About two years ago, I sat in a different place in the sanctuary and happened to notice an acquaintance of mine sitting near the back center of the building. This man is about my age and stands ramrod straight at six foot six. I do not like to look around in worship, since it distracts both me and others who are trying to worship. I had not seen him worshiping before. However, this day I couldn't miss such a tall man because of where I was seated. When the worship began, without causing a scene or any type of distraction, up stood this giant with his long arms raised high over his head as if trying to touch the top of our high ceiling—or God himself. All of him in total must have risen about eight feet or more into the air. In my twenty years of attending that church, I had never seen this man do this in worship. I wondered if he did this every Sunday or just today. His eyes were closed, and for the next twenty minutes he worshiped God in that position, never once lessening the reach of his arms.

I am ashamed to say that I envied him that day. I sat down after about ten minutes and never raised my arms once. I can't even clap effectively with that one hand being as numb as it is. The next Sunday I was in my usual spot again and had to turn slightly and look behind me to my right in order to see him. And there he was, like a cedar of Lebanon, stretched toward God and the skies. This time, however, when I sat down early in worship, something happened inside of me. I don't know how this happened, but I think it may have been a prayer that I never verbalized, only one that I felt. His tall worship posture was no longer a point of envy for me but one through which I slowly came to offer worship to God for myself. His worship in that physical stance has, for the past two years, become my worship stance—at least in my heart. I have "borrowed" from him what I could not do myself, what I could not physically give to God. I know that God looks at the heart of a worshiper much more than the physicality of one's posture, but my heart wanted so desperately to offer to God praise and worship *like that*. Somehow, I am able to worship vicariously through him. It makes little theological sense to me, but in a practical way I see it as my brother in Christ providing me something in worship that I cannot provide to God. He always stands as a physical witness to me of a servant of God who worships his Lord with abandonment. He has no clue how powerfully his way of corporate worship has helped another part of the body of Christ—and I don't plan to tell him since I don't want to make him self-conscious about it.

My point in sharing this story is this: God places his people in the context of a community so that we may receive strength from others when we have no strength; we may offer peace to others who have lost their peace; we may encourage others—and be encouraged by them—to stay the course of faith when the wind has stilled our sails and there is no sign of God's Spirit anywhere to start the wind to blow again. To be sure, all of this body ministry may happen by talking to each other one-to-one, but something powerful occurs when we worship together: we begin to feel strengthened by the Spirit of the Lord's presence among us *and* by seeing others stand in worship, despite the challenges they face. My own faith is made stalwart and my own wobbly knees are strengthened by this corporate expression of faith in God when we worship him together despite our circumstances. Worshiping together allows us to glorify God *and* build up each other.

Engaging Spiritual Disciplines Together

The church glorifies God when it worships God together, making room for the very presence of God in our midst. As we have described it thus far, worship is a *response* to God's initiative toward us. In view of God's mercies, we lay down our lives in sacrifice and renew our minds (Rom. 12:1–2). Now we move toward a second arena of glorifying God together: the spiritual disciplines. Where do the spiritual disciplines fit into this scheme? They are usually viewed as *individual* habits, not *community* ones. However, in this section I wish to expand the common notion of spiritual disciplines and ask why and how these habit-forming actions in community work toward building up the entire body of Christ.

Part of how we glorify God comes in our response to him. This is not only personal and individual but also public and corporate. Because God has graciously and powerfully encountered us, we respond by praying, reflecting, meditating, studying the Scripture, fasting, and so forth.[53] Why do we do these

---

53. Clearly these are not the only spiritual disciplines for Christians, but they are some of the more prominent ones we are going to consider. Dallas Willard suggests two categories with fifteen different disciplines. The categories are disciplines of *abstinence* and disciplines of *engagement*. How these may be handled as corporate acts is my concern here. See Dallas

things? We do them in response to the grace that God has given us, which causes us to participate in his divine nature (2 Pet. 1:3–4); because of this, we "make every effort" to add to our faith goodness, knowledge, self-control, perseverance, mutual kindness, and love (1:5–7). God has encountered us, so we respond by doing things that increase our relationship with him and make us more like him. We "share" in his nature and find ourselves motivated to build virtues onto our faith, virtues that belong to Christ.

Performing these disciplines individually creates a habit of life; performing these disciplines together in community creates a force in life. What do I mean by this? I know what a positive thing prayer by myself can be, but I also know from experience how potent a group of people from the same local church consistently praying every Tuesday morning from six to seven can be in transforming both them and the body with which they are connected. Engaging in these disciplines develops a united people in the local body of Christ. The same is true of Bible reading and studying together on a consistent basis. Such group actions are transformative. They also give us the chance to "make room for God's presence" among a few so that we are better prepared to "make room for God's presence" when the entire local body comes together to worship.

However, the mere performance of these disciplines can also create legalism and rigidity. Understanding the motive and purpose underlying these actions is crucial for the resultant transformation of believers. Dallas Willard, a philosopher writing on the spiritual disciplines, has compared them to nutrients for a living organism. Just as an organism maintains itself by "continually sucking orderliness from its environment," so too believers immersed in God's presence take in the orderliness of their environment—namely, the very nature of God.[54] The result is a pervasive transformation: "as a corn stalk in drought is transformed by the onset of drenching rain—the contact with water transforms the plant inwardly and then extends it outwardly. In the same way, people are transformed by contact with God."[55]

The rain of God's Spirit has fallen on us in an encounter of an "I" with a "Thou" and continues to fall on us in an encounter of "we" and "Thou." Together, we respond to this divine thunderstorm of his presence either by running away from the rain or by opening ourselves up to this downpour. However, like a living organism extending its roots and branches, we must perform certain practices in order to extend ourselves together as we continually feast

---

Willard, *The Spirit of the Disciplines: Understanding How God Changes Lives* (San Francisco: HarperCollins, 1988), 158.

54. Willard, *The Spirit of the Disciplines*, 65.

55. Willard, *The Spirit of the Disciplines*, 65.

on God's grace and transforming presence. Therefore, these disciplines are "activities of mind and body purposefully undertaken, to bring our personality and total being into effective cooperation with the divine order."[56] To this statement by Willard I would simply add that these activities are most effective when served up together so that all our personalities and total beings are offered to God's plan in an effective cooperation with God *and* each other. Having been encountered by God's presence, we cooperate with his grace and practice disciplines that continue to make us open to God's transforming power. We continue to make room for God to create the character of Christ within our natures personally and collectively.

The people of God pray together. Perhaps a primary spiritual practice of God's people is prayer. Frequently understood as petition sent heavenward, prayer is more than such requests. Instead of prayer being our speaking on a one-way phone without any return conversation, *prayer is primarily being in God's presence individually and collectively in order to pay close attention to God*. It is a stance of openness to hear God together as well as share in dialogue with him personally. Only in a secondary manner is prayer petitionary.

As Diogenes Allen notes, substantial effort is involved in this type of prayer: "It can be performed only as one gains some freedom from the competing desires which pull us in diverse directions, but which all conspire to feed our inordinate desire for significance, so that we cannot attend properly to what is before us."[57] Prayer is focused attention on God; it is waiting in God's presence, becoming aware of another reality beyond oneself.[58] Karl Barth describes the context of such prayer as one of interest: the Christian is *interested* in God.[59] Prayer focuses Christians' attention on God so that they understand God as the center of life—both corporate and individual life.

A key to prayer is learning to "wait on God." This waiting in God's presence produces a life that is in a position for moral transformation. For this reason, Steven Land can rightly state that prayer is the "primary theological activity" for a people of God's presence.[60] Waiting on the Lord can transform our nature *and* can color our knowledge of God together. Land states, "Prayer, therefore, is the most significant activity of the Pentecostal congregation. It suffuses every other activity and expresses the affective richness of the believer

---

56. Willard, *The Spirit of the Disciplines*, 68.

57. Diogenes Allen, *Finding Our Father* (Atlanta: John Knox, 1974), 69.

58. Simone Weil, a philosopher of the twentieth century, has helped shape this definition for me. See Simone Weil, *Waiting for God*, trans. Emma Crawford (New York: Harper & Row, 1973), 105, 115, 197.

59. *CD* IV/2:793.

60. Steven J. Land, *Pentecostal Spirituality: A Passion for the Kingdom* (Sheffield, UK: Sheffield Academic, 1993), 166.

and the church. All prayer is in the Spirit, and all who truly pray continually open themselves to receive what the Spirit is saying and doing in and among them. . . . This indwelling and constant receptivity constitutes the church as a fellowship or participation in God and, at the same time, a missionary force."[61] Prayer, in its private and corporate dimensions, is fundamental to the life of the people of God's presence because it focuses attention on God and opens our spirits to being encountered by him.

Iris Murdoch, a twentieth-century moral philosopher and novelist, summarizes our main point well with these words: "Prayer is properly not petition, but simply an attention to God which is a form of love."[62] Martin Luther engages in a discussion on the benefits of corporate prayer in his *Treatise on Good Works* (1520). Luther describes common prayer as a great force against the "evil spirit," who does everything to hinder such prayer.[63]

> [The evil spirit] lets us build pretty churches, create numerous endowments, play instruments, read and sing, celebrate many Masses, and promote unlimited pomp. It has no regrets about this but even encourages us to imagine such things are the finest and to think that with them we have done everything just right. When prayer that is communal, strong, and effective dies out, such hypocrisy smothers it. . . . But when it sees that we do want to engage in this prayer, whether it happens in a thatched cottage or a pigsty, the evil spirit cannot ignore it but has more fear of that sty than of any tall, beautiful churches whatsoever, with their steeples and bells, in which such prayer is not present. The places and buildings in which we assemble do not matter, but rather only this invincible prayer that we truly offer in common and lift up to God.[64]

In whatever way contemporary Christians may understand evil spirits or forces that work against the cause of Christ in the world, Luther has rightly pointed to the spiritual challenge to such evil that corporate prayer brings. Luther knew well the harassment that evil can bring to the church. If our worship only circulates around the ceiling of our chapels, then how can we connect to the exigencies of the real lives of people in the world? As practical theologian Don Saliers has said, "Unless the forms, the language, and the style of our worship of God as a gathered community can confront and

---

61. Land, *Pentecostal Spirituality*, 166–67.
62. Iris Murdoch, *The Sovereignty of the Good* (London: Routledge & Kegan Paul, 1970), 55.
63. Martin Luther, *Treatise on Good Works* (May/June 1520), trans. Timothy Wengert, rev. and trans. Scott Hendrix, in *The Annotated Luther*, ed. Hans J. Hillerbrand, Kirsi I. Stjerna, and Timothy J. Wengert, vol. 1, *The Roots of Reform*, ed. Timothy J. Wengert (Minneapolis: Fortress, 2015), 315.
64. Luther, *Treatise on Good Works*, 1:315–16.

live honestly with these disparate features of our life-world, our liturgies become, sooner or later, a self-serving flight from what is real."[65] Rather than ignoring the sufferings and tragedies of life, the body of Christ gathers to honor and glorify God through worship that focuses grateful attention on God by lifting up our hearts and minds to the Lord. The reciprocal movement of worship turns God's attention to us so that our petitions naturally follow our initial focus on God. Having lifted up our hearts together, we find ourselves lifted up by the Spirit to perform our priestly function of intercession for the world. This intercession parallels the intercession of our High Priest, the risen Christ, who lives to intercede for us. "Christ, in and through the Spirit, prays for the world and for us in and through our prayers in his name. Hence, Christian liturgy both forms us in certain characteristic ways of being human, and brings these things to expression through the arts of worship."[66]

What happens in personal and corporate prayer? Our moral dispositions are radically transformed by the recognition of the reality of God, who comes to encounter us. Contemplating this transcendent perfection affects our own moral development. God is *the* vital transformative force in sanctification, which itself stems from our love for God and spills over into love for neighbor. This attentiveness may be labeled variously: prayer, contemplation, or meditation (or all three).

It is immediately evident that most modern Protestant prayer is a form of self-love, *not* love or regard for God. Modern prayer is swallowed in requests about personal problems rather than waiting on God's presence. However, such attentiveness not only begins the process of moral growth but also characterizes it throughout life. Learning to be *attentive to God* is a form of loving God, *and* it becomes a mode of learning to love others. Our oft-used phrase "making room for God's presence" is just such a discipline as "waiting for God." The reason we can speak of prayer together being transformative of our moral imaginations and lives is that by making room for God we experience the transforming nature of God's being, thereby propelling us into an attentiveness for others.

Without such an encounter with God's transforming presence, we would be left to ourselves, and our moral vision would be selfish and distorted; the love for God would be a self-love dressed in some form of idolatry. Yet the Holy Spirit produces fruit that develops our personalities (Gal. 5:22–23) and

65. Don E. Saliers, *Worship as Theology: Foretaste of Glory Divine* (Nashville: Abingdon, 1994), 24.
66. Saliers, *Worship as Theology*, 28.

aids in the removal of extreme self-centeredness, thereby propelling us into the byways and hedges to invite all people to God's kingdom.

The people of God meditate on God together. In addition to prayer, the people of God reflect on God—we meditate on God. This is a natural extension of prayer. For some, it takes the form of theological reflection and writing. For others, it takes the form of preaching or teaching. For still others, it takes the simple form of meditation. Karl Barth has reminded us that "the first and basic act of theological work is prayer."[67] Being open to heaven and the things of God naturally opens our minds to receive from God the truth of his Word and to be encountered by the Holy Spirit. True theology can never be divorced from spirituality. Indeed, a praying person naturally becomes a reflective person. The people of God's presence meditate on God and his law day and night. This act of thoughtful reflection makes them solid in times of trouble, like trees planted by running water (Ps. 1:2–4). We worship God in our reflection.

In our hurried society, meditation requires us to slow down and listen for the voice of God. This may mean that as individuals we turn off electronic devices that beep or ring at us all day long; as a gathered community it may mean that we provide constructive periods of silence in our services so that we may lessen the noise of everyday living, over which God's voice can rarely be heard. Slowing down to listen, to pay attention to God by meditating on him, is one of the healthiest things believers can do, both individually and corporately. However, beyond slowing our heart rates and calming our nerves (as any form of meditation might do), Christian meditation focuses on God and listens for his voice. Richard Foster, a well-known writer on spiritual disciplines, has commented on this: "That is why meditation is so threatening to us. It boldly calls us to enter the living presence of God for ourselves. It tells us that God is speaking in the continuous present and wants to address us. Jesus and the New Testament writers make clear that this is not just for the religious professionals—the priests—but for everyone. *All* who acknowledge Jesus Christ as Lord *are* the universal priesthood of God and as such can enter the Holy of Holies and converse with the living God."[68] Intense discipline is required for such meditation on a personal basis, but even more so when the entire congregation is gathered. The one affects the other. If we cannot pay attention to God by meditating on God in private, then how can we meditate on God corporately without losing

---

67. Karl Barth, *Evangelical Theology: An Introduction* (Grand Rapids: Eerdmans, 1963), 160.

68. Richard Foster, *Celebration of Discipline: The Path to Spiritual Growth* (San Francisco: Harper & Row, 1978), 19.

our attention to the sounds, smells, and people around us? Unfortunately, we do not meditate nearly enough in our corporate meetings. The result seems to be that we focus more on ourselves and our problems and what we will do next week than on God. Was the worship service one that became transformative because we encountered the very presence of God? To make it so, I think that people must learn to sit quietly together and operate with the discipline of listening to God. When we meditate, we "withdraw into silence where we prayerfully and steadily focus" on what God brings to our thoughts.[69]

What would our church gatherings look like if we worked hard at finding ways to be silent—not just so our minds could wander but so that we could spend time cleaning out our spiritual ears and listening carefully for the voice of the Spirit? When we do this together, we glorify God because we give God one of our most costly gifts: our focused attention.

The people of God fast together. In this context of focused attention in prayer and meditation, we consider another spiritual discipline: fasting.[70] Some have used fasting as a way of twisting God's arm into doing something for them. There is no biblical or theological reason for considering this a legitimate purpose for fasting. However, others fast as an action within particular seasons of the church-year calendar (e.g., Lent). Fasting is not unique to Christianity. Other world religions go without food for a period of time for religious reasons. Why, then, would Christians fast as an aspect of spiritual discipline?

Fasting forces our flesh (especially our stomachs!) to submit to our spirits' desire to focus on God. Fasting is *not* a means for earning God's favor. It does not place God at our disposal or in our debt. The only biblical requirement for fasting was in the Old Testament on the Day of Atonement. Therefore, in the new covenant, I see no requirement for Christians to engage in fasting,

---

69. Willard, *The Spirit of the Disciplines*, 177. Simone Weil has suggested that school studies, however trivial or meaningless they feel to us presently, build the discipline of focusing attention on detail. The honing of this skill assists us in prayer and meditation. For my part, Simone Weil has "redeemed" every algebra equation or chemistry formula I needed to learn, since these skills improved an essential skill in the Christian life: focused attention. Even the rigorous task of paying attention while learning the conjugational endings of different languages can assist us in learning the focused skill of paying attention to others beyond ourselves. See Simone Weil, "Reflections on the Right Use of School Studies with a View to the Love of God," in *The Simone Weil Reader*, ed. George A. Panichas (New York: David McKay, 1977), 44–52.

70. For one of the very few book-length monographs on the topic of fasting, see Lee Roy Martin, *Fasting: A Centre for Pentecostal Theology; Short Introduction* (Cleveland, TN: CPT, 2014). This book covers various arenas, such as fasting in the Old Testament, New Testament, Christian history, and early Pentecostalism and then proposes some biblical guidelines for fasting.

especially since Jesus completely fulfills the atoning sacrifice without any need on my part to help him.

Why, then, should the people of God's presence fast *together*? First, fasting was used throughout the Scriptures to show one's solemn, humble approach to God. It often accompanied sorrow for sin or a plea for God's mercy (consider David's fast at the death of his and Bathsheba's infant son). Fasting does not earn God's favor, but it shows God and us that we are serious about the nature of our lives lived out before him. Such fasting is more than a religious ritual; it is a realignment of the heart. It is not for God's benefit but for ours. Isaiah 58 speaks of God's "chosen fast" as not one of a mere ritualistic performance but one of honesty in paying wages, kindness to one's relatives, and justice in relationships. What good is fasting if there is no change of heart and life? It becomes a mere ritual without significance for our daily living. Fasting, then, is an important spiritual discipline because it tames our flesh by causing us to focus on God rather than our natural and selfish desire to eat. Arising from the fast, one has a sense of clarity and focus due to the nature of attention given to God instead of one's gustatory delights.

Again, this feels like an individual discipline. To be sure, it is primarily that, but it can also be used corporately when the church agrees to fast for a period of time in order to show more careful attention to God *as a group*. From my own experience, this cannot be a requirement across the community since everyone's personal health is different, and some may not be able to miss meals by fasting (e.g., those with diabetes or gastrointestinal problems). Also, it does not seem to be a requirement in Scripture but is presented more as a voluntary act. Furthermore, when an entire community fasts, it is most helpful if there is teaching about corporate fasting that shows clearly the purpose for fasting at that time. The result of fasting together for an agreed-upon purpose is one of the most unifying factors I have ever witnessed among local congregations. Fasting together causes us to be more sensitive and aware of God, thereby denying our own self's need to consider the needs of others.

However, prayer, meditation, and fasting by themselves do not complete the corporate task of glorifying God. As medieval monks used to say, "*Orare est laborare*" (To pray is to work). Prayer leads to reflection and meditation but never to individualistic quietism. When we encounter the living God in prayer, we rise transformed to serve our King in this world. We do not return from God's presence to sit by ourselves in some kind of self-congratulatory satisfaction. Prayer assists us in moving out into the world by lifting our eyes off ourselves and focusing our attention on God. By paying attention to God, we rather naturally are able to focus on others when we return to the everyday world. It is this transformation that occurs in the divine presence: we become less self-centered and more other-centered, thereby reflecting the nature of the Triune God. And so we rise to study the Word of God with diligence, to write theology with passionate excellence, to feed the poor and clothe the needy, to visit the sick and imprisoned, and to side with the righteous causes of justice in the world. Prayer does not cause us to retreat into some interior world but propels us outward to advance into God's world to do the will of God there. In so doing, we worship and glorify our God.

To Enjoy God Forever

We return to the Westminster Confession in order see the *second* goal of humans after glorifying God: to enjoy God forever. Given the disciplined and serious nature of the spiritual practices we have just considered, one could misunderstand the nature of the Christian way of life as being a type of ascetic sadness. While it is true that discipline and focus require sustained effort, it is equally true that participating in the divine nature produces immense joy and pleasure. The psalmist has struck the precise tone with this statement: "Thou wilt shew me the path of life: in thy presence is fulness of joy; at thy right hand there are pleasures for evermore" (Ps. 16:11 KJV). In God's presence is *fullness of joy*! The inner life of the Trinity is so rich in fellowship and joyful relatedness that when we are caught up into God's presence by the Spirit, we too become overcome with joy. Using the imagery of Clark Pinnock, "We join the dance and begin to experience the movement and interplay of the trinitarian persons."[71]

The Trinity overflows in such rich fellowship and joy that the world is created as a spillover of this richness. We are called to participate in this joyous life. The people of God's presence are filled with joy because "at thy right hand are pleasures for evermore." The Spirit lifts us up to join the joyous communion in the Son and with the Father. "Designed for mutuality, we are destined for the dance, destined to be married to Christ and share in the triune life."[72]

Tasting God

The life of the people of God's presence, then, should reflect the life of communion in God's nature. In this personal union, we *enjoy* God. How do we as humans do this? Obviously, we can only do so because through the incarnation of Christ and the power of the Spirit, the Infinite One has opened

71. Clark Pinnock, *Flame of Love: A Theology of the Holy Spirit* (Downers Grove, IL: InterVarsity, 1996), 46.
72. Pinnock, *Flame of Love*, 47.

up the possibility for finite creatures to enter into the life of his trinitarian fellowship. And yet what do we mean when we say we can "enjoy" God? On a human level, we enjoy each other's presence by participating and interacting with each other. As my wife poignantly describes such interactions, we "don't just sit and stare at each other." We communicate, interact, and truly enjoy each other's presence by being actively engaged with one another. In some analogous way, this is true of our joy in God. We are lifted up by the Spirit to share in the nature and life of God. We enjoy God by participating in and interacting with God's presence. Through the Spirit, we become actively engaged in the fellowship that is the Trinity. Since God himself is the source of true joy, merely engaging in his presence triggers a response of joy in our lives.

Therefore, the people of God celebrate our life with God in utter joy, joy that is unspeakable and full of God's glory (1 Pet. 1:8). This is not merely a spiritual celebration but one that impacts our embodied living on this earth. Being a Christian is a life of joy and pleasure because we first and foremost enjoy God. It is also a life of joy because we celebrate and enjoy the people and things God has made. It is a mistaken view of the Christian life that true spirituality bogs us down in the mire of solemnity and morose seriousness.

"'Spiritual people do not play.' That is the usual view. For one thing, they are too serious ever to play. . . . For another, play might be pleasurable. And while spiritual people can have *joy*, they probably should stay away from just plain pleasure."[73] Such a view misunderstands God's creation of the body and, without any thoughtfulness, accepts the ancient, extreme asceticism of early monasticism as the more spiritual, classic way to follow Christ. Within appropriate bounds, God has designed us for pleasure, even in our "sensation" of enjoying him.

To enjoy God, then, does not require some disembodied spirit. We are a unit—a whole person who experiences the presence of God. The biblical imagery of "taste" expresses this experience with God; it is used in both Testaments. This underscores the almost physical experience of God that is available. The psalmist calls us to "taste and see that the LORD is good" (Ps. 34:8 KJV); the writer to the Hebrews and Peter speak of believers who have "tasted the heavenly gift" (Heb. 6:4) and have "tasted the kindness of the Lord" (1 Pet. 2:3 RSV).[74] It is also no accident that God gave the Israelites numerous feasts to celebrate their common life with him. As a unitary whole (both body and soul/spirit), we enjoy God.

---

73. Willard, *The Spirit of the Disciplines*, 79.
74. Geoffrey Wainwright has pointed out that these writers' biblical imagery is a key insight for understanding what it means to "enjoy" God. See Wainwright, *Doxology*, 17.

Celebrating God and Each Other with Feasts

In the common life of the people of God's presence, we are called to enjoy God together by celebrating God's presence among us. Therefore, we share the Eucharist in communal celebration of Christ's love for us. We celebrate certain days in the life of the church, not because they are so commanded in Scripture but because when we gather together, we find ways to remember Christ's life, death, and resurrection for us. Each Sunday, we gather to celebrate Christ's resurrection. It is the "Lord's Day" (Rev. 1:10) not a Sabbath. It is the day when early Christians chose to move forward from their Jewish heritage and toward a Christian one. What, then, should be the centerpiece of the week? It is the day of resurrection, the day that belongs to the Lord. We celebrate our own feast of the resurrection every Sunday, reminding ourselves to rejoice in the new life given to us through the resurrection. As the early church father Athanasius preached to baptismal candidates, "Christ, rising from the dead, has made the whole life of humans into one feast without end."[75] And so it is that God's people celebrate, needing only the slightest reason to rejoice in God and in this life given to us by God.

Some Christian traditions celebrate many "feast days" while others choose to celebrate very few. The point here should be *celebration*, not the frequency or infrequency of these feasts. The people of God's presence, however, are a people of joy, a people who love to throw a lavish feast in God's presence among us. The people of God should know how to throw the best parties in town for the sake of celebrating their God!

We enjoy not just God's presence but also the presence of God's creation. In other words, the people of God celebrate not only God but also each other, the animals he has made, and the realm of nature created by his very Word. The celebrating spirit in the people of God spills over from our sacred feasts to feasts for and with each other. Therefore, we celebrate around family meals, around birthdays, around anniversaries, around almost anything we can find for an excuse to express our joy of life in God.

Such joy enters with us into every worship gathering because it is with us constantly. The Spirit pours out of us in expressions of joy just like the rivers

---

75. Athanasius, "Sermo: In sanctum Pascha et in recens illuminatos, seu baptizatos sabbato in albis," in *Athanasius: Opera Omnia quae exstant, Tomus Quartus*, Patrologiae Cursus Completus: Patrologiae Graecae, ed. J. P. Migne (Paris: 1857), 28, col. 1081B. I was made aware of this quote from Jürgen Moltmann, *Der lebendige Gott und die Fülle des Lebens: Auch ein Beitrag zur Atheismusdebatte unserer Zeit*, 2nd ed. (Gütersloh: Gütersloher Verlagshaus, 2015; orig. ed., 2014), 192. The Greek is located on 1081B, not 1061B as Moltmann's n. 2 for this chapter alludes. It reads as follows: Χριστὸς ἐγερθεὶς ἐκ νεκρῶν ὅλην τῶν ἀνθρώπων τὴν ζὴν ἑορτὴν ἀπειργάσατο μίαν.

that flow out of believers' insides (John 7:38). As a people of God's presence, we live in joy and thus come to celebrate his presence each Sunday. Worship can have moments of solemnity and reverence, just as life itself has occasions of solemnity and reasons for serious reflection. However, the overwhelming song of life for the church is not a dirge in a minor key but a pattern of celebratory joy in God's presence. So we gather to bless God and honor his name. We worship him with joyous shouts of praise; we "enter his gates with thanksgiving and his courts with praise" (Ps. 100:4). We celebrate in worship through song and dance, through prayer and praise, through banners waving and hands raised. Whatever our creative minds and celebratory hearts can offer in the form of worship to God is what he desires (and deserves) from us. In worship, we express our joy of God's presence with us in the midst of this life, even in the midst of the suffering in this life.

As God's people, we glorify God and enjoy him forever. In whatever manner we glorify and enjoy God here and now, it is only a foretaste of the heavenly worship and celebration in which we will participate throughout eternity. And so we find ourselves tasting of the powers of the age to come in the here and now. We rejoice even in our trials because we know such suffering will produce for us an eternal glory (1 Cor. 4:17). We worship in the present by faith, knowing we will one day see God face-to-face and worship him with the multitudes of his people through the ages. We enjoy God's presence now, but only in a partial, proleptic sense. Nonetheless, when we walk in this life in the presence of God, we experience joy in the journey. We are the happy people of God.

5

The Tasks of the People
of God in Missional Outreach

The Church in Fellowship

Moving beyond the first two major aspects of the church's mission (to glorify God and to enjoy him forever), we turn to consider how the mission of the church relates to fellowship. It is my belief that by gathering to glorify God and enjoy him, we are brought together in a bond of fellowship by the Holy Spirit. From this center of our communal being, we spiral toward God's mission for his people to minister to others. Without worship and fellowship as the core of our communal existence, we will spiral inward toward ourselves and do activities that have little connection with God's intended purpose for us. We will become a society of like-minded individuals whose gathering only serves to further our like-minded cause. We will oscillate around each other, never moving outside of ourselves to those in genuine need. Without the center of our communal lives being the worship of God, we will warp the *missio Dei* (the sending or mission of God) into a *missio mei* (a mission of me).

When we share in the divine nature as a local part of the body of Christ, we enter the fellowship of the Triune God, who lives in richest communion as Father, Son, and Spirit. This unity does not cause uniformity; there is diversity within this unity. So it is with God's people; the fellowship we share is not of human design but is etched in our beings by the power of the Spirit to link us to other human beings in the community of faith. The *koinōnia* of the Trinity becomes the basis for the *koinōnia* of the saints assembled. We have unity in the

Spirit and yet diversity; we are not made to look alike or be alike in this unity but to live as God intends with others so that our own gifts and calling can be enhanced by being within the community of others. This union is caused by the Spirit, the person of the Trinity whose characteristic is to sponsor fellowship or commonality (*koinōnia*; 2 Cor. 13:14). Thus the Spirit assumes the lead in sponsoring *koinōnia* among humans. We might call the Spirit's task here one of "taking point" in the work of connecting humans to God in the divine dance and of causing humans to participate in each other's lives with authentic love.[1]

The type of fellowship described here is not simply communal because believers are human beings who are relational. There is a communion held between the church and Christ, between gathered believers and the Trinity, wherein we participate in the life of God, having been made sons and daughters in his family through Christ's work and having been—and continually being—drawn into the dance of God's triune fellowship. These are not just intriguing metaphors but a reality for believers. As Robert Jenson noted years ago, the "intrinsic order" of having fellowship in the body of Christ is *not* the rather accepted notion of Western modernity that humans are relational and that they therefore obviously become believers and join groups (churches) that contain other similar believers. Rather, the "intrinsic order" is the Johannine one described in 1 John 1:3: "that you also may have [*koinōnia*] with us. And our [*koinōnia*] is with the Father and with his Son, Jesus Christ." Further, Jesus's words in John 17 remind us of that perichoretic nature of God's fellowship: "As you, Father, are in me and I am in you, may they also be in us. . . . [May they] be one, as we are one" (John 17:21–22 NRSV).[2] It is the prior fact that the Triune God is one and three, three and one, in such fellowship of persons that brings us into that common life of Trinity. Our unity is established in the unity of the Triune God. Jenson says, "The communion that is the church is not primally the communion of believers among themselves; it is primally God's communion with us in the incarnate Christ; and because the God who thus admits us to communion is in himself

---

1. With the phrase "taking point" I am using a quasi-military term to describe the specific functions of the members of the Trinity. To "take point" is also a term used in team management among corporations to describe the leadership one takes (or is given) to direct the team. At another time, however, that very leader may step back while another member of the team "takes point." It may also conjure up the image of the "V" formation of geese in flight. No one goose takes the lead position throughout the entire migration; as the lead goose tires, another goose flies up to take point. Whatever image might be used to describe the Trinity's operations, it will always fall short of an accurate depiction. The Trinity is so unified, even in their separate functions, that it is inaccurate to suggest that one person performs one function alone while the other persons stand by.

2. Robert W. Jenson, "The Church and the Sacraments," in *The Cambridge Companion to Christian Doctrine*, ed. Colin E. Gunton (Cambridge: Cambridge University Press, 1997), 215.

a *koinonia*, the *perichoresis*, the 'mutual inhabiting,' of the Father, Son and Spirit, we are drawn also to mutual love of one another."[3] The love that we have for God exists in us as a *response* to Christ's own initiative to seek and save that which was lost. The love that we have for brothers and sisters in Christ is due to the Spirit's initiative to draw us into the rich communal life of God so that we may *respond* to this divine and intimate initiative by loving them from the love of God that we imbibe in the Spirit's presence. This love that we have for those who do not know God—even those who seem not to care about knowing God—is birthed in us by the Spirit's plunging us into the very being of the Triune God's life, from which we rise to seek others on God's behalf like the woman who lost one coin (Luke 15:8–10). Living in God's rich love, breathing the pristine air of God's *agapē*, infuses God's own love for others into our hearts as it is poured into us by the Holy Spirit (Rom. 5:5). The church is not merely a collection of similarly interested people. The church consists of humans who have been drawn into the life of God and who come out of that love-enriched environment with power to breathe that love in the face of hatred, bigotry, persecution, and injustice. We are drawn *together* into God's presence to swim in the triune fellowship as if it were a deep ocean of life-giving oxygen so that we may enter the polluted world of sin, where toxicity spews forth. We are called to witness to a different way of living from the noxious one that is all around us, giving others a taste of what it means to breathe the life-giving air of the Spirit of God.

The Spirit continues the work of establishing fellowship by creating community among us within the church. The Holy Spirit joins humans from every race and socioeconomic status in the world into the one body of Christ. The people of God's presence come together in unity, not because they share common interests, hobbies, or other things that usually bring people together but because the Spirit joins us in fellowship within the presence of God. Paul describes this aspect to the Corinthians: "Just as a body, though one, has many parts, but all its many parts form one body, so it is with Christ. For we were all baptized by one Spirit so as to form one body—whether Jews or Gentiles, slave or free—and we were all given the one Spirit to drink" (1 Cor. 12:12–13). The Spirit weaves a pattern of unity and diversity within the church in a manner similar to the triune life. Clark Pinnock clarifies the Spirit's role in this regard:

> The Spirit is central for ecclesiology because he is the source of fellowship among humans in history and the bond of love between Father and Son in eternity.

3. Jenson, "The Church and the Sacraments," 215.

Fellowship on earth corresponds in a measure to fellowship in heaven. The Trinity is an open, inviting fellowship, and the Spirit wants the church to be the same, responsive in the same sort of way. . . . The Church is meant to resemble the triune life by being itself a place of reciprocity and self-giving. The fellowship that we have with one another is related ultimately to our fellowship with Father and Son (I John 1:3). *Fellowship* refers both to divine life and to community life, because the community is meant to reflect the communion of the Trinity, which is the ontological basis of the Church.[4]

The church, then, is not just any association of people but a community created and sustained by the Holy Spirit. While the people of God cannot reflect the inner trinitarian fellowship perfectly in this life, we are lifted up by the Spirit to create an intimate communion with humans here and now. "En route to the consummation of his purpose, therefore, God calls the church to mirror as far as possible in the midst of the brokenness of the present that eschatological ideal community of love which derives its meaning from the divine essence."[5]

The People of God Edify Each Other

A fundamental point for our proposal about glorifying God first before entering into God's mission in the world is simply this: the gathered people of God must engage and edify each other *before* and *while* engaging the world with the love of God. In God's community we learn to love and live with other human beings in something like a spiritual family. Within the community of believers, we learn how to make room for God and also for "the other." This is requisite for any movement outward. Hence, the mission of God does not begin with evangelism but with gathering in God's presence for worship, learning how to open space for God in our lives as well as for others. Only when we have been encountered and empowered by God's presence can we reach out to other human beings without pride, paternalism, or condemnation. It then becomes the love of God that "constrains us" to offer the ministry of reconciliation (2 Cor. 5:14 KJV). From the centerpiece of worship in glorifying God, we turn naturally to the other in our midst—the "household of faith" or "family of believers" (πρὸς τοὺς οἰκείους τῆς πίστεως | *pros tous oikeious tēs pisteōs*), as Paul calls it. "Therefore, as we have opportunity, let us do

4. Clark Pinnock, *Flame of Love: A Theology of the Holy Spirit* (Downers Grove, IL: Inter-Varsity, 1996), 117.
5. Stanley Grenz, *Theology for the Community of God* (Grand Rapids: Eerdmans, 1994), 483.

good to all people, especially to those who belong to the family of believers" (Gal. 6:10). From that home base of worshiping fellowship, we spill over into making room for others outside the family of God.

This is no simple task. By nature, all humans have felt the dizzying effects of sin's force in us by the ever-constant self-absorption that colors almost everything we do (even the "good" things). Martin Luther offered a metaphor for sin that is filled with richness: sin is the self "curved in on itself" (*homo incurvatus in se*).[6] This is not a mere dallying with one's appearance or thinking about where one might eat lunch while sitting in a boring 11:00 a.m. committee meeting. This inheritance of sin consumes every part of us, warping the love inward that was meant to be directed outward. Other-centered love was the original reflection of God in us; after sin, however, that love has become perverted, twisted into a centripetal force that sucks everything around it into the center of our little universe—namely, the self. Sin is the spiritual black hole that pulls all orbiting objects into its dark and mysterious center. It is a force that is difficult to tame, let alone master.

When we rest in God's presence together during worship, prayer, meditation, Bible study, singing, or any type of effort that glorifies our God and makes room for his presence, we gradually find the centripetal, center-pulling gravitation toward the self to be reversed to a centrifugal, outward force[7] that reconstitutes the genuine unconditional love of God in us so that we become other-centered in our thoughts and actions rather than self-centered.[8] Worship is at the center of this transformation because it makes room for God's presence to encounter us as we really are—even our sinful, private selves—and then makes room in our individual and corporate lives for *growth in character*. Such a central place for corporate worship in the mission of the church

6. Martin Luther, *Luthers Vorlesung über den Römerbrief, 1515/1516: Die Glosse*, ed. Johannes Ficker (Leipzig: Dieterich'sche Verlagsbuchhandlung, Theodor Weicher, 1908), "Corollarium on Romans 8:3," 184, line 18. The entire sentence in Latin and the following one provide explanation and context for this claim: "*Et hoc consonat Scripture, que hominem describit incurvatum in se adeo, ut non tantum corporalia, sed et spiritualia bona sibi inflectit et se in omnibus querit. Que curvatas est nunc naturalis, naturale vitium et naturale malem.*" Here is my translation of this into English: "And this harmonizes with the Scripture that describes a human being as curved in upon itself to such a degree that they bend toward themselves not only bodily things but even spiritually good things and in all things seek themselves." Cf. Luther, *Lectures on Romans*, Ichthus ed., trans. and ed. Wilhelm Pauck, Library of Christian Classics 15 (Philadelphia: Westminster, 1961), 218–19.

7. Technically, this outward tendency in the laws of motion is not a "force" but a result of inertia. Nonetheless, the characteristic feature of centrifugal "force" is that the center is fleeing outward, following a curved path from the center to an object outward.

8. There are flaws in this analogy from physics, but the general point seems similar enough to the reality of sin and its reversal in salvation/sanctification to make this a beneficial comparison.

may seem odd, but little else besides a direct encounter with God will suffice to uproot our habitual nature of self-centeredness. William Willimon has noted that worship does transform us, creating in us a character that lives in response to God's gracious actions toward us by developing gratitude in us. Worship molds us into creatures who are thankful, and this transformation opens up the way for us to live an "ethics of gratitude."[9]

Therefore, we turn now to consider some specific ways in which God's people edify each other, and then we will examine ways that they reach out to others beyond the local community of faith.[10]

Edifying Relationships

The psalmist reminds us that God "sets the lonely in families" (Ps. 68:6). The NIV's marginal reading expands the notion: God sets "the desolate in a homeland." Another translation reads, "God gives the desolate a home to live in" (NRSV). Whatever the precise meaning of these Hebrew words, the context seems clear that God is a "father to the fatherless and a defender of widows" (68:5) and therefore is looking out for those who are orphans, widows, or lonely. In each case, God provides for those in need whatever is most necessary: a father to those without fathers, a defender of those widows who may have been swindled or mishandled, and a maker of families in which solitary or lonely people may live.

Allow me to expand that notion to suggest that God is well aware of the needs of human beings. Just as God said after creating Adam, "It is not good for the man to be alone" (Gen. 2:18), so here he is said to be a creator of the family household so that people will not be alone. In other words, God made humans to enjoy relationships with other humans. I suggest that this idea could be extended to the family of God: God sets individuals together in a community of faith and love so that they may live in the fullness of God's purpose and that they may reflect the nature of God's triune society of love. We reach our fullest potential in relational community, which is why God sets us in families *and*, I believe, why God sets us in the local church. However, because of the fall, sin has broken our capacity for genuine relationality. Relationships today are characterized by alienation,

---

9. William Willimon, *The Service of God: Christian Work and Worship* (Nashville: Abingdon, 1983), 194. This book is extremely suggestive in the relation of ethics and worship. It develops an ethics of character and then proceeds to show how worship makes a difference in one's moral life.

10. This list is not exhaustive but points to several of the major tasks that I deem relevant for the twenty-first century *and* connected to what it means to be the people of God's presence in both the past and future.

distance, and enmity, as well as love, intimacy, and friendship. Even the best of our human relationships are tainted by some sort of self-interest. Yet God has "set us" in the family of church so that we give of ourselves to other believers and may also take from them what is lacking in us. Indeed, our own identity as a human being who follows Christ and has been transformed by God's presence.awaits us only in communal relationships, not in the idolatry of isolated self-centeredness. As Daniel Migliore says, "In the light of Jesus Christ, to be fully human is to be in relationship with God and others. Christian identity is found in a community that is open to and inclusive of the stranger. Growth in Christian life is measured by an increasing ability to affirm the worth of others who are different in important ways from us."[11]

So, does becoming a Christian really make any difference in our relationships, or does the transforming power of Christ not extend to this interpersonal arena of our lives? Although building human relationships within the context of the fall is hard work, it is possible to overcome the alienating forces by the power of God's Spirit, thereby forging relationships in the body of Christ that point (even in a limited way) to the healthy and fully functional relationships that we will share together in God's eternal presence.

Building relationships is not always easy. Sometimes when we meet other people, something "gels" with us. In these cases, relationship building merely requires intentionality so that we build on the foundation of similar likes and dislikes. Yet there are other cases where people do not readily appeal to us as someone we would like to know better. We do not imagine ourselves eating lunch with them or having them over to the house and appreciating every minute of it. We have a strong tendency to categorize people according to how we *perceive* they might match our personalities. Unfortunately, this human impulse to congregate around similar likes and dislikes is quite ubiquitous, even in the church. We were not brought into the body of Christ in order to pigeonhole people into categories of those with whom we will or will not associate. God brings us into a spiritual family so that we might bring our gifts and calling to that family and thereby help it grow into the full measurement of Christ. At the same time, others in that family exercise their own strengths and gifts, creating a growing environment for all of us in the body. While we may not be able to be close to every person in the local church, we can be intentional about building close relationships that edify each other and the entire community.

---

11. Daniel L. Migliore, *The Power of God and the gods of Power* (Louisville: Westminster John Knox, 2008), 105.

A crucible for developing and growing relationality that reflects the nature of our God is a good way to describe the local church. It is through building relationships with other human beings that our own idiosyncrasies become prominent and then can be dealt with. This activity also is done in a community where there are always different levels of spiritual and emotional maturity. Loving each other in relationship becomes a crucible where God places a purifying flame under us to raise to the surface the dross that has settled in hidden crevices of our hearts. This is actually a gracious gift that God gives us through our sisters and brothers in Christ. It is in this community, whose foundation is love, that we begin to understand the unconditional love of God for us because we have witnessed such love shared with us when we did not deserve it. Daniel Migliore uses another metaphor to describe the church: it is "essential for growth in Christian life because it provides the training ground for a new humanity."[12] In the context of loving relationships drawn together by the Spirit in the bond of peace, believers *learn how to deal with other humans in a Christlike manner in the training ground of the Christian community*, thereby acquiring much-needed skills for the mission of outreach assigned to the church.

Here is why this task—building relationships that edify—is so crucial for mission: if we cannot show love for each other in the local assembly of the people of God, how can we expect to show love to people outside of that community? How can we expect the world to believe our witness to Christ's unconditional love if they never see it evidenced in our lives? If we build edifying relationships in the local body of Christ, we will be better prepared to make relationships that are meaningful and important for the cause of Christ with those who do not know this love that compels us to share it.

A final thought on edifying relationships in the church is necessary. While I have called for the local church to be a place where the Spirit teaches us what it means to be a new creature in Christ Jesus with other believers who are learning the same thing, I do not mean to imply that this inward, one-another focus is a permanent location for the people of God. True mission is birthed in the rich fellowship of the Triune God with God's people in a particular location, but if it only circulates around itself, it has lost the purpose for its existence. In the end, the "training ground" or "crucible" for learning how to relate to other humans is only meant as a station along the way to everyday mission. It is true that believers go out and come in, go out and come back in, but the going out

---

12. Daniel Migliore, *The Power of God*, Library of Living Faith, ed. John M. Mulder (Philadelphia: Westminster, 1983), 88. This comment did not remain in the revised edition of 2008, so I have cited the first edition.

must be based on the skills learned and motivations received when one comes "back in" the local gathering. The richness of Christian fellowship *always* seeks other people to join its joyous dance. It causes us to move into the corridors of hate with the light of God's love, into the gutters of despair with the hope of change, into the abuse of power with a servant's heart. It is not God's intention for the church to be the goal, the end of all things. It is to be a step toward the goal of representing the kingdom of God to the world. In this process, then, there is joy in reaching out to others, especially others who are most unlike us. I prefer to call these people the "radical other," since it underscores the sense of extreme difference between us. It also is precisely how God came to us from his rich fellowship of divinity, reaching out to us who are not divine in any sense of the word. When Christ came to seek and save the lost, he came to the most radically other possible. Therefore, our mission is not to build relationships in the church in order to "be blessed" by them, excluding all future participants from our group and denying access to those with whom we do not prefer to commune. The church is based on the love of God, which is the most inclusive love ever known. Diversity among the body of Christ prepares us for dealing with people who are not part of our racial ethnicity or socioeconomic stratum or whatever self-inscribed standard might apply to others. God loves diversity— and so should God's people! Indeed, as Migliore emphasizes, "Homogeneity in the Christian community is a contradiction of the gospel of God's powerful love, which frees us to accept as brothers and sisters those from whom we were previously estranged. A community that calls itself Christian and is complacent about its economic, racial, and cultural homogeneity is a community without the power of the Spirit."[13] Amen.

Operating with Gifts of the Spirit

Sandwiched between two chapters on the gifts of the Spirit lies a profound and rich description of the need for love in the body of Christ so that the gifts themselves may operate properly (1 Cor. 13). The Corinthian church possessed many spiritual gifts but did not possess them in love (1:7). Upon the foundation of love, the Spirit distributes gifts as he wills (12:11). Love knows that the purpose for the gifts is the edification of the body. The gifts of the Spirit descend on our gatherings for the benefit of the people of God, to make room for God's presence to accomplish what he wills.

It is not a coincidence that the body of Christ is the context for listing the gifts found in Romans 12 and 1 Corinthians 12. As our bodies are units with

---

13. Migliore, *The Power of God* (2008), 88.

a variety of parts, so the body of Christ is one yet with many members who perform various functions. A specific description and commentary on the gifts of the Spirit is not our purpose here; rather, we are focusing on the fact that the Spirit dispenses gifts among us *individually* so that the *whole* might be encouraged and strengthened. As we make room for the presence of God among us, the Spirit makes room among us for a diversity of gifts to operate so that the people of God may fulfill the mission to which God has called them. "Gifts are divine actions that build up the community and advance its mission. They demonstrate the power of the Spirit, who is at work in the church. They are manifestations of the Spirit's presence" (1 Cor. 12:7).[14]

In the midst of intensive instruction from Paul on how the Corinthians should change their worship agenda in their meetings, there is a surprising clue about worship in the first-century church: "When you come together, each of you has a hymn, or a word of instruction, a revelation, a tongue or an interpretation. Everything must be done so that the church may be built up" (1 Cor. 14:26). From these words it appears that people gathered together with something already deposited in their hearts by God's Spirit during the previous week. They came prepared to share. That was *not* the issue that Paul had with them! The fact that they all possessed every spiritual gift among them was something Paul praised (1:7). So they came and exercised the gifts with exuberance and ecstatic utterance, but not with much love for the other. They made room for *themselves*, not for God or for the others among them. How is this selfishness seen? They confused almost everyone who came into their meetings because of the popcorn-like jumping to speak a revelation or pray in a tongue or proclaim prophecy. Paul calls for order in their chaotic worship, for the purpose of building up the body not for the purpose of squelching their enthusiasm or the presence of the Spirit in their midst. Sadly, many have read 1 Corinthians 14 as a manual for shutting down *any* operation of spiritual gifts among the people of God. Instead, this passage needs to be read from the perspective of the entire epistle, where Paul has chided the Corinthians for numerous problems—all of which seem to be traced back to abnormal self-centeredness. They had all kinds of gifts but lacked love for others. So rather than shutting down the gifts of the Spirit entirely, he asked that, for the sake of the people attending, everything be done in a more orderly manner so that everyone could benefit.

The manner in which we *make room for* the Spirit's presence among us is not to open our church meetings to chaos, rendering unintelligible whatever it might have been that God wanted to do or say in our midst. At the other

14. Pinnock, *Flame of Love*, 130.

extreme, the manner of making room for God's presence is also not to close our gatherings to the Spirit—the very One who binds us to Christ and to each other. It should be no strange thing for a Christian to believe that God speaks to him or her, yet I find rather large numbers of people today feel that such "speaking" is really in one's head or a result of medication (or lack thereof). When Jesus said, "[The shepherd] goes on ahead of [the sheep], and his sheep follow him because they know his voice" (John 10:4), isn't it reasonable to think that this style of intimate communication between sheep and a shepherd is at the very least the *point* of the metaphor in this verse? God is talking to his children. This should not seem strange. God is talking to his church, his gathered people; this, too, should not seem strange. To relegate such communication from God solely to the pastor or priest of the congregation misses the variety and richness of the Spirit's distribution of the gifts among the congregation. I should think that the people of the world who have grown calloused to our preaching and teaching would find it astounding (and convincing!) if while someone is prophesying, "an unbeliever or an inquirer comes in, . . . [and] they are convicted of sin and are brought under judgment by all, as the secrets of their hearts are laid bare. So they will fall down and worship God, exclaiming, 'God is really among you!'" (1 Cor. 14:24–25). That might draw people back to the church—certainly it is vastly more appealing than rotating lights and dried ice! People want—no, desperately need—God's presence. The church must demonstrate that God's presence is in the midst of his people, and it is a marvelous thing in everyone's sight. Therefore, the church of the twenty-first century needs greater openness to freedom of participation on the part of *everyone* in the community; it needs greater welcoming of the Spirit's presence, the ministering through fellow believers not simply through paid or professional clergy. The Spirit falls on whomever the Spirit wills, distributing to one this particular gift and to another a different gift, but giving to all the full array of the Spirit's arsenal so that every person in the community—believers and unbelievers—may benefit.

There is much in our history as the Christian church that has reacted against emotionalism and fanaticism—and appropriately so in many cases. Is it possible, however, that by tamping down too firmly on these excesses we have choked our attention to the Spirit? Have we lost the joy of bathing in God's presence together? Do we really believe what we *say* about who God is and how he communicates with us? Or are Sunday gatherings for ourselves and not for this God? It is impossible to tame or domesticate our God. The Spirit will "out" where and when the Spirit will. This is especially true when what is at stake is the well-being of God's people. Our task today as the people of God's presence is to make room for God among us.

When we gather as the people of God, we should come ready to be used by God's Spirit and ready to receive from God's Spirit. The people of God's presence commune with the Spirit during the week and therefore are in tune with the Spirit when assembled for worship. They are ready and willing to be used by the Spirit in order to edify the body of Christ.

Nurturing Discipleship

Another task that relates to how the people of God show their love for one another is training one another in ways of following Christ. Frequently, this can be the older training the younger, but training does not need to flow in only one direction. Discipleship is learning how to follow after Christ. Unfortunately, churches in North America have lessened their focus on training believers *how* to live the Christian life in today's society. While we have concentrated efforts on preaching, evangelism, and potluck dinners, we have left discipleship to the Sunday school or some other educational arm of the church—if there is one.

One aspect of the Great Commission is to "make disciples" (Matt. 28:19–20). We are to train new converts, to be sure, but we are all responsible for each other in the body of Christ, both young and old. A principle that Paul used was to have the older train the younger—a rather natural process of training.[15] Outside of the formal training that any local church might offer through a Christian education program, the people of God's presence open up their lives and homes to other believers so as to experience mutual nurturing and accountability. The people of God make room for God's people.

The Christian walk is better "caught" than "taught." Authentic Christian living is not merely the dissemination of information but the learning of spiritual disciplines and being formed by habits of life. I learned *about* prayer in Sunday school, college, and seminary. However, I really learned to pray at my grandparents' feet as a little boy. I learned to pray from the Ladies Willing Worker Band of our little country church when my mother took me along as a four-year-old to their house meetings. I learned to pray by hearing other faithful saints pray, both inside and outside the church building. Without knowing it, many believers influenced the nurturing of my Christian walk. And so we also influence more lives than we can imagine by the way we live out our spiritual relationship with God in the presence of others in the community of faith.

The "heart habits" of the Christian life are best learned in a relationship with other believers. The church of Jesus Christ is in desperate need of people

---

15. See Titus 2:3–8. Also, consider Paul's own mentoring of Timothy and Titus.

who have time (or are willing to sacrifice time) to mentor other believers by sharing their lives with them. No one person can perform this task of mentoring. The body of Christ grows as each part does its assigned task (Eph. 4:11–16). I cannot grow into the person of God that I am meant to be without others in the body doing their part.

Sharing Testimonies

Another way God's people edify each other is through testimonies. This is a form of verbal witness in a public setting—usually when the church is gathered for worship. Testimonies may be a strange task of the church to consider here since such witness may not be part of the official liturgy of every tradition in Christianity. It was a part of my church life when I was younger; given the importance of witness and storytelling, which is part of reflecting on the encounter with God's presence that believers have experienced, it probably should become a central feature of our gatherings again.

Each of us has a story with God that can be shared. Whether we share it verbally during a worship gathering or in written form for a magazine or flyer, it is important that we offer witness to the presence of God in our lives. Such testimonies of God's faithfulness and presence are an old tradition among God's people. Consider some of the psalms. Many of them rehearse the stories of God's goodness and faithfulness to his people (e.g., Pss. 106; 107). Consider the personal stories told from the Acts of the Apostles, such as Stephen's words before the Sanhedrin and Paul's words before Roman governors concerning his own conversion. Indeed, a good part of the biblical narrative weaves stories of humanity's experience with God along with other information, thereby offering a vast amount of knowledge about our God and even about humanity itself. Stories, therefore, are part of the Christian experience and tradition.

It is fitting that we should speak the praises of God in the midst of the congregation. Doing this is a vital way that we magnify the Lord before others. From my earliest days as a child, I recall hearing the saints in our little country church stand each Sunday evening, sometimes even on Sunday morning, to testify. Like witnesses called to the stand, one after another they spoke the truth of what they saw or experienced that week in their relationship with God. Some people told lengthy stories about God's intervention; other people were short and terse, thanking God for helping them find their car keys that week or reminding them of an important task or even healing their child from fever. Some were lurid, describing in detail the mess they were in when God found them and how grateful they were now that they were walking in the light; others gave quotations of a favorite Bible verse that was particularly comforting to them at that moment. The point is that *life stories* with and about God were woven into the fabric of our church community. This was not a God in a far-off, distant place but a God who intervened and labored alongside of these hardworking people, just like the God of the Bible. I grew up with a sense of expectation that God could work in my life as well.

While most of the stories were uplifting and positive, there were times when people exposed the lament of their souls. They stood and revealed their grief at the passing of a loved one or poured out their fear over the son who had just been sent overseas to a war in Vietnam. These stories were not fairy tales with predictable happy endings. Some people rose to speak *in spite of* the circumstances of their lives, testifying to the goodness of the Lord in the land of the living. Like Job, they testified to God's faithfulness amid their pain. Yet always they ended with a note of praise and expectation that God knew best and that he was going to work everything for the good. These stories were different in tone and substance from the victorious testimonies of other saints, but they were not different in their conclusions. There is a God who loves us when things are going well and when things are going poorly. This I learned in a small, rural church while listening to the people of God testify.

What a pity that many church meetings today do not allow for such openness and honesty, such vulnerability and sharing from the heart. When I ask my students why people in their twenties do not want to attend church (but usually want some form of spirituality), the answer is varied but frequently includes this: they do not like the lack of authenticity they sense in churches. Perhaps the church today needs to return to simple storytelling from God's people to God's people. Somehow we feel embarrassed or tense when someone stands in the pew to speak. Only those on the platform should speak—or so we think. In larger sanctuaries, people in the pew cannot really be heard, yet all of the microphones are on the platform, giving the message that the important things said today will come from the front, not from the pews. By silencing the testimonies of God's people, we mute the faithful voices that would bear witness to all who might hear of the love and faithfulness of God. We need the voices of fellow believers to remind us of God's presence in the darkness, and we need to stand in the midst of God's faithful people to tell of God's presence in the darkness! Testimonies build up the people of God by telling the stories of God's work in our lives. The people of God witness to the God who encounters them by telling stories about those events, thereby making room for God to be glorified.

Confessing Sins

A number of liturgies for Christian worship begin with a general confession of sins or some form of acknowledgment that we have sinned in what we have done and not done. Such confession is usually followed by some type of pronouncement or reminder of the grace and forgiveness of God. Congregations that do not allow for such public admission that we are not all we can be in Christ are the lesser for it. James reminds us, "Confess your sins to each other and pray for each other so that you may be healed" (James 5:16). We cannot be whole without confession of our sins to each other. Admitting that we are imperfect and at times overcome by the sin nature helps us all to understand the instability of the human heart and forces us to rely on God's grace within the context of a community of believers who are also imperfect and in need of God's grace.

It is a pillar of Protestantism that we have one mediator for our sins, Christ Jesus. In 1520, Martin Luther struggled over whether the sacrament of penance should be held on to in the new reforming movement. Along with baptism and communion, he felt that it may have necessary elements to assist believers in understanding the thing it signifies—namely, gracious forgiveness. However, in the end he opted to keep confession of sins to the minister and others but not as a sacrament.[16] One aspect of the Lutheran Church that I admire is this very point. A minister who hears someone's confession announces that God forgives. It isn't absolution per se (as in Roman Catholicism), but it is a pronouncement of the good news in their lives and over their sin. Perhaps evangelical Protestants today have sidestepped the confessional in favor of Christ as our only mediator, but by so doing we may have overplayed this point and bypassed the benefit of admitting our sins to one another for the sake of our emotional, spiritual, and physical health. Moreover, hearing another human being pronounce forgiveness based on our repentance and God's Word can be an invigorating and inspiring release from our sins and the burden of the guilt that we carry.

The people of God's presence edify one another by being this vulnerable, unmasking the pretensions of spiritual pride and opening the heart for honest relationality. Too frequently we walk in self-assured righteousness, assuming

16. See Martin Luther, *The Babylonian Captivity of the Church [1520]*, trans. Erik H. Herrmann, in *The Annotated Luther*, ed. Hans J. Hillerbrand, Kirsi I. Stjerna, and Timothy J. Wengert, vol. 3, *Church and Sacraments*, ed. Paul W. Robinson (Minneapolis: Fortress, 2016), 127. Luther notes that baptism and communion fulfill the requirements for a true sacrament— namely, divine institution and promise of forgiveness of sins. While penance does not meet the requirement for divine institution, it does function as a "return to baptism." Therefore, it has a somewhat nebulous life as a quasi-sacrament at this point in Luther's career.

that no one knows or needs to know the trouble we have in our lives or, indeed, the sin we may carry. We pretend to be people we are not, thereby hindering the possibility for God to work through us since we cannot admit there is a problem. A people who live in God's presence understand the need for confessing sins and know the grace of God's forgiveness to cleanse them. When we walk with each other in this life, we need to confess our sins to others and open our lives to the inspection of the Spirit for "hidden sins." To be sure, confessing before random people or even before the whole congregation may not be helpful or wise. We should seek out relationships where we learn to trust that there is unconditional love among us and attempt to walk in the light as he is in the light. To do so will inevitably require us to confess our sins, as John tells us (1 John 1:9). Confessing sins to one another is one more way the body works to edify or build itself up in love, making room for the joy of transparency before God and others.

Anointing with Oil

In the same passage where James speaks of confession of sins (James 5:16), there is a call for those who are sick to receive prayer and anointing with oil. "Is anyone among you sick? Let them call the elders of the church to pray over them and anoint them with oil in the name of the Lord. And the prayer offered in faith will make the sick person well; the Lord will raise them up. If they have sinned, they will be forgiven" (5:14–15). The people of God edify each other through praying for one another, especially in times of illness. Sickness can drag one through the depths of depression and may produce absorbing self-centeredness, even in the most selfless person. Pain has a way of bringing one's attention entirely onto the self, as if the whole rest of the world does not even exist—except as mute witness to one's pain. At these times we should call for the elders of the church to pray for us and anoint us with oil.[17]

Notice that the context of this call for elders is in a passage related to the body of Christ. In a manner reminiscent of Paul's encouragement to the Corinthian church (if one suffers, all suffer), we hear James asking, "Is anyone among you in trouble? Let them pray. Is anyone happy? Let them sing songs

---

17. I deal with the issue of who elders are in *Serving the People of God's Presence*. For issues related to the problem of pain and sickness, especially in relation to the promise of healing, see Terry L. Cross, "The Doctrine of Divine Healing," in *Transforming Power*, ed. Yung Chul Han and Wanda Griffith (Cleveland, TN: Pathway, 2001), 179–231. Also, see John Christopher Thomas, *The Devil, Disease and Deliverance: Origins of Illness in New Testament Thought*, Journal of Pentecostal Theology Supplement Series 13, ed. John Christopher Thomas, Rickie D. Moore, and Steven J. Land (Sheffield: Sheffield Academic, 1998), esp. 19–37 on James 5.

of praise. Is anyone among you sick? Let them call the elders of the church" (James 5:13–14a). Listing the variety of circumstances within which believers might find themselves, James encourages us to pray, sing, and be anointed with oil. The context seems to imply that this is done in the congregation so that "if one part suffers, every part suffers with it; if one part is honored, every part rejoices with it" (1 Cor. 12:26).

In times of trouble or joy, we need each other. In such times, *we are to do something*—sing or pray. However, in times of sickness, we especially need others in the body of Christ. In such times we are to call for the elders of the church and let them do something. While they are on this earth and within the frailty of human existence, the people of God's presence will probably become ill from something in their lives. By making room for the leadership of the church to know about their illness and to pray for them, the people of God create space for God's presence to heal and forgive them.

In ancient times, oil was equated with medicinal properties. It was a soothing salve on a wound or even assisted in the healing process. James uses it here undoubtedly because it was a practice among the disciples of Jesus, as in Mark 6:13: "They drove out many demons and anointed many sick people with oil and healed them." However, it should not be viewed as magical. Chris Thomas has offered insight into anointing with oil: "Inasmuch as the anointing is to function alongside prayer, and healing is not dependent on the anointing with oil (as v. 16 makes clear), it is likely that the anointing with oil serves as some kind of sign. . . . Given its many associations with medicine, it seems natural that oil would serve as a sign of healing."[18]

This is not the place to discuss why God seems to heal some believers in this life and not others. It is enough to say that certain Scriptures balance this out so that we should come to God expecting entire healing, but if that is not granted us, we still remain God's servants and live out our days in faithful submission to his will, which is hidden from us in mystery at this time. The crucial aspect for our concern here is that we tell the people of God when we are not well; we are prayed for by the elders and those around us. The people of God's presence are a praying, believing people who are open to the move of the miraculous hand of God in their midst. Such prayer for the sick is an essential ingredient in the life of the church. The people of God's presence make room for the sick by praying for God's intervention, either for physical healing or the grace to endure the suffering without losing faith.

18. John Christopher Thomas, "The Prayer of Faith in James 5:14–16," in *Ministry and Theology: Studies for the Church and Its Leaders* (Cleveland, TN: Pathway, 1996), 106.

Going to the Altar

The architecture of many church buildings has changed and is still changing. Some local churches have auditoriums or buildings that do not possess any of the "trappings" of Christian architecture or art. Other local congregations take great care to reflect their theological understanding of worship in their architecture and art. In most churches, there is an altar of some kind. In some churches, it is a barrier between the people of God and the priest who ministers on their behalf. In other churches, it is a rail at which people come forward to pray or receive communion.

Whether or not there is an actual physical altar in the building where the people of God meet, there needs to be a place where we can gather for prayer *together*. It is true that we can pray in our seats or in isolated prayer rooms off of the side of the sanctuary or even in our own homes, but the point of the people of God assembling to glorify God and edify each other should not leave out this integral ingredient: praying for one another, not in the silent isolation of our minds but in the communal presence of brothers and sisters in Christ before our God. In whatever building we meet, there should be space and time for praying together. Here I am not referring to carving out time in the liturgy for responsive lines nor the much-used "pastoral prayer" in which Protestant pastors offer prayer for the people as if they, the pastors, were priests. These may have necessary and even important functions within the framework of worship, but they miss an ingredient that seems necessary for any local body of Christ: praying with each other and for each other. To do this, I must have some idea of another's needs; I also must have space and time to reach out to others in the body of Christ and touch them in their need. I must have space and time *within the gathering of the people of God in God's presence to pray for others*. It is vital that members of the body of Christ hear others speaking their names out to God on their behalf; further, it may be just as necessary that this type of praying *not* be done by those whom we expect should pray for us (the pastors or elders or leaders). The type of prayer that I am proposing with this metaphor of the altar is an outgrowth of body ministry; it requires making room for people to minister to each other and to be ministered to. This type of praying cannot be equated with the greeting of one another in the pew behind or in front of you. It must be *prayer—communication with God in a petitionary, intercessory manner for the needs of fellow believers*.

It is this laying on of hands and praying for one another that I find symbolized by the use of the word "altar." Indeed, part of the reason for using this word is my own Pentecostal heritage. The altar was not where the Eucharist was shared; it was not the communion table. The altar was not just a rail at the front where only sinners came to pray (the old-time "mourners' bench," leftover from the revival years in the 1800s). The altar was a place of prayer where I could go to pray over my own failings and weaknesses and expect to find another brother or sister praying next to me for my needs. It was also the place where I prayed for others. In the body of Christ, we edify each other when we join together in prayer for one another.

The altar was also a place of surrender to God. The Old Testament imagery of sacrifice was never far from my mind when I went forward to the altar. I knew that there were things I needed to lay down on the altar—things I needed to slay and sacrifice to God. And there were things God needed to slay in me at the altar—things that I could not see or that I would not acknowledge. At the altar, I knew God would meet me directly, and that was not always a comfortable thing!

For all of this to function well, I needed my sisters and brothers in Christ to pray with me. Their physical presence and their verbal support raised heavenward on my behalf encouraged me to offer my whole life to God. Rising from that altar, I always walked away a better believer and usually found a way to be with someone else the next time the altar was open for prayer, assisting them in surrendering all.

Using this example from my personal life and offering a metaphor like the altar is risky in that the reader may be primed to think of this task of God's people as a *place* rather than an *image for what happens at that place*. I believe that we do not pray together enough in our churches—we have relegated that to the professionals. I believe that we do not "tarry" long in God's presence, be that at a physical altar rail at the front of the sanctuary or kneeling in a pew in the back. As a child I vividly remember "tarrying" meetings, where the church—the whole church!—would gather to wait on God. I remember these well because as a four- or five-year-old, I thought they were talking about me (my first name is pronounced the same as "tarry"). I must admit that for a preschooler, these meetings that were named after me (or so I thought) did not end up being very appealing. There were usually people all over the church, kneeling at the altar or in the pews. There was no preaching, no singing, no testimonies, no public Bible reading; we had come to wait . . . on God. I never did understand what it would look like if God showed up. Frankly, I thought the older folks of the church were just too tired to do anything else but kneel down and talk in a low voice to God. Little did I know what was really going on! When I was a teenager, I do not recall attending any more tarrying services. We were too busy—and by then some of the oldest among us, who had found that tradition essential for anyone's Christian walk, had passed on to their reward.

What would happen in our churches today if anyone called for a "tarrying service" like in the old days? Many of us who lead or have led churches know the answer: perhaps two or three people would show up, but it would not become a consistent experience in the life of every believer in that church. How do we make room for God if we are not praying together? How do we make room for each other if we do not "tarry together" over burdens we carry, if we do not voice the name of our brother or sister and their needs aloud so that their ears can hear our own cry to God on their behalf? How do we expect the next generation of Christians to *be the church* when we do not demonstrate the power of unity in Christian relationships—something perhaps most powerfully demonstrated when we *pray one for another*?

The People of God Reach Outward

The Eccentricity and Ecstasy of God and God's People

We have already established that the church is not just another social club among human institutions. We are brought together by the will of the Spirit, not by the common interests we may hold. Therefore, we gather not simply to enjoy our God and each other's company but to do the will of the Father as Jesus did. By being drawn into the trinitarian fellowship of Father, Son, and Spirit, our own natures and wills come to align with God's. Baptized into his loving presence, we rise, dripping with the aroma of unconditional love, and enter a world that is desperate for such love. We edify each other, to be sure, but that is not the final purpose of our salvation or of our gathering together. Just as it is the nature of God to reach out to the radically other (that is, humanity), so it becomes our nature as we participate with him to reach out to those who are the despised, rejected, and marginalized of society. The love of God that is poured out in our hearts by the Spirit (Rom. 5:5) compels us to share the message of love and reconciliation with others (2 Cor. 5:12–21). If the people of God only circulate around each other, they have missed a vital feature of their reason for existence: to share the gospel in word and deed with others who do not know Christ.

Why have I placed a discussion of reaching out to others with the section titled "The Church in Fellowship"? Does not this discussion on outreach merit a section all its own? To place the missionary work of the church under the section of fellowship is not to demean or replace this outward directed work but rather to place it precisely within the outgrowth of the fellowship of the Triune God and the fellowship of the people of God. As Elton Trueblood has noted, "Christians may indeed *come in*, but they do so only that they may, in consequence, *go out*, and furthermore, that they may go out with greater effectiveness."[19] Out of the richness of trinitarian fellowship, the Spirit reaches out to the humans of the world that God has created. It seems clear that there is a necessary connection between our fellowship with each other in the Spirit and our natural impetus to reach out to others. As Clark Pinnock describes the Spirit's role in this work, fellowship is a central aspect of the Spirit's work in trinitarian relations. The rich fellowship there overflows in the work of the Spirit, who "takes point" in reaching out in fellowship to humanity. Pinnock suggests that the Spirit completes the trinitarian circle and "opens it up to the world outside God."[20] To describe this reaching out, Pinnock uses the term "ecstasy," which comes from the Greek words meaning to "stand outside of one's self." The Spirit is the ecstasy of the Triune God, the One who "makes the triune life an open circle and a source of pure abundance. Spirit embodies and triggers the overflow of God's pure benevolence, fosters its ecstatic character and opens it up to history."[21] God becomes a "missionary" in the sense that he reaches out to foreign and alienated humans, sending his Son for the sake of our salvation and for an opportunity to invite humans to participate in the fullness of his trinitarian fellowship.

Since the God of the people of God is a missionary God, the life of the church should reflect this calling. We are to reach out, to send out, to be "ecstatic" toward the radically other, offering them the reconciliation of the Son to the Father through the Holy Spirit. "The reconciling mission of the incarnate Word and the transforming mission of the Spirit identify the God of Christian faith as a missionary God. A proper understanding of the church and its mission begins with this recognition: that the Triune God initiates mission and the church is called to participate in that mission."[22] In this reconciling mission, God is especially interested in the outcast and marginalized, the stranger, the Other, the "alien and disturbingly different."[23]

Godly mission in this world does not promise to be free from the mud and grime of sinful reality. Stepping into the world to minister to it without

19. Elton Trueblood, *The Company of the Committed* (New York: Harper & Brothers, 1961), 69.

20. Pinnock, *Flame of Love*, 38.

21. Pinnock, *Flame of Love*, 38.

22. Daniel Migliore, "The Missionary God and the Missionary Church," *Princeton Seminary Bulletin*, NS, 19, no. 1 (1998): 14–25, here 18.

23. Migliore, "The Missionary God and the Missionary Church," 20. Migliore makes it clear that here we are dealing with a paradox. God causes the rain to fall on the just and unjust alike, so it appears that he shows no favorites and treats no one with favoritism. The paradox is that God is able to treat people with this "wideness of mercy" and yet especially embraces the downtrodden and despised (cf. Deut. 24:17–18).

pretense or self-righteous pride is the call of the church. We are at our highest when we stoop into the gutters of this world to minister to those in need because we more perfectly reflect the true nature of the Triune God, who sent his Son to stoop into the stables, taverns, and gutters of this world to win those who were lost. The church that has a plethora of programs and is clothed in purple but does not take the gospel to the streets should expect to receive the same judgment from our Lord as the church of Laodicea (Rev. 3:17).

Why do the people of God's presence reach out to other human beings? What is the motivation and rationale for outreach? At this point the Swiss theologian Karl Barth can assist us greatly. In the fourth volume of his *Church Dogmatics*, Barth divides his discussion of reconciliation into three sections (with one volume for each section). In each of these sections, he addresses a doctrinal component of reconciliation along with an ecclesial component that describes the concomitant effect for the community (*Gemeinde*) of believers.[24] These are divided as follows: *CD* IV/1: the doctrine of justification and the *gathering* of the community; *CD* IV/2: the doctrine of sanctification and the *upbuilding* of the community; *CD* IV/3: the doctrine of vocation and the *sending* of the community. Barth's point here seems to be that these two doctrinal aspects (soteriology and ecclesiology) are related to each other *and* are connected at some basic level to the doctrine of the Triune God. How is this the case? Barth establishes a clear connection between God's being and God's doing. It is the nature of God to be other-centered, first within the fellowship of the persons of the Triune God and second toward the persons for whom he has "made room" in creation. It is the task of the church to exist in reflection of the other-centeredness of its God.

---

24. There are several terms in German that couch Barth's ecclesiology in a very different "feel" for German readers than the English translation has provided (or perhaps can provide?). The term most prominent throughout Barth's ecclesiological considerations is the persistent use of *Gemeinde*, or "community/congregation," instead of or in addition to *Kirche* (church). To be sure, Barth does not eliminate *Kirche* entirely from his vocabulary in *CD* IV, but the predominance of *Gemeinde* is frankly head-spinning. Barth notes that Luther had wanted to make this word, *Gemeinde*, the only word for church but in the end did not do so. "What is certain is that Luther preferred not to use the word [*Kirche*] at all, but to speak of the 'community' [*Gemeinde*], the 'congregation' [*Sammlung*], the 'company' [*Haufen*] or 'little company' [*Häuflein*], or even 'Christendom' [*Christenheit*]." *CD* IV/1:651. Also, *Die Lehre von der Versöhnung*, in *KD* IV/1:728. However, Barth notes that finding appropriate translations for *ekklēsia* (church) is fraught with difficulty. In an earlier address (1947), he provides a lengthier description of the linguistic problem concerning "church" and admits there as well that "the mere substitution of 'congregation' or 'community' for the word 'Church' would not be worthwhile." See Barth, "The Church: The Living Congregation of the Living Lord Jesus Christ," in *God Here and Now*, trans. Paul van Buren (London: Routledge, 2003; 1st English ed., 1964), 75–104, here 82.

God is a being whose action perfectly corresponds to his being. When God stoops to earth to reconcile sinful humans through the incarnate ministry of the Son, God is revealing Godself in human history in a way that corresponds to God's own other-regarding life in the triune fellowship. This means that "as God was in Christ, far from being against himself, or at disunity with himself, . . . he has done that which corresponds to his divine nature" (CD IV/1:186). How God acts in our history is already shaped by how God exists in eternity.

We may call this "bent" of God's character toward the creature by a mathematical term: eccentricity.[25] In English, the word "eccentric" can have two meanings: (1) off-centered, out of kilter, elliptical, not having the same center; not concentric; and (2) an oddball, someone exhibiting old-fashioned traits. It is the more mathematical first definition that we are using here when speaking of God's character as eccentric. When an orbit does not spin or move from a central location for its axis, its movement becomes more elliptical than circular. It is almost as if the orbit becomes elongated toward something. When used in theology with reference to God, we are referring to God's outward movement toward others, which causes his "orbit" of influence to reach out beyond a circular pattern, which might be expected, to an elliptical pattern, which includes those unreachable within a regular circular extension. Just as God's own life is marked by this eccentric pattern, leaning toward humanity in love, so too must the church's life be eccentric—that is, "bent" or "elongated" toward other humans.

In the same eccentric style of love with which God acts, the people of God operate with a human counterpart to the divine action. The Spirit gathers us together, shaping our "being" as a community of humans; from this "being" as a communion of other-regarding people, the Spirit sends us out to be a witness to God's life in Jesus Christ. To describe this community accurately, Barth suggests, "We must abandon the usual distinctions between being and act, status and dynamic, essence and existence. Its act is its being, its status its dynamic, its essence its existence" (CD IV/1:650).

In and from eternity, God chose *for humankind*. This is the eternal basis of God's historical action in Christ. Within the triune life of God, there is a teleologically oriented movement toward the human being as revealed in the economy of salvation. God's life and eternal decision anticipate this movement into historical reality *for* the human. The being of God has determined

---

25. It comes from the Greek, *ek* + *kentros* which means "out of the center." When referring to an orbit, it speaks of not having its axis placed centrally, thereby creating an orbit that is not circular but elliptical or irregular to some marked degree. Similar to how *ecstatic* (*ek* + *stasis* = to stand outside of oneself) is used of God to describe the Trinity's other-centered focus, *eccentric* is used to describe God's unusual extension to reach out to the other.

its own act and life by a "deliberate act" of begetting the Son, which is not a second step alongside who God is in and for himself but the determination of his own life.[26] Contained *within* the social life of the Triune God is the *missio Dei*—the movement and orientation for the Other. Such insight is absolutely crucial for one's ecclesiology. Here the point for Barth is that God's own eternal being is in unison with God's historical action in Jesus Christ. God's acting corresponds with God's being. The life, death, and resurrection of Jesus Christ correspond to the being of the Triune God so that becoming a human was not a "second step" alongside a first—not an afterthought—but indeed consonant with God's own nature. God's eternal decision to be for and with the human is not an add-on to his character but has been determined already *within* the eternal character of the living God. Colin Gunton has noted that the consistency between God's being and acting may be seen as the "holiness" of God's character, so that the actions reflect the being with integrity and wholeness.[27] God is in God's doing (mission) precisely what God is in God's being (nature). Therefore, "God's act in reconciling the world to himself is not a second step alongside his being in and for himself."[28]

However, as John Flett has masterfully shown, any bifurcation between an understanding of God's being and action has negative ramifications for one's doctrine of the church. How can this be? If there is a "breach in the being and act of God," then that rupture becomes replicated as a "breach in the being and act of his community."[29] If it is God's eternal decision to choose for God-self to be the God who is for and with humans, then we must grasp that this God is at the very core a "missionary God." Therefore, mission (outreach) is not incidental to God's own life. In the same way, God has chosen the people of God to reflect this bent toward the world; hence, the *being* or *nature* of the church reflects the being or nature of its God in this core aspect of its identity—namely, "leaping out or on the verge of leaping out to those to whom it is sent" (*CD* IV/3.2:780 [alt.]; *KD* IV/3.2:892). In this way, the orientation of the church in all of its activities is always *ad extra* or *extra muros*, "to the outside" or "outside the walls" (*CD* IV/3.2:780; *KD* IV/3.2:892).

The Lord of the church was *sent* on a mission from God the Father to this earth in order to seek and save the lost. Such an orientation to search out the radical other exists in the core of God's eternal being. It was this

---

26. John Flett, *The Witness of God: The Trinity, missio Dei, Karl Barth, and the Nature of Christian Community* (Grand Rapids: Eerdmans, 2010), 292.

27. Colin E. Gunton, *Act and Being: Towards a Theology of the Divine Attributes* (Grand Rapids: Eerdmans, 2002), 117.

28. Flett, *The Witness of God*, 292.

29. Flett, *The Witness of God*, 292–93.

very other-directed orientation of God in Jesus Christ that was passed on to his *ekklēsia* in its structural DNA. In this way, the mission of Christ continues in the mission of the church. From the source and origin of its being in Jesus Christ, whose presence is brought to us today by the Holy Spirit, the Christian congregation is called to "live in active participation in Jesus's own mission by the power of the Spirit."[30] The very root of the existence and service of the community is found in its *sending*, its mission (*CD* IV/3.2:872; *KD* IV/3.2:981). On several occasions Barth speaks in this way: "The community is as such a missionary community, or she is not the Christian community" (*CD* III/4:504–5; *KD* III/4:578).[31]

To Witness and to Serve

The people of God's presence participate in the nature of God so that they begin to take on the missionary nature of the Trinity. "The church is the instrument of Christ, called to carry on his mission in the power of the Spirit."[32] But what precisely is this mission? It is at least twofold in relation to nonbelievers: (1) *to witness*: offering the gospel (the good news) of reconciliation to those who do not yet believe (2 Cor. 5:12–21); and (2) *to serve*: providing material help among the poor and marginalized of the world, sharing the love of Christ through the power of the Spirit (Matt. 25:31–46).

To Witness

For Barth, the Christian community is essentially defined by this task of witness.[33] The church is a witness to Christ because Christ causes the community of believers to join in his *prophetic office*. In this way, the church shares in the "divine ministry of the Word of God," preaching and teaching the gospel of our living Lord to fellow believers and the world (*CD* IV/3.1:482). In this way, Christ's own prophetic office and work continues uninterrupted through the community. Barth states, "There is no pause or vacuum in the exercise of His prophetic function. He Himself is fully present and active" (*CD* IV/3.1:349–50). Jesus Christ confronts humans here and now "by the Word spoken not only then and one day, but also directly here and now. And in this confrontation [humans are] sustained, shielded, comforted, nourished and guided in all the obscurity of [their] way" (*CD* IV/3.1:350 [alt.]).

30. Flett, *The Witness of God*, 271.
31. Also, see *CD* III/3:64.
32. Pinnock, *Flame of Love*, 116.
33. Joseph L. Mangina, *Karl Barth: Theologian of Christian Witness* (Louisville: Westminster John Knox, 2004), 143.

Indeed, the Christian community is the *herald* of the Lord, always pointing to him with its communication. However, we cannot be true witnesses in the Christian community as Barth establishes it unless we are also liberated— transformed to *speak* on behalf of God to the people of the world and to *live* as a testimony to the world of the transforming power of the new reality that God has established in history through Jesus Christ. It is the Spirit of God who liberates believers to have freedom to pick up the mantle of witness to the One whose life, death, and resurrection have ushered a new age into this old system of things.

The mission of the church, then, is essentially shaped by the stance of its Lord; the community bends in the shape of its Lord's being, making our own actions *correspond* to his actions. Thus Barth can speak of each in-dividual in the community as a "messenger of God," or one who is sent, an "apostle" (*CD* II/2:415; *KD* II/2:458). Christians are therefore *social by nature* in that they "cannot cease to testify that God in Christ has found [them]" (*CD* I/2:370 [alt.]). Barth's next line after this statement is crucial to understanding the being/doing relationship inherent within the nature of the church: "Therefore [the Christian's] being makes necessary a very definite doing. [Christians] simply cannot suppress or conceal or keep to themselves what they are. They are human beings found by God. . . . This is the irresistible summons to action. This is what they have to reveal and declare" (*CD* I/2:370 [alt.]). Hence, the change in status for the new creation in Christ impels the Christian forward into the world as one who lives *for the sake of the world*. In their service as heralds, they point beyond themselves to Jesus Christ (*CD* IV/1:724; *KD* IV/1:809). Believers are "liberated" by God in order to "be a witness of Jesus Christ" (*CD* IV/3.2:663; *KD* IV/3.2:760). "Therefore, the Christian existence is not an end in itself [*Selbstzweck*]. As fellowship with Christ it is in principle and essence a service [*Dienst*]. It is witness [*Zeugnis*]" (*CD* IV/3.2:647–48; *KD* IV/3.2:742). Barth has provided a substantial foundation for building a theology of mission here.

Among some traditions, the task of witness has been typically called "evangelism." Just hearing the word raises horror stories from my past. Some believers apparently think they have to pressure someone into believing in God; others believe they have to foster a sense of fear (of hell, in particular) in order to "win" people into God's kingdom. Some see a necessity of speak-ing a word of witness to everyone they meet; others believe their lives are the only witness they need.

Much confusion and coercion has reigned in this task of the church for many years. I believe evangelism is something that naturally spills over out of one's fellowship with the Spirit and with other believers. We are ambassadors

The Great Commission

The Great Commission has an intriguing point of Greek grammar at the beginning of it: "Therefore go and make disciples of all nations" (Matt. 28:19a). The first word of the sentence in Greek (and therefore the one that is strongly emphasized) is πορευθέντες | *poreuthentes*, which is an aorist passive (middle) participle meaning "to travel, depart, go forth, take a journey, or walk." Here this participle is combined with an imperative ("make disciples"). This grammatical construction happens three other times in Matthew's Gospel with *poreuthentes*.[a] Daniel Wallace argues that this aorist participle is a special form called "attendant circumstance." Such a participle is semantically dependent on the main verb, which means it cannot exist alone but piggybacks on the mood of the main verb (in this case "make disciples," μαθητεύσατε | *mathēteusate*, which is an aorist active imperative). In such situations, the participle takes on the force or mood of the main verb, so "Go . . . and make disciples" is the result. The aorist passive participle *poreuthentes* morphs into an imperative mood like the main verb, *mathēteusate*, on which it relies. So, combined together this verbal construction can describe a simple action revealing a commitment to a decisive choice; it can also operate as a command to "do this thing!" It can even mean "Begin to do this right now! Make it happen!" So, it may be read in this way to mean: "Travel (take a journey), then, and disciple all the nations—make it happen! And continually baptize them in the name of the Father and the Son and the Holy Spirit, continually teach them to honor all things I have commanded of you." The theological point that may be drawn from this grammatical possibility is that when we go or travel or move ourselves from one place to another, we are to make disciples by means of baptizing and teaching all humans what Christ has taught us.[b]

[a] See John Nolland, *The Gospel of Matthew: A Commentary on the Greek Text*, New International Greek Testament Commentary, ed. I. Howard Marshall and Donald A. Hagner (Grand Rapids: Eerdmans, 2005), 1265.
[b] See Daniel B. Wallace, *Greek Grammar beyond the Basics: An Exegetical Syntax of the New Testament* (Grand Rapids: Zondervan, 1996), 640 for a participle as attendant circumstance, and 645 for an extended discussion of how it operates in Matt. 28:19.

for Christ, persuading the world that God was really in Christ, reconciling or healing the brokenness between God and humans. As ambassadors, we represent the Triune God to the world in every action we do and every word we say. Having been transformed by the presence of God and continuing to be transformed in God's presence privately and corporately, we walk through the world differently from those who do not believe. This walk should rather naturally cause unbelievers to inquire about our lives; at this point, the Spirit empowers us not only to live the life of God before the world but also to speak the truth of the gospel in love. We talk about our relationship with God because it is by far the most defining relationship of our lives as believers. We can share our experiences in God's presence with those who do not realize such a personal relationship with God is available. We evangelize (share the good news) *as we go* through the world of our everyday affairs. God does not call us to convict or convince people of their sins (that is the work of the Holy Spirit). God does call us to witness to the Light, to point to the cross and declare as did John the Baptist, "Look, the Lamb of God, who takes away the sin of the world!" (John 1:29).

To Serve

It may sound odd to place service as a task in the mission of the church. Witness may indeed be a central feature of the church's task, but service? Within the context of loving God and loving our neighbor, we show our love for both God and neighbor through serving them. Once again, Karl Barth provides some insight into such ecclesial service. While this "service" (*Dienst*) is toward God primarily, for Barth it necessarily involves service to the world. Using the command to "love God" and "love thy neighbor," Barth engages in a lengthy discourse on how these two loves relate. One cannot love God and ignore one's neighbor, precisely because the nature of God is such that it shapes us *toward* the "other"—namely, toward humans in the world. Thus, to "serve God is to live in service to the world" (*CD* III/4:504; *KD* III/4:577). However, such service cannot mean "cooperation" or synergy between the human and God. Instead, it must mean something like work in which the divine action does not exclude the human action (*CD* IV/3.2:600–601; *KD* IV/3.2:688). We are not dealing with any type of synergism here in Barth's thought but rather a level of cooperation whereby the divine action stirs in the human being a corresponding response/reaction. As Barth makes clear, all living expressions of the Christian community can have only the character of service (*dienenden Charakter*) (*CD* IV/2:712; *KD* IV/2:807). We serve God, and we serve the world for the sake of God.

Related to the concept of service, Barth also provides an important insight in his ecclesiology that Christian "service is not the privilege or concern of a few" (*CD* IV/2:693). Each one is called to represent Christ by serving. This view works against any type of "practical clericalism" in the church (*CD* IV/2:694). The ranking or hierarchy that frequently divides the body of Christ cannot be part of Christ's *communio*. While I clarify my own approach to the clergy/laity divide in *Serving the People of God's Presence*, it is enough to say here that Barth's sense of removing the practical sense in which clericalism divides the church is right along the lines I will be developing. The language Barth uses helps to emphasize his point: he uses the German word *Dienst*, which as we have seen can mean "service" or "ministry." But as John Flett rightly notes, on many occasions the English translators of *Die kirchliche Dogmatik* used "ministry" where "service" would have better rendered the idea.[34] In English the word "ministry" has too many overtones of work done by professional clergy, not laity. Barth clearly de-emphasizes all such "practical clericalism" (*allem praktischen Klerikalismus*) and even wants to "avoid the fatal word 'office,' [*Amt*] and replace it by 'service' [*des Dienstes*]," thereby allowing it to be a term "which can be applied to all Christians" (*CD* IV/2:694; *KD* IV/2:787). Therefore, "quite simply," the best term for this aspect of the community's mission is "*Dienst*" (service) (*CD* IV/3.2:601; *KD* IV/3.2:688).[35]

The Spirit of God empowers and initiates the work of service among the people of God. Believers cooperate with God's action in the world, joining the work that God is already doing as the Spirit leads. It is this cooperation between God and humans that can best be described as "service" (*Dienst*). From this description, Barth draws several important ramifications. First, *Dienst* is the task of every single Christian within the community of believers. Everyone is called to serve God and the world. This service takes the form of humbly and gratefully responding to the grace offered by God to individuals by fulfilling their vocation to be "in Christ." Such a response to grace will be shaped by the Lord's own nature and command but will be primarily characterized by "service." In this sense, everyone is called to minister—to serve! All of God's people are meant to witness and serve—not just a few elected and educated clergy. Clericalism tends to make both calling and ministry into gifts and tasks reserved for a select few, whereas the Spirit of God distributes the gifts according to his own will. The people of God's presence must be characterized by the Spirit's gifting upon all individuals within a congregation, not only for the benefit of the local body but also for the sake of the world. Since the Lord of the church is not some omniscient spectator watching the goings-on in the body, the people within the community cannot be detached

---

34. Flett, *The Witness of God*, 261n21. This has also been an emphasis in several discussions had with the Barth Translators Group in the Center for Barth Studies at Princeton Theological Seminary since 2007. Darrell Guder has frequently noted the confusion created in English by translating *Dienst* as "ministry" when Barth's term seems clearly to require "service."

35. The translation at *CD* IV/3.2:601 of the *KD* IV/3.2:688 reads as follows in English: "This is quite simply the term 'service' or 'ministry.'" However, the German leaves out the phrase "or ministry" altogether: "*es ist schlicht der Begriff des Dienstes.*"

spectators watching the chosen few offer their gifts without offering (or even considering) their own.

Second, as we noted in the previous chapter concerning worship, the idea of service (*Dienst*) as characteristic of all the activities of the community reveals itself most clearly in the service of worship (*Gottesdienst*), where worship of God draws together God's people to remind them of and energize them for service in the world. Worship is service to God, which inevitably leads directly to service of the world. Worship is *the center*, but it radiates outward into the *daily activities* of our lives and relationships. Barth is most poignant in making clear that some forms of Pietism revolved too much around the inner life, focusing only on what was happening in the *spiritual, inward world*. He sees this as a potential danger for the contemporary church as well. Some forms of the church also turn inward and revolve around themselves by focusing attention on their own lives and needs to the exclusion of any ministry to those outside of the building or Christian community. These inward-focused latter groups are diseased, off-centered churches that do not deserve to be called churches. Their function is lopsided, and therefore their service becomes no longer acceptable to both God and the world. Churches in Western societies today can learn well from Barth's caution, especially since the last few decades have seen a rise in a style of self-centered focus in the church: *What can I get from attending? Does the sermon tell me how to get by this week? Does worship make me feel better about my relationship with God?*

Third, Barth's use of *service* in distinction to (or perhaps elucidation of) *ministry* allows believers within Christian communities to see more of their actions in the world as part of their calling to love God and neighbor. *Dienst* does not refer to supraspiritual, invisible endeavors but to clearly visible, concrete actions that can bring God's love to others in tangible ways. The task of service to which the church is called in relation to unbelievers is to serve their physical, emotional, and social needs. By so doing, we acknowledge the fact that humans are more than "souls" to be won; they are persons who are embodied in their existence here and now. Jesus points to this in his parable of the sheep and goats (Matt. 25:31–46). Without recognizing Christ's presence among the poor, naked, prisoners, sick, and marginalized, the people of God's presence served in faith to all who were in need. Christ did not announce his presence thus: "I am here—minister to me!" Rather, Christ was hidden in the weak and despised humans so that his people might serve everyone without discrimination—especially, however, those whom we might usually pass by. James points to this as well when he asks how someone who has faith can walk by those in physical need without meeting their needs (James 2:14–16).

"Suppose a brother or a sister is without clothes and daily food. If one of you says to them, 'Go in peace; keep warm and well fed,' but does nothing about their physical needs, what good is it?" (2:15–16). If we are to feed and clothe fellow believers (brothers or sisters) in order to reveal the true nature of our faith, then we are to feed and clothe unbelievers (our human brothers and sisters) just as surely to reveal our faith.

Such interest in social concerns overwhelmed many denominations in North America in the early part of the twentieth century. By emphasizing benevolent service to present needs of people, the "social gospel" seemed to eliminate any need for sharing the gospel. However, equally problematic was the evangelical response: all talk and very little physical help for those in need. A people of God's presence understands that both elements are necessary tasks since God's mission is concerned not only about the people's spiritual well-being but also about their physical condition in this world.

Yet this second task (service) is not just benevolent giving of clothing or food to help the poor. It is also identifying with the poor and marginalized in such a way that they are not made into "objects of our attention" but are people for whom Christ died and who therefore are worthy of great respect and love. The people who dwell in God's presence understand this task. They also recognize that social justice and equity of treatment for all people are crucial fights in this world, but ones for which the church must find itself on the side of the oppressed and downtrodden.

Daniel Migliore directs our attention to Christ incarnate as a way to understand this twofold interest in the people of the world. He says,

> If we see the missionary activity of God centered in Christ the incarnate Lord, we will understand our own mission as an incarnational mission. We will understand who we are and what we are called to do wholistically and will not allow our understanding of church and mission to be driven by pernicious dualisms. Among these dualisms are the views that the mission of the church is directed toward the salvation of souls *or* toward the care of the hungry and the homeless; that the mission of the church is concerned about the well-being of humanity *or* about the well-being of nature; that the mission of the church is to worship God *or* to be an advocate for justice and peace in our homes, our communities, and our world.[36]

The two tasks of the church directed toward the unbelieving world are really two prongs of one mission—namely, God reaching out through his people to share the love of Christ to the world.

36. Migliore, "The Missionary God and the Missionary Church," 19.

Richard Shaull has offered some insight into the difficulty the church has in fulfilling its mission in the world today, especially in relation to solidarity with the poor and marginalized. He traces the history of theology and the church in modern times by demonstrating the church's capitulation to modernity's narrow definition of truth. The realm of experience in God, he claims, has been lost to much of the church in modern times.[37] "As a result of all this," he suggests, "we have practically lost the ability to connect to, enter into, and live out the realm of the Spirit so central to the biblical witness."[38] He suggests that Western churches (especially in North America) could learn something from Pentecostals in this arena. But why would they want to do what Shaull proposes? Simply because most churches talk, think, and live in a manner that excludes them from ministering effectively to the poor and marginalized. In addition, he suggests that such churches cannot minister to the people of postmodernity, "who live in a quite different reality and are searching for spiritual resources capable of ordering their lives and providing them with meaning and hope in their existential situation."[39]

The upshot for Richard Shaull is that churches in the West must enter a "more radical theological reconstruction"[40] than theologians in the academy and pastors in the field have been willing to take thus far. He suggests that they could learn well from those Pentecostals who rather naturally understand and experience the presence of God and therefore rather naturally relate to the poor and marginalized.

> If we are committed to the struggle of the poor for life and recognize how far our theological conceptualization has departed from the biblical witness to the realm of the Spirit, we can go forward only as we undergo a much more radical process of unlearning, of "self-emptying," which will prepare us to perceive dimensions and realities of faith that have thus far been closed to us. To do this, I believe that nothing short of immersion in Pentecostal and other popular religious movements, and openness to the experience of those being transformed by them, will enable us to perceive and respond to the moving of the Spirit, to be free to reread the Bible, and to engage in an ongoing task of theological re-creation in dialogue with such grassroots communities. As we do this, we may find ourselves embarking on a new journey of faith and participating in

37. Richard Shaull and Waldo Cesar, *Pentecostalism and the Future of the Christian Churches: Promises, Limitations, Challenges* (Grand Rapids: Eerdmans, 2000), 168–71. Shaull writes from his recent experience with Pentecostals in South America, especially Brazil.

38. Shaull and Cesar, *Pentecostalism and the Future*, 170.

39. Shaull and Cesar, *Pentecostalism and the Future*, 170.

40. Shaull and Cesar, *Pentecostalism and the Future*, 170.

the formation and development of communities of faith living and struggling in solidarity with the poor.[41]

The people of God's presence are gradually transformed into the nature and likeness of the Triune God. Since the nature of our God is characterized by love that reaches out of Godself toward those who are radically other, the new nature of God's people is characterized by a love that reaches out to un-believers and is committed to the poor and marginalized. The church clothes the naked and feeds the poor without regard for what it might receive in return (which is the very same way that God loved us in Christ—without regard for what God might receive in return). The church sides with the oppressed and attempts to fight against structures of social injustice, racial prejudice, and institutions that marginalize the needy. Jesus did not come to save those who thought they were well; he came to save those who were sick, rescuing them from their plague of sin. Christians will attempt to meet the physical and social needs of people everywhere without regard for what they may or may not be able to give back. This is as much the task of the church as the proclamation of the gospel, since the gospel itself proclaims good news to the poor, liberty for the captive, recovery of sight for the blind, deliverance for the oppressed, and the year of the Lord's favor (Luke 4:18–19). In the hands of God's people, this gospel is not merely proclamation but also action. The people of God do not step into this mission with arrogance, lording it over those in need with some kind of Christian "paternalism." With genuine hu-mility and love, the church moves together to worship God, share things in common with fellow believers, and then from this rich bond of unconditional love, they move outward to those who are in need. The mission of the church is an extension of the mission of God; indeed, our mission is a continuation of the incarnational ministry of Christ our Lord, who became a servant among us, living at our level in order to minister to us (Phil. 2:5–7). We become one with God in his presence so that we may become "little Christs" in this world, bringing Christ with us into the darkness wherever we go, especially to those in need. Given the missionary nature of God and the extent to which God went to reach humans, can the people of God expect to do anything less?

41. Shaull and Cesar, *Pentecostalism and the Future*, 171.

6

The People of God Proclaim
the Word of God
and Hear It Proclaimed

Introduction

New England grows old tombstones almost as prominently as the Midwest
grows cornstalks. From Connecticut to Maine, cemeteries are filled with
standing stones—tall or short, granite or red sandstone. For almost fifty years
I have been interested in genealogy—not just my own but anyone's family
history. When I discovered that one of my early ancestors came from Connecticut near where I was living at the time, I trudged through the woods to the
broken-down markers of my great-great-great-great grandfather, Barnabas
Ford, and his son, Ebenezer, in the "Ancient Burial Grounds of Plymouth
(Connecticut)." Both lived in the area in the mid-1700s. The stones were
worn but readable.

I made it a habit to stop in the town greens of New England to search for
old gravestones. What a fascinating hobby! My wife thought it was always a
bit morbid, but I delighted in finding poems, Scripture verses, or in some cases
the story of a person's death on the stones themselves. On one clear fall day,
I stopped to walk through the North Haven Cemetery on the green. In clean,
discernable rows, the stones tried to stand upright where tree-root buckling
had done its best to unearth these markers. Some had fallen to the forces of
nature; others stood ramrod straight as if newly planted.

239

Near the back of the cemetery, I sauntered past a very tall red-sandstone marker. It was one of the tall, straight ones that had remained upright for over two hundred years despite the Connecticut winters. The etching of the words remained clearly visible and readable on the four-foot-high stone. It read as follows (with the old English lettering and verbiage slightly modernized):

Sacred
To the Memory
of
Mrs. Sarah Blakslee
late Comfort of ye Revd Edward
Blakslee & Daughter of Rev^d
Richd Mansfield of Derby who
Departed this mortal life Dece^r 23
AD 1790. Aged 32.
She left behind a deeply afflicted
Husband to mourn ye loss of a discreet,
amiable, & affectionate Companion &
exercise alone Parental affection towards
the Infant of her last moments A
Parent of a virtuous and beloved daughter
Brothers & Sisters of a Dear & most
Kindly affected Sister & the Poor & Needy,
of a liberal & most cordial Benefactress
The unvaried tenour of her life was
Exemplary & truly Christian & She is
now gone to receive a crown of Im-
mortal Glory.

I was quite overcome by the tragedy of this woman's death in childbirth. At the grave directly beside Sarah's stood a stone about half as tall as hers, yet the wording was almost entirely effaced. The red sandstone that had so carefully preserved the sentiment on Sarah's stone had somehow been wiped clean from that gravestone. No story. No dates. No name—except the letters "Mo . . ." and "Abi . . ." and the word "late" running down the left side. I could not even tell if this was her husband's stone. It stood mute, unable to speak anything to me about the person lying below. The contrast between the two stones was expansive. Clearly, the weather had worn down one stone while (somehow) not fazing the other.

Walking to my car I began wondering about words—words like those on Sarah's tombstone that struck something deep within me about my own mortality and the importance of family, kin, and the "poor and needy" among us. Then I thought about the wordless stone next to it. I remember stopping in my tracks when my mind wandered on to the next thought. One day even Sarah Blakeslee's tombstone will be just as effaced as the other stone, without a name or date or story. It may last another hundred years or even five hundred years, but at some point the words will dissolve into the reddish sand background. I stood looking at the back of that tall tombstone and allowed the truth of the thought to sink in. All those words will one day be gone.

As I turned again toward my car, another thought came from nowhere: "Heaven and earth will pass away, but my words will never pass away" (Matt. 24:35; Mark 13:31; Luke 21:33). *Some words* will never be effaced by weathering or dissolved over time. The earth may melt with a fervent heat and the mountains fall into the sea, but the words of Christ will remain forever. The "sturdiest" things known to humans (the heavens and earth) will come to an end, but the words of Christ will by no means whatsoever come to an end.

The words of Christ will not disappear, because they are "Spirit and life" (John 6:63). However, the words from the law will pass away: "For truly I tell you, until heaven and earth disappear, not the smallest letter, not the least stroke of a pen, will by any means disappear from the Law until everything is accomplished" (Matt. 5:18). The written words of the former covenant *could pass away* once the Law and Prophets are fulfilled and "everything is accomplished." The written law is not eternal; its purpose will be accomplished someday, and at that point the need for a written law will be over. However, Christ asserts the opposite about his own words. Using the same verb here (Matt. 5:18) for "pass away" (παρέχομαι | *parechomai*) that he uses in Matthew 24:35, Jesus declares that his words will never pass away, disappear, or be invalid.

Why is this the case? It is because Jesus the Christ is the *Logos*, the eternal Word of God residing in human flesh. Hence, the eternal Word must refer primarily to the voice of God: the Logos from heaven—namely, the eternal Son, who from all eternity has been associated with the Word or Communication of God. It was this eternal Word who became flesh and thereby subject to mortality—to the same defacing and erasing of identity, just like the tombstones in North Haven. Yet when Christ conquered death, his eternal life shone through and offers us hope for our own deaths—namely, that *we* will not be forgotten.

What, then, is the meaning of this eternal Word? How are the people of God's presence to handle the word of life and hold it forth like a torch in the darkness (Phil. 2:16)? What is the relation of the Word of God to the Spirit of God and both of these to the people of God's presence? To these questions we now turn.

The Church as a Creation of the Word and Spirit

The church of Jesus Christ is a "creature of God's Word" (*creatura Verbi*), which functions as a "living voice" to create and nourish the church through the ages.[1] Why is the church a creation of God's Word? It is because faith is "called forth by the Word of God" and "is brought about by the action of the Holy Spirit."[2] Hence, the church of Jesus Christ is also a "creature of the Holy Spirit" (*creatura Spiritus*).[3] The Word of God and the Spirit of God operate together to spawn faith in humans so that they can believe that Jesus the Christ is the Son of God who suffered, died, and rose again for their salvation. The Spirit incorporates believers into the body of Christ and then uses the Word of God to continue nourishment and strengthening through reading, preaching, and teaching of the Word. Therefore, the church is both a divine and human reality.[4]

God calls people to Godself through an invitation or summons via the preaching of the good news (gospel). In the New Testament, "calling" is primarily used to speak of an invitation to become a Christian, not to discover one's vocation or career.[5] God's Word calls us to Christ (2 Thess. 2:14) and calls us to hope (Eph. 1:18; 4:4).[6] Indeed, God the Father gives good and perfect gifts. "He chose to give us birth through the word of truth, that we might be a kind of firstfruits of all he created" (James 1:18). The Word summons us to respond to the gospel message of reconciliation.

Since faith comes as a result of "hearing the message" of the Word of God, there must be "preachers" of the message in the church and world so that people can believe (Rom. 10:17). Believing in one's heart and confessing with one's mouth that Jesus is Lord and has been raised from the dead by God is the path to salvation (10:9). Such reception of the Word of God must

---

1. *The Nature and Mission of the Church: A Stage on the Way to a Common Statement*, Faith and Order Paper 198 (Geneva: World Council of Churches, 2005), 14, §10.

2. *The Nature and Mission of the Church*, 14, §11.

3. *The Nature and Mission of the Church*, 14, §11.

4. *The Nature and Mission of the Church*, 15, §13.

5. See Terry L. Cross, *Answering the Call in the Spirit: Pentecostal Reflections on a Theology of Vocation, Work and Life* (Cleveland, TN: Lee University Press, 2007), 30–31.

6. Everett Ferguson, *The Church of Christ: A Biblical Ecclesiology for Today* (Grand Rapids: Eerdmans, 1996), 162.

be based on the power of the Spirit to break up the hardened ground and allow the seeds of the implanted Word to come to sprout. "Therefore, get rid of all moral filth and the evil that is so prevalent and humbly accept the word planted in you, which can save you" (James 1:21). It is the divine Word of God that can "save" us. "For you have been born again, not of perishable seed, but of imperishable, through the living and enduring word of God. For, 'All people are like grass, and all their glory is like the flowers of the field; the grass withers and the flowers fall, but the word of the Lord endures forever.' And this is the word that was preached to you" (1 Pet. 1:23–25). Faith, then, is a gift of God, wrought in the human heart by hearing the Word of God (the gospel message about Jesus Christ); God takes the initiative in doing things that can generate faith in human hearts. Yet faith is not entirely a gift of God; it is also a human response to the proclaimed Word of God.[7]

Faith grasps or apprehends (*apprehensiva*) Christ.[8] And so Luther can say, "Thus faith justifies because it takes hold of [*apprehendit*] and possesses [*possidet*] that very treasure, namely, the present Christ."[9] What does this apprehension of Christ by faith do to us? It makes us miserable! We agree with God's judgment that we are sinners, bereft of anything good as we stand before our Maker. Wrought by the Holy Spirit in us, faith makes us no longer satisfied with ourselves. Thus, faith works in us a clear understanding of how displeasing to God we are—and therefore how displeasing we are to ourselves!

Faith brings us the righteousness of Christ—an alien righteousness. Only because the Holy Spirit causes faith to rise in us can we enter into a relationship with the "present Christ." Through the preaching of the gospel, the Holy Spirit causes Christ to dwell richly in our hearts, thereby justifying us because of his presence in us.[10] Our hearts are made righteous (justified) because of the imputation of Christ's own righteousness. Indeed, our hearts become righteous because God's Spirit has poured Christ's righteousness into our hearts. This alien righteousness poured into our hearts by the Spirit of Christ spurs us to walk in obedience to the commands of God, thereby fulfilling the Law. Indeed, it is the Holy Spirit dwelling in us who enables us to follow Christ and his commands. First, the Law is fulfilled and set aside through Christ (*per*

---

7. Ferguson, *The Church of Christ*, 164.

8. WA 39¹:45. This is from "Theses on Faith" (1535), Thesis 12.

9. WA 40¹:229, from his *Galatians Commentary* (1531/1536), with my translation from the Latin.

10. Paul Althaus, *The Theology of Martin Luther*, trans. Robert C. Schultz (Philadelphia: Fortress, 1966), 232. Also, Althaus, *Die Theologie Martin Luthers* (Gütersloh: Gütersloher Verlaghaus Gerd Mohn, 1962). Hereafter cited as *Theology of Martin Luther* and the German as *Die Theologie Martin Luthers*.

Christum) outside of us (*extra nos*). Second, "he fulfills it in us through his Holy Spirit, since when we believe in him, he gives us the Holy Spirit, who begins this new and eternal obedience in us, but in the resurrection from the dead, a perfected obedience."[11]

This faith spawned by the Spirit in our lives is focused on the reality of Christ's presence within us. It is to Christ alone (*solus Christus*) that our faith holds. The present Christ (*Christus praesens*) is mediated to believers in their moment of despair, creating faith in their Savior, but then also causing them to turn back to their real-life situations whereby their own sin becomes dominant to their consciousness. There is something of a back-and-forth motion to this Spirit-mediated faith: it looks to Christ and then to one's sins (and eventually to the needs of one's neighbor). Luther means to present a view of the Christian life that is moment-by-moment dependent on the presence of the risen Christ mediated by the Holy Spirit. In this state, we can never become self-righteous in our own efforts, but rather we must be humble and submitted to the fact that we are always and ever sinners who have been saved by grace through faith.

John Calvin (1509–64) frequently speaks of the work of the Spirit as "secret" (*arcana operatione Spiritus*) or "hidden" or even "inner."[12] While the effect of the Spirit's hidden work may become visible, the actual activity of the Spirit itself is not. The Spirit is God's own invisible presence and activity in the world. For Calvin, the Spirit is God in action.[13] Michael Beintker, a contemporary German theologian, has understood this concept as so important for Calvin that he has remarked, "God in action—that is the most apt brief description for the work of the Holy Spirit."[14] Thus, from Calvin's perspective we can expect that God's action will be energetic and efficacious—it will accomplish what it intends to do. Therefore Calvin speaks of the "secret efficacious work of the Spirit" in our lives (*arcana Spiritus efficacia*).[15]

It is this active, energetic work of the Spirit that brings Christ and his benefits to believers. So important is the Spirit's work that without it "Christ, so to speak, lies idle because we coldly contemplate him as outside ourselves—indeed, far from us."[16] Therefore, we must come to understand that "as long

---

11. WA 39¹:435. This is from the treatise *The Second Disputation against the Antinomians* (1538), with my translation from the Latin.

12. *Inst.* 3.1.1 (538–39). For the Latin, see OS 4:1.

13. *Inst.* 1.13.18 (143); OS 3:132.

14. Michael Beintker, "Calvins Theologie des Heiligen Geistes," *Tydskrif vir Geesteswetenskappe: Spesiale Uitgawe—Johannes Calvyn* 49, no. 3 (September 2009): 487–99, here 493, my trans. from the German. The journal is in Afrikaans, but Beintker's article is in German.

15. *Inst.* 3.1.1 (537); OS 4:1.

16. *Inst.* 3.1.3 (541); OS 4:5.

as Christ remains outside of us, and we are separated from him, all that he has suffered and done for the salvation of the human race remains useless and of no value for us."[17]

It is no mistake, therefore, that Calvin introduces his discussion of salvation with an entire chapter on the Spirit's work in binding Christ to us through the instrumentality of faith. Faith is the "proper and entire work of the Holy Spirit."[18] Only as the Spirit, our "inner teacher," moves through the promises of the gospel and "penetrates into our minds" can the work and benefits of Christ be effective.[19] Furthermore, since faith "rests not on ignorance, but on knowledge" concerning Jesus Christ, humans are entirely dependent on the Spirit to teach them inwardly the truth of Christ's work and benefits.[20]

Yet what does this faith spawned by the Spirit do for us? The foremost benefit of Christ's work that is applied to our hearts by the Holy Spirit through the instrumentality of faith is our being "engrafted into the body of Christ."[21] The Holy Spirit works inside of us through faith in order to bring us into communion with Christ (*communio cum Christo*). The Spirit unites us to Christ and Christ to us in this prominent way. Hence, Christ is not distant from us, but by the Spirit's presence and work, Christ has been brought near. As François Wendel has said, "Calvin never tires of repeating that 'the Holy Spirit is the bond, as it were, by which the Son of God unites us to him effectually.'"[22]

Without this work of the Spirit, we are disconnected from Christ. As Charles Partee says, "God's special gift is that we possess Christ and he possesses us. . . . In this way Calvin strongly and essentially identifies faith and union with Christ."[23] Calvin himself says, "For we hold ourselves to be united with Christ by the secret power of his Spirit" (*qui tenemus nos cum Christo uniri arcana Spiritus eius virtute*).[24]

---

17. *Inst.* 3.1.1 (537); OS 4:1.

18. *Inst.* 4.14.8 (1284); OS 5:265.

19. *Inst.* 4.14.8 (1284). Calvin says that without the Spirit producing faith in us by illumining our minds, the promise of salvation would "only strike our ears and appear before our eyes, but not at all affect us within" (*aures duntaxat percellerent, et oculis obversarentur, interiora minime afficerent*). See *Inst.* 4.14.8 (1284); OS 5:266.

20. *Inst.* 3.2.2 (545); OS 4:10.

21. François Wendel, *Calvin: Origins and Developments of His Religious Thought*, trans. Philip Mairet (Grand Rapids: Baker, 1997), 240.

22. Wendel, *Calvin*, 239.

23. Charles Partee, *The Theology of John Calvin* (Louisville: Westminster John Knox, 2009), 201.

24. *Inst.* 3.11.5 (730); OS 4:185. This is in the context of Calvin's debate against Andreas Osiander, a Lutheran theologian who tended to see a substantial union of Christ's divine nature with ours. Calvin had to clarify the difference between Osiander's view of union and his own.

How does the Spirit relate to the Word of God in Calvin's thought? Of the many things Calvin has written about the Spirit, one doctrinal point was his own original contribution—namely, the "internal witness of the Spirit" (*internum testimonium Spiritus Sancti*) as related to Scripture.[25] For Calvin, the Spirit is the author of Scripture. Moreover, the same Spirit who authored the Scriptures is the One who penetrates our hearts to assure us that the Scripture proclaims what God commanded.[26] While Roman Catholics viewed the authority of Scripture as coming from the church, and some Radical Reformers viewed Scripture's authority as coming from special revelation within one's inner being, both Luther and Calvin attempted to balance the Word with the Spirit. It was Calvin, though, who carefully laid out the Spirit's role in the authority of Scripture.

First, Calvin stresses that the Spirit "wishes to be joined" to God's Word by "an indissoluble bond" (*individuo nexu cum verbo Dei coniunctus esse velit*).[27] Only as the Spirit illumines our minds can believers understand the Word of God itself.[28] Second, Calvin offered the concept that Scripture is self-authenticating (αὐτόπιστον | *autopiston*).[29] This means that for believers there is certainty that the Word of God is true through the "conviction" (*persuasio*) offered through the Spirit by means of an internal testimony (*internum testimonium Spiritus Sancti*).[30] Since it was the Spirit who inspired the writers of Scripture, this same Spirit speaks with an internal assurance for believers that these are truly God's words. In this way, the testimony of the Spirit is "more excellent than all reason."[31] Thus, an assurance penetrates our hearts "to persuade us that they [the authors and words] faithfully proclaimed what had been divinely commanded."[32] We are drawn to obey God due to the Spirit's persuasion that "requires no reasons" (*persuasio quae rationes non requirat*).[33] The result is a "feeling" (*sensus*) of certainty, which is "experienced" (*experitur*) in one's self, that comes only from "heavenly revelation."[34]

In addition to this inner witness of the Spirit that testifies to believers that the Scripture is authoritative and God's own Word, Calvin spoke of the

---

25. *Inst.* 1.7.4 (78–79); OS 3:69–70. John Hesselink notes how Luther had alluded to this concept, but Calvin first developed this idea into a doctrine. See I. John Hesselink, *Calvin's First Catechism: A Commentary, Featuring Ford Lewis Battles's Translation of the 1538 Catechism*, Columbia Series in Reformed Theology (Louisville: Westminster John Knox, 1997), 179.

26. See *Inst.* 1.7.4 (79); OS 3:70.

27. *Inst.* 4.8.13 (1165); OS 5:148.

28. *Inst.* 1.9.3 (96); OS 3:84.

29. *Inst.* 1.7.5 (80); OS 3:70.

30. *Inst.* 1.7.4 (78); OS 3:69.

31. *Inst.* 1.7.4 (79); OS 3:70.

32. *Inst.* 1.7.4 (79); OS 3:70.

33. *Inst.* 1.7.5 (80); OS 3:71.

34. *Inst.* 1.7.5 (80); OS 3:71.

more commonly understood "witness"—namely, the witness of the Spirit to believers that they are the children of God (Rom. 8:16). The Spirit who leads believers (8:14) and who teaches believers that they are children of God (8:15) is the same Spirit who assures us that we may call God our Father. Calvin asks how we could pray to Abba Father if our hearts did not have the assurance that we are legitimate children of God. Therefore, "except the Spirit testifies to our heart respecting the paternal love of God, our tongues would be dumb, so that they could utter no prayers."[35]

While Calvin spoke of assurance of our salvation, John Wesley (1703–91) enlarged the meaning of it under the category of the witness of the Spirit. There are two spirits here involved in this witness: (1) God's Spirit and (2) our human spirit.[36] In two sermons on "The Witness of the Spirit" and in another on "The Witness of Our Own Spirit," Wesley lays out the importance of these two aspects for assurance of salvation.[37]

First, it is the Spirit of God who testifies to our spirit. This testimony of the Spirit is not the same as our own spirit's testimony to our consciences. The Spirit's testimony is "immediate and direct," while our own testimony is indirect (perhaps even inferential).[38] Wesley states, "The testimony of the Spirit is an inward impression on the soul, whereby the Spirit of God directly 'witnesses to my spirit that I am a child of God,' . . . that all my sins are blotted out, and I, even I, am reconciled to God."[39] The immediate result of this testimony is "the fruit of the Spirit" as listed in Galatians 5:22–23.[40] If the fruit does not arise in us, then the testimony of the Spirit cannot continue. This testimony of the Spirit, then, is so important for humans to acknowledge that if anyone denies it, they are denying justification by faith itself![41] Hence, this testimony of the Spirit must come *prior to* any witness of our own spirit. We love God because he first loved us. We know within ourselves that we belong to God, have been reconciled with God, and now are children of the Father.

---

35. John Calvin, "Romans 8:16" in *Commentaries on the Epistle of Paul the Apostle to the Romans*, trans. Christopher Fetherstone, ed. Henry Beveridge, Calvin's Commentaries 19 (Grand Rapids: Baker Books, 2009), 299.

36. John Wesley, "The Witness of the Holy Spirit," in *The Holy Spirit and Power*, rev. and ed. Clare Weakley (Gainesville, FL: Bridge-Logos, 2003; rev. ed. of 1976 ed.), 125. Here Wesley states that there is a "double witness in the new birth experience. There is both the testimony of God's Spirit and the testimony of the Christian's own spirit that he is a child of God."

37. *Sermons*, 1:271–310.

38. Kenneth J. Collins, *The Scripture Way of Salvation: The Heart of John Wesley's Theology* (Nashville: Abingdon, 1997), 134.

39. "The Witness of the Spirit, I," in *Sermons*, 1:274.

40. "The Witness of the Spirit, II," in *Sermons*, 1:286.

41. "The Witness of the Spirit, II," in *Sermons*, 1:292.

But how do we *know* for sure whether the Spirit has witnessed to our spirits concerning this joyous truth? For Wesley the answer lies in the soul's perceptions of its feelings: when God's Spirit testifies to our spirits, our souls know a delight and love of God hitherto unknown. We now have a double proof: the truth of the Scriptures (which the Spirit has impressed on our hearts) and our inward experience of joy and love for God.[42] Here Wesley is attempting to guard against a twofold extremism: first, a fanaticism of the Spirit whereby we rely only on some vague internal witness and have no fruit or reasonable evidence at all; second, a legalism that justifies the self by means of its works.[43] Therefore, our assurance of salvation can rest neither in the fruit alone without the Spirit's witness nor in the Spirit's witness without the fruit.

Second, the witness of the *human* spirit is the "rational evidence" that we have truly heard the Spirit's voice and have begun to follow it.[44] From the Spirit's speaking to our spirits, God's grace produces the first "rational evidence"—namely, the fruit of the Spirit. The fruit displays itself in love and joy toward God as well as toward one's neighbors.

Another "evidence" is found in our clear consciences. Indeed, when reading Wesley's sermon on "The Witness of Our Own Spirit," it almost seems that he has conflated the meaning of our spirit with the human conscience! Using 2 Corinthians 1:12 for his text, Wesley explains the phrase there "the testimony of our conscience" (KJV) as demonstrating the connection between the Spirit's testimony and our own spirit's testimony to itself.[45]

The result of the Spirit's initial inner testimony to believers' spirits is the foundation for the continued work of the Spirit in our lives. The Spirit's work issues forth in uncontainable joy and loving obedience. Both the Spirit's witness and our own spirit's witness produce evidence (and therefore assurance) that we are God's children. The Spirit brings to our hearts a "double proof"—namely, the truth of the Word of God and our inward love for God.

The Forms of the Word of God

Before going further in our understanding of the Word of God, we need to clarify what is meant by this phrase. In his *Church Dogmatics* (I/1), Karl Barth posed a model for gaining clarity of the way Christians use the phrase "Word

---

42. Wesley, "The Witness of the Spirit," in Weakley, *The Holy Spirit and Power*, 130.
43. Collins, *The Scripture Way of Salvation*, 135–36.
44. "The Witness of the Spirit, I," in *Sermons*, 1:272.
45. Wesley, "The Witness of Our Own Spirit," in Weakley, *The Holy Spirit and Power*, 139–40.

of God." He suggested that the "Word of God" consists of three unified concepts that can be drawn as if concentric circles. The innermost circle is the Word Revealed (Jesus Christ in the flesh); the second circle surrounding the first circle is the Word Written (the Scriptures that point to the God of revelation in Jesus Christ); and the third, outermost circle is the Word Proclaimed (the Word given to the church through preaching).[46] While Barth's discussion starts from the outermost circle of preaching and then moves inward through Scripture and finally the incarnate Christ, I will reverse that order in explaining these "decisive connexions" here (CD I/1:89).

The Word Revealed (Jesus Christ)

The core of revelation from God is found in the Word Revealed—namely, the incarnate Son of God, Jesus Christ. What has been revealed through Christ? It is the reality that God is with us in the history of humanity (CD I/1:116). Revelation is the unveiling of what has been previously veiled (CD I/1:118–19). Therefore, the revelation to us from God is that "The Word became flesh" (CD I/1:119). In this revelation, God himself speaks in revelation so that Jesus Christ speaks for himself "and needs no witness apart from His Holy Spirit and the faith that rejoices in His promise received and grasped" (CD I/1:120). In the incarnation, God's Word "comes to [humans] as a human word" (CD I/2:699). Therefore, we can know the Word of God because God has chosen to reveal Godself in this human way. "God's Word has for our sakes stepped forth out of the unapproachable mystery of its self-contained existence into the circle of those things which we can know" (CD I/2:699–700).

That the Word became flesh is a powerful fact of history and eternity. It is the reality of God's speaking, of God's Word, of the *Deus dixit* (God has spoken) (CD I/1:120).[47] It comes to humans from the freedom of God's grace.

---

46. *CD* I/1:88–124, which is §4 (2nd ed.).

47. This phrase, *Deus dixit*, was frequently used by Barth in his prior attempt at dogmatics in 1927 and also as early as the 1924 Göttingen dogmatics. See Karl Barth, *Die christliche Dogmatik im Entwurf*, vol. 1, *Die Lehre vom Worte Gottes: Prolegomena zur christlichen Dogmatik, 1927*, ed. Gerhard Sauter, Karl Barth Gesamtausgabe 2, Akademische Werke 1927, ed. Hinrich Stoevesandt (Zurich: Theologischer Verlag Zürich, 1982), 65, esp. n. 8. The editor (G. Sauter) notes that Barth may have taken over this Latin phrase from the Dutch theologian Herman Bavinck. Also, see Karl Barth, *The Göttingen Dogmatics: Instruction in the Christian Religion*, vol. 1, ed. Hannelotte Reiffen, trans. Geoffrey W. Bromiley (Grand Rapids: Eerdmans, 1991), 10. Cf. Barth, *"Unterricht in der christlichen Religion," Erster Band: Prolegomena 1924*, ed. Hannelotte Reiffen, Karl Barth Gesamtausgabe 2, Akademische Werke 1924 (Zurich: Theologischer Verlag Zürich, 1985), 12, 13, and 18. *"Deus dixit"* is the section title in chap. 1 for §3 (53–82); ET, 45–68. See esp. subpoint 3 in §3, which remains untitled in the German edition (68) but is titled by the editor of the ET as "The Meaning of *Deus Dixit*" (58). Hereafter the

In the 1932 *Church Dogmatics* (I/1), Barth wrote about the *Deus dixit* in the section of the Word of God revealed (namely, the innermost form). The basic point he attempted to make in this section was that the *event of revelation* in Jesus Christ *is* the *Deus dixit*. "The fulfilled time which is identical with Jesus Christ, this absolute event in relation to which every other event is not yet event or has ceased to be so, this 'It is finished,' this *Deus dixit* for which there are no analogies, is the revelation attested in the Bible" (*CD* I/1:116). This revelation of Jesus Christ is "the superior principle," whereas the Bible is primarily "the subordinate principle" (*CD* I/1:114). In other words, Scripture is *not* revelation; Scripture attests to the revelatory event in Jesus Christ. Therefore, "revelation engenders the Scripture which attests it" (*CD* I/1:115). However, God can take the human words of witness offered by the writers of Scripture and let them become God's own Word to humanity. When God chooses, *Paulus dixit* can become *Deus dixit* in the "event of the Word of God" (*CD* I/1:113, 120). "Thus in the event of God's Word revelation and the Bible are indeed one, and literally so" (*CD* I/1:113).

In the earlier *Göttingen Dogmatics* (1924–25), Barth wrote extensively about the meaning of *Deus dixit*.[48] While Barth still uses the concept "God has spoken" in both the 1927 and the 1932 prolegomena, he increasingly diminishes its role in establishing an understanding of revelation. This may be due to the gradual recognition that Christ must be the centerpiece of revelation. As long as *Deus dixit* refers clearly to Christ, then it is usable. Whatever may be the reason for this change, it is fruitful to engage Barth on this very point from the 1924 lectures in Göttingen.

Barth offers six points on the meaning of *Deus dixit* in 1924. We shall examine a few of them that relate to our discussion. First, *Deus dixit* is "an address" (*eine Anrede*).[49] "The presupposition of the Bible is not that God *is* but that he *spoke*."[50] We do not discover God as God is in Godself (*an sich*) but as God communicates or shares Godself (*mitteilt*).[51] Such communication is *personal* in nature. Hence, there is in the address of God an "I-Thou

German edition will be cited as *Unterricht* and the ET as *Göttingen Dogmatics*, with volume and page numbers.

48. Barth, *Göttingen Dogmatics*, 1:58–68; *Unterricht*, 1:68–82.

49. Barth, *Göttingen Dogmatics*, 1:58; *Unterricht*, 1:69.

50. Barth, *Göttingen Dogmatics*, 1:58; *Unterricht*, 1:69. It must be noted that the ET lacks some of the precision that is needed to convey Barth's emphases as well as some of his points. For example, in this section, none of the underlined words in the handwritten manuscript, which are italicized in the German edition, are emphasized in the ET. I have done so here (and hereafter) in order to point to what Barth wanted to emphasize in his lectures. Hence, the emphasis here is Barth's in the German, but not the ET.

51. Barth, *Göttingen Dogmatics*, 1:58; *Unterricht*, 1:69.

encounter" (*Begegnung auf Ich und Du*).[52] This encounter requires one to speak and another to be spoken to—a communication and reception. "When we do not think of revelation as such, that is, one person speaking and another spoken to, God revealing himself to us and we to whom he reveals himself; when revelation is seen from the standpoint of the noninvolved spectator, then it amounts to nonrevelation."[53] Hence, receiving revelation means being addressed by God.

Moreover, the *Deus dixit* is God's revelation as "qualified history" (*qualifizierte Geschichte*); that is, while it happens "there and then" in Palestine in the years 1–30 CE, it is not something that we can discover through some reading of history where Jesus is the end result.[54] In some sense, Barth seems to be describing revelation as both *in* history and yet *beyond* it. Therefore, the "history of *Deus dixit* has, as *qualified* history, no such links with the rest of history. It must be understood *in and for itself* or *not at all*."[55] Further, God is always the *subject* of the revelation.[56] If we have knowledge of God, it is only because we have knowledge "through God and from God" (*durch Gott und aus Gott*).[57] After all, it is *God* who speaks to us in revelation. This means that God is at work in us. "*God* is the subject even when we hear his Word in the witness of the prophets and apostles."[58] Indeed, this early in his career, Barth can say, "*God* is subject even in Christ, precisely in Christ, of whom the prophets and apostles witness."[59] Hence, the content of God's self-revealing is "a *dicere*, its content is *Word*."[60] This Word is the *Logos*—an "*intellectual* communication, a revelation of *reason*" (*Geistesmitteilung*,

52. Barth, *Göttingen Dogmatics*, 1:58; *Unterricht*, 1:69. This seems to be a clear reference to the writing of Martin Buber, *I and Thou*.

53. Barth, *Göttingen Dogmatics*, 1:58; *Unterricht*, 1:69.

54. Barth, *Göttingen Dogmatics*, 1:59, 60; *Unterricht*, 1:70, 72.

55. Barth, *Göttingen Dogmatics*, 1:61, with emphases from the German text; *Unterricht*, 1:73. The word "history" is here always *Geschichte*, not *Historie*.

56. While Bromiley's translation here is adequate, I prefer to allow the sentence to retain some of the stark yet emphatic order of the German: "In this hidden, singular address, which is standing in continuity with no other events, *God* is and remains subject and God is and remains *subject*." *Unterricht*, 1:73–74.

57. Barth, *Göttingen Dogmatics*, 1:61; *Unterricht*, 1:74.

58. Barth, *Göttingen Dogmatics*, 1:62; *Unterricht*, 1:74.

59. Barth, *Göttingen Dogmatics*, 1:62; *Unterricht*, 1:74. Unfortunately, Bromiley left this sentence out of the ET. It seemed to be Barth's pivotal point here, so I have translated it and included it.

60. Barth, *Göttingen Dogmatics*, 1:62; *Unterricht*, 1:74. In contrast to *dixit*, which is a present perfect tense in Latin (and therefore Barth said he chose it to express an "eternal perfect"; p. 59), *dicere* is a present active infinitive denoting a more continuous present, especially when it is used, as I believe it is here, as a gerund (a verbal noun). Hence it should be translated "speaking" and not the infinitival "to speak."

Offenbarung von <u>*Vernunft*</u>).[61] We cannot think God's thoughts, but God can communicate them to us by faith. Hence, we cannot have certainty about this self-revelation of God, just confidence. "We can *only* believe."[62] In this regard, Calvin's secret testimony of the Holy Spirit is helpful since the witness of Scripture "becomes God's self-witness [*Selbstbeweis*] to us" through it.[63] Through the Holy Spirit, says Barth, God is "in the present, in the church, and in us," assisting us who preach the Word that God himself will bear witness to Godself, even in preaching. Barth declares, "Here is the knowledge, courage, and authority of the Christian preacher. Even for those of us who are not prophets, here is the *coal* from the altar which the seraph took with tongs and with which he touched the prophet's lips when he confessed that he was *lost* in the presence of the Lord of Hosts on account of the *unclean* lips of himself and his people (Isa. 6:5–7)."[64] God has spoken to humans in Jesus Christ, the Word Revealed.

The Word Written (Scripture)

Now we move on to the second concentric circle in Barth's threefold form of the Word of God. From the inner core, the witness to the revelatory event in Christ was written down in the form of the Scriptures. The Bible is "not in itself and as such God's past revelation" (*CD* I/1:111). The revelation occurred in the "event" of Jesus the Christ. However, the Bible "attests" to this revelation, and our acceptance of this good news is taken by faith. The apostles and prophets (writers of Scripture) do not write for their own sakes, but "they speak and write, as ordered, about that other" (*CD* I/1:112). Thus, the biblical witnesses "point beyond themselves" (*CD* I/1:111). Once we are outside of this inner core of the threefold form of the Word of God and enter the second and third forms (Scripture and preaching), we arrive at a twofold movement that is based on the inner core of revelation in Christ. This twofold movement is found in the written Word of "past recollection" of the event (Scripture) and in the "future expectation" of God's revelation (preaching; *CD* I/1:109).[65] According to Barth, the witnesses of the Old Testament pointed to a "time of expectation" in which the Word would become flesh (*CD* I/2:71–72). The witnesses to God's revelation in Jesus Christ in the New Testament point to

---

61. Barth, *Göttingen Dogmatics*, 1:62; *Unterricht*, 1:74. I have underlined the emphasized words or partial words in Barth's German.
62. Barth, *Göttingen Dogmatics*, 1:67; *Unterricht*, 1:81.
63. Barth, *Göttingen Dogmatics*, 1:68; *Unterricht*, 1:82.
64. Barth, *Göttingen Dogmatics*, 1:68; *Unterricht*, 1:82 (emphasis from the German text).
65. These ideas are developed in more detail in *CD* I/2:70–122.

a "time of recollection" (*CD* I/2:101–4). Both Testaments are witnesses to revelation but point in different directions (one ahead and one back).

Scripture is not God, although it is "God-breathed" (2 Tim. 3:15–17). However, we cannot make this written text into the Word of God at our own power of recollection; to do so would be a violation of God's freedom. "It is not in our own power to make this recollection, not even in the form of our grasping at the Bible. Only when and as the Bible grasps at us, when we are thus reminded, is this recollection achieved. . . . The Bible is God's Word to the extent that God causes it to be His Word, to the extent that He speaks through it" (*CD* I/1:109).

Therefore, the written text *becomes* the Word of God for some of its readers when the Sovereign God causes it to be so. *Deus dixit* is true "where and when God" lets it become true (*CD* I/1:120). In this way, the Word of God is not some magical written formula providing spiritual cures through incantation or repetition of words but becomes God's Word in this renewing event of revelation. When we acknowledge the truth of the witness of revelation by faith as recorded in Scripture, a genuine miracle occurs. The written Word has spoken to us just as if God himself had spoken to us. We humans are spiritually blind and deaf, unable to interpret God's message to us by ourselves. Therefore the Spirit of God exposes our helplessness and performs a miracle—the opening of our eyes and ears by God so that we can hear from God (*CD* I/2:244). By recognizing that we humans are not free already (because we are not free "for God"), the Spirit begins the miraculous work to open our selves to freedom in God. "We must make room for the miracle of acknowledging the Word of God" (*CD* I/2:258).

The Word Proclaimed (Preaching)

As we move outward from the inner core of *the* Word of God revealed in Jesus Christ to the attestation of the Word of God in written record, we come to the third circle: the proclamation of the Word of God. Here, Barth does something unusual. He lifts up preaching the Word to a level almost equal to the written Word—or even to the Word of God itself. Whereas the Bible bears witness to past revelation and may become for us the Word of God by God's grace, proclamation "promises future revelation" (*CD* I/1:111). Preaching is human talk about God "on the basis of God's own direction, both in the written revelation and in Jesus Christ" (*CD* I/1:90). It is connected to the written and revealed Word of God and thereby is not merely human talk of God. It too can become the occasion for a continuing event of revelation. In other words, the speech of a human preacher may *become the Word of God*, just as the written Word. When God speaks through our human speech, then "the Word of God is the event itself in which proclamation becomes real proclamation" (CD I/1:93). This event is nothing less than the "miracle of revelation and faith" (CD I/1:93). Barth's creative approach combines this threefold form into one unit of God's communication to humans. "Real proclamation, then, means the Word of God preached and the Word of God preached means in this first and outermost circle man's talk about God on the basis of God's own direction, which fundamentally transcends all human causation, which cannot then, be put on a human basis, but which simply takes place, and has to be acknowledged, as a fact" (CD I/1:90). God takes up human words in true proclamation and makes use of them, transforming them miraculously into the Word of God for that time and moment. Barth cites Luther positively when he says, "I am sure my word is not mine but Christ's Word and so my mouth must also be His whose Word it speaketh" (CD I/1:96).[66] Amid the frailty and sinfulness of human preachers, the Word of God takes place miraculously on a human level (CD I/2:750). So in answer to his own dilemma posed in a lecture in October 1922, it is the Spirit who takes human words about God and allows them to become the very Word of God for hearers. Barth had posed the question this way: "As theologians, we ought to speak of God. But we are humans and as such cannot speak of God. We ought to do both, to know the 'ought' and the 'not able to,' and precisely in this way give God the glory."[67] Because God has spoken definitively in Jesus Christ and has allowed witnesses to this event of revelation in Scripture, human preachers (or theologians) can proclaim the Word of God with the expectation that the sovereign God will determine how and when our words can become God's Word. "For what happens is that [humans] are really able to speak of God, and to let others hear of Him" (CD I/2:751).

Toward a Theology of the Word of God

There is much in Barth's proposal that I want to consider further as we ask what all of this discussion about the Word of God has to do with the people of God's presence. Engaging his ideas and criticisms of them will assist us in homing in on the importance of the Word of God for the church. Divine

66. This is from Martin Luther, *Eine treue Vermahnung* (1522), WA 8:263, line 13.
67. Karl Barth, "The Word of God as the Task of Theology," in *The Word of God and Theology*, trans. Amy Marga (Edinburgh: T&T Clark, 2011), 177. Cf. Barth, "Das Wort Gottes als Aufgabe der Theologie," in *Das Wort Gottes und die Theologie: Gesammelte Vorträge* (Munich: Kaiser, 1924), 158.

speech is not only communicating information but is also the "typical mode of [God's] presence and power."[68] As Carl Trueman says, "Speech is how God is present or, to use a more modern idiom, how he makes his presence felt."[69] Since through this book we have been focused on the nature and meaning of God's presence among his people, it is especially relevant to our discussion to deepen our consideration of the implications of divine speech-act for the people of God's presence.

What Does It Mean to Say God _Has Spoken_ (Deus Dixit)?

The God of Scripture is a God who has spoken to human beings. This is the incontrovertible fact of the witnesses recorded in Scripture. God has revealed Godself to humans in various ways, making God's own presence known. At least one dimension of the record of Scripture is the testimony of the writers and compilers that God was communicating to them.[70]

If we consider the revelation of God in Jesus Christ to humanity, then it seems to make little sense to narrow the field of revelation down to what God _says_. Indeed, that is not quite the point of this Latin phrase. _Deus dixit_ refers not only to God's words but also to the Word—the _Logos_—made flesh. The Word of God has always existed and indeed was God (John 1:1). Therefore, the nature of making this kind of statement about God's speech is more like describing the English word "communicate." The old English word "communicatio" has a basic meaning derived from the Latin (_communicatio_), which means "a communicating or imparting or the act of sharing in something," from _communico_, the verb, which means "to share, impart, inform, confer with, take a share in, or participate in." Over time this developed into _verbal_ sharing or communication that offers an "exchange of information" through verbal or mechanical means. The older definition of communicating something (such as heat, motion, feeling), as well as that of sharing in something, has become obsolete.[71] Instead, the connotation of exchanging information verbally or by other means is the most common usage today.

---

68. Carl R. Trueman, "The Word as a Means of Grace," _Southern Baptist Journal of Theology_ 19, no. 4 (2015): 59–78, here 65.

69. Trueman, "The Word as a Means of Grace," 65.

70. While I will not engage with a particular text in the footnotes, I want to acknowledge the benefit I have received from Nicholas Wolterstorff, _Divine Discourse: Philosophical Reflections on the Claim That God Speaks_ (Cambridge: Cambridge University Press, 1995). Especially helpful for me have been the segments relating to Ricoeur, Derrida, and the "speech-act" theory of J. L. Austin.

71. From the _Oxford English Dictionary_, accessed Oct. 31, 2018, http://www.oed.com/view/Entry/37309?redirectedFrom=communication#eid.

When Barth used *Deus dixit* to describe God's revelation, he was referring not simply to the speaking of God to us but also to the entire revelatory event whereby God *communicates* to us and with us. To say *Deus dixit* is to say revelation. It is to say God *communicates* in these two senses: (1) in personal terms where God reveals Godself through the Word, Jesus Christ; and (2) in relational terms where God reveals Godself through addressing humans with an expectation of some response from them. God desires to communicate with humans, both in the sense of sharing God's own self with them and in the sense of speaking to and with them. In this way, we might view God's speech through the lens of J. L. Austin's "speech-act" theory, which argues that words have three dimensions: (1) locutionary acts, which are words as they are simply uttered; (2) illocutionary acts, which are what words are doing; and (3) perlocutionary acts, which are what the words are bringing about.[72] Perhaps we can understand the "speech" of God more in line with this complexity of "speech-act."[73] In whatever form it may come to humans, the Word of God demonstrates something of the character of the God who speaks.

This is aptly described by Jonathan Edwards in one of his miscellaneous entries in a journal notebook. The disposition of God—the core of who God is—is "to incline to communicate himself."[74] Since this was written in the 1700s, one must hear intonations of the older sense of sharing in these words: God inclines to share something of himself as well as say something about himself. The God of the Christian faith is a communicating God. The Word of God became flesh and lived among us, communicating both his knowledge of the Father and his mirror image of the Father in bodily form.

With Barth, I see the central event of revelation from God in the person of Jesus Christ. If we want to see God, we must look at the clearest expression of God given to us in Jesus Christ (Col. 2:9). The Word of God is clearly identified both as *God* and as *the particular human, Jesus Christ* (John 1:1, 14). In a very real sense, therefore, when we speak of the Word of God, we are speaking of a person, Jesus the Christ. All other aspects of this central event of revelation must tie into this innermost circle: the Word Revealed.

---

72. Amos Yong, *Spirit-Word-Community: Theological Hermeneutics in Trinitarian Perspective* (Aldershot, UK: Ashgate, 2002), 254.

73. Wolterstorff suggests that the biblical narrative falls in line with the illocutionary dimension of speech-acts. See Wolterstorff, *Divine Discourse*, 240–45.

74. Jonathan Edwards, *The Miscellanies, 1153–1360*, ed. Douglas A. Sweeney, Works of Jonathan Edwards 23, ed. Harry A. Stout and Kenneth P. Minkema (New Haven: Yale University Press, 2004), entry no. 1218. For denoting Edwards's view of God as incorporating a "dispositional ontology," see Sang Hyun Lee, *The Philosophical Theology of Jonathan Edwards* (Princeton: Princeton University Press, 1988).

The Word Written (Scripture) reveals the purposes of God in this revelation through the words recorded by witnesses of it.

However, here is my first concern with Barth's three concentric circles of the Word's threefold form. Can one so easily describe the witnesses in Scripture as witnesses to the event of Jesus Christ (either as *expectation*, as with the Old Testament, or as *recollection*, as with the New Testament)? Barth's line of thinking seems to truncate everything in the written text to the person of Christ. The difficulty is that in so doing there may be themes that are inspired by God among words and genres of Scripture that do not readily point to Christ. Are these non-Christ words, which seem to point neither in expectation nor recollection to Christ, not actually the Word of God? What of psalms of lament? What about genealogical records (the "begats")? One needs to stretch rather far to make the story of Job show any expectation of Jesus Christ. Nicholas Wolterstorff has called Barth's attempt to get the Old Testament writers to fit under the category of witness as showing "visible signs of strain."[75] I agree.

What may be the problem here is that Barth defines the revelation of God solely in terms of Jesus the Christ—that is, in terms of "self-revelation." Is there not more revealed to us about God and life than Jesus the Christ? It seems that way to me—and perhaps to many other Christians throughout history who have used the Scriptures as a blueprint for our lives before this God. Squeezing all of the witness of Scripture into expectation and recollection of the Jesus Christ event of revelation denigrates the variety and diversity found in the genres throughout Scripture as well as denies the ability for God to say something about Godself that is not directly related to Jesus Christ. To be sure, Barth has pointed us in a *Christian* direction by focusing attention on Christ, but he has also left us without much clarity on what to do with those passages in the Bible that do not point to Christ.

What Does It Mean to Say God Has Spoken through the Scriptures?

The primary purpose of the revelation of God to us in Jesus Christ is to introduce us to a person. In this respect, I believe that Barth has provided us with a helpful discussion on the Word Revealed. However, as noted already, it has some areas that are problematic, especially for understanding the written text of the Word of God. The narratives of Scripture provide us with an understanding of who this God who encounters humans at a core level of their being is. They also provide us stories that reflect the biblical witnesses'

---

75. Nicholas Wolterstorff, *The God We Worship: An Exploration of Liturgical Theology* (Grand Rapids: Eerdmans, 2015), 134.

attempt to testify to their own experiences of these encounters with God. As we saw in earlier chapters, sometimes the best way to talk about such core-level encounters is through narrative or storytelling. Some aspects of the narrative genre of Scripture, then, seem to be crafted to draw us into the scene of the story in order to understand something about the God who engages us. "Revelation is addressed not only to the intellect but to the whole person."[76]

To say that revelation is addressed to the whole person is not to say that all revelation is personal, but surely some of it is. This is also not to say that all revelation in Scripture is propositional, but surely some of it is.[77] The complexity of Scripture in terms of God speaking is augmented only by our attempt to hear what God is saying *together in community*. Such a movement brings us into interpretation, which inevitably requires some consideration of inspiration and illumination.

Donald Bloesch offers a thought that is reflective of what we have discussed up to this point and that is provocative for where we are headed in our consideration of the Spirit and Scripture: "Some theologians have erred by subordinating the Spirit to the Word; others by elevating the Spirit over the Word. If we mean by the latter the living Word, Jesus Christ, then we must view him as equal to the Spirit, though he has a certain priority in the economy of salvation. If we are thinking of the written Word, however, the Spirit clearly has precedence, since the Bible was produced by the inspiration of the Spirit, and the Spirit uses the Bible to bring sinners to the knowledge of Jesus Christ."[78] This last clause is an *evangelical* understanding of the Spirit and Scripture. The purpose of Scripture is primarily to be used by the Spirit to share the good news (*euangelion*) to the world, revealing God's self to humanity. Scripture is useful for teaching, reproving, and correcting in the church, but its primary service is in the *re*telling and *re*-presenting of the story of God in Scripture through the Spirit. Obviously, the heart of that story is the good news of the revelation of Jesus the Christ, who for our sin and salvation came to earth, lived as a human being, died, and was raised to life by the Spirit of the living God. Surely the Spirit who inspired the writers of Scripture can also be present throughout history to engage, inspire, and illuminate the readers and hearers.[79]

76. Clark H. Pinnock, *Flame of Love: A Theology of the Holy Spirit* (Downers Grove, IL: InterVarsity, 1996), 226.

77. Pinnock, *Flame of Love*, 226.

78. Donald G. Bloesch, *The Holy Spirit: Works and Gifts*, Christian Foundations (Downers Grove, IL: InterVarsity, 2000), 57–58. This is one of the best statements I have seen among evangelicals on these relationships.

79. As Clark Pinnock notes, F. F. Bruce suggested that we not separate the Spirit's work of inspiration from the subsequent work in illumination. I am following that line here. See Pinnock,

In the past decades some evangelical discussions of Scripture have focused on what I consider to be a debate revolving around issues of modernity more than issues of foundational importance for the Christian faith.[80] Questions of the authority of Scripture, the inerrancy of the Bible, and the appropriate model of evangelical interpretation have blown up a "perfect storm," overwhelming the broad tent of evangelicalism and threatening to send the coalition of evangelicals into splintered, smaller tents of their own.[81] What I attempt to craft in this section is a different approach to Scripture that hopefully posits a high view of the text and its authority but *in the Spirit*, not in some propositionalist sense of proof that would cause one's mind to submit to the truths therein. Moreover, arguing with the postmodern world over the perfection of the original writings (the *autographa*) of the Bible is simply a nonstarter, especially since the *autographa* do not exist. The Christians who wanted to support the modernist cry of "inerrancy" were really concerned to support the authority of the canon of Scripture. On what basis can we *trust* the documents we have as *reliable* instruments of God's intention? What I attempt to craft here is a high view of inspiration and illumination in which the Spirit of God uses the vessel of Scripture to speak to humans the truth about the God who is recorded therein.[82] While evangelicals have always stressed a "high" view of Scripture, we have also become less than "generous" in our orthodoxy regarding various views of how Scripture is to be regarded and what each particular group will approve as "high" enough.[83] To be sure, there

"The Role of the Spirit in Interpretation," *Journal of the Evangelical Theological Society* 36, no. 4 (December 1993): 491–97, here 492–93.

80. For a more extended discussion of what I mean by this statement, see Terry L. Cross, "A Proposal to Break the Ice: What Can Pentecostal Theology Offer Evangelical Theology?," *Journal of Pentecostal Theology* 10, no. 2 (2002): 44–73, esp. 51–57 and 56n25, where I state, "Inerrancy is a dead theological term; it is non-Scriptural and hearkens back to an era when *evidences* and *rationales* were meant to offer apologetic proof."

81. Here I use the imagery of a large tent, borrowing the idea from Donald Dayton, "Some Doubts about the Usefulness of the Category 'Evangelical,'" in *The Variety of American Evangelicalism*, ed. Donald Dayton and Robert K. Johnson (Downers Grove, IL: InterVarsity, 1993). Diversity is stretching the tent of evangelicalism; now, twenty-five years after Dayton's description of the stretching, the movement seems splintered into political divisions as well.

82. Here I follow Calvin, who sounds strangely Pentecostal: if one wants *proof* for the authority of Scripture, one need not look for debates or human ratiocinations but to the One who assures our hearts that we can trust the Scriptures as being God's Word via the "inner testimony of the Spirit."

83. The phrase "generous orthodoxy" apparently originates with Hans Frei, a professor at Yale, in dialogue with Carl F. H. Henry. It refers to an openness of spirit in the dialogue of theology so that we can arrive at a better understanding of truth. See Frei, "Responses to Narrative Theology: An Evangelical Proposal," in *Theology and Narrative: Selected Essays*, ed. George Hunsinger and William Placher (New York: Oxford University Press, 1993), 207–8. Also, it is described by George Hunsinger, "What Can Evangelicals and Postliberals Learn from

is a danger of reducing Scripture to mere human writing, but a rationalistic argument of inerrancy alone will not stem this tide.

Instead of engaging in the particularities of this debate, allow me to sketch a broader approach to Scripture that includes consideration of the Spirit's role beyond the traditional understanding of inspiration that is common to so many evangelicals.[84] There are two prongs in this broader approach that initiate our discussion. First, since the Spirit testifies of Jesus Christ and has inspired the Scriptures, an essential goal of the proclamation of Scripture is to portray the good news of Jesus Christ. How is this done? We realize that God the Spirit has inspired (breathed into) the writers with the content and (perhaps) intent of what God wanted humans to know (2 Tim. 3:15). The Spirit carries along the writers of Scripture so that the words they write are not their own but portray—with all their humanness—the content and intent of God (2 Pet. 1:21). But does the extent of the inspiration apply only to the written documents? To respond affirmatively to this latter idea is to limit the action of the Spirit in Scripture to time past. Surely the same Spirit who inspired the writers of Scripture can also be present throughout history to engage, inspire, and illuminate the readers and hearers.

Each Other?," in *The Nature of Confession: Evangelicals and Postliberals in Conversation*, ed. Timothy Phillips and Dennis Okholm (Downers Grove, IL: InterVarsity, 1996), 141–42.

84. The classic statement and portrayal of this comes to fruition in the writings of B. B. Warfield and A. A. Hodge of the Old Princeton School. For an excellent portrayal of this approach and its influence on fundamentalism and the eventual evangelical movement, see Stanley Grenz, "Nurturing the Soul, Informing the Mind: The Genesis of the Evangelical Scripture Principle," in *Evangelicals and Scripture: Tradition, Authority and Hermeneutics*, ed. Vincent Bacote, Laura Miguélez, and Dennis Okholm (Downers Grove, IL: InterVarsity, 2004), 21–41, esp. 30–32. Also, I recognize that some evangelicals "in the tent" will be uncomfortable with my bypassing the inerrancy discussion in this way, but there are just as many (if not more) evangelicals who will see this as a legitimate direction. Pentecostals, for example, do not seem to have a need to engage modernism per se. As Nancey Murphy has observed, Mennonites and Pentecostals attempt to hold a more middle position in relation to fundamentalism versus liberalism. See Murphy, *Beyond Liberalism and Fundamentalism: How Modern and Postmodern Philosophy Set the Theological Agenda* (Harrisburg, PA: Trinity Press International, 1996), 6n8. Hans Frei has noted that liberalism and fundamentalism are really "siblings under the skin." See Frei, *Types of Christian Theology*, ed. George Hunsinger and William Placher (New Haven: Yale University Press, 1992), 84. And Joel Carpenter has shown that "many holiness Wesleyans came to accept the doctrine of biblical inerrancy even though that belief is not a Wesleyan way of understanding the Bible's inspiration and authority." See Carpenter, *Revive Us Again: The Reawakening of American Fundamentalism* (New York: Oxford University Press, 1997), 237. I would add that Pentecostals also find themselves influenced by a fundamentalist DNA that is not part of their true genetic composition. Some of this "unease" with fundamentalist approaches to Scripture is portrayed well by Donald Dayton, "The Pietist Theological Critique of Biblical Inerrancy," in *Evangelicals and Scripture*, ed. Bacote, Miguélez, and Okholm, 76–89.

It is for this reason that I find Karl Barth's approach to the threefold form of the Word of God to be engaging. As humans proclaiming the Scriptures and pointing to Jesus Christ, we rely on the Holy Spirit to present the good news to the hearts and minds of hearers. The preacher's task is to witness to or to "herald" the good news in a way that reiterates God's speaking in Jesus Christ in the past (*Deus dixit*) and to present the future promise of salvation because of this past event (*CD* I/2:70–121). Humans may *acknowledge* God's Word to them when they truly "hear" it in the Spirit. As Barth states, "We must make room for the miracle of acknowledging the Word of God" (*CD* I/2:258). It is in the Holy Spirit alone that humans are truly "free for God" (*CD* I/2:243). However, this message that the Spirit brings to humans is not an understanding devoid of content; it is instruction brought by the Spirit, "for the Word is never apart from the Holy Spirit" (*CD* I/2:244).

The Spirit *re*-presents to us Jesus Christ through the proclamation of Scripture. In some mystical manner, the Spirit reaches over the time and space of several thousand years of human history and brings us face-to-face with Jesus the Christ, whom we may acknowledge in faith or deny in doubt. Such a *re*-presentation is crafted not by a preacher's own human abilities—such as homiletical or teaching skills, personal charisma, eloquence in communication—but rather by the power and presence of the Spirit (1 Cor. 2:4–5). It is the Spirit who "mediates the *Christus Praesens*," presenting the crucified and risen Lord and opening the heart to "see" and believe in him.[85]

This approach seems to offer a great deal to Christians today by reinvigorating the role of the Spirit in the *hearing* and *preaching* of the Word of God—two aspects that are vital to the future of Christianity. Yet some may think that this approach is too mystical. Perhaps such concern is too tied to a rationalism that requires the truth of Scripture to respond with mere mental assent yet not also with one's entire life. Indeed, Jesus is *re*-presented to us by and in the Spirit in such a way that our *whole person* is asked to respond (Matt. 22:37–39). Jesus imparts himself to us in the Spirit, and we in turn are able to respond with our entire selves in the Spirit.[86]

---

85. In describing Karl Barth's view of the Spirit, George Hunsinger has captured this aspect masterfully. See Hunsinger, "The Mediator of Communion: Karl Barth's Doctrine of the Holy Spirit," in *Disruptive Grace: Studies in the Theology of Karl Barth* (Grand Rapids: Eerdmans, 2000), 148–85, here 161.

86. Hunsinger, "The Mediator of Communion," 161. Also, Donald Bloesch writes in these terms quite frequently. For example, he says, "For biblical evangelicals, the truthfulness of the Bible cannot be determined by historical investigation, since this truth is inaccessible to human perception and conception." He continues by stating that the truth of the Bible "is the revelational meaning of the events that are described, not the events in and of themselves."

In order to consider more carefully the concept of "hearing" the Word of God that is read or preached in the congregation, a word needs to be said concerning *how we approach* the reception of the Word. As mentioned previously, James McClendon has proposed a "baptistic vision" for an approach to reading and hearing the Bible in a way that is clearly not Catholic or Protestant. There is much here that I find resonating with my own theology of the Word of God and the Spirit's re-presentation of Christ offered above. The phrase "baptistic vision" is purposely written with a small *b* because McClendon sees this view tied mainly to free-church movements, including Baptists of various stripes as well as holiness and Pentecostal churches. What is the baptistic approach to Scripture? First, it accepts the "plain sense" reading of Scripture, seeing some continuity with the hearers' lives today and the story Scripture tells. Second, it acknowledges that some point of the story of Scripture will lead them to its application. Third, it "sees past and present and future linked by a 'this-is-that' and 'then-is-now' vision, a trope of mystical identity binding the story now to the story then, and the story then and now to God's future yet to come."[87] This final aspect of the baptistic vision, as McClendon calls it, seems to be precisely what we have been describing, except without the acknowledgment of the Spirit's role in this re-presentation.[88] Therefore, from the human "hearing" side of the Word of God, we listen for the voice of God in the Word in ways that expect God to be present today just as God was present in the days of the biblical events. This mind-set, then, is enhanced by the Holy Spirit, who awakens the Word in us so that its seed can sprout on good ground, ultimately alerting us to the reality of Jesus the Christ as the Son of God. This is what I call my first "prong" in our approach to Scripture: the baptistic vision.

In addition to this approach, I offer a second prong. John Webster has provided a provocative dogmatic treatise on Scripture, addressing primarily the concepts of revelation, sanctification, and inspiration. Although Christians may use the adjective "holy" before "Scriptures," we usually do not

---

See Bloesch, *Holy Scripture: Revelation, Inspiration and Interpretation* (Downers Grove, IL: InterVarsity, 1994), 19.

87. James McClendon Jr., *Systematic Theology*, vol. 2, *Doctrine* (Nashville: Abingdon, 1994), 45.

88. Originally, I came upon this thought of re-presentation in the writings of Wilhelm Hermann, a teacher of Barth in theology. I read him as sketching a way to overcome the historical "ditch" of Lessing by speaking of the way the "inner life of Jesus" forms a stream in which believers may now stand and participate, almost as if they were in the historical past with him. This triggered my thoughts about a spiritual "stream" and the way the Holy Spirit may work to re-present this Jesus Christ to us. See Wilhelm Hermann, *The Communion of the Christian with God: Described on the Basis of Luther's Statements* (Philadelphia: Fortress, 1971).

think of sanctification in relation to the Scriptures themselves. Since one of the essential works of the Spirit is sanctification, it seems appropriate to ask what such a work might look like in relation to the Bible. Frustrated with the deistic or dualistic approaches to the divinity/humanity framework for considering Scripture, Webster posits sanctification by the Spirit as a potential way to reconsider the whole question without the baggage of previous attempts. He describes sanctification as a process in which God, who is entirely free, commands and molds the "creaturely element" to enter divine service.[89] For Webster, sanctification does not imply a cooperative effort between God and the creature, as if building "upon some inherent holiness of the creature's own."[90] Holiness belongs solely to God as an incommunicable attribute. If creatures become holy, it is because God has chosen to *make* them holy—a *sanctitas aliena*. Yet the story does not end here. The sanctifying Spirit who is Lord is also the giver of life. God the Spirit pours this life into the horizontal dimension of creatureliness without abrogating it, thereby infusing it with holiness—a *sanctitas infusa*. Webster suggests that this "making holy" of human creatures may be conceived analogously with the way the Spirit operates in making Scripture "holy." The accent seems to be on the divine gift of grace to scriptural authors to write God's words, but almost equally important is the human response to that grace to write those words in all their creatureliness. Sanctification may then be broadened to consider the work of the Spirit in the lives of the community of faith—the fellowship of believers who hear, read aloud, and proclaim the Scriptures. The people of God are being sanctified by the Spirit of God, who is also at work in making the Scriptures holy.

This has interesting and powerful implications for theology. By considering how Webster deals with the question of inspiration, we may see this theology of the Word of God in its broader context. The Word Written was "God-breathed," or "inspired," by the Spirit of God (2 Tim. 3:16). What does this mean? With the help of Webster's discussion of 2 Peter 1:20–21, we can see some clear directions for understanding inspiration. "Above all, you must understand that no prophecy of Scripture came about by the prophet's own interpretation of things. For prophecy never had its origin in the human will, but prophets, though human, spoke from God as they were carried along by the Holy Spirit" (2 Pet. 1:20–21). What is clear from this description is that Scripture does not derive from one's own interpretation of things. Prophets (writers of Scripture) speak "from God." As John Webster notes, "Inspiration

---

89. John Webster, *Holy Scripture: A Dogmatic Sketch*, Current Issues in Theology 1, ed. Iain Torrance (Cambridge: Cambridge University Press, 2003), 27.

90. Webster, *Holy Scripture*, 27.

is not primarily a textual property but a divine movement and therefore a divine moving."[91] Further, Scripture is not a creation of human ingenuity or creativity. It is not from "human will." Instead, the prophets "were carried along" by the Spirit. The writers were "moved" by God.[92] Finally, the prophets so moved by the Spirit *spoke* in human language.[93] Revelation from God moves the writers to write, the prophets to speak. The "communicative self-presence of God" impels such activity.[94] Yet this does not entail pure passivity on the part of the writer. The Spirit offers the suggestion of words, and human writers respond accordingly. As Webster describes these, they are "concursive rather than antithetical."[95] The presence of God in the writing process is the "sanctifying work of the Spirit" that brings the texts to a place "fitting vessels of the treasure of the gospel."[96] Therefore, the text of Scripture "enjoys a privileged position" among Christians.[97]

Returning to Barth's threefold form, there is another difficulty with his portrayal of the Word Written. The fact that Scripture may *become* the Word of God provides clearly for the sovereignty of God over the written Word but at the same time sets up the reception of this writing as quasi-authoritative. How does the community of believers know collectively when some words in the text *become* God's Word for us now and therefore need our greater attention? Further, Barth's description of both the written and preached Words as *becoming* the Word of God seems "occasionalistic." If there is no constancy to the written Word as being the Word of God, then the Christian faith and indeed the communal Christian life seem to lack constancy as well. Saying that God has spoken to us but that we can never quite tell which part of Scripture is God's Word or at what time God's Word will resonate through the human words of Scripture crafts a recipe for confusion within the body of Christ.

Although I argue against Barth's occasionalism, I admit that God is sovereign over how humans receive the words of Scripture. I still believe that the Spirit, who breathed into the writers the message to speak, can bring those words to life again. Why does this enlivening work need to be described as the Word of God? It is the Spirit, not our intellect or ingenuity, that provides occasions for humans to hear the Word of God and respond in obedience (or disobedience). This is what the church has traditionally called illumination.

91. Webster, *Holy Scripture*, 36.
92. Webster, *Holy Scripture*, 37.
93. Webster, *Holy Scripture*, 37.
94. Webster, *Holy Scripture*, 38.
95. Webster, *Holy Scripture*, 38–39.
96. Webster, *Holy Scripture*, 39.
97. Pinnock, *Flame of Love*, 229. Webster thinks even the process of canonization of Scripture is sanctified by the Holy Spirit.

It is the work of the Spirit to provide assistance to the body of Christ in its interpretation of the written Word. As Pinnock says, "If inspiration secures Scripture, illumination is meant to enable readers to recognize Scripture's timely meaning."[98]

Here we can see that both the text and reader require something of the Spirit's work in inspiring and illuminating the text for understanding in today's world. The text of Scripture can be used by the Spirit as a transforming instrument. "The text projects a world and clears a space into which we enter and experience transformation. It projects an alternate world and invites us to follow Jesus in it."[99] When we gather as a community of believers to hear God's Word together, we must "make room" for the presence of the Spirit to illumine our minds and hearts. "This means that my listening to what the Spirit is saying includes my being open to being transformed by what is said, and not just myself, but all those [who] claim to be of the Spirit of God and are claimed by that same Spirit."[100] Making room for an awareness of the presence of the Spirit in the congregation is crucial to corporate understanding of the Scriptures. This process is overseen by the Spirit, not by humans, and therefore remains somewhat "unseen." The Word of God working in our midst, then, is "a complex interactive process between God, the prophet, the inspired utterance, and the audience to which such utterance is directed."[101] It is in this sense that I understand Hebrews 4:12: "For the word of God is alive and active. Sharper than any double-edged sword, it penetrates even to dividing soul and spirit, joints and marrow; it judges the thoughts and attitudes of the heart." The Spirit makes the Word alive to us, demanding from us a response. Therefore, while the community interprets the Word by the illumination of the Spirit, the Word interprets the community.[102]

What Does It Mean to Say God Is Still Speaking (Deus Dicit)?

While Barth used *dixit*, the present perfect tense (a form of the Latin past tense), to describe that God *has spoken* in the past, he did not use the present tense (*dicit*) to describe that God *is speaking*. It may be that Barth saw in *dixit*

---

98. Pinnock, *Flame of Love*, 229.
99. Pinnock, *Flame of Love*, 230.
100. Yong, *Spirit-Word-Community*, 255.
101. Yong, *Spirit-Word-Community*, 255. Yong focuses his words here on "the prophetic Word of God," but as we have seen in 2 Pet. 1:20, prophecy and Scripture (writing) are frequently interchanged.
102. A provocative and intriguing proposal in relation to interpretation of Scripture comes from Chris E. W. Green, *Sanctifying Interpretation: Vocation, Holiness, and Scripture* (Cleveland, TN: CPT Press, 2015), esp. chap. 8.

an action in the past that has ramifications into the present.[103] God has spoken in Jesus Christ and is still speaking through Christ. Perhaps that is how Barth intended it to be understood. However, for Barth, through the human words of preaching, God is still speaking! The "foolishness of preaching" can be elevated by the Spirit of God so that our words become God's words (1 Cor. 1:21). In some miraculous way, God speaks about himself through human words of preaching (*CD* I/1:95).

Heinrich Bullinger established a Reformed understanding of preaching, from which Barth surely derived his thinking in this matter. "The preaching of the Word of God is the Word of God."[104] When "preachers lawfully called" preach in the church, the "very Word of God is proclaimed, received by the faithful."[105] Speaking against "inward illumination of the Spirit" as the only source of hearing from God, Bullinger crafts a strong argument for the need of "external preaching," based on the premise that it is the "will of God" that such preaching occur.[106]

As Karl Barth says in a work about preaching the gospel, "Preaching is the Word of God which he himself has spoken; but he makes use, according to his good pleasure, of the ministry of [humans] who speak to their fellows, in God's name, by means of a passage from Scripture."[107] Preachers offer their human remarks on Scripture between the twin poles of "whence" and "whither"—that is, between the incarnation of Christ and the future parousia of Christ.[108] Preachers do not need to add anything to the revelation of God but simply lift up the event of revelation and believe that God's presence will be there when they do so. Barth states, "But if God speaks through our words, then in fact that same situation is produced: the prophets and apostles are present even though the words are spoken by an ordinary minister. But we must not think of ourselves as uttering prophecies; if Christ deigns to be present when we are speaking, it is precisely because the action is God's, not ours."[109] Again, I do not see the necessity for labeling this action of the Spirit

103. This could be Barth's meaning of his statement in 1924 that *dixit* was used because it spoke of the "eternal perfect." See Barth, *Göttingen Dogmatics*, 1:59.

104. Bullinger, *The Second Helvetic Confession* (1566), chap. 1, ¶4, in *The Book of Confessions: The United Presbyterian Church USA* (New York: Office of the General Assembly, UPCUSA, 1970), 5.004.

105. Bullinger, *The Second Helvetic Confession* 5.004.

106. Bullinger, *The Second Helvetic Confession* 5.005.

107. Karl Barth, *The Preaching of the Gospel*, trans. B. E. Hooke (Philadelphia: Westminster, 1963), 9 (alt.).

108. Karl Barth, *Homiletics*, trans. G. W. Bromiley and Donald E. Daniels (Louisville: Westminster John Knox, 1991), 51–52.

109. Barth, *The Preaching of the Gospel*, 14.

as "the Word of God." Why cannot the same Spirit who inspired the writers of Scripture also speak to our hearts through the exposition of texts in the voice of human preachers? There is no need to divinize the preached Word.

The people of God's presence gather to hear from God through the voice of humans. It is not that believers cannot hear from God on their own, but the nature of being human requires us to hear from God together so that we will not pervert the Word into our own schemes or receive the Word and never do anything with it. Hearing the Word of God within the context of our local community of believers lays upon us certain demands and responsibilities.[110] "[Scripture] is read in community, the community we call church, because that is the Spirit's primary residence. It is read, not in isolation, but in conjunction with the saints of the church, who provide our best insight into how that word can take shape in our own lives."[111] Thus the people of God proclaim God's Word and hear it proclaimed in their midst. If they listen "in the Spirit" and "make room" for the presence of God, they will be able to hear God through the words of the preacher. God has chosen that through the foolishness of preaching, the message from God and about God would be offered to humans.

A well-known homiletician, Thomas Long, has suggested that the image of "witness" is an important descriptor for the preacher. In many ways this coincides with Barth's understanding of the church as witness to the self-revealing God. The preacher is a *witness* to the good news. Thomas Long declares that the Christian preacher is a unique speaker in not only pointing to the gospel but also needing to experience the gospel in order to be a credible *witness* of the things God has done and can do.[112]

Within the context of *witness*, Long offers five points that support the idea of preacher as witness; we will note several of them that specifically relate to our discussion. First, witness emphasizes the authority of the preacher. This authority does not come through rank or power, "but rather because of what the preacher has seen and heard."[113] Such credibility of one's own experience of God is crucial for preaching in the postmodern era. Long's comments have special impact for anyone who has struggled through a text to preach: "When the preacher prepares a sermon by wrestling with a biblical text, the preacher is not merely gathering information about that text. The preacher

---

110. This idea is well described by Martin Copenhaver, Anthony Robinson, and William Willimon, *Good News in Exile: Three Pastors Offer a Hopeful Vision for the Church* (Grand Rapids: Eerdmans, 1999), 38.

111. Copenhaver, Robinson, and Willimon, *Good News in Exile*, 38.

112. Thomas G. Long, *The Witness of Preaching* (Louisville: Westminster John Knox, 1989), 41.

113. Long, *The Witness of Preaching*, 44.

is listening for a voice, looking for a presence, hoping for the claim of God to be encountered through the text. Until this happens, there is nothing for the preacher to say. When it happens, the preacher becomes a witness to what has been seen and heard through the scripture, and the preacher's authority grows out of this seeing and hearing."[114] Notice that the quest in this description is for a personal encounter with God so that what is found in the text and in one's life is God's presence and voice.

Second, the image of witness provides a way of approaching the Bible itself. Witnesses testify to things they have seen or heard, and similarly preachers testify to the event of the encounter between God and humans.[115] "We go to scripture, then, not to glean a set of facts about God or the faith that can then be announced whenever and wherever, but to encounter a Presence, to hear God's voice speaking to us ever anew, calling us in the midst of the situations in which we find ourselves to be God's faithful people."[116] The written Word opens us up to a Presence. If that Presence is experienced by the preacher, then it will come out in the pulpit.

Preachers, then, are witnesses to the God of the Scriptures and the cross. They have been transformed by this personal experience (event) and therefore speak out of their own lives concerning the God who encounters humans. They soak themselves in prayer and study of the Word in order to hear what God is saying to the church that week. Then they find the best way to speak those words with as much skill as they can muster. Finally, they recognize that their mere human words and efforts are nothing unless punctuated by the presence of God the Spirit when the message is delivered.[117]

One reason I am drawn to Barth's discussion of preaching in *CD* I/1 and I/2 is that he gives substance to Bullinger's idea that preaching *is* the Word of God. While the two thinkers undoubtedly mean different things by their similar ideas, the fact that Barth can recognize the miraculous nature of God's

---

114. Long, *The Witness of Preaching*, 44.

115. Long, *The Witness of Preaching*, 45.

116. Long, *The Witness of Preaching*, 45.

117. While it may be unnecessary for some to state this caveat, I believe it is an essential *theological* and *pragmatic* part of the church in the world today. Effective preachers require training in a variety of skills and competencies. In my grandfather's day, one could receive a call to preach and spend one's life fulfilling that calling without much formal education. (Indeed, my grandfather was educated through only the fourth grade but preached for fifty-five years.) Today, the world and culture are much more complex. I am convinced that training ministers requires a formal education of some sort so that preachers can offer to congregations more than some pabulum from their own flow of consciousness. What do preachers need (here I'm considering just the *preaching* aspect, not also the skills and training required for pastoral ministry today)? I return to this question more thoroughly in the companion volume, *Serving the People of God's Presence*.

Spirit taking up human words into divine purpose resonates with much of how I understood preaching as a child *and* how I have come to understand preaching after having done it hundreds of times. Preaching is a human act, to be sure, yet it has the potential of becoming an instrument in the movement of the Spirit's presence to drive home the point that God wants to get across to his people. In this way, one part of a sermon may be brought home to one or two people in the congregation while another part may be driven by the Spirit into several other hearts. When people respond to my preaching, I find it amazing that in the same sermon one person was struck by one point and another by an entirely different point. My comment here is to illustrate the Spirit's power to channel the Word of God spoken by human instruments to different hearts for different reasons. In this way, I do believe that preaching *becomes* a word from the Lord for the congregation at that moment in time because the Spirit of God makes it effective in its delivery to individual needs. I am not saying that preaching *becomes* the Word of God (as would Barth) but that God the Spirit *uses* the human instrument of preaching to illumine Scripture for the point to be made for each person.

Further, the ministry of preaching is focused not just on a believing community but also on unbelievers who may hear it. When the gospel of Jesus Christ is proclaimed, the Spirit of God is present to *re*-present the life, death, and resurrection of Jesus Christ to the unbeliever, thereby creating a sacred space in the human heart where faith *can* and *may* arise. Just as I discuss with the sacraments (or participatory Christian practices) in the companion volume, *Serving the People of God's Presence*, there is a twofold purpose for preaching of the Word of God: (1) for nourishing and strengthening the body of Christ in doctrine and life; and (2) for public witness to the reconciling gospel of Jesus Christ: the life, death, and resurrection of Christ and its meaning for humans.[118]

In preaching, the presence of Christ is made real by the power of the Spirit, making the Word-become-flesh alive for us today. Further, when we preach the truths from God in the Scriptures, we bring clarity and application to our congregation's current situation. It is the Spirit who makes the Scriptures alive for us, driving God's Word home to a depth of heart that is beyond cognitive,

---

118. What I say about preaching here is not meant exclusively for "clergy." I believe that all Christians are preachers, heralds of the good news, and therefore should be listening to God through the Word in order to hear God's voice for others. Paul reminded the Corinthians that in a church worship service, it was important to allow for the voices of everyone who had received "a hymn, a lesson, a revelation, a tongue, or an interpretation" (1 Cor. 14:26 NRSV). Each one was to come with some form of God's Word for the gathered community. The purpose of such sharing within the congregation is primarily so that the body of Christ may be edified.

informational instruction. Through the Scriptures and the preaching of them, the Spirit engages our spirits to be conformed to the Word Revealed in Jesus Christ. While teaching is a large part of the task of preaching, it is not the whole part. Teaching frequently requires the transmission of *information* to the mind, but the goal of Christian teaching is also directed toward the entire human being for the purpose of *formation*. The power of the Spirit brings about the enlivening of the preached words so that believers may grow in understanding and in spiritual character. As Martin Luther described in a 1523 sermon on Luke 2, "Christ is wrapped through and through in the Scripture just as the body was wrapped in swaddling clothes. The crib in which he lies and in which he is placed is now preaching, and from this one receives food and provision."[119]

However, one further point of importance regarding preaching needs to be considered. In addition to preaching as public witness to the gospel of Christ and as nourishment for the strengthening of gathered believers, preaching may also be *prophetic*. I am not suggesting that preachers become prophets or apostles on which the foundation of the church is built (Eph. 2:20). What I am suggesting is that the prophetic aspect of preaching today is found in its capacity to deliver timely messages for the people of God from God's Word to the historical setting of the day. In this way, the preacher is a messenger "who speaks a word other than his own."[120] Prophets heard messages from God that shaped the content and method of delivery for their "words." I am not proposing such a role for modern-day preachers but am instead proposing one that relates to the power of the written text itself; namely, preachers can deliver sermons that address various aspects of contemporary life in terms of God's vision for both this life and the one to come. This prophetic edge of the church's witness in the world comes from the radical difference between principles in the kingdom of God and principles in the kingdom of darkness. When the church confronts racism, injustice, corrupt governmental leaders, and systems through its preaching, it is speaking the Word of the Lord to the powers that be. In so doing, it uses its prophetic edge to address the current systems of corporate sin. In its preaching, the church says that injustice is not the way it is supposed to be in God's world. This does not mean that preachers are to be politicians. It does mean, however, that preachers are to

119. Martin Luther, "Ein Sermon auff Euangelion am Sontag nach Ephiphanie, Luce 2 (1523)," in *Predigten des Jahres 1523*, WA 12:418, line 24, my trans. from Luther's old German: "Christus ist yun der schrift eyngewicklet durch und durch, gleich wie der leyb yun den tuchlen. Der krippen ist nu die predigt, daryun er ligt und verfasset wirt, und daraus man essen und sutter nympt."

120. Walter Brueggemann, *Theology of the Old Testament: Testimony, Dispute, Advocacy* (Minneapolis: Fortress, 1997), 629.

be messengers of God's vision of shalom for the world, where (eventually) everyone will live up to the full potential of their being as God created them and relationships will flourish along with justice.[121]

Nicholas Wolterstorff has offered several descriptors to expand the meaning of shalom. Shalom is usually translated as "peace" or "well-being." While it is "intertwined with justice," says Wolterstorff, it is more than justice.[122] Cornelius Plantinga adds further dimensions: shalom is a "universal flourishing, wholeness, and delight—a rich state of affairs in which natural needs are satisfied and natural gifts fruitfully employed, all under the arch of God's love. Shalom, in other words, is the way things are supposed to be."[123] Preaching that is prophetic speaks to the powers of the age, exposing them for precisely what they are in God's eyes. The basis for our knowledge of these powers and for the content within them so as to recognize them is clearly the Word and the Spirit—Scripture as understood in the community of believers, who are illumined by the Spirit. Preaching that is prophetic takes to heart God's burden for the world, engaging the brokenness fostered by sin and pointing out injustice nurtured by hate. Preaching that is prophetic directs our attention to the realms of our world where the reign of God is hindered and where the purposes of God are thwarted (at least temporarily, not ultimately). Preaching that is prophetic reminds hearers that we live in this present world as sojourners and strangers, indeed as aliens whose true homeland is not here but with God. Preaching that is prophetic raises the hearers' sights above the brokenness, oppression, and hurt of our world to the justice, peace, and flourishing of God's future kingdom. Preaching that is prophetic directs hearers to the despised, rejected, and marginalized humans among us so that we may together work to bring hope and healing to "the least of these" (Matt. 25:45). Preaching that is prophetic reaches to heaven in order to pull back to earth a glimpse of how we are to live here and now in anticipation of God's future kingdom. The people of God's presence will respond to such preaching by working to eliminate structures that oppress others and destroy their humanity. The people of God's presence will respond by treating others as we would prefer to be treated ourselves.[124]

---

121. Nicholas Wolterstorff, *Until Justice and Peace Embrace: The Kuyper Lectures for 1981 Delivered at the Free University of Amsterdam* (Grand Rapids: Eerdmans, 1983), 69.

122. Wolterstorff, *Until Justice and Peace Embrace*, 69.

123. Cornelius Plantinga Jr., *Engaging God's World: A Christian Vision of Faith, Learning, and Living* (Grand Rapids: Eerdmans, 2002), 15.

124. I find the writing of Ron Sider to be most helpful in this regard. See Sider, *Good News and Good Works: A Theology for the Whole Gospel* (Grand Rapids: Baker, 1993); Sider, *The Scandal of the Evangelical Conscience: Why Are Christians Living Just Like the Rest of the World?* (Grand Rapids: Baker Books, 2005).

Summary

This chapter began with reflections on words etched on gravestones. A thoughtful walk through a cemetery reminds us of our own mortality—and the fact that we may not always be remembered in this life. Even the clearest inscriptions today will one day fade into the ground and be effaced—much like our bodies. Death and decay face us all. "All people are like grass, and all their glory is like the flowers of the field; the grass withers and the flowers fall" (1 Pet. 1:24). Our lives here are momentary and fragile. We come and we go. Yet as we have seen from Jesus's own words and now hear from the prophet Isaiah, "The grass withers and the flowers fall, / but the word of our God endures forever" (Isa. 40:8). There is constancy in God's life that endures throughout eternity; this permanence of life is reflected in the permanency of God's Word. Since God is "inclined to communicate himself" (as Jonathan Edwards has so brilliantly described God's disposition), the Word of the Eternal One has always existed and will always exist. The Word of the Lord endures forever.

Beyond our genuine fears and anxiety over our mortality and what happens when we die, the Triune God of the Christian faith has shown himself as the Lord over life and death. "For none of us lives to ourselves alone, and none of us dies for ourselves alone. If we live, we live for the Lord; and if we die, we die for the Lord. So, whether we live or die, we belong to the Lord. For this very reason, Christ died and returned to life so that he might be the Lord of both the dead and the living" (Rom. 14:7–9). The resurrection of our Lord points to a day when our own mortal bodies will be resurrected to a new life. In the meantime, Christians live in faith concerning God's promises for our future, based on the eternal Word of the Lord. While our bodies and even the memory of our lives here on earth may quickly fade from the annals of human history, there is One who knows our name and who holds us throughout our lives here and even in the sleep of death. In life and death we belong to this Lord. One day our faith will be made into sight, and we shall all realize that the *Logos*, the Word made flesh, has truly been raised for our justification (Rom. 4:25) and glorification. We shall not be lost—God holds us and our lives in the palm of his hand. For, as the eternal Word made flesh, Christ is Lord of both the living and the dead. May we remember this truth about the Word and words the next time we walk through a graveyard—or through any yard.

Conclusion

For the Sake of the World

As we conclude this volume on the nature and mission of the people of God's presence, it is good to recall the initial motivation for this theological engagement. For decades, the church in Western societies has declined significantly in effectiveness. In some areas, the church's influence has descended slowly and steadily; in other areas, the church's influence has taken a crashing dive in an accelerated tailspin. In the United States, all regions seem to be affected by the diminution of the church's influence—except, perhaps, the southeastern region, previously known as the "Bible belt." The reasons for this fall from a position of respect are multifarious, but rehearsing these is not our present task. Potential solutions for reversing the tailspin have arisen in churches small and large, urban and rural. In my experience, the attempts by churches to retrieve a voice amid the circus-like cacophony of postmodern societies have generally revolved around two major methods: (1) changing church programs to garner interest and people; or (2) changing church messages to appear more compatible with people in the world. As I noted in the introduction, I do not believe either of these are viable options.

What can the church do? This book is one attempt to provide a third response to the increasing marginalization of influence in which the church finds itself in Western societies. I believe that the initial response must be to return to biblical and theological inquiry into the intended nature and purpose of the church in the world and then to reshape our practice of being and doing Christianity in community in the world. By reconsidering the nature of the church as a *people of God's direct presence*, this book has attempted to propose one potential answer to the biblical and theological inquiry regarding its nature and mission. It remains my persistent belief that unless a biblical and theological reconsideration of the nature of the church is developed for our local churches and the church at large, then we will populate the pews with people who come out for the "bread" but not for the "bread of life" (with reference to John 6:26). And this is true only if the people *come out*! Programs can always be effective to some extent in reaching some people with the benefits of a church's life. However, programs usually appeal to something that benefits humans in order to get them to come out; they do not always help to shape true followers of Christ. The tragedy of many local churches in this century is that they sit on past achievements, when society used to be friendlier and more receptive to the message concerning Christ. A return to the biblical and theological roots of who the church is and how the church is to operate is *the* agenda for the church in this day.

Yet such a theological study quickly becomes irrelevant if it is not "doable." For this reason I have written *Serving the People of God's Presence*, in which I discuss the theological theme of ecclesiology in terms of practical application. What might a church that reflects the theological understanding I have sketched in this volume look like? How might body ministry operate within the umbrella of leadership functions? How can we put into practice what has been sketched in theory? That is the goal of *Serving the People of God's Presence*. While these two books can be read separately, they are companion volumes that compose a cohesive theology in which theological inquiry informs the practical application in the local church.

What is at stake in this ecclesiological quest is the future of the church of Jesus Christ in North America in particular, but also throughout the increasingly post-Christian world in which we live. While I realize that the proposals for implementation of my theological and practical suggestions may be ill received by some, my plea is that at least something needs to be done along these lines to retrieve our witness to the gospel of Jesus Christ. After all, the church exists not only for the edification of communities of believers but also for the sake of the world. Here I should like to highlight one of my favorite sections from Barth's *Church Dogmatics*:

> The community of Jesus Christ is for the world, i.e., for each and every man, for the man of every age and place who finds the totality of earthly creation the setting, object and instrument and yet also the frontier of his life and work. . . . First and supremely it is God who exists for the world. And since the community of Jesus Christ exists first and supremely for God, she has no option but in her own manner and place to exist for the world. How else could she exist

for God? The centre around which she moves eccentrically is not, then, simply the world as such, but the world for which God is. For God is who He is, not in abstracto nor without relationship, but as God for the world! (*CD* IV/3.2:762)

Therefore, in concluding my thoughts, I want to gather a few key points. In the previous chapters, I have made the internal working of the community to be prominent in my ecclesiological endeavors. While one should not get the impression that this ecclesiology is about only the church and not the world, I do see how it might seem that way. By placing such emphasis on the importance of engaging worship and the Word *in* the gathered community, the concomitant focus on the world seems muted. Allow me to clarify my rationale for this again as we close.

As the people of God's presence, the church gathers to engage in fellowship with God and each other. On these occasions of gathering, worship and the Word open opportunities for God's presence to be among us through the Spirit. I need not rehearse the details of these ideas from earlier chapters here. However, the point is important: *believers together experience encounters with the Spirit at our assembling, giving us the motivation and character to engage in the task of witness to our God outside of our assembling.* This means that gathering is a crucial aspect for growing in Christ because it is one part of our character development that God has set in place for us. It has been my contention that, for example, as we focus our eyes on God in worship, God's presence covers us and we experience God at a core level of our being. Such an experience with God sets the stage for transformation and sanctification of our character. We are different when we have been encountered by God's presence among God's people.

Further, I see the local community as a training ground for learning how to love and fellowship with other human beings. As each person in the body of Christ does their work or exercises their gifts, then and only then does the body grow (individually and corporately). We are tied together in the bond of the Spirit so that we might learn how to love as Christ loves within the family of God. This is crucial because loving each other in Christ becomes the foundation for building a genuine, loving relationship with those who are not in Christ. In other words, how can we love the people of the world if we have not first learned to love the people of God?

What I have not stated as clearly in this book is that the presence of God in our corporate and individual lives has missional purpose. We are continuing the mission of God through our own reaching out to the people in our neighborhoods. Experiencing an encounter with God is not for our own personal spiritual enjoyment but for the purpose of bringing Christ to the world. It is this dimension of the work of the church that occupies much of my writing in *Serving the People of God's Presence*. However, in order to bring Christ to the world, we need to "get our act together" in the household of faith. Therefore, I reflect on how to put the theology of the church, which I describe in this book, into practice in the companion volume. Alongside that goal, I develop a "theology of ministry" that also derives from this ecclesiology of God's presence.

The encounter with the presence of God increasingly transforms us into the image of Christ. In some way, we become Christ-bearers to the people of the world. Two books by three writers have greatly influenced my thinking on this. The first is a book by Kenda Creasy Dean and Ron Foster titled *The Godbearing Life: The Art of Soul Tending for Youth Ministry*.[1] Yes, it is a youth ministry book! The creative and yet profound idea that I took from them is that "God calls each of us to become a Godbearer through whom God may enter the world again and again."[2] Using the ancient theological title for Mary—namely, "the Godbearer" (*theotokos*)—Dean and Foster craft a view of ministry and life that is *incarnational* in its approach. While we cannot *be* Christ to the world, we can *bring* Christ to people.

This dimension of ministry as Christ-bearing is a necessary counterweight to the programmatic style of ministry that has become rampant in so many places in North America today (especially in youth ministries). It is particularly fruitful when paired with our theological discussion concerning the church as the people of God's presence.

From the gathering of the body of Christ in worship and Word, the people of God experience God's presence in the person of the risen Lord, who is brought to the core of their being by the Holy Spirit's direct work. Ministry, then, engages both people in the church and in the world as carriers of the presence of Christ, as Godbearers. By the work of the Holy Spirit, the presence of Christ can be made alive and real to those with whom we are ministering.

The third author is Ray S. Anderson. In his book *The Shape of Practical Theology*, he offers a sketch of what he calls "paracletic ministry of the Spirit."[3] "Paracletic" here is an anglicized form of speaking about the Paraclete, the One called alongside to help. This is the Spirit's role. Therefore, in ministry in the world today, Anderson suggests features that should reflect the

---

1. Kenda Creasy Dean and Ron Foster, *The Godbearing Life: The Art of Soul Tending for Youth Ministry* (Nashville: Upper Room Books, 1998).

2. Dean and Foster, *The Godbearing Life*, 18.

3. Ray S. Anderson, *The Shape of Practical Theology: Empowering Ministry with Theological Praxis* (Downers Grove, IL: InterVarsity, 2001), 195–98.

Spirit's role among Christians. The full details of these authors' influences are developed in *Serving the People of God's Presence*.

Here is the point of this conclusion: we are called by God not to sit in a pew but to go forth into the world, continuing the ministry of Jesus Christ through the power of the Spirit, bringing God's holy presence into unholy situations, broken relationships, systemic sin, and individual suffering. A fundamental assumption of my model of worship (in which it is the center of the life and ministry of the church) is that the *presence of the living Lord of the church* always transforms us into the image of Christ when we make room for Christ's presence in our everyday living. Only through carrying the presence of God among the people of God and into our everyday lives in the world can we expect to continue the ministry of Christ.

Thus, the ministry of Christ continues in the ministry of the people of God's presence through the paracletic empowerment of the Spirit to action, thereby ministering the presence of the crucified and risen Lord to a world broken by sin, for the purpose of glorifying God the Father.

Select Bibliography

Allen, Diogenes. *Finding Our Father*. Atlanta: John Knox, 1974.

Alston, William P. *Perceiving God: The Epistemology of Religious Experience*. Ithaca, NY: Cornell University Press, 1991.

Anderson, Ray. *On Being Human: Essays in Theological Anthropology*. Pasadena, CA: Fuller Seminary Press, 1982.

Augustine, Daniela. *Pentecost, Hospitality, and Transfiguration: Toward a Spirit-Inspired Vision of Society Transformation*. Cleveland, TN: The Centre for Pentecostal Theology, 2012.

Baillie, Donald M. *God Was in Christ: An Essay on Incarnation and Atonement*. London: Faber & Faber, 1961.

Baillie, John. *Our Knowledge of God*. New York: Charles Scribner's Sons, 1959.

Balthasar, Hans Urs von. *Creator Spirit*. Translated by Brian McNeil. Vol. 3 of *Explorations in Theology*. San Francisco: Ignatius, 1993.

———. *Spirit and Institution*. Translated by Edward T. Oakes. Vol. 4 of *Explorations in Theology*. San Francisco: Ignatius, 1995.

———. *Spiritus Creator*. Skizzen zur Theologie 3. Einsiedeln: Johannes Verlag, 1967.

———. *Theology: The Old Covenant*. Translated by Brian McNeil and Erasmo Leiva-Merikakis. Edited by John Riches. Vol. 6 of *The Glory of the Lord: A Theological Aesthetics*. San Francisco: Ignatius, 1991.

Barth, Karl. *Church Dogmatics*. 13 vols. Edited by T. F. Torrance and G. W. Bromiley. Translated by G. W. Bromiley et al. Edinburgh: T&T Clark, 1936–68.

———. "The Church: The Living Congregation of the Living Lord Jesus Christ." In *God Here and Now*. Translated by Paul van Buren. London: Routledge, 2003.

———. *Credo*. Eugene, OR: Wipf & Stock, 2005.

———. *Die Hauptprobleme der Dogmatik dargestellt im Anschluß an das Apostolische Glaubensbekenntnis, 16 Vorlesungen gehalten an der Universität Utrecht im Februar und März 1935*. 3rd ed. Munich: Kaiser, 1935.

———. *Die Lehre vom Worte Gottes: Prolegomena zur christlichen Dogmatik 1927*. Edited by Gerhard Sauter. Vol. 1 of *Die christliche Dogmatik im Entwurf*. In Karl Barth Gesamtausgabe 2, Akademische Werke 1927, edited by Hinrich Stoevesandt. Zurich: Theologischer Verlag Zürich, 1982.

———. *Evangelical Theology: An Introduction*. Grand Rapids: Eerdmans, 1963.

———. *The Göttingen Dogmatics: Instruction in the Christian Religion*. Vol. 1. Edited by Hannelotte Reiffen. Translated by G. W. Bromiley. Grand Rapids: Eerdmans, 1991.

———. *Homiletics*. Translated by G. W. Bromiley and Donald E. Daniels. Louisville: Westminster John Knox, 1991.

———. *The Preaching of the Gospel*. Translated by B. E. Hooke. Philadelphia: Westminster, 1963.

———. *Unterricht in der christlichen Religion, Erster Band: Prolegomena 1924*. Edited by Hannelotte Reifen. Karl Barth Gesamtausgabe 2, Akademische Werke 1924. Zurich: Theologischer Verlag Zürich, 1985.

———. *The Word of God and Theology*. Translated by Amy Marga. Edinburgh: T&T Clark, 2011.

Beintker, Michael. "Calvins Theologie des Heiligen Geistes." *Tydskrif vir Geesteswetenskappe: Spesiale Uitgawe—Johannes Calvyn* 49, no. 3 (September 2009): 487–99.

Bellah, Robert N., Richard Madsen, William M. Sullivan, Ann Swidler, and Steven M. Tipton. *Habits of the Heart: Individualism and Commitment in American Life*. Berkeley: University of California Press, 2008.

Bloesch, Donald. *Holy Scripture: Revelation, Inspiration and Interpretation*. Downers Grove, IL: InterVarsity, 1994.

Bonaventura. *Sententiarum*. Vol. 1 of *Opera Omnia*. Edited by A. C. Peltier. Paris: Ludovicus Vives, Bibliopola Editor, 1864.

Bonhoeffer, Dietrich. *Act and Being: Transcendental Philosophy and Ontology in Systematic Theology*. Edited by Wayne Whitson Floyd Jr. Translated by H. Martin Rumscheidt. Vol. 2 of *Dietrich Bonhoeffer Works*. Minneapolis: Fortress, 1996.

———. *Christ the Center*. Translated by Edwin H. Robertson. San Francisco: Harper & Row, 1978.

Bosch, David J. *Transforming Mission: Paradigm Shifts in Theology of Mission*. 20th anniv. ed. Maryknoll, NY: Orbis, 2016.

Brunner, Emil. *Das Mißverständnis der Kirche*. Stuttgart: Evangelisches Verlagswerk, 1951.

———. *The Misunderstanding of the Church.* Translated by Harold Knight. Philadelphia: Westminster, 1953.

Buber, Martin. *I and Thou.* Translated by Walter Kaufmann. New York: Simon & Schuster, 1970.

Bulgakov, Sergei. *The Comforter.* Translated by Boris Jakim. Grand Rapids: Eerdmans, 2004.

Calvin, John. *Institutes of the Christian Religion.* 2 vols. Edited by John T. McNeill. Translated by Ford Lewis Battles. Library of Christian Classics 21–22. Philadelphia: Westminster, 1975.

Collins, Kenneth. *Theology of John Wesley: Holy Love and the Shape of Grace.* Nashville: Abingdon, 2007.

Cross, Terry L. *Answering the Call in the Spirit: Pentecostal Reflections on a Theology of Life and Work.* Cleveland, TN: Lee University Press, 2007.

———. "The Divine-Human Encounter: Towards a Pentecostal Theology of Experience." *PNEUMA: The Journal of the Society for Pentecostal Studies* 31, no. 1 (2009): 3–34.

Dalferth, Ingolf U. "Representing God's Presence." *International Journal of Systematic Theology* 3, no. 3 (November 2001): 237–56.

de Lubac, Henri. *Catholicism: Christ and the Common Destiny of Man.* Translated by Lancelot C. Sheppard and Sr. Elizabeth Englund. San Francisco: Ignatius, 1988.

———. *The Motherhood of the Church.* Translated by Sergia Englund. San Francisco: Ignatius, 1982.

———. *The Splendor of the Church.* Translated by Michael Mason. San Francisco: Ignatius, 2006.

Derrida, Jacques. *Adieu to Emmanuel Levinas.* Translated by Pascale-Anne Brault and Michael Naas. Stanford, CA: Stanford University Press, 1999.

Dowey, Edward A., Jr. *The Knowledge of God in Calvin's Theology.* Expanded ed. Grand Rapids: Eerdmans, 1994.

Dulles, Avery. *Models of the Church.* Expanded ed. New York: Doubleday, 1987.

Fee, Gordon. *God's Empowering Presence: The Holy Spirit in the Letters of Paul.* Peabody, MA: Hendrickson, 1994.

Ferguson, Everett. *The Church of Christ: A Biblical Ecclesiology for Today.* Grand Rapids: Eerdmans, 1996.

Fiddes, Paul, S. *Participating in God: A Pastoral Doctrine of the Trinity.* Louisville: Westminster John Knox, 2000.

Flett, John. *The Witness of God: The Trinity, missio Dei, Karl Barth, and the Nature of Christian Community.* Grand Rapids: Eerdmans, 2010.

Ford, David F. *Self and Salvation: Being Transformed.* Cambridge Studies in Christian Doctrine 1, edited by Colin E. Gunton and Daniel W. Hardy. Cambridge: Cambridge University Press, 1999.

Foster, Richard. *Celebration of Discipline: The Path to Spiritual Growth*. San Francisco: Harper & Row, 1978.

Grenz, Stanley J. *Theology for the Community of God*. Grand Rapids: Eerdmans, 2000.

Guder, Darrell L., ed. *Missional Church: A Vision for the Sending of the Church in North America*. Grand Rapids: Eerdmans, 1998.

Gunton, Colin. *Act and Being: Towards a Theology of the Divine Attributes*. Grand Rapids: Eerdmans, 2002.

Gunton, Colin, and Daniel W. Hardy, eds. *On Being the Church: Essays on the Christian Community*. Edinburgh: T&T Clark, 1990.

Harrison, Nonna Verna. "Perichoresis in the Greek Fathers." *St. Vladimir's Theological Quarterly* 35, no. 1 (1991): 53–65.

Heidegger, Martin. *Being and Time*. Translated by Joan Stambaugh and Dennis J. Schmidt. SUNY Series in Contemporary Continental Philosophy, edited by Dennis J. Schmidt. Albany, NY: State University of New York Press, 2010.

———. *Sein und Zeit*. 7th ed. Tübingen: Max Niemeyer Verlag, 1953.

Hendry, George. *God the Creator: The Hastie Lectures in the University of Glasgow, 1935*. London: Cokesbury, 1938.

Herrmann, Wilhelm. *The Communion of the Christian with God: Described on the Basis of Luther's Statements*. Philadelphia: Fortress, 1971.

Hilbert, Gerhard. *Ecclesiola in Ecclesia: Luthers Anschauungen von Volkskirche und Freiwilligkeitskirche in ihrer Bedeutung für die Gegenwart*. Leipzig: A. Deichert, 1920.

Hodgson, Leonard. *The Doctrine of the Trinity: Croall Lectures, 1942–1943*. London: Nisbet, 1943.

Hunsinger, George. *Disruptive Grace: Studies in the Theology of Karl Barth*. Grand Rapids: Eerdmans, 2000.

Jenson, Robert W. "The Church and the Sacraments." In *The Cambridge Companion to Christian Doctrine*, edited by Colin E. Gunton. Cambridge: Cambridge University Press, 1997.

Jewett, Paul K. *Man as Male and Female*. Grand Rapids: Eerdmans, 1975.

Johnson, Luke Timothy. *Religious Experience in Earliest Christianity: A Missing Dimension in New Testament Studies*. Minneapolis: Fortress, 1998.

Kärkkäinen, Veli-Matti. *Introduction to Ecclesiology: Ecumenical, Historical and Global Perspectives*. Downers Grove, IL: InterVarsity, 2002.

Kelsey, David. *Eccentric Existence: A Theological Anthropology*. 2 vols. Louisville: Westminster John Knox, 2009.

Kierkegaard, Søren. *Practice in Christianity*. Edited and translated by Howard V. Hong and Edna V. Hong. Kierkegaard's Writings 20. Princeton: Princeton University Press, 1991.

King, Magda. *Heidegger's Philosophy: A Guide to His Basic Thought*. New York: Macmillan, 1964.

Knight, Henry H., III. *The Presence of God in the Christian Life: John Wesley and the Means of Grace*. Pietist and Wesleyan Studies 3. Lanham, MD: Scarecrow, 1992.

Küng, Hans. *The Church*. Garden City, NY: Doubleday, 1976.

LaCugna, Catherine Mowry. *God for Us: The Trinity and Christian Life*. San Francisco: Harper & Row, 1991.

Ladd, George Eldon. *A Theology of the New Testament*. Grand Rapids: Eerdmans, 1974.

Land, Steven J. *Pentecostal Spirituality: A Passion for the Kingdom*. 2nd ed. Cleveland, TN: CPT, 2010.

Levinas, Emmanuel. "The Ego and the Totality." In *Collected Philosophical Papers*, translated by Alphonso Lingis. Phaenomenologica. Dordrecht: Martinus Nijhoff, 1987.

———. "Freedom and Command." In *Collected Philosophical Papers*, translated by Alphonso Lingis. Phaenomenologica. Dordrecht: Martinus Nijhoff, 1987.

———. "Meaning and Sense." In *Collected Philosophical Papers*, translated by Alphonso Lingis. Phaenomenologica. Dordrecht: Martinus Nijhoff, 1987.

———. "Philosophy and the Idea of Infinity." In *Collected Philosophical Papers*, translated by Alphonso Lingis. Phaenomenologica. Dordrecht: Martinus Nijhoff, 1987.

———. *Totality and Infinity: An Essay on Exteriority*, translated by Alphonso Lingis. Pittsburgh: Duquesne University Press, 1969.

Littell, Franklin H. "The Concept of the Believers' Church." In *The Concept of the Believers' Church: Addresses from the 1968 Louisville Conference*, edited by James Leo Garrett Jr. Scottsdale, PA: Herald Press, 1969.

Loder, James E. *The Transforming Moment*. 2nd ed. Colorado Springs: Helmer & Howard, 1989.

Long, Thomas. *The Witness of Preaching*. Louisville: Westminster John Knox, 1989.

Lopes, Dominic Ives. *Sight and Sensibility: Evaluating Pictures*. Oxford: Clarendon, 2005.

Lumen Gentium. In Heinrich Denzinger, *Enchiridion symbolorum definitionum et declarationum de rebus fidei et morum / Compendium of Creeds, Definitions, and Declarations on Matters of Faith and Morals*, edited by Peter Hünermann, Robert Fastiggi, and Anne Englund Nash. 43rd ed. San Francisco: Ignatius, 2012.

Luther, Martin. *The Babylonian Captivity of the Church (1520)*. Translated by Erik H. Herrmann. In *Church and Sacraments*, edited by Paul W. Robinson. Vol. 3 of *The Annotated Luther*, edited by Hans J. Hillerbrand, Kirsi I. Stjerna, and Timothy J. Wengert. Minneapolis: Fortress, 2016.

———. *Lectures on Romans*. Ichthus ed. Translated and edited by Wilhelm Pauck. Library of Christian Classics 15. Philadelphia: Westminster, 1961.

———. *Luthers Vorlesung über den Römerbrief, 1515/1516, Die Glosse*. Edited by Johannes Ficker. Leipzig: Dieterich'sche Verlagsbuchhandlung, Theodor Weicher, 1908.

———. *Treatise on Good Works (1520)*. Translated by Timothy J. Wengert. Revised translation by Scott Hendrix. In *The Roots of Reform*, edited by Timothy J. Wengert. Vol. 1 of *The Annotated Luther*, edited by Hans J. Hillerbrand, Kirsi I. Stjerna, and Timothy J. Wengert. Minneapolis: Fortress, 2015.

Macaskill, Grant. *Union with Christ in the New Testament*. Oxford: Oxford University Press, 2013.

Macmurray, John. *Persons in Relation*. The Gifford Lectures, 1953–1954. Amherst, NY: Humanity Books, 1991.

Maier, Walter A. "The Divine Presence within the Cloud." *Concordia Theological Quarterly* 79 (2015): 79–102.

Maltese, Giovanni. *Geisterfahrer zwischen Transzendenz und Immanenz: Die Erfahrungsbegriffe in den pfingstlich-charismatischen Theologien von Terry L. Cross und Amos Yong im Vergleich*. Göttingen: V & R Unipress, 2013.

Mangina, Joseph L. *Karl Barth: Theologian of Christian Witness*. Louisville: Westminster John Knox, 2004.

Marcel, Gabriel. *Faith and Reality*. Vol. 2 of *The Mystery of Being*, translated by G. S. Fraser. The Gifford Lectures, 1949–1950. South Bend, IN: St. Augustine's Press, 1950.

———. *Homo Viator: Introduction to a Metaphysic of Hope*. Translated by Emma Crauford. New York: Harper & Brothers, 1962.

———. *The Philosophy of Existentialism*. Translated by Manya Harari. New York: Citadel, 1956.

———. *Reflection and Mystery*. Vol. 1 of *The Mystery of Being*, translated by G. S. Fraser. The Gifford Lectures, 1949–1950. South Bend, IN: St. Augustine's Press, 1950.

Marshall, Molly Truman. *Joining the Dance: A Theology of the Spirit*. Valley Forge, PA: Judson, 2003.

———. "Participating in the Life of God: A Trinitarian Pneumatology." *Perspectives in Religious Studies* 30, no. 2 (Summer 2003): 139–50.

McClendon, James W., Jr. *Doctrine*. Vol. 2 of *Systematic Theology*. Nashville: Abingdon, 1994.

———. *Ethics*. Vol. 1 of *Systematic Theology*. Nashville: Abingdon, 1986.

———. *Witness*. Vol. 3 of *Systematic Theology*. Nashville: Abingdon, 2000.

Migliore, Daniel L. *Faith Seeking Understanding: An Introduction to Christian Theology*. 3rd ed. Grand Rapids: Eerdmans, 2014.

———. "The Missionary God and the Missionary Church." *The Princeton Seminary Bulletin*, NS, 19, no. 1 (1998): 14–25.

———. *The Power of God and the gods of Power*. Louisville: Westminster John Knox, 2008.

Minear, Paul S. *Horizons of Christian Community*. St. Louis: Bethany, 1959.

———. *Images of the Church in the New Testament*. The New Testament Library, edited by C. Clifton Black, John T. Carroll, and Beverly Roberts Gaventa. Louisville: Westminster John Knox, 2004.

Moltmann, Jürgen. *The Church in the Power of the Spirit: A Contribution to Messianic Ecclesiology*. Translated by Margaret Kohl. Minneapolis: Fortress, 1993.

———. *Der Geist des Lebens: Eine ganzheitliche Pneumatologie*. Vol. 7 of Werke. Gütersloh: Gütersloher Verlagshaus, 2016.

———. *Der lebendige Gott und die Fülle des Lebens: Auch ein Beitrag zur Atheismusdebatte unserer Zeit*. 2nd ed. Gütersloh: Gütersloher Verlagshaus, 2015.

———. "Perichoresis: An Old Magic Word for a New Trinitarian Theology." In *Trinity, Community and Power: Mapping Trajectories in Wesleyan Theology*, edited by M. Douglas Meeks. Nashville: Abingdon, 2000.

———. *The Spirit of Life: A Universal Affirmation*. Translated by Margaret Kohl. Minneapolis: Fortress, 1992.

———. *Trinität und Reich Gottes: Zur Gotteslehre*. Munich: Kaiser, 1980.

———. *The Trinity and the Kingdom*. Translated by Margaret Kohl. San Francisco: Harper & Row, 1981.

Mulhall, Stephen. *Routledge Philosophy Guidebook to Heidegger and* Being and Time. London: Routledge, 1996.

Murdoch, Iris. *The Sovereignty of the Good*. London: Routledge & Kegan Paul, 1970.

Nature and Mission of the Church: A Stage on the Way to a Common Statement. Faith and Order Paper 198. Geneva: World Council of Churches, 2005.

Newport, John P. "The Purpose of the Church." In *The People of God: Essays in the Believers' Church*, edited by Paul Basden and David S. Dockery. Nashville: Broadman, 1991.

Ogden, Greg. *The New Reformation: Returning the Ministry to the People of God*. Grand Rapids: Zondervan, 1990.

Orr, Robert P. *The Meaning of Transcendence: A Heideggerian Reflection*. AAR Dissertation Series 35, edited by Wendell Dietrich. Chico, CA: Scholars Press, 1981.

Pinnock, Clark. *Flame of Love: A Theology of the Holy Spirit*. Downers Grove, IL: InterVarsity, 1996.

———. "The Role of the Spirit in Interpretation." *Journal of the Evangelical Theological Society* 36, no. 4 (December 1993): 491–97.

Plantinga, Cornelius. *Engaging God's World: A Christian Vision of Faith, Learning, and Living*. Grand Rapids: Eerdmans, 2002.

———. *Not the Way It's Supposed to Be: A Breviary of Sin*. Grand Rapids: Eerdmans, 1995.

Pohl, Christine D. *Making Room: Recovering Hospitality as a Christian Tradition.* Grand Rapids: Eerdmans, 1999.

Polan, Gregory J. "Divine Presence: A Biblical Perspective." *Liturgical Ministry* 3 (Winter 1994): 13–21.

Reynolds, Thomas E. *Vulnerable Communion: A Theology of Disability and Hospitality.* Grand Rapids: Brazos, 2008.

Rust, Eric C. *Religion, Revelation and Reason.* Macon, GA: Mercer University Press, 1981.

Saliers, Don E. *Worship as Theology: Foretaste of Glory Divine.* Nashville: Abingdon, 1994.

Schleiermacher, Friedrich D. E. *Christian Faith: A New Translation and Critical Edition.* Translated by Terrence N. Tice, Catherine L. Kelsey, and Edwina Lawler. Edited by Catherine L. Kelsey and Terrence N. Tice. 2 vols. Louisville: Westminster John Knox, 2016.

Shaull, Richard, and Waldo Cesar. *Pentecostalism and the Future of the Christian Churches: Promises, Limitations, Challenges.* Grand Rapids: Eerdmans, 2000.

Smith, James K. A. *Desiring the Kingdom: Worship, Worldview, and Cultural Formation.* Cultural Liturgies 1. Grand Rapids: Baker Academic, 2009.

———. *Thinking in Tongues: Pentecostal Contributions to Christian Philosophy.* Pentecostal Manifestos, edited by James K. A. Smith and Amos Yong. Grand Rapids: Eerdmans, 2010.

Snail, Thomas. *The Giving Gift: The Holy Spirit in Person.* Eugene, OR: Wipf & Stock, 1994.

Snyder, Howard A. *The Problems of Wineskins: Church Structure in a Technological Age.* Downers Grove, IL: InterVarsity, 1975.

———. *Signs of the Spirit: How God Reshapes the Church.* Eugene, OR: Wipf & Stock, 1997.

Starr, James M. *Sharers in the Divine Nature: 2 Peter 1:4 in Its Hellenistic Context.* Coniectanea Biblica New Testament Series 33, edited by Birger Olsson and Kari Syreeni. Stockholm: Almqvist & Wisell, 2000.

Stump, Eleonore. *Wandering in Darkness: Narrative and the Problem of Suffering.* Oxford: Clarendon, 2010.

Tanner, Kathryn. *The Economy of Grace.* Minneapolis: Fortress, 2005.

Taylor, Charles. *Sources of the Self: The Making of the Modern Identity.* Cambridge, MA: Harvard University Press, 1989.

Taylor, John V. *The Go-Between God: The Holy Spirit and Christian Mission.* 2nd ed. London: SCM, 2004.

Terrien, Samuel. *The Elusive Presence: Toward a New Biblical Theology.* San Francisco: Harper & Row, 1978.

Trueblood, Elton. *The Company of the Committed*. New York: Harper & Brothers, 1961.

Vandervelde, George. "The Challenge of Evangelical Ecclesiology." *Evangelical Review of Theology* 27, no. 1 (2003): 4–26.

Vanier, Jean. *Becoming Human*. New York: Paulist Press, 1998.

———. *Encountering "the Other."* Dublin: Veritas Publications, 2005.

Vatican Council II: The Conciliar and Post Conciliar Documents. Edited by Austin Flannery. Translated by Colman O'Neill. Collegeville, MN: Liturgical Press, 1980.

Volf, Miroslav. *After Our Likeness: The Church as the Image of the Trinity*. Sacra Doctrina: Christian Theology for a Postmodern Age, edited by Alan G. Padgett. Grand Rapids: Eerdmans, 1998.

———. *Exclusion and Embrace: A Theological Exploration of Identity, Otherness, and Reconciliation*. Nashville: Abingdon, 1996.

Vondey, Wolfgang. *Heribert Mühlen: His Theology and Praxis—a New Profile of the Church*. Lanham, MD: University Press of America, 2004.

Wainwright, Geoffrey. *Doxology: The Praise of God in Worship, Doctrine and Life*. New York: Oxford University Press, 1980.

Webster, John. "The Church and the Perfection of God." In *The Community of the Word: Toward an Evangelical Ecclesiology*, edited by Mark Husbands and Daniel J. Treier. Downers Grove, IL: InterVarsity, 2005.

———. "'Eloquent and Radiant': The Prophetic Office of Christ and the Mission of the Church." In *Barth's Moral Theology: Human Action in Barth's Thought*. Grand Rapids: Eerdmans, 1998.

———. *Holy Scripture: A Dogmatic Sketch*. Current Issues in Theology, edited by Iain Torrance. Cambridge: Cambridge University Press, 2003.

Weil, Simone. *Waiting for God*. Translated by Emma Crauford. New York: Harper & Row, 1973.

Wesley, John. *The Works of John Wesley*. Edited by Thomas Jackson. 14 vols. Grand Rapids: Baker, 1978.

Whale, J. S. *The Protestant Tradition: An Essay in Interpretation*. Cambridge: Cambridge University Press, 1955.

Willard, Dallas. *The Spirit of the Disciplines: Understanding How God Changes Lives*. San Francisco: HarperCollins, 1988.

Williams, George H. *The Radical Reformation*. Philadelphia: Westminster, 1967.

Willimon, William. *The Service of God: Christian Work and Worship*. Nashville: Abingdon, 1983.

Wolterstorff, Nicholas. *Divine Discourse: Philosophical Reflections on the Claim That God Speaks*. Cambridge: Cambridge University Press, 1995.

———. *The God We Worship: An Exploration of Liturgical Theology*. Grand Rapids: Eerdmans, 2015.

————. *Until Justice and Peace Embrace: The Kuyper Lectures for 1981 Delivered at the Free University of Amsterdam.* Grand Rapids: Eerdmans, 1983.

Yong, Amos. *Spirit-Word-Community: Theological Hermeneutics in Trinitarian Perspective.* Ashgate New Critical Thinking in Religion, Theology & Biblical Studies. Burlington, VT: Ashgate, 2002.

Author Index

Scripture Index

Subject Index